a special gift

presented to:

Mary, with much love

from:

Mom

date:

Dec. 14, 2012

"And sing, sing your hearts out to God! Let every detail in your lives—words, actions, whatever—be done in the name of the Master, Jesus, thanking God the Father every step of the way."

—Colossians 3:16, 17, Message

The Women's Devotional Series

Among Friends

The Listening Heart

A Gift of Love

A Moment of Peace

Close to Home

From the Heart

This Quiet Place

In God's Garden

Fabric of Faith

Alone With God

Bouquets of Hope

Colors of Grace

Beautiful in God's Eyes

A Word From Home

Morning Praise

Heaven's Whisper

Grace Notes

Sanctuary

Love Out Loud

Renew

Blessed

Blessed

Ardis Dick Stenbakken, editor

REVIEW AND HERALD® PUBLISHING ASSOCIATION
Since 1861 | www.reviewandherald.com

12501 Old Columbia Pike
Silver Spring, Maryland 20904, U.S.A.

Published by Review and Herald® Publishing Association, Hagerstown, MD 21741-1119

Review and Herald® titles may be purchased in bulk for educational, business, fund-raising, or sales promotional use. For information, e-mail SpecialMarkets@reviewandherald.com.

The Review and Herald® Publishing Association publishes biblically based materials for spiritual, physical, and mental growth and Christian discipleship.

The author assumes full responsibility for the accuracy of all facts and quotations as cited in this book.

This book was
Edited by Penny Estes Wheeler
Copyedited by Judy Blodgett
Designed by Patricia Wegh / Review & Herald® Design Center
Cover photo by Joel D. Springer
Typeset: 10.5/13.5

PRINTED IN U.S.A.

16 15 14 13 12   5 4 3 2 1

Library of Congress Cataloging-in-Publication Data
Blessed / Ardis Dick Stenbakken, editor.
        p. cm.
1.   Seventh-Day Adventist women—Prayers and devotions. 2.   Devotional calendars—
Seventh-Day Adventists. I. Stenbakken, Ardis Dick.
    BV4844.R46 2011
    242'.643—dc22

                                2010041816

ISBN 978-0-8280-2654-3

Scholarshipping Our Sisters
Women Helping Women

There is an aspect of this book that is unique . . .

None of these contributors has been paid—each has shared freely so that all profits go to scholarships for women. As this book goes to press, 1,748 scholarships have been given to women in 115 countries.

For more current information, or to contribute to these scholarships, please go to http://adventistwomensministries.org/index.php?id=60. In this way you too can renew the dreams of some woman—or even your own—in seeking a higher degree.

General Conference Women's Ministries Scholarship Fund

The General Conference Women's Ministries scholarship program supports higher education for Adventist women globally. Recipients are talented women of vision who are committed to serving the mission of the Seventh-day Adventist Church.

Among Friends, published in 1992, was the first annual women's devotional book. Since then, proceeds from 22 of these devotional books have funded scholarships for Adventist women seeking to obtain higher education. However, as tuition costs have risen and more women have applied for assistance, funding has not kept pace with the need. Many dedicated women who apply must be turned down.

Recognizing the importance of educating women—to build stronger families, stronger communities, and a stronger church—each of us can help. Together we can change lives!

There are many ways to support our sisters, such as . . .

- Praying for women worldwide who are struggling to get an education.
- Telling others about the Women's Ministries scholarship program. (Materials are available to share.)
- Writing for the women's devotional book. (Guidelines are available.)
- Your gift or pledge to support women's education.

To make a gift or receive materials, send us a postcard with the following information. (Our address is on page 7.)

Name _____

Street _____

City _____ State/Province _____

Postal Code _____ Country _____

E-mail _____

To contact us:

Women's Ministries Department
General Conference of Seventh-day Adventists
12501 Old Columbia Pike
Silver Spring, MD 20904

Phone: 301-680-6636

Fax: 301-680-6600

E-mail: womensministries@gc.adventist.org

Web site: http://adventistwomensministries.org

Scholarship application and devotional book writers' guidelines are available at our Web site.

Make Me an Instrument

Open my eyes that I may see.
Ps. 119:18, NIV.

FIVE MINUTES into my presentation I noticed the woman enter and take the last vacant seat on the front row. From the corner of my eye I sensed the intensity of her gaze. After the seminar she came up to me and said, "I'm Maya. Two hours ago I had never heard of you, and I was getting ready to overdose on these." She held up a large bottle of pills. "But I had the strangest impression," she continued, "that I needed to surf the Internet one last time. Within seconds I had stumbled onto your Web site and discovered you were speaking at the university, just minutes from my home." She tossed the bottle into a nearby receptacle and added, "You're a miracle worker, you know. You've saved my life."

"I may be an instrument," I replied, "but God is the miracle worker. Who do you think impressed you to surf the Internet? Who directed you to my Web site? And," I continued, smiling, "who prompted you to attend the seminar and to discard your pills?" The ghost of a responding smile dawned on Maya's face.

As we chatted about the role of providence in our lives, a counselor I had been introduced to earlier that evening joined in the conversation. Within minutes it was obvious that the two women were on the same wavelength. *Great,* I thought as they walked away together, exchanging contact information. *Miracle number two. Thank You!*

Driving back to the hotel, I pondered the ways in which God answers prayer, even those that are as yet unspoken. Often the answer comes as an impression to take some action, or when an individual with vital information crosses our path. Sometimes I have recognized these opportunities and followed through on them. Other times I have failed to act. And, more is the pity, some were undoubtedly missed altogether because I didn't grasp that they were an answer to my prayer.

As we begin a new year, let us each open our eyes that we may see the opportunities God has for us. As God opens our minds, let us respond to His impressions. We have a whole year of opportunities to be an instrument of God's peace. God may have miracles to work in your life or in the lives of those around you.

Arlene R. Taylor

Beluga

Consider its ways and be wise. Prov. 6:6, NIV.

HE WAS BORN IN OUR HOUSE and was named a few seconds after his birth. "This kitten is all white," exclaimed our 5-year-old son, "except for the black spot on his head that looks like a blowhole. Let's call him 'Beluga'—just like the white whales!"

Beluga lived with us for almost 16 years, and I learned many things from him.

He was accepting. His mother died when he and his littermates were only 4½ weeks old—just old enough to lap milk. However, one of his brothers missed their mother so much that for the next four months Beluga patiently allowed him to try to nurse.

He was sociable. If he was looking for frogs beside the lake and saw our family enjoying the early-evening shadows, he would chirrup and rush up the hill to sit beside us. Occasionally he even wanted his own chair so he could be on the same level with my husband and me. He would also wait in the hallway until he saw us get into bed, and then he'd jump onto the bed and snuggle next to my knees.

He was happy, ready to purr whenever he was stroked. Often he joined me as I graded student essays, stretching out, purring and bumping my arm to call attention to his presence.

As an adult he weighed about 13 pounds, but slowly—and then with horrifying rapidity—he began to lose weight. The veterinarian said that he had kidney and liver problems. He would grow weaker and eventually die. Soon he weighed only five pounds, but still he was sociable. Still he seemed happy. Still he purred.

One night I turned over in bed and bumped Beluga, who was curled up at my knees. Sleepily I reached down to pat his head in a brief, automatic apology. He didn't respond with a purr. Had he died? If he were alive, surely he would have purred. I didn't want to turn the light on and awaken my husband, so I touched him again. He opened his eyes, and then tucked his chin down on his paws and resumed his interrupted sleep.

A few months later Beluga died, but not before I thought about his qualities: flexibility, sociability, and the ability to show his happiness and contentment to others.

If I were more catlike, I'd be more Christlike.

Denise Dick Herr

9

Just the Hem of His Garment

But Jesus said, "Someone touched me; I know that power has gone out from me." Luke 8:46, NIV.

PERHAPS YOU KNOW THE STORY told in Luke 8:40-48 of the woman who needed Jesus. Do you realize how low you have to stoop to touch the hem of a long, flowing robe? Very low, maybe even crawling on the ground. At the very least, kneeling. So there she was—weak, discouraged, probably hungry and thirsty, and quite literally bleeding to death. I picture her among that crowd, maybe scooting along on her knees behind Jesus, desperately hoping He would stop so she could tell her story. But Jesus kept moving. Jairus and his people were urging Him along for a very different reason. The throng was pushing and shoving, the noise deafening as everyone tried to get closer to Jesus. But Diana—as I have named her—couldn't keep up. Tears filled her eyes. With trembling lips she muttered to herself, "I've failed again. There is no hope." But something within her rallied, and she realized that with just one more push at least the hem of His robe would be within her reach. "I believe with all my heart that if I just touch the hem of His garment, I will be healed." No more doubt, no more hesitation. Reach out, reach out. *Reach out!* With a last effort she grasped a handful of the robe of righteousness—the very hem—and she was healed. Her body was whole again! *Now I just need to hide in the crowd for a few minutes, and He'll be . . .* But wait! Jesus was looking around. He was looking straight at her. Diana's body went limp. *What have I done? I shouldn't have touched Him.* But Jesus' voice was kind, gentle, encouraging. "I know someone touched Me, because I felt power go out from Me."

Ladies, do you see? The throng pressed against Him on all sides, but no power went out from Him. No one was healed by simply bumping into Him. Diana had it right—she reached out!

We too can touch the robe of His righteousness, and He doesn't ask us to crawl around on the ground. Just kneel and pray, "Lord, I need strength for this day."

"Daughter, do you love Me enough to humble yourself and reach out? Reach out and take the power that will go from Me. You can have courage, and you can have hope in your heart."

Diana "came trembling and fell at His feet."

Carol Wiggins Gigante

Runaway Boat Dock

When you pass through the waters, I will be with you; and when you pass through the rivers, they will not sweep over you.
Isa. 43:2, NIV.

JUST WHEN I THINK I pretty much have a handle on life, I'm thrown a curveball. In this case it was a runaway floating boat dock. It happened on one of the windiest days in January, and the temperature had plummeted into the 20s. Brrr! That's cold for Tennessee!

I remember thinking as I looked out over Norris Lake from the warmth of our living room how fortunate that we could be inside and that our furnace worked. Then I took a closer look. The shoreline in front of our house was empty. It couldn't be! Where was our boat dock? It didn't take me long to spot it drifting in the middle of the lake. The cables had come loose.

What was I going to do? I prayed, "Lord, help me! Let the wind bring the dock back to land." And just like that the wind shifted and the dock began drifting toward the shore. Even so, it was a long way from our house—across a muddy inlet.

I had to rescue that boat dock before it hit the bank. The last thing I wanted to do was to wade into the frigid water after it—or worse yet—swim for it! I gave Kari (my daughter who lived next door) an SOS, and flew down our 88 steps to the lake. As I plunged through the muddy inlet, I thought, *What am I, a 65-year-old woman with an injured ankle, doing trying to catch a runaway floating boat dock? This is crazy!*

Just as I was about to give up, Kari came running. Somehow the two of us managed to catch the dock and secure it.

Three hours later, as I was trying to warm my icy hands and feet, I thought, *This was not on my list of things to do today! I didn't have time for this!* I never wanted to be a boat dock chaser—nor had I trained for it. But isn't that the way it is in life? Many of the things we have to do we may not want to do, nor do we like doing.

That's why I've found I must give my day totally to the Lord and trust Him that He means what He says in Jeremiah 29:11: "'For I know the plans I have for you,' declares the Lord, 'plans to prosper you and not to harm you, plans to give you hope and a future'" (NIV). Otherwise, so many things that I end up having to do would seem to be a senseless waste of time!

Kay Kuzma

I Will Go With You

Cause me to hear thy lovingkindness in the morning; for in thee do I trust: cause me to know the way wherein I should walk; for I lift up my soul unto thee. Ps. 143:8.

MANY YEARS AGO I worked in a technology equipped and fully automated public relations office. Though I was not overly excited about using all this technology, there was no choice, and I loved my job. However, when that company moved to another state I decided not to move, and I changed careers. Imagine my surprise when I learned that the new company had limited technology. *This is amazing in this day and age,* I thought. Because of this change my skills quickly diminished.

But then I faced another problem. The church I attend has a strong technology team, and most of the information for committees, presentations, and planning is given via technology. So I was pressured to get involved to stay in the loop. After much resistance I asked someone for assistance and was kindly given printed information on how to choose the equipment I needed. Several months went by, and I'd made no progress. Then someone told me, "When you're ready to get your equipment, I will go with you." One week later everything I needed had been bought and installed. I was then given a quick refresher's course and my friend's assurance that if I experienced any problems, I should call.

The words spoken by my friend have never left my mind: *I will go with you.* They remind me that each day, as I make my plans, I need not fear, because Jesus has promised to go with me and to show me the way wherein I should walk. And just as my earthly friend was able to answer all the technical questions I was asked by the store assistant, so Jesus is able to answer all my questions and help me make the right decisions.

Those words have also caused me to regret the many times when, in answer to a question, I've told someone what to do or where to go, when it would have been better to say, "I'll go with you." I think of the times I've told a new Christian *about* Jesus instead of saying, "Let me walk with you until you know the way."

My prayer for each of us today is that we seek divine guidance to walk or go with those in need of help rather than merely telling them where to go or what to do.

Maureen O. Burke

Vertical Vision

And when these things begin to come to pass, then look up,
and lift up your heads; for your redemption draweth nigh. Luke 21:28.

WHEN LIFE BECOMES DIFFICULT, when pain becomes too hard to bear, we often find ourselves focusing on that pain and the circumstances that surround us. As long as we do that, we will not see the "big picture." We are locked into our own little worlds, our own pain, our own trials and tribulations. Soon Satan has convinced us that there is no hope, that there is no way out of our depression and pain.

What can we do? I am reminded of a 1915 piece of art that I acquired from my father. It was my grandmother's, and I obtained it long after her death. It depicts a realistic "photo" of Daniel in the lions' den. In the image Daniel stands in the den, surrounded by lions. It is dark. The lions are hungry. Yet they do not come near him. Daniel stands with his back to the lions. His face is turned up toward the shaft where a light, streaming as it were from heaven, shines down upon his countenance.

I fell in love with this image the moment I saw it. As I reflect upon it, the lesson is so very clear. We are to look up—we are to look to Jesus. Jesus is the Light of the world. Here is Daniel, surrounded by lions, the "problems" in his life. Is he looking at the problems? No. Daniel has chosen to look toward the heavens. He is choosing to look to Jesus, the solution.

Our natural human tendency is to focus on ourselves and on our problems. Yet, if we will look to Jesus, if we will go to Him in prayer and seek His wisdom, we will find comfort, hope, and courage. We know we shall have tribulation in this world, but that doesn't mean we can't have hope. Titus 2:13 states, "Looking for that blessed hope, and the glorious appearing of the great God and our Saviour Jesus Christ." We have hope in Christ!

We need to look up, to have a "vertical vision"—a vision that directs our eyes to our Savior, not to those troubling circumstances on our every side. Hebrews 12:2 describes what our actions should be: "Looking unto Jesus, the author and finisher of our faith, who for the joy that was set before Him endured the cross, despising the shame, and has sat down at the right hand of the throne of God" (NKJV). I don't know about you, but I choose to look to Jesus.

Samantha Nelson

The Illusion of Control

A man's heart plans his way, but the Lord directs his steps.
Prov. 16:9, NKJV.

HOW MANY OF US struggle to control ourselves and our environments? For most of us this need to control leads to stress and frustration. In some it leads to eating disorders or other destructive behavior. One day as I was lying on the bed with my 6-month-old son he reached up and began to play with my hand. I relaxed and let him explore as he moved my hand closer and then pushed it away. He would move it left and right, and try twisting it now and again. If he tried to move it in a way that was uncomfortable I simply moved my elbow or shoulder to remove the pressure or gently corrected him. He played this way for quite a while as he is a very curious little boy.

Suddenly it occurred to me that he might think he was in control. After all, if he wanted my hand to go left, it went left. Logically, he could reason that he was in control. As he was only 6 months old, I doubt he actually came to this conclusion, but others might have—not about my son moving my hand, but about their ability to control the hand of God. We are told to pray and ask God for the desires of our heart—for healing, help, and comfort, as well as anything else. However, God is not a magical genie in a bottle, and many times, even though we ask, He says, "No," or "Wait." But there are times that what we pray for is the will of God, and the answer is yes. If we are blessed to have many of those prayers answered time after time, we may feel that our diligent prayers or some other activity that we are doing is causing God to do as we ask.

This is dangerous thinking. Like Peter, when he was walking on the Sea of Galilee, it can cause us to sink, and if we aren't careful, we will drown. Why? Because Satan loves to encourage these types of thoughts. They cause us to take our eyes off Jesus and to put them on ourselves. We must never forget that God is always in control. When our prayers are answered with a "Yes," of course we rejoice. But instead of the answer indicating that God is doing *our* bidding, we know that we are doing His will.

Each day, as we hold the hand of God in faith, it is important to remember that though we hold God's hand, we don't control it. Rejoice in the joy and peace of knowing that God is in control—always.

Juli Blood

Words Without a Voice

In the beginning was the Word, and the Word was with God, and the Word was God. John 1:1.

YEARS AGO I was in an emotional crisis. I drove into my driveway and broke down in tears. Suddenly, "words without a voice" filled my head: *It will be OK.* And I was filled with a feeling of being loved, of calm, of peace, and of confidence.

That afternoon I joyfully told my minister about that reassurance. He looked serious and drew away from me. "Don't be deceived by the devil," he said. "You are not a prophet! You did not hear the voice of God. He has not directly communicated with man since Malachi!"

I was horrified. The thought of being a prophet had never crossed my mind. I immediately thought of Christ's many lessons recorded in the New Testament. Were those not the direct communication of God with people? I left the minister's office in a state of shock and bewilderment.

Later I remembered Isaiah 8:20: "To the law and to the testimony! If they do not speak according to this word, it is because there is no light in them" (NKJV). So I decided to test my experience. I found John 14:27: "Peace I leave with you, my peace I give unto you: not as the world giveth, give I unto you. Let not your heart be troubled, neither let it be afraid" (KJV). My experience in the driveway stood up to the Bible criteria. God had spoken to me to give me peace in a time of trouble.

But God has always communicated with people. I believe that He speaks quietly to our souls, but not with a voice we have heard before. His words of love and comfort, reproof, teaching, guiding, and instruction are not audible, but nevertheless they are from Him. The problem is we do not recognize the "words without a voice" because we do not believe that God will personally "speak" to us. We don't expect to hear from God, so we don't listen for Him.

Know that God does speak to you in love and comfort every day of your life. Learn to listen for God's "words without a voice," and you too will be able to hear Him. If the "words without a voice" you experience pass the test of Isaiah 8:20, then believe, learn, and obey. One must listen for God's "words without a voice" to learn to recognize them. Please listen!

Darlenejoan McKibbin Rhine

Adoration

I will extol you, my God and King, and bless your name forever and ever. Every day I will bless you, and praise your name forever and ever. Great is the Lord, and greatly to be praised; his greatness is unsearchable. Ps. 145:1-3, NRSV.

ONE SABBATH MORNING I felt the presence of God come upon me. In my ministry life I've become aware that in my spiritual disciplines, adoration to God isn't always part of my devotional life. However, as I examined Psalms and Proverbs, I noticed a theme of adoration to God the Father, Son, and Holy Spirit.

In the lives of biblical characters—particularly David—we see substantial moments of time dedicated to adoring God. I too have discovered that there is something therapeutic about adoration and praise to God. As I hear the incredibly poignant stories of precious people walking the Christian journey, they tell me that they aren't always in adoration of our Father. Listening to their diverse journeys, I sometimes detect that their faith and trust in God has been challenged. If your faith and trust is being challenged, it will be more difficult to come before God in adoration. However, with your adoration, your struggle with faith and trust will begin to change.

In my own personal experience, knowing God and searching for Him with all my heart, soul, and mind is the preface to adoration. When I've been greatly stressed during the days or weeks of my multifaceted life—giving and emptying of myself to people—I've encountered the truth that adoration lifts me to a higher plane of life.

According to Webster's dictionary, "adoration," as a noun, means an act of adoring. Webster says further that the root word, "adore," is: "1: to worship or honor as a deity or as divine; 2: to regard with loving admiration and devotion; 3: to be extremely fond of."

"O Lord, I will honor and praise your name, for you are my God. You do such wonderful things! You planned them long ago, and now you have accomplished them" (Isa. 25:1, NLT). God created us with the yearning to adore Him as Creator, Lord, and Redeemer—longing for Him to be Lord of our lives. I challenge you today: Take time to adore Him. He is our King of kings and Lord of lords. He is— Jesus Christ our Lord!

Mary L. Maxson

Letting Christ Shine Through

I can do all this through him who gives me strength.
Phil. 4:13, NIV.

MY SISTER DIED LAST WEEK. When at my sister's house, I noticed her walker-on-wheels by the garage door. I took a picture of it to remind me that in heaven she will literally run and not get weary. Yes, Lynne without hospice, IVs, prosthesis, surgeons, neurologists, prescriptions, canes, and pain. As I said the day she died, "I'll have a sister again on resurrection morning. She'll be better than new!" And as I said to her at her casket, "I'll see you in the morning."

Lynne's death gives new life to the Scriptures for me. The night before she died she requested to hear the hymn "Blessed Assurance." And now she indeed rests assured. Lynne resides in a gravesite on a hilltop that overlooks a river. It's her well-deserved rest. There was no cure for her cancer and neuromuscular disease, but I remember reading that rest was the only remedy that could alleviate her symptoms. She is now resting. But not for long!

The week before Lynne died I received a story of grief and gratitude. It was a testament to Lynne, who was a quilter herself. It seems that a woman faced her Maker at the last judgment. Before her, and other women, their lives lay like the squares of a quilt. An angel sat sewing the quilt squares into a tapestry of the life. The woman reported, "But as my angel took each piece of cloth, I noticed how ragged and torn my squares were. Each was labeled with a part of my life that had been difficult—the challenges and illnesses that I'd faced, the hardships making the biggest holes of all. I glanced around. Nobody else had such squares. Other than a tiny hole here and there, the other tapestries were filled with bright hues of color. My heart sank.

"Finally, it was time for each life to be displayed, held up to the light. Each woman held up her tapestry. Their lives seemed so filled. Then my angel nodded for me to rise.

"When I stood and lifted to the light the combined squares of my life, everyone gasped. As I looked upon my life's tapestry I saw that light flooded through the many holes, creating an image. It was the face of Christ. 'Every time you gave your life over to Me, it became My life, My hardship, My struggle,' Jesus said. "'Each point of light in your life is when you stepped aside and let Me shine through.'"

So loved ones, may all your quilts be threadbare and worn, so Christ can shine through!

Diane Shellyn Nudd

You've Got Mail

Now unto him that is able to do exceedingly abundantly above all that we ask or think, according to the power that worketh in us. Eph. 3:20.

DURING A SLOW DAY AT WORK I randomly began checking my e-mail and saw that one of them stated "Check out my cosmetics sale." *This must be junk mail,* I thought, *as so many of them are these days.* I was very close to deleting it when something made me stop, and I clicked on it instead. The message invited anyone interested in purchasing cosmetics to dial the contact number. I hastily wrote down the number and stuffed it into my purse.

A couple of weeks later, when I ran out of foundation, I found the discarded note. I picked up my cell phone and made an evening appointment. When I got to the house the cosmetic consultant introduced herself as Ella. Her house was in disarray. The kitchen was filled with boxes of all kinds of products for nails, skin types, and much more.

Ella's demeanor told me that her heart was also in shambles, outwardly seeping with sadness and grief. As we continued talking, she confided the story of the abuse she and her two children had endured during the past couple years. My heart went out to her as she told me about her husband's drug use. I then asked if I could pray with her. She readily took the inspirational tract I gave her, let me hug her, and smiled when I said that I'd stay in touch.

In the midst of her trials, the Lord brought Ella and me together. Our friendship strengthened over time as I helped her address her needs of moving to a shelter, finding a job, and obtaining transportation. She then told me the truth: that she was also doing drugs. At last, events caused her to end up in the prison system. Even though I had never been to a jail facility, I went to visit her. In the loneliness of her prison cell, Ella called out to God. God was gracious and answered Ella's prayers. She was able to get into a rehabilitation program to deal with the debilitating issues that arose from her dysfunctional relationships.

I asked her one day how she got my e-mail address. She had no idea. In her dire straits, she had simply sent out a mass mailing, hoping for anyone to respond. As we look back, we both marvel at the way God worked to bring us together in such a miraculous way.

Does God know your e-mail address? You bet He does.

Karen Phillips

He Was Buried Alive

Praise ye the Lord . . . Praise the Lord; for the Lord is good. Ps. 135:1-3.

ON TUESDAY, JANUARY 12, 2010, an earthquake (7.0 on the Richter scale) hit Port-au-Prince, Haiti, collapsing numerous buildings and killing more than 300,000 people. Many of them were buried under the concrete rubble. At first, recovery efforts were slow, for experts from other countries had to be flown in to help. People began to be unearthed, some alive, some dead. By the third day, hope started to fade. It was known that without food and water and often injured, people would begin to die under that rubble.

On the seventh day a miracle occurred. An 8-year-old boy was unearthed—alive! I watched on TV as they lifted him into the air. His face was beaming with an ear-to-ear smile, and his hands were lifted up to heaven as he praised and thanked God. To me it was a touching scene. His attitude almost seemed more important than his miraculous rescue. I was moved to tears as several thoughts raced through my mind.

This young boy, who was buried so deep that it took seven days to get to him, should have been hungry, thirsty, weak, and terrified. No doubt he wondered where everyone was! Seven days equals one week, which equals 168 hours, equaling 10,080 minutes, the approximate time that he was down there alone. Did he panic? Was he conscious of day or night? Did he cry? If he did, that was acceptable. Yet, as he was lifted up and out, his face showed no evidence of torture or fear. He was eternally thankful to be out.

I couldn't help comparing him to so many of us. We too are buried under the rubble of the sin and evil caused by another earthquake, Satan's temptations, which probably read 100 on God's Richter scale. Unlike that little boy who didn't know if he would be rescued, we *know* that Jesus died to rescue us. Yet we go through life morose, complaining, and unthankful, bemoaning our poor, unhappy lot. I can't help wondering, *How does that make God feel?*

It is my hope that we remember that one day we too will be lifted up and out into eternal freedom. May we so live that our hearts are ready, that our faces exhibit our faith and gratitude to God so that others will also be drawn to our Lord and Savior.

Joyce O'Garro

Broken Dreams

Joseph dreamed a dream.
Gen. 37:5.

CLOSETS ARE MUSEUMS of broken dreams: dresses we bought in hopes of having an occasion to wear them, shoes we wore only once. And there are outfits that almost fit when we bought them, thinking we would lose a few pounds—but never did.

Recently I had to make more space in my cramped closet. As I ruthlessly discarded items that were too old or no longer fit me, I came across *the dress.* I had bought it 15 years earlier because it was the perfect dress for a special occasion. Even though I didn't need it at the time, I bought it because it made me feel young, slim, and attractive.

As the years passed, I wore it only once, but it was so beautiful that I kept it, thinking there would surely be another occasion when I would wear it and again feel young, slim, and attractive. But as I studied it a few days ago, I was forced to admit that my wonderful dress was not only out of style, but no longer fit my middle-aged body.

I cried as I put the still-beautiful dress in the bag to take to the thrift store—cried for dreams that never came true, for the times I wanted to feel young and attractive, times that never happened. Life is littered with broken dreams, and that dress is a symbol of mine.

I'm reminded of another person who had broken dreams: Joseph, the dreamer, the favorite son of his father, Jacob. Joseph surely shed tears when he was betrayed by his brothers and sold into slavery. He must have cried, if only inside, when Potipher's wife lied about him, and he was put in prison. But despite disappointments and injustices, he did not turn his back on God. Eventually God used Joseph's dreams in a much bigger way than he imagined—to save an entire nation from famine. In the process God gave Joseph new dreams and bold new realities—prime minister of Egypt, savior of his own family, and finally, reunion with his beloved father.

From Joseph's story we learn that God is interested in our dreams, but His dreams for us are much bigger than our own. God sometimes delays making our dreams come true so that greater good may come about. As I cried about my dress, I realized that God's dreams for me have always been bigger than a dress. Countless times He has taken my broken dreams and used them for the good of others and for His glory. I am safe giving my dreams to God.

Carla Baker

Distress in the Big City!

A hostile world! I call to God, I cry to God to help me. From his palace he hears my call; my cry brings me right into his presence—a private audience! Ps. 18:6, Message.

I JOKINGLY SAY TO MY FRIENDS, "God gives us children to keep us on our knees." I recently proved once again how real God is and how He hears our cries for help. My husband's niece was getting married in New Jersey, and we all were excited about traveling there to be with family and friends once again. Those of us from the Caribbean islands always look forward to visiting the United States. Weeks before we left, I asked God to protect us as we traveled. Our second daughter who attended college in Tennessee would meet us in New Jersey. She would be traveling alone from Atlanta, Georgia. Of course, this made her feel grown-up—she was 20—but this did not make her mother feel any less worried.

We arrived in New Jersey ahead of our daughter and had a wonderful time shopping and spending time with family. On the day of her arrival we traveled by limousine to the hotel where we would stay. However, the fare was more than we had anticipated, and we still had to get our daughter from the airport. We decided to use the same limousine service, but to our chagrin we were told that the fare would be $175 if we went along, but only $85 if the driver went alone.

I began to panic. Suddenly my once-perfect trip was unraveling right before my eyes. My pastor-husband suggested that we ask the driver to pick up our daughter. Even though I was very uncomfortable with this idea, I couldn't think of another solution. So off the limousine drove, leaving us to do the only thing we could do—pray! And pray we did! We immediately called our daughter and explained the situation to her. You may know how a mother's mind works: scenes of TV cop shows—girls found dead in the big city—danced wildly in my head. But I continued to pray that God would protect our girl. Meanwhile, as she rode in the limo, I kept her on the phone, constantly checking the front door of the hotel. That was the longest 45 minutes of my life! When she finally walked through the hotel lobby, I thought I would burst from sheer thankfulness and joy. God had given me a private audience in His presence!

As our text says in another version, "I was in terrible trouble when I called out to you, but from your temple you heard me and answered my prayer" (CEV). He will do it for you, too!

Lynn C. Smith

Fitting Shoes

And thine ears shall hear a word behind thee, saying, This is the way, walk ye in it, when ye turn to the right hand, and when ye turn to the left. Isa. 30:21.

WHENEVER I ASK MY HUSBAND to buy shoes for me, I can't just tell him the size, because not all companies number the sizes the same way. So to be safe, I trace my foot on paper, cut out the shape, and give it to my husband. Even then I have had to ask him to return shoes and bring the next size. Actually, I need to go shopping myself so I can try them on.

When I was much younger, I was more interested in the style of the shoes than the right size alone. I must confess that I had a passion for shoes. I bought shoes mainly for style and the fashion of the day. I admit that was rather vain on my part. Now that I'm old and retired I look for comfort. I need to be secure when I walk, and I also want to keep my feet warm.

On our recent trip to Thailand our son took us to a night market that sold secondhand shoes. I am not one who would be interested in old shoes, so I was not at all interested in buying any. I just looked around at the women's section while the men selected theirs. However, I did end up convinced to buy a pair that was practically new. I checked them carefully, and there was no indication that they had ever been worn. Whoever the owner had been, I was impressed that she must have been very careful and particular with her things. So whenever I wear these shoes, I feel I must prove worthy to own them.

As I think about shoes, my mind goes to Jesus when He was here in this world. I feel sure He must have owned only one pair at a time. And perhaps that one pair had to be repaired often. In His ministry Jesus must have worn the local, common sandals. Such shoes allow the dust to pass through easily, but they couldn't keep the feet clean or warm. Those sandals took Him to distant villages and towns. He went about doing good, seeking and saving the lost. My favorite author calls such shoes the "gospel shoes." She writes, "Let all see that your feet are shod with the preparation of the gospel of peace and good will to men. Wonderful are the results we shall see if we enter into the work imbued with the Spirit of Christ" (*Evangelism*, p. 564).

My prayer is that I wear the gospel shoes that I may go where the Spirit leads me.

Birdie Poddar

Safe and Secure

Thou shalt not be afraid for the terror by night; nor for the arrow that flieth by day; nor for the pestilence that walketh in darkness; nor for the destruction that wasteth at noonday. A thousand shall fall at thy side, and ten thousand at thy right hand; but it shall not come nigh thee. Ps. 91:5-7.

SOMEONE ONCE READ a poem to me that I have not been able to find again. The poet would leave mansions near paradise for others; he wanted a cabin in the gates of hell so that he could maybe stop and turn some people around at the gates. I want my ministry to be like that. I would like to snatch people from the devil's clutches just as they are on the verge of entering hell.

After nearly five years at Miracle Meadows School (a program for at-risk youth), I have found that the gates of hell can be a pretty hot place. The devil does not like for anyone to be tugged from his grasp. It is by the grace of God that he doesn't destroy both my cabin and me.

I recently had an illustration of God's care when I went to a teachers' training session with four other teachers. I was driving, thinking about other things, when all of a sudden the van started to shake. I smelled burning rubber, so I thought we'd blown a tire. But I was able to safely steer the van onto the shoulder.

We all got out to see the damage, and found transmission fluid pouring out. Our tires were intact, but a damaged tire was rolling after us. We had not seen it, but we had hit it.

"Well, I guess I need to call Mr. Weber to pull the van," the principal said. We had been on the road for four hours—our destination was still four hours ahead.

A patrolman came and drove us to a convenience store where we could get something cool to drink and wait in relative comfort. We called AAA to bring the van. When my colleagues walked back to meet the tow truck, they found our driveshaft in three pieces on the highway. The broken shaft had dented the gas tank. If it had hit a little harder, we probably would have burned or exploded.

"You know," one of the other teachers said, "I hadn't had any near scrapes until I started to really follow God. Then . . ." She let herself trail off. She is right, of course. Our enemy attacks when he sees us close to God. But our Father is bigger than all the plans of the enemy.

Paula Graham

"I Like Christians"

For he shall give his angels charge over thee, to keep thee in all thy ways.
Ps. 91:11.

HERMIE MUNEZ, his wife, Daniela, and two children were jolted awake very early one morning when five men with guns burst into their home. The Munez family are missionaries in Africa.

Quickly the thieves tied Hermie's hands and neck and ordered Daniela to collect the things they wanted—mainly money. The problem was that the Munez family had very little cash. Again and again the robbers slapped Daniela's face and hit her on the head, demanding she get them more money. The 11-year-old daughter, Joanne, and 4-year-old son, Zuriel, cowered in the corner, praying earnestly throughout the two-hour ordeal.

When the men turned to start their looting, Daniela and the children began singing "Jesus Keep Me Near the Cross." Soon they noticed that each time they sang the word *Jesus* the robbers stopped what they were doing. However, after ransacking the house, one of the robbers angrily slapped Daniela hard in her face, again demanding money. Another plugged in the iron and turned on the stove. Daniela's heart jumped into her throat. She had heard that the robbers often tortured their victims by holding a hot iron on their face, or holding their head against the red-hot burner on the stove.

"Dad," she whispered, fear gripping her heart, "they are going to iron me."

Hermie, who was having trouble breathing with the rope tight around his neck, managed to squeeze out a raspy whisper: "Ma, just pray. Keep on praying."

And they did. Daniela and the children prayed and started reciting Psalm 23. As he heard the words of that familiar chapter, one of the robbers turned to his friends and said, "Oh, they are Christians. Let's go."

As they started gathering up the things they wanted to take, the other robbers demanded that the entire family lie on their stomachs, heads down. Daniela covered herself and the children with a blanket, thinking that it would be better not to see what the men did next. Those were the longest moments in their lives—waiting for the sound of the gun. But it didn't come. Then they heard one of the men say, "Don't worry, we will not kill you. I like Christians."

Jemima Dollosa Orillosa

The Master Designer

Our Lord and God, you are worthy to receive glory, honor, and power. You created all things, and by your decision they are and were created. Rev. 4:11, CEV.

WHAT A GLORIOUS PLACE Eden must have been! How fulfilling and enjoyable for Adam and Eve to inhabit and tend it, along with the creatures living there. But we've come a long way from Eden. Sin has taken its toll. But marred as it is, the imprint of God still exists.

From our family room slider we get a panoramic view of our backyard and the woods beyond it. To me, God's imprint is evident there. From the mighty oaks, towering high above our two-story house, to the smallest maple sapling, one can see the details that are unique to each species. The shapes of the leaves, the texture of the bark, and the contour of the branches identify them. The leaves and blossoms of the smaller plants vary in size, color, and shape, distinguishing themselves from each other and showing their unique beauty.

Bushy-tailed gray, black, and red squirrels and tiny little chipmunks, wearing handsome coats, choose our yard as a place to get a drink and eat the seeds dropped from the bird feeders. Their antics delight us. Only a Master Designer can give a squirrel the ability to climb vertically and jump at dizzying heights from one tree to another without falling. And how do those tiny chipmunks have the strength to dig holes under the earth?

Who tells the fawns with spotted coats and the adult deer when to change the color of their hides?

Feeding the birds gives us joy beyond measure. They come in all sizes, from the huge wild turkeys strutting out of the woods with their young to the tiny hummingbirds gathering nectar from the flowers on the deck. The many varieties with their beautiful colored feathers grace our feeders. Each is equipped with just the right kind of beak, feet, and wings to meet their needs. How do they know when the feeder is supplied with food and when it's empty?

When examining nature closely, how can anyone believe there is no God? We don't have to look far to see abundant evidence of a master designer. In my mind evolution is a hoax. The God of the universe is the Creator of all nature. That is my belief, and I am sticking to it. I hope it is yours, too!

Marian M. Hart

My Father's Glasses

But blessed are your eyes, for they see: and your ears, for they hear.
Matt. 13:16.

MY FATHER DIED IN 2005. Since my mom could not bring herself to clean out his stuff, it was not until after her death two years later that we started the clearing-out process. Going through my dad's top dresser drawer, I found a few personal items such as a pocket watch from our grandfather, newspaper clippings, and glasses. Six pairs of glasses.

He probably kept all these glasses so that if he broke one pair, he could easily return to the "old pair," and so save a little money, or perhaps use them until he got another pair. Out of curiosity I decided to try them on to see what kind of vision my father had.

Was I ever shocked! My father, who sat up late nights reading books, the newspaper, or the latest *Reader's Digest,* was apparently legally blind in one eye. I could see through the lens on one side, but the second lens looked like a thick fog. I started to cry. Daddy really did have bad eyes. Probably that was why he so often insisted that I get my kids' eyes checked.

It was then that a story Dad had told me as a child, about his "lazy eye," came to mind. "I remember riding in a buggy with Dad and Mother when I was about 5," he'd said. "I could put my hand over one eye and see fine, but when I covered the other eye, everything was dark, with just a little light shining through. When I got older, my parents got me some glasses, but my vision was poor in one eye. If only someone had put a patch on the good eye and made my poor eye work a little harder to strengthen it, I could possibly have had better vision in this one eye."

So for 90 years my father had not had good vision. Yet he had reared a family, kept a job, and lived normally. We never thought about how his eyesight was less than perfect.

How often do we look at a person and not really know how they see the world? Do they "see" things through cloudy eyes, eyes that make their life bitter? Or do they have clear eyesight, having a joy reflected in the brightness of their eyes? It's likely that Helen Keller, who had lost her eyesight by the age of 2, never remembered seeing anything. But her inner sight was one of happiness, delight, and positive thoughts. If we could look through others' eyes, it might help us better understand how their decisions were made. We might even see things the way God wants us to see the world.

Charlotte Robinson

Mission to Chile

Let us run with patience the race
that is set before us. Heb. 12:1.

IT STARTED AS A DREAM—a daydream—that one day I would go on a real mission trip. It was an impossible hope in many ways. So for years I contented myself with teaching the church's elementary school and the knowledge that right here was a mission field too. As group after group of children passed through my hands I prayed that I had been able to make a difference in their lives, that somehow my presence had led them to the foot of the cross. When years went by and many former students told me of their service to God, I was filled with a sense of accomplishment. Yet that did not fill my need to go on a mission trip of my own.

Years later, on a Christian TV station, I watched stories of people doing mission trips with a group called Maranatha, and my hopes returned that one day I could do it myself.

Then sometime ago I learned of a mission trip to Chile, and my thoughts and hopes went into high gear. I laid my hopes out to God: *God, I am willing to work every day to earn the money for a mission trip.* So I did substitute teaching for a few months. Every day that I worked I dreamed of that day when I would be in Chile.

Then came the biggest disappointment of my life. That mission trip was canceled. I kept my grief inside and smiled outwardly. I asked God, *Why?* But I got no answers. Someone suggested that my mission trip money could be used elsewhere, but I refused to spend it. I didn't know why plans had changed, but I have learned that sometimes God has even better plans.

The phone call came late in 2008. "Mother, would you still like to go to Chile?"
"Yes!"

"Well, our church is going, and there's space for you if you'd like to go."

Suddenly God's plan became clear. Not only would I get to go on a mission trip, but I would be going with my son. A double blessing indeed!

I am home now, and my experience was all and more than I had ever hoped for. My thoughts often go back to the new friends I made, to the opportunity to hear my son preach an evangelistic series, and to see tears of joy on the faces of people who appreciated the efforts we had made on their behalf. Truly God has marvelous plans for each of us.

Patricia Cove

A Lesson in Waiting

Wait on the Lord: be of good courage, and he shall strengthen thine heart: wait, I say, on the Lord. Ps. 27:14.

WHEN I MOVED TO CHARLOTTE, North Carolina, little did I know that faith would be greatly tested in that lovely town. After unsuccessfully job hunting, I decided to return to my job in New York. However, just three days before my return, a part-time teaching position at a college became available. Should I give up a job with benefits and years of experience for a part-time job with no benefits? I asked God to have the director offer me a position immediately. Well, she did, and after a day of praying, I accepted. I had no way of knowing that the Lord had plans to use this part-time job to help me learn a lesson in waiting.

I began teaching six classes in September, was cut to three in March, and had no classes after April. Again I was unemployed! In October, however, one of my colleagues told me about a full-time position at another college. I applied, but heard nothing from them. Disappointed, I went through the summer on unemployment until the part-time director asked me to return to work in September. However, it would be the same routine—six classes in September and no classes after April.

I prayed for a full-time teaching position with benefits, but became discouraged listening to the news about the heavy layoffs in education. I wondered how long God was going to keep me waiting. Through it all I decided this was a good time to build my relationship with the Lord, to trust Him fully. He would come through one day.

When the part-time job was about to end in April, I did not know if I would be able to make it through another summer, even with unemployment benefits. Then three days before this job ended, I received a call from the administrator of the college that I had applied to the previous October. "Agnes, are you still interested in a position at our college?" Shocked, I could hardly stammer a reply. After the interview God gave me that full-time job.

I understand now that when God says to wait, He does not answer in our time, but in His. During that time of uncertainty, thanks to my God and family I never went hungry, and my bills were always paid. I thank God for teaching me a real lesson in waiting.

Agnes Vaughan

My Time Is in Your Hands

I trust in you, Lord; I say, "You are my God." My times are in your hands.
Ps. 31:14, 15, NIV.

THERE ARE MANY INTERESTING WAYS to spend our time. While reading a magazine a few days ago, I found out that in a lifetime the average American will spend six months sitting at traffic lights waiting for the light to change. They will spend one year searching through desk clutter looking for misplaced objects, and eight months opening junk mail. They will spend five years of their life waiting in lines. Three years in meetings. I think it is a whole lot more than that! We get interrupted 73 times a day. It seems like such a waste, doesn't it? It is crazy. Think about what really matters in life, and then think about all of those real meaningful relationship activities that we are doing—or could or should be doing. We need to get control of our time and begin spending it wisely.

Ministering to the women in different cultures, one of the challenges a woman faces—and it does not matter what culture she lives in—is *not* to orchestrate her life or to plan her year, but to order each day, allowing for sufficient rest, proper nourishment and exercise, and quiet time spent exclusively with the Lord.

I like to think that our lives are like a train. Like trains, our lives have a starting point and final destination. It runs on a divinely appointed schedule and makes important stops along the way. We have a powerful engine, the Holy Spirit, who moves us along the tracks of faith and obedience. And like the train, we are well cared for and maintained by God's Word.

Today is a special day because you are exactly where God wants you to be in your journey. Maybe you are waiting for a miracle or a promise that needs to be fulfilled, or you are eager to move on to something new. Maybe you are crying and praying for someone, or asking God for healing—or any other desire. Do not forget: just because you are waiting, it does not mean that God is not working. There may be obstacles that first need to be removed before God moves you on in His will.

The truth is, if you are waiting at a station or moving on, the important thing to remember is that your times are in His hands and that He knows what is best for you because His eyes are fixed upon you.

Raquel Queiroz da Costa Arrais

The Prophet's Room

One day Elisha went to Shunem. And a well-to-do woman was there, who urged him to stay for a meal. So whenever he came by, he stopped there to eat. She said to her husband, "I know that this man who often comes our way is a holy man of God. Let's make a small room on the roof and put in it a bed and a table, a chair and a lamp for him. Then he can stay there whenever he comes to us." 2 Kings 4:8-10, NIV.

NOW THAT MOST OF OUR CHILDREN have left home we have more space in our house. So we prepared a guest room on the top floor under the rafters. It is decorated with the many exotic items my parents had collected. It's a beautiful room, with an Asian flair. The only problem is that it is in the attic and can be reached only by a ladder and a trap door.

We had friends from another country visiting, a pastor with his family. I considered giving them our bedroom for their stay, but we sleep on a waterbed. From my personal experience I know that you cannot sleep well on a waterbed if you aren't used to it. But how should I explain to them the access to the guest room?

I thought about the Bible story of the room on the roof for the prophet, so I told them that we had prepared the prophet's room for them. They understood the allusion and had no problems with the ladder and slept well in the attic room.

The woman of Shunem wanted to care for the needs of the prophet because she saw in him a man of God. She always invited him in for a meal, but she felt she should do more. She wanted him to stay longer in her house. That is why she added another room to the top of the house. Am I as interested in having God live in my house? Do I want to involve Him in everything that happens in our home? Do I have room for Him in my everyday life? Is my house a house of the Lord? "Unless the Lord builds the house, the builders labor in vain" (Ps. 127:1, NIV).

In the end, the most beautiful house without the Lord is worthless. But if, today, the Lord lives in our home, we will one day live in the house He is preparing for us right now. "My Father's house has many rooms; if that were not so, would I have told you that I am going there to prepare a place for you? And if I go and prepare a place for you, I will come back and take you to be with me that you also may be where I am" (John 14:2, 3, NIV).

Hannele Ottschofski

Answered Prayers

Before they call I will answer; while they are still speaking I will hear.
Isa. 65:24, NIV.

RECENTLY TODAY'S TEXT became a reality in my life. I was walking to town after a spirit-filled prayer and fasting service at one of the local churches. I had used my computer for a presentation during the service, and now I struggled along, carrying it. The island's heat was sweltering and the humidity high as I walked under the midday sun. I felt weary just thinking of all the errands I had to do in town.

By the time I got to the supermarket I was very tired. I prayed desperately that God would provide a ride for me to get home with my groceries. Otherwise I would have to catch a bus, which would leave me two blocks from home. That would mean a struggle with the groceries up an incline to get to my apartment. My funds were so low that I couldn't afford a cab. Now, I must point out that only divine intervention could provide a ride home for me, as I was relatively new to the island and had recently relocated to this apartment. At the checkout I still had no answer to my prayer. So as I walked from the supermarket with the extra load, I changed my request: *Lord, if You will not provide the ride, then give me the strength to bear this load.* I felt peace and reassurance as I continued the short walk to the bus terminal.

Then, hurrying to catch the bus, I almost bumped into Rose, the wife of one of my colleagues. We exchanged pleasantries, and then she rushed on, explaining that she was trying to meet her husband, who, incidentally, was parked in front of the supermarket. I continued down the street when I heard someone behind me shouting my name. It was Rose. "My husband wants to give you a ride home," she told me. They lived in the city, and to take me home was a huge diversion. I later learned that they had gotten their meeting place mixed up because of my colleague's "momentary amnesia." So instead of meeting his wife at the center of town he ended up in front of the supermarket.

Mixed-up plans? I don't think so. I clearly see the hand of God in that situation. "Ask and it will be given to you; seek and you will find; knock and the door will be opened to you" (Matt. 7:7, NIV). I need to always remember as I go through each day that God is just a prayer away.

Tamar Boswell

It's Hard to Wait

Meanwhile, the people were waiting for Zechariah and wondering why he stayed so long in the temple. Luke 1:21, NIV.

TO ME, "WAIT" IS A CRUEL WORD. I don't like to wait for anything! With this attitude, I cannot understand the female dove in the garden outside my bathroom. She remains seated on her nest for weeks, waiting for her eggs to hatch. I can watch her while I'm taking my shower. How can she be so patient, waiting so long? Seated there all the time without even going to look for food! But all things have their own schedule. And if you try to hurry up the hatching of a baby bird or chick, you only destroy the baby waiting to be hatched.

When I have to accompany my husband somewhere, I always carry a book or crossword puzzles because I don't like to just sit in the car and wait for him. So while he runs his errands, I can read without feeling the impatience of waiting.

Most of our frenetic, frenzied, whirling world sees the word "wait" as unmerciful. We are so often impetuous and impatient, wanting things to be our way and to take place within the time frame that we stipulate. Why should I write a letter if I can e-mail or text my message? We expect instant results and instant action.

The truth is that we think we can't wait. We want people to understand now! We want people to change now! We want people to perform smoothly and in a vivid way! Now. The wise Solomon has already said that "there is a time for everything, and a season for every activity under heavens" (Eccl. 3:1, NIV). The fact is that we don't have the patience to wait for the right time for things to happen.

But we should not run ahead of God. If we don't wait on Him, we will run with no power and with disastrous results. We will destroy the wonderful plan He has in mind for us. During my life I have learned that every day I have to study God's Word with prayer and ask Him to give me power and patience like the people who waited for the priest Zechariah to come out of the Temple. I think they waited a long time. Maybe they grew tired of waiting, and they worried about what had happened to their priest. But the Bible says that they "waited."

We have waited for the second coming of Jesus for a long time. I pray that God may give us patience to continue waiting, because He knows the right time—and it's actually very near.

Ani Köhler Bravo

Isn't It Just Like God?

If you declare with your mouth, "Jesus is Lord," and believe in your heart that God raised him from the dead, you will be saved. Rom. 10:9, NIV.

They replied, "Believe in the Lord Jesus, and you will be saved—you and your household." Acts 16:31, NIV.

SINCE I WAS 6 YEARS OLD I knew I was God's kid, and from that time on I have believed in the Father, Son, and Holy Spirit, and that Jesus is my Savior. One day on my way home from school, I was trapped by some older, bullying kids who had surrounded me. I could see no way out, but I felt faith also. Suddenly I was pulled backwards by my coat collar, and those mean kids were scattering. One of my four older brothers (I was one of the youngest of 10) was driving by from work and saved me. He gave me a ride home in his work truck, and I felt very safe and delighted. Isn't it just like God to send someone to save me when I was really scared and praying inside my head?

There were times I did have to fight (which I hated) while walking home, but I had quite a temper, and many got hurt. I got in trouble more than once because my glasses got broken. With so many children my parents did not have what some call "spare money." Soon I grew older and was walking my younger sister home from school and had to protect her. She was my sister!

When the Israelites were leaving Egypt with Moses, they felt their backs against the wall at the Red Sea. But God made a path of dry land with walls of water on each side. I'm sure it was by His mighty and wondrously strong hands. Then He told them, "Go!" The way God protects should reassure His people for a long time, but in a short time that assurance is easily forgotten.

Jesus has shown me again and again how He saves me, not just from my sins, but from myself and bad situations. My sisters in Christ and I pray for each other so that faith and grace are ours. We meet after the luncheon at church and go over our list of prayer requests. When I feel "trapped" in a group of people in controversy and chaos, my head is busy with internal prayers for simple answers. The more simple the answer the better, and prayers are answered perpetually. Isn't that just like God? I'm so thankful.

Sally J. Aken-Linke

The Golden Strands of Love

For God so loved the world that he gave his one and only Son, that whoever believes in him shall not perish but have eternal life. John 3:16, NIV.

OFTEN WE CHRISTIANS FOCUS on the things in life that separate and make us different rather than on the similarities we share and the attributes that make us one in Christ.

Aunt Dolly's life exemplifies true Christianity. She gives generously of herself, her time, her talents, and her financial resources to the needy and not-so-needy. Her recipients often have no religious or familial connection to her. She lives a life of constant prayer and thanksgiving, even for the trials that come her way. This was evident to my family and me on a recent trip to Jamaica, where we were guests in her home for an extended period of time.

Hers is not an easy life. Shortly after my aunt and uncle retired and moved back to their homeland, Uncle Herman suffered a severe stroke that greatly affected his speech and motor skills. Aunt Dolly's professional nursing skills became a priceless gift in caring for him. Her devotion to his care, however, leaves little time for herself. His inability to travel also means her inability to travel. Despite this seeming hardship, she tends to my uncle with praise and thanksgiving to God for His wonderful care.

While my aunt and I do not share the same religious doctrines as far as certain tenets go, we have developed a deep bond through our mutual Christian beliefs that are wound together by the golden strands of love. The commonalities we share include a deep faith in Jesus Christ as our Lord and Savior. We also share the belief that prayer is our only medium of communication with God through Christ Jesus, through whom we have eternal life.

As I reflect on our visit on the hill in Montego Bay, the devotions and meditations we shared, I must conclude that the things that bind us together are far greater than the things that divide us as Christians. Today, let us endeavor to find in each other those common threads that make us uniquely Christian women and avoid the differences that would bring discord and separate us. Jesus told His disciples, "Other sheep I have which are not of this fold; them also I must bring, and they will hear My voice; and there will be one flock and one shepherd" (John 10:16, NKJV).

Avis Mae Rodney

Wake Up!

Awake thou that sleepest, and arise
from the dead. Eph. 5:14.

THE DAZZLING LIGHT and the soft padded footsteps of the nurses brought me out of a heavy sleep. "Wake up, sleepyhead," they coaxed. "It's time to get you ready for surgery. Let us help you onto this gurney," I noticed the clock. It was 6:00 a.m. My brain slowly registered—colon cancer!

What lies ahead? Just two days previously I had experienced an unusual discomfort in my abdomen, and my doctor felt I should have a CAT scan. It revealed a large mass in my bowel area, and now I was in the hospital, preparing for surgery. I had informed the doctor that if it was cancer I didn't want chemo or radiation treatments. I was prepared to die without all the chemicals that I knew would make me very sick and then still might not cure me. I had asked the surgeon if he was a Christian, and he assured me that he was. I felt surprisingly at peace, though everything around me was so weird and perplexing.

The room into which the nurses rolled me buzzed with activity. They took all the necessary information, hooked me up to numerous machines, and took my vital signs. The anesthesiologist came in and calmly explained all about his job and what was going to happen. Then he put a mask over my nose and told me to breathe slowly.

Seemingly, the next instant I heard, "Frances, wake up! It's all over."

Another voice added, "The surgery is over, and you are in the recovery room." I opened my eyes. Nurses were all around me—I was still alive! The nurses rolled me back into my room. Now awake and in my room, I heard the doctor explaining the details to my son. I knew I was well cared for. However, my brain kept hearing the call, "Frances, wake up!"

I could visualize the resurrection morning and what it will be like when Jesus returns and calls the righteous from the graves to life again. What a beautiful day that is going to be! Oh, how I want to hear that voice and hear Him call my name! Job says it so well: "And after my skin has been destroyed, yet in my flesh I will see God; I myself will see him with my own eyes—I, and not another. How my heart yearns within me!" (Job 19:26, 27, NIV).

Frances Osborne Morford

I Know Just How You Feel

This is what the Lord Almighty said: "Administer true justice; show mercy and compassion to one another." Zech. 7:9, NIV.

HAVE YOU EVER told someone who's going through a difficult time, "I'm so sorry. I know just how you feel"? But as we say these words, do we really know how that person feels? And do they know how *we* feel when they say the same to us? Three months after I had my first knee replacement surgery, I made a trip to New York City to attend a women's conference at the United Nations. My hotel was about four blocks from the United Nations building. I knew I could not walk that distance each day, so I rented a mobile chair to use. What I did not count on was the reaction most people had to someone in a wheelchair.

Each day of the conference, as I wheeled through the streets and into the U.N. building, I found myself amazed at the insensitivity of some. Many people opened the door and walked right through it, letting it close back on me. When I would try to reach for something on a shelf people would reach *over* me for their own wants, never asking if I needed assistance. I was appalled at how rude and uncaring the average person could be.

Then there were those few who did stop and smile and ask if I needed assistance. It was such a stark contrast between what these few people did for me and what the majority of people did or did not do. This experience, even though for only a few days, taught me so much about how difficult it must be for those who are disabled or physically challenged. Do they find, as I did, most of us "able" people to be rude and uncaring?

The week following my trip to New York, as I sat thinking about my experience, I understood that one of the reasons God allows us to go through difficult trials is to help us develop compassion. Having personally experienced pain or suffering should help us feel compassion for those who are now hurting or suffering.

The Bible tells us that we should "show mercy and compassion" to each other. One definition of compassion is to "feel for or share the suffering of others." How can we do this? How can we truly feel the suffering of others? By asking God to give us the heart of Jesus, and to let our own personal suffering and pain give us a heart of love to help someone else. That way, no trial is in vain.

Heather-Dawn Small

The Prodigal Cat

As the Father hath loved me, so have I loved you: continue ye in my love.
John 15:9.

"TEACHER! We have to help Sunshine!" begged my students as they rushed in from recess. I ran outside and scanned the playground, but could not see a thing.

The children pointed to the edge of the school property. "Up there!"

There, perched high atop a telephone pole, I saw the round shape of my orange tabby tomcat. Sunshine came to school with me every morning believing that books, desks, and daily hugs from boys and girls were pleasing even though mundane. Today, though, Sunshine decided to add some adventure, and my students were worried about their best furry-friend's safety.

A quick call to the phone company, and Sunshine was rescued. Peace and quiet returned to the classroom, and Sunshine returned to napping on desks.

Yet one week later I again heard, "Teacher! We have to rescue Sunshine again!"

This time it was pole number two. About 10 poles skirted the school's 20 acres. *What will the phone company think of driving their bucket truck to our school again?* Fortunately, no complaints came, and once again Sunshine stood on solid ground.

"When is Sunshine going to learn?" asked one student poignantly. "Doesn't he know he could die doing something like that?"

Regardless of our hopes and best interest for Sunshine, the day soon came when freedom found Sunshine up pole number three. How could I call the phone company a third time?

"Sorry, students, but we need to let Sunshine stay up there. He has made his choice." Tough love wasn't easy, especially when snow began to fall. The flakes grew thicker and thicker, and my students' concern grew deeper and deeper. School would soon be dismissed, and Sunshine still perched on the pole. My oldest student checked our door one last time.

"Sunshine! You've come home!" The students ran to circle Sunshine and give him warm hugs. "I'll get him some food! Get the snow off his ears!" They rushed to care for Sunshine, who wisely never again chose to climb a telephone pole.

Someday, in heaven, we will all learn what it was like for God when we ran away from Him. I long for the day when God welcomes me home. Only then will we begin to understand how much God loves us.

Jodie Bell Aakko

37

The Vidalia Onion

And if your eye causes you to stumble, pluck it out. It is better for you to enter the kingdom of God with one eye than to have two eyes and be thrown into hell. Mark 9:47, NIV.

WHEN SHOPPING, I always buy onions by the mesh bag so I'll have them readily available for recipes. Recently, while getting my aromatic vegetables chopped and ready to add with other ingredients, I noticed that the onion was bruised-looking on one end. If it had been a small yellow onion or a scallion, I would have disposed of it and gotten another. However, this was a big sweet Vidalia onion and too big just to go to waste.

On the cutting board little by little I cut away the bad portions in order to salvage as much of the onion as possible. Finally I ended up with about an eighth of it fit for the trash. I then chopped and diced the rest of the onion in preparation for the intended dish. While I was sautéing it, it smelled so delicious that I was indeed glad that I had saved some of it, as the portion saved was certainly better than none at all.

As a health-care professional, I sometimes must talk to patients in preparation for some nondesirable surgery, such as an amputation of a limb or removal of another part of their body. I like to say to them, "It will be better for you to have the part that is offensive removed than not have you at all!" And thinking of my sweet Vidalia onion, I am also reminded of Mark 9:47: "If your eye causes you to sin, pluck it out" (NKJV).

When we accepted Jesus as our Savior, we had offensive parts in us that needed pruning, trimming, or even removing entirely so that the Lord could use us in His service. Some of us have had greed, jealousy, strife, or envy—or other sins—in our hearts. These things should be cut out of our lives, as the Lord in His infinite mercies can see that what is left of us can be used in His service.

"When we are judged in this way by the Lord, we are being disciplined so that we will not be finally condemned with the world" (1 Cor. 11:32, NIV). All we have to do is say, just like the old hymn, "Just as I am, without one plea but that Thy blood was shed for me" (Charlotte Elliott). The Lord has His own mysterious and awesome way of preparing us to be of service here on this earth and for the new heaven and new earth.

Betty G. Perry

"Rabbi, Who Sinned?"

His disciples asked him, "Rabbi, who sinned, this man or his parents, that he was born blind?" "Neither this man nor his parents sinned," said Jesus, "but this happened so that the works of God might be displayed in him." John 9:2, 3, NIV.

WHY DO SOME PEOPLE suffer so much? Why is my child healthy while another mother has *two* children with disabilities? Why does God give some people such a heavy burden? In my church in South America was a mother with two children in their 20s. They both had cerebral palsy. Their mother was not able to take care of them both, so she had to place her son in a nursing home. He had his own little room, and he had a sunny, happy disposition. He studied his Bible diligently and insisted that he be baptized by immersion, as His Savior had been. I feel sure that was the happiest day of his life.

The brother was able to communicate perfectly, but his sister's mobility and speech were both impaired. Bedridden, she was so difficult to understand that it was not clear if she was also mentally challenged. I always treated her as if she understood everything, even though I was never sure that was the case. Then I moved away, not returning for 10 years. When I returned, I went to visit this brother and sister again. Church members visited the brother but told me not to bother about the sister, as she "was belligerent" and did not want to see any of them.

The brother was delighted to see me, and he insisted that I visit his sister. As I walked into her room, she looked at me and formed the words "Happy birthday, Sister Sinikka." I had actually forgotten that it was my birthday! How was it possible that she recognized me and even remembered my birthday after so many years? I felt very small and humbled, at the same time grateful that I had treated her with respect.

God does not miraculously heal all believers or their children. But He wants us to be mindful of the suffering ones. He wants us to treat them with love and compassion. God is glorified, not only through a miraculous healing, but also through the words and actions of His children. Maybe God has not taken away all disabilities so that we have a chance to develop the character of Christ, who cares even for the sparrow.

Sinikka Dixon

Crash!

And call upon me in the day of trouble: I will deliver thee.
Ps. 50:15.

ONE MOMENT I WAS DRIVING from a parking lot into a very dangerous section of highway, and the next there was a crash, my car spinning around and around, finally landing in a parking lot across the street. All the time I was thinking that this couldn't be happening, that surely I had not been hit that hard. I sat behind the wheel dazed, hardly noticing that my left arm was bleeding profusely. Later I realized that my left leg was also bleeding. At the moment I was trying to get my breath and sort out my jumbled thoughts. I had never before been involved in a serious accident and couldn't grasp the fact that it had actually happened.

A small crowd gathered, and a kind young man appeared at my window, assuring me that I was going to be all right. Others asked if I thought I should go to the hospital. I foolishly said that I didn't think I needed to. However, someone called for an emergency vehicle, and soon I was strapped onto a hard backboard with a collar on my neck, an IV in my right arm, a blood pressure cuff around my left arm, and oxygen in my nostrils. I was loaded into the ambulance for a bumpy ride to the hospital, where I was wheeled into the emergency department.

Several hours later, after many X-rays, a tetanus shot, and other procedures, I learned that although I was battered and bruised, I had no broken bones.

Not having family nearby, I called my friend Marilyn and without explanation asked if she could pick me up at the hospital emergency room. Soon she was there. I had been told where my car had been taken, so she took me to see it and to rescue its contents. The car, a sad sight, was later declared totaled. I had groceries in the trunk, and about half of them were smashed beyond use, but we salvaged the rest.

Marilyn's daughter, Lori, a wonderful nurse, came every day as long as she was needed, to change the dressings on my wounds. My sister Lila came from another town to stay for a few days. I couldn't have asked for better care.

Later Marilyn mentioned to Lori that it was too bad I didn't have family here. Lori responded, "She does. She has us." She was right. I do have family here. My friends. My church family. The family of God. If you have that, you are blessed.

Mary Jane Graves

Sudoku Parable

You will seek Me and find Me, when you search for Me with all your heart.
Jer. 29:13, NKJV.

SOMETIME AGO I found myself in a situation with a little too much time on my hands, yet with a need for activities that would reduce or at least not add to my stress level. My patience for otherwise enjoyable short-term activities was somewhat diminished until one day I saw a newspaper with a Sudoku puzzle. I had seen other people working on such puzzles before, but they had never appealed to me.

The puzzle was popularized in 1986 by a Japanese puzzle company under the name Sudoku, meaning *single number.* In the United States the first Sudoku puzzle was in a New Hampshire newspaper in 2004. The puzzle has nine squares, each of which has squares for nine digits. The idea is to place numbers 1 to 9 in each small square only once and in each line horizontally and vertically.

On that particular day, as I glanced at the puzzle, I noticed that the solution to the one from the previous day was given. *What do I have to lose?* I mused to myself. *I can work at my own pace, stop and start when I like, and if I really get stuck, I can check the solution tomorrow.* Having mentally psyched myself up for the challenge, I picked up a pencil with an eraser, read the instructions, and started. At first I used the eraser frequently, but soon realized that I was not only making progress but deriving great pleasure from this newfound activity. Soon I was using Sudoku as a stress reliever or just for fun during limited free time.

It has occurred to me that there are several lessons to be learned from Sudoku. One is that there are often several ways to approach and find solutions to life's situations. I realized, too, that while sometimes elusive, there is *always* a solution, but one has to look in several directions as well as in and "out of the boxes." Another lesson is that sometimes "sleeping on" the challenge is necessary so that one can "wake up" with a fresh perspective.

In our spiritual lives we can ask God to help us to continually look for new ways to meet Him and serve Him. We need help to look outside the boxes of our mundane lives more often so that we can truly find and serve God.

Doreen Evans-Yorke

Flowers Always Bring a Smile

Oh, give thanks to the Lord, for He is good! For His mercy endures forever.
Ps. 136:1, NKJV.

I HAVE ARRANGED flowers for many functions, homes, and meeting halls. I became interested in floral art and received the necessary training to become a flower-arranging art designer. Flowers give me peace and always bring about relaxation and rest. Even if I am tired, I take every opportunity to do flower arrangements because I always feel cheerful and sleep peacefully afterwards.

Comments I've received from others made me realize that my flower-arranging artwork is also a ministry. One of the first was a Sabbath after fellowship. An elderly woman said, "I missed your flower arrangements last week. I always look forward to seeing them. They lift my spirit and always bring a smile." I have had many such comments since then, but whether or not anyone comments, I do the arrangements from my heart.

As I think of the emotions and thoughts that flowers can bring, I recall a conversation I had yesterday with an associate. She spoke of spending time in Holland, and I shared the story of my visit to Great Britain. She painted a word picture of endless gardens of tulips, like a sea of colors in every form. That reminded me of a summer in the East Midlands, and the endless farmlands of yellow rapeseed plants in its countryside. The beauty and calm that comes with these memories always brings a smile, and I could not help but smile as she spoke.

I often use flowers such as roses, tulips, carnations, chrysanthemums, lilies, gypsophila, and birds of paradise in my arrangements. Colorful flowers are always interesting, and placed in an arrangement, they can both brighten or give calm. When Jesus and His disciples went from village to village they brought cheer to hearts and smiles to faces. Think of the many people whose lives were changed through healing, deliverance, restoration, fellowship, needs met, and the gift of hope for the future.

Jesus still touches our lives today. Be like Him. Try touching someone, or nurture the plants and flowers around you. You are bound to see a response. It's a wonder and a marvel that God has given *us* the ability to touch hearts and bring a smile to others. I'm sure He wants us to do so often.

Elizabeth Ida Cain

"I Don't Do . . ."

For it is God which worketh in you both to will and to do of
his good pleasure. Phil. 2:13.

And we know that all things work together for good to them that love God,
to them who are the called according to his purpose. Rom. 8:28.

ARE THERE THINGS in your life that you categorize as "I don't do"? Surely we all do this at some point or another, irrespective of whether our reasons are well founded or substantial. As we look through the Bible, however, we find dozens of people who easily could have chosen to say, "I don't do . . ." during critical moments but who, under conviction and humility, chose the opposite for the greater good.

Consider for a moment the loss of opportunity and the lasting spiritual loss if the following Bible characters had chosen this attitude. Imagine what would have happened if Naomi had said, "I don't do daughters-in-law," or if Ruth had responded, "I don't do gleaning in Boaz's field"? And if Rahab had declared, "I don't do spies," her entire family would have been lost. What would have happened if the widow at Zarephath had said, "I don't do prophets," or if the Samaritan woman at Jacob's well had said, "I don't do Jews"? Rebekah could have pouted, "I don't do camels," and missed her place in history. And finally, the woman with the issue of blood would have lost all if she had determined, "I don't do hems."

And similarly, what would happen today if God were to say, "I don't do healing—spiritual, mental, social, emotional, or physical"? Or "I don't do widows anymore." What if God declared, "I don't do divorced people or broken homes either"? Imagine if God decided, "I don't do loneliness or helplessness or hopelessness." Worst of all, what if He decided, "and finally, I don't do sinners anymore!" What a catastrophe this would be. But God's love and care is so far-reaching and encompassing that He crosses all human barriers of race, color, gender, status, and religious persuasion. He "does" all of us, every day.

It seems obvious that we might need to reexamine our "don't do" list. We might need to add the very things God has been asking us to do for a while now. You know what yours are. And yes, it might take all of our humility, but it will be worth it.

I am reorganizing my "to do" list. Will you?

Althea Y. Boxx

February 6

A Pleasant Morning Trip

If you listen carefully to the Lord your God and do what is right in his eyes, if you pay attention to his commands and keep all his decrees, I will not bring on you any of the diseases I brought on the Egyptians, for I am the Lord, who heals you. Ex. 15:26, NIV.

EVERY MORNING my husband and I go for a walk. It's always exciting, for we live where we can see the luxuriant green of an Atlantic forest, where squirrels dart around looking for something to fill their tummies, where the strident shrieks of little monkeys call for our attention, and birds sing to announce a beautiful day. All this makes us feel closer to God. Also on our walk we see geese paddling on a lake after receiving a free breakfast. Sometimes children throw food in the lake and the geese hurry to get it with great determination.

As I walk I like to remember eight natural remedies, principles that can bring more health to us. I find them helpful in my life. The first is pure air, and I try to breathe deeply in the open air. To be able to continue to enjoy this, we need to keep the air clean. Clean water is important too. Our bodies, like our planet, are two-thirds water. Thus, we should drink water all day long, except during meals. We also need water to keep our bodies clean. Sunlight is an efficient germicide, and our homes should be airy and bathed by sunbeams. We need to get out in God's sunlight, but we also should protect our skin from harmful rays. A healthy diet comes from God, who created the heavens and the earth. Eating fruits, brightly colored vegetables, and whole grains all contribute to our overall health. We also need regular strenuous exercise. This helps keep our heart healthy, helps keep cholesterol low, and also controls our blood pressure. Self-control, or temperance, in all things is another essential in living a well-balanced life. And although God gave us six days for work, rest is also important.

After a week of activity, we receive from our Creator a wonderful present, the Sabbath, in which we can rest as He did after He finished creating the world.

Studies reveal that people who live closer to God, who have the assurance of being helped by Him, live happier and have more positive relationships—and better health. As Solomon wrote: "A cheerful heart is good medicine, but a crushed spirit dries up the bones" (Prov. 17:22, NIV).

Neide Balthazar de Oliveira

"You Aren't a Christian!"

And ye shall know the truth, and the truth
shall make you free. John 8:32.

WHEN I CAME HOME from church, my husband was finishing making the dinner I'd started earlier. However, he was making brown gravy instead of the tomato-based gravy I'd requested.

"You never listen," I exploded angrily. "You just do what you want to do. It doesn't help me if you can't do what I ask."

My husband looked at me, then retorted, "You aren't even a Christian!"

I backed into the corner of the kitchen cupboards. I was shocked. Usually I would have discounted his comment. What did he know? Did he go to church every week and study the Bible every morning? No! But this time I sensed the Holy Spirit speaking through his lips.

Why do I so often react in anger toward my husband lately? I asked myself.

Then I felt as though God told me, "Yes, you are a Christian, or you wouldn't care if you misrepresented Me. But your anger doesn't represent Me. I want to take you to another level of becoming like Jesus." I knew that Satan the accuser never speaks words of hope along with his accusations, so I was sure it was God speaking.

"OK, Father," I prayed silently, "I'm going to fast and pray until You show me what my problem is."

As I read, studied, and prayed for wisdom, God led me to the story of David and Saul. I realized I was full of resentment; no, it was deeper than that. I was full of envy, and like Saul, that led to some ugly, irrational behavior and words. But what was I envious of? Then God showed me that I was envious of the accepting relationship my husband and my adult daughter had with each other. I felt left out, and was making myself—and everyone else—miserable.

Instead of being devastated by this insight, I was thrilled to finally understand. I almost shouted, "Yes, Lord, take it away. Heal me!" And He did. I am free. The truth about myself set me free. God knew that I needed to see this before my daughter came for the summer. Then I was able to enjoy the pleasure she and my husband had working together without my feeling left out. What a gift from God!

Lana Fletcher

The Brown Sweater

The Lord is my light and my salvation.
Ps. 27:1.

I HAD DECIDED beforehand what I would wear to work that Thursday—a brown long-sleeved sweater, brown slacks with a tiny brown and black pattern, and brown boots. This would save me a little time in the morning. As usual, at 5:45 a.m. I slid out of bed onto my knees for prayer, washed up, and went to my special place to study the day's Bible lesson and write in my journal before getting dressed and heading downstairs for breakfast.

I thought I looked OK and was dressed adequately for the wintry morning when the temperature hovered just above 20° Fahrenheit. Then I took one final look in my bedroom mirror, under a different light than the one in the bathroom. Only then did I see that though I'd been certain my sweater was brown, it was actually a dark wine color, and certainly did not match my brown slacks and boots. Now I had to scurry to be on time for work. Instead of changing the sweater, I decided to wear black slacks and boots.

Under the scrutiny of better lighting, the true color had been revealed. Life can be just like that. Sometimes we feel good about ourselves—we attend church regularly; we give to charities to help the poor, sick, needy, and those we think are less fortunate than ourselves. We look into the mirror and think we're OK, or at least not as "bad" as some others to whom we compare ourselves.

I once heard a saying: "We're who we really are under pressure." When things go bad or someone "rubs us the wrong way," the ugliness that often lies beneath our coiffured exterior comes out, and we find that we are not exactly who we thought we were, or who we would have others think we are. Rather, we realize how far short we measure up to the real standard: Christ Jesus. In the light of the Scriptures, we see ourselves as we really are and recognize that we're not all that "good" after all. We realize that we must look to Jesus for strength at all times. As we stand in His light to see our true colors, necessary changes can be made to bring us in line with Jesus, our high standard and true light.

Would you join me today as we submit ourselves to His light so that we might see ourselves as we really are and be willing to change as He deems necessary?

Gloria Stella Felder

Selah!

I will meditate in thy precepts, and have respect
unto thy ways. Ps. 119:15.

SELAH. A TERM that we often just run past as we stumble upon it in the reading of Psalms or ignore it entirely as we move along to more "interesting" information. Many of us do not even say it when reading aloud. Similar to so many other things in life that we seem to miss, *Selah* bears a profound and inescapable significance. Many believe it is an exaggerated pause for meditation upon that which was stated, and an emphasis upon that which is to come! In the irreducible minimum of explanations, *Selah* can be compared to a time when you finally have a bite of a wonderful milk chocolate after you've craved it for the last three hours. You pause to savor its goodness.

When a hammer slams onto the wrong target and you scream with excruciating pain, the soothing feel of cold water running over your still-throbbing thumb brings hope. *Selah!* When you finally use the restroom after you have long struggled to suppress the need—you almost melt with the relief. And when you've waited patiently for the love of your life to come home after a long trip, and you're surprised because they arrived earlier than you had expected—and with gifts, you stand for a moment stunned by a plethora of excitement, happiness, disbelief, and gratitude! *Selah!*

In all of these experiences you are forced to pause for a moment and meditate on that which has just occurred and to embrace that which is to come.

Here are some of those verses on which to pause and ponder: Psalm 85:2: "Thou hast forgiven the iniquity of thy people, thou hast covered all their sin. *Selah.*" Psalm 3:8: "Salvation belongeth unto the Lord: thy blessing is upon thy people. *Selah.*" Psalm 60:4: "Thou hast given a banner to them that fear thee. . . . *Selah.*" Psalm 62:8: "Trust in him at all times; ye people, pour out your heart before him: God is a refuge for us. *Selah.*" Psalm 24:10: "Who is this King of glory? The Lord of hosts, he is the King of glory. *Selah.*"

It is my hope that each of us will pause for a moment today to meditate upon the promises in God's Word. Let us choose to abide in His presence today and to trust Him with our every undertaking. I proclaim to Him, "Thou alone art my God. *Selah!*"

Shanter H. Alexander

The White Peacock

For now we see through a glass, darkly; but then face to face: now I know in part; but then shall I know even as also I am known. 1 Cor. 13:12.

THERE ARE BEAUTIFUL glass panels in our front doors. I like the elegance the embossed patterns project. Mom likes the fact that while we can see out, no one can see in. This morning we found another reason to enjoy our glass-paneled doors.

Through these doors I saw what I thought was our neighbor's pure white cat on the porch. But when I went to open the door, I found a stunning display of color. Three peacocks—two of which bore the iridescent emerald and vibrant blue plumage that's made them famous—had come to call. But even more eye-catching was the pure white peacock with them. His dark eyes assured me that he was no albino. I was charmed as I watched him strut through our rose garden, noting the differing varieties—or so it seemed. But when he started eating rosebuds, my delight unraveled to displeasure, and I had to shoo him away.

But what a blessing! When I watched him with the other two, a phrase in today's text came to mind: "For now we see through a glass darkly." Though the word "glass" in this text is usually translated as "mirror," I felt the power in its literacy. I was being reminded that my understanding and my relationship with God was shadowy at best. I did not really know Him.

In her most popular book, Ellen White reminds me of one way to get to know Him better. "Nature speaks to our senses without ceasing. The open heart will be impressed with the love and glory of God as revealed through the works of His hands" (*Steps to Christ,* p. 84).

I thanked God that He had bound this precious lesson with the white peacock. He had linked that bird with a truth reminding me that beauty is more than looks; that purity is reflected in character and actions; that His love is constant, overarching, and supreme.

Now whenever I pass those glass-paneled doors, I remind myself of the need to spend more time with God. But today's text doesn't stop there. It is followed with the assurance that one day I will get to know Him as intensely as He knows me. And that's an enormous promise.

"But now ask . . . the birds of the air, and they will tell you. . . . The hand of the Lord has done this" (Job 12:7-9, NKJV). The white peacock showed me.

Glenda-mae Greene

The Heaven-bound Train

Blessed are those who do His commandments, that they may have the right to the tree of life, and may enter through the gates into the city. Rev. 22:14, NKJV.

I LOVE TRAVELING BY TRAIN. In England trains are more expensive than buses, but they are faster and more punctual. I love the way they glide their way through valleys, mountainous areas, towns, and villages. I can take every bag that I want with me on my journeys, for there is no restriction of how many kilograms you can carry, as there is on planes. Trains carry a lot of people, too. Food and drinks are sold, so you don't go hungry. In England most people who use trains in the early morning are on their way to work. Late-morning and early-afternoon riders are usually going shopping or connecting to other cities. Evening riders are, of course, mostly people coming home from work.

But there is another train that I long for. Its coming is more anticipated than the trains of this world. No one knows the day or the hour that the train will arrive, but it will definitely arrive. This train will take on board everyone who is willing to ride—free of charge regardless of color, race, age, or gender. On this train, however, you have to be very careful about the bags you carry. The bag marked gossip won't be allowed on board. The suitcase marked adultery won't be allowed on. The small bag with a label of unforgiveness will not go anywhere. The box marked fornication will be thrown out. The suitcase of anger must remain behind. The small bag marked thievery or lying won't be allowed near the train.

However, the big bags of kindness, forgiveness, longsuffering, love, purity, and patience will have plenty of room on this train. And as we travel, food and drinks will be served at no price. Whenever you are hungry or thirsty you just have to put your hand up, and waiters in white will come to serve you.

We will pass through so many countries. We will cross so many rivers, seas, and oceans. We will pass deserts and through mountains, and on into outer space. Perhaps the most amazing thing is that we won't need passports or visas to go on this journey. One's heart is one's passport. Whatever your plans in life, plan to travel on this train, for this train is heaven-bound. Don't you want to invite your whole family, your friends, and neighbors to join you too?

Peggy Rusike

The Power of a Signature

Jesus said to him, "Have I been with you so long, and yet you have not known Me, Philip? He who has seen Me has seen the Father; so how can you say, 'Show us the Father?' Do you not believe that I am in the Father, and the Father in Me? The words that I speak to you I do not speak on My own authority; but the Father who dwells in Me does the works. Believe Me that I am in the Father and the Father in Me, or else believe Me for the sake of the works themselves." John 14:9-11, NKJV.

WHEN I SAW the catalog from a Christian media program, I decided to order a few of its Christian books. So I filled out the order blank with my name, address, phone number, the book titles, numbers, and prices, and added it up. I wrote a check to send with it, put it in their self-addressed envelope, stamped it, and mailed it. A few days later I received a phone call saying that I had not signed the check! "How could that be?" I asked. I must have been in a hurry, because I always sign my checks. The kind woman said they could get permission from the bank to sign for me if they put their initials by the signature. Would I agree to that? I said "Of course."

I prayed that it would work for their sake and for my peace of mind. Later, when I received the package of books and checked the bank record, I saw that the check had cleared the bank. I was relieved to know all was well with that, and thanked God for His intervention in that matter. Then I vowed, with God's help, not to make that mistake again. How important a signature is! Your name, my name, anyone's name, when signed by the hand, is a sign of authority.

That started me thinking about the power of a signature. As I understand it, in today's verse Jesus told His disciples that He was the *signature* for God, His *authority!* I looked up the word "signature" in the Oxford dictionary, and it can mean a "characteristic," which indeed fits our Lord, God's Son. Powerful, isn't it!

Next time you or I go through an airport check-in, a border crossing, a customs line with our passport, or even a store check-out where we pay with currency, let's remember the importance of that *authority, a signature,* and let's thank God for His *authority* given to us through His Son, our Lord and Savior Jesus Christ, and His Holy Spirit. Even more trustworthy!

Bessie Siemens

"You Love Me, Don't You?"

This is love: not that we loved God, but that he loved us and sent
his Son as an atoning sacrifice for our sins. 1 John 4:10, NIV.

We love him, because he first loved us. 1 John 4:19.

"GRANDAD, YOU LOVE ME, don't you?" asked 2-year-old Damien as he snuggled up close to his grandfather on the sofa.

"Yes," replied Grandad, at which Damien jumped up onto his lap and smothered him with hugs and kisses. "I love you, Grandad! I love you, Grandad!" he exclaimed. It was one of those special moments of innocence and joy that young children bring into our lives.

We know that God, our heavenly Father, loves us far more than any of our earthly family does. He has told us so, and has shown His love in so many ways, the greatest of which is in giving us Jesus. "God showed how much he loved us by sending his one and only Son into the world so that we might have eternal life through him" (1 John 4:9, NLT). Jesus told us not to worry about our everyday needs, because our heavenly Father already knows what we need and gives it to us (see Matt. 6:31, 32; Acts 17:25). Not only that, He gives us things that are beyond our wildest dreams or imaginings (see Eph. 3:20; 1 Cor. 2:9).

So what is our response to God's love? Do we return that love like Damien did to his granddad? "We love him because he first loved us." And how do we show our love for Him? The answer is simple, given by the Lord Himself: "Love one another the way I loved you. This is the very best way to love" (John 15:12, Message). If anyone "won't love the person [she] can see, how can [she] love the God [she] can't see? The command we have from Christ is blunt: Loving God includes loving people. You've got to love both" (1 John 4:20, 21, Message).

Valentine's Day is a perfect time to share love. So an act of kindness to a loved one or neighbor, words of appreciation to a relative, friend, neighbor, work colleague, or church member, offering a helping hand or encouraging word to a discouraged companion, going the second mile, sharing what you have with those in need—all of these are ways of saying to God, "I love You."

Have you given God a hug lately?

Antonia Castellino

My Secret Valentine

I have loved you . . . with an everlasting love.
With unfailing love I have drawn you to myself. Jer. 31:3, NLT.

SEVENTH GRADE. That wonderful, awful, awkward time of thinking such thoughts as *Am I pretty? Do I matter? Oh, no! A new pimple! Ahhh!* And last, but certainly not least, *I wonder if anyone will send me a valentine this year.*

All of those questions danced in my head that crisp February afternoon right before Valentine's Day. After school I walked through the back door of my house and went into the front room to pick up the mail. Our mailbox was not outside the house. Instead, our mail was delivered through a little slot in the wall by the front door. Incoming mail was pushed through the slot and landed on the floor. Today only one envelope lay on the floor. I picked it up. I turned it over. *My* name was written on it! There was no address—just my name. Someone had hand-delivered something *just for me!* Eagerly I opened it and found, to my delight—a valentine! There was no flowery message on the front. In fact, there were no words at all. Curious beyond belief, I opened my card. "Happy Valentine's Day," I read. But it had no signature. Just a code: GL2. What? Nothing in my brain registered GL2. I didn't know anyone with those initials. I had no clue what my secret admirer meant by this unknown code! My heart raced as I tried unsuccessfully to figure it out. Someone thought *I* was special! Someone liked *me!* Captivated by this small card from an unknown sender, I knew, right there in my awkward, seventh-grade heart, that I mattered.

Have you ever wondered, "Do I matter?" Has there ever been a time when you felt less than special? Well, sweetheart, I have good news! Today a valentine came with your name on it. It's signed with all the love your heart can hold, and it's just for *you!* It says: "I have loved you with an everlasting love." In fact, "before you were even born I knew you" (see Ps. 139:15). I delight in you—I even sing songs about you! (see Zeph. 3:17). I am enthralled with your beauty! "You are mine!" (Isa. 43:1, NLT). Find those words hard to believe? Better double-check the signature. There's no mistaking or hiding it. This valentine *is* for *you,* girlfriend! I never did discover the identity of my secret admirer, but there is no secret as to the sender of this valentine for you! The Lover of your soul sent it. *You* matter!

DeeAnn Bragaw

The Benefit of Wisdom

Trust in the Lord with all your heart and lean not on your own understanding; in all your ways submit to him, and he will make your paths straight. Prov. 3:5, 6, NIV.

THE SOUND OF MY husband's voice still rang clearly in my ears as I sat alone, in silence, to pray. He had spoken with wisdom and great assurance. "You can only do your best," he'd told me. "You must trust God to do the rest." This was just the reminder I needed, and it relaxed me just like drinking a tall cold glass of lemonade on a hot sunny day. I had organized a women's conference for 90 women leaders from across the country. But it was easy to see that more women had arrived than I'd planned for. It was now lunchtime. And I'd ordered only 100 plates of food.

I had instructed the women to leave the Radisson Hotel conference hall and go to the nearby Animal Park, where we'd have lunch together. As I prayed alone, I asked God, "Just as You multiplied the five loaves and two fishes, would You please multiply this lunch so that no one is left without a plate of food?"

I walked over to the Animal Park to meet the women waiting there. As soon as I arrived the cook approached me and said nervously, "I thought you told me to bring 100 plates of food, but I've already served 101. I need some more plates."

In her mind, she had cooked to feed 100 people, with an extra plate just in case. But God already knew that that was not going to be enough, and He had multiplied it. The cook served 20 more women from the food that still remained in the pots she had brought to the park. There was enough for every woman there.

The disciples were also perplexed over food and cried out to the Master. "'This is a remote place,' they said, 'and it's already very late. Send the people away so that they can go to the surrounding countryside and villages and buy themselves something to eat'" (Mark 6:35, 36, NIV). But Jesus took a few loaves and fishes, gave thanks, and gave everyone there a hearty meal. Our God is a God of miracles. When we cannot see because of a mountain, we need to have faith and rely on His promises. Our explicit faith in the Father is the only thing of value to hold on to when troubles arise.

Velda M. Jesse

Healing Time!

Beloved, I pray that you may prosper in all things and be in health,
just as your soul prospers. 3 John 2, NKJV.

I HAVE NEVER MET anyone who has not been sick at one time or another. Have you? While living on earth, Jesus came in contact with countless persons who were sick. In fact, many who were sick went in search of Jesus. He was full of compassion, and among His numerous titles is that of the Great Physician. I am fascinated by the many narratives recorded in the Gospels, but I have found the ones pertaining to healing to be particularly intriguing. There seems to have been so many ill that Jesus was kept busy in the healing ministry. No one was ever turned away.

In the time of Christ leprosy was a serious scourge. The ultimate! If you had leprosy, you were considered cursed by God and rendered ceremonially unclean. You were an outcast of society and had to keep a safe distance from everyone. Whenever they were near civilization lepers were required to cry, "Unclean," so that others could hurry away.

The Gospels record two instances in which Jesus healed lepers, but I feel certain He must have healed many more. Matthew tells the story of a single leper courageous enough to approach Him. He fell at the feet of Jesus "and worshipped Him, saying, 'Lord, if You are willing, You can make me clean'" (Matt. 8:2, NKJV). Jesus defied the law of the day and touched him, assuring him, "I am willing; be cleansed" (Matt. 8:3, NKJV). The 10 lepers were healed differently. When Jesus drew near to a certain village they met Him but stood a long way off and called loudly, "Jesus, Master, have mercy on us!" (Luke 17:13, NKJV). Notice that Jesus did not touch them. Instead He told them to go to the priest. Their obedience in setting out to see the priest shows that they had faith that they'd be healed. A leper could go to the priest only after being cleansed. Verse 14 tells us that "as they went, they were cleansed." Notice that only one returned and thanked their Healer.

Today many of us stand in need of the healing touch of Jesus. Some of us are physically unwell, others socially and emotionally ill. But most, if not all of us, are spiritually sick. Spiritual sickness is often likened to leprosy. I am thankful that Jesus is still passing by and so we too can be made well

Jacqueline Hope HoShing-Clarke

God's Protection

For it is written: "He will command his angels concerning you to guard you carefully." Luke 4:10, NIV.

JUST BEFORE LUNCH my husband turned on the TV so we could watch the news. One of the first stories surprised me. A reporter announced that a big crash had occurred in a municipality next to ours. An ambulance had crashed while taking a mother and her newborn son to the hospital, and that tiny baby had been thrown out of the vehicle into the jungle. I cried and prayed to God, asking Him to protect that precious, vulnerable child. I then prayed that God would help me find them. Were they now in a hospital, and if so, which hospital? Where were they? The place where the accident had happened was some distance away and a little difficult to access. So I prayed for them. Somehow I felt especially drawn to the child. The next day I called the hospitals in my city and the city of the TV channel that had reported the story, but I was not able to get any information about the accident or the baby.

As the days passed by I often thought about that tragedy. I would wonder what had happened to the newborn that had been thrown into the jungle and how he was now doing. Then about a month later, as I sat in church on a Sabbath morning, meditating, praying, and thanking God for the infinite blessings in my life, a woman came up and asked if she could sit beside me. Of course I promptly gave her a seat. I asked if she was visiting our church, because I had not seen her before. She said yes, and I welcomed her, saying that I was pleased to meet her. I love babies and saw she held a baby in her arms. Then she looked at me and asked, "Did you hear about an accident that happened last month with an ambulance? I am the woman who was in it, and this is my baby, who was thrown out of the vehicle." I began crying and took that little baby on my lap. As I hugged and caressed him, I told her, "You cannot imagine how much I prayed to God for your lives. I wanted very much to have news of you."

At that very moment I felt and saw God's presence in my life—and in the life of those for whom I had prayed. He obviously cares about our daily incidents and accidents. I am sure God sent angels to guard and protect this mother and her son.

Ester Loreno Perin

Leaving My Net

As Jesus was walking beside the Sea of Galilee, he saw two brothers, Simon called Peter and his brother Andrew. They were casting a net into the lake, for they were fishermen. "Come, follow me," Jesus said, "and I will send you out to fish for people." At once they left their nets and followed him. Matt. 4:18-20, NIV.

THEY ANNOUNCED more reductions of hours at work and mandatory work on Saturday. And I was planning to be baptized the very next day.

I knew that dark forces would be working hard to claim me. Nevertheless, I quickly found myself thinking, *God will understand if I decide to work Sabbaths.* It would be so much easier to stay working. No job meant no house, and the rent was about to take a huge hike. And what about my daughter?

I did not sign the papers agreeing to these conditions. I was angry that after working this job for eight years I was being put in this impossible position. Refusing a half-time position amounted to a layoff. The state, however, said I had quit my job, so I was not entitled to unemployment benefits. I moved out of the house, and my daughter and I stayed 30 miles away with my best friend—because I couldn't rent an apartment without income. Nobody would hire me. My daughter had to start a new school. My mother missed her granddaughter. My church missed me when I began attending the church close to my friend's home.

It took five months to secure unemployment benefits, but the state accepted my "quitting" on religious grounds. Rejection after rejection for work hurt, but my daughter and I remained active in our church. I made use of the extra time by helping out in her first-grade classroom.

I found another job. Now married, we have moved into an apartment to house three, and with some help from the church my daughter was enrolled in the church-sponsored school.

God has not let me down! I am in a job I love. There's always an uncertain future, but I feel assured we will be provided for whatever happens. I think of when Jesus called Peter and his brother Andrew to be His disciples. Did they worry about their jobs? Did they worry about where they would live? The Bible clearly states that they dropped what they were doing and followed. If we truly have faith, we never need worry.

Jennifer Burkes

He Supplies My Needs

This same God who takes care of me will supply all your needs from His glorious riches, which have been given to us in Christ Jesus. Phil. 4:19, NLT.

IT WAS FRIDAY, 10 days before the Board of Governors banquet, at which I would be awarded for long service. I had gone through my closet to see what I could wear, but found nothing that I considered appropriate. Everything had been worn, and worn, and worn. I really needed a dress for the occasion, but could not afford to buy one at that time. So I spoke to my Father about my need.

That very afternoon a friend in the United States called to say hello. After we chatted for a while, she asked if there was anything I needed her to bring for me, since she would be coming to the island a few weeks later. I told her there was nothing I really needed, but did mention the banquet I was to attend. Soon we said goodbye, wishing each other a pleasant Sabbath.

About an hour later my phone rang, and when I answered, I again heard the voice of my friend. She told me that she had bought me not only a dress for the banquet, but matching shoes, bag, and scarf. I was speechless, but when I found my speech, I thanked her extravagantly, and asked how I was going to get them since she lives in the United States and I live in Jamaica. She assured me that there was plenty of time for her to get them to me. She would take them to church the next day and was confident that she would find someone coming to Jamaica who could take them.

Saturday night she called to say she had given the package to a young man who would be attending a funeral in the island the next weekend. Two days before the function I collected the package and found that it contained all that she said that it would: a gorgeous black dress with matching shoes, bag, and scarf.

As I thanked God for hearing and answering my prayer so quickly, I reflected on today's text: "My God shall supply all your need according to His riches in glory in Christ Jesus." God is truly awesome! He is concerned about every detail of my life, and seeks to attend to my needs.

God often demonstrates His great love to me in tangible ways. Has He done that for you too? Have you given God the glory by sharing your story?

Carol Joy Fider

A Narrow Escape

The angel of the Lord camps around those who fear God, and he saves them.
Ps. 34:7, NCV.

IT WAS WEDNESDAY MORNING, a public holiday, and I had just returned some of my "church daughters" to their homes after an evening of fellowship. Before I left for the half-hour drive home, my friend Pauline suggested that I have a sleep and go home later. *I'm fine,* I thought, *and when I get home I can sleep without thinking about having to drive later.* So I thanked her and was on my way.

About halfway home I felt very tired. I opened the car windows for fresh air and turned on the radio, hoping to stay alert. I remember hearing the radio commentary on the cricket game—not my favorite sport. Then without warning, in a matter of seconds, I fell asleep. The car drifted from the lawful left side of the road (we drive on the left side in Jamaica) to the far right. The next thing I knew, I was startled awake by the impact as the car hit and climbed the embankment on the opposite side of the road.

I was literally shaking like a leaf. As I regained my composure and steered the car to the left side of the road, there was no vehicle in sight. But no sooner had I completed my maneuver than a speeding taxi came up behind me. It was filled with people, and some of them shouted to me as they passed, asking if I was OK. Clearing the corner, I stopped where it was safe, and thanked the Lord for sparing my life.

Driving requires much vigilance, especially on rural Jamaican roads! But I had slept. Because it was a holiday, that winding road, which was usually very busy with speeding vehicles, was clear. The accident happened at one of the deepest blind corners in that area. No one would want to be caught there, especially on the wrong side. Without a doubt the Master was at work.

Friends, we serve a God who is all loving and caring. It is not because of our goodness, but because of His mercy, that we live each day. My experience reminds me that that morning could have been my last. Was I ready? Are we ready for Jesus to come? Then I thought, *Maybe the Lord still has some work for me.* May we allow ourselves to be used by Him. May we be ready, stay ready, and live each day as if it is our last. We know not when it will be.

Donette James

Humbled

Therefore let him who thinks he stands take heed lest he fall.
1 Cor. 10:12, NKJV.

LANGUAGES FASCINATE ME. I love books and words, and I'm meticulous about spelling. More often than not, I am a good speller, and it used to annoy me when others failed to check for spelling mistakes. Then one night I wrote a document that I was to present to a school staff the next morning. It was late, and as I reread and revised the document, I left the phrase "all expects" instead of the phrase "everyone expects."

The technology director projected the PowerPoint on the screen, and as soon as the offending phrase appeared, a coworker shouted that there was a grammatical error! I didn't believe that I was corrected out of love, but I thanked my coworker and with a heavy heart continued and completed the rest of the presentation.

Later that day I was seething. I was furious at myself for not catching the mistake, and I was mad at my coworker for embarrassing me. I drove home murmuring in my heart and making excuses for why I had erred. The more I grumbled, the more I felt the Spirit of God speaking to me. God's love smothered the fire in my heart, and I began to listen.

I realized that I was not just angry. I was humbled! I thought I could not—or should not—make mistakes. I also felt ashamed as I wondered how many times I had pointed out the faults of others in public and left them broken. *Well,* I thought, *I could have been corrected in private!* But again I felt the gentle voice guiding and calming me. I finally understood that the incident happened to remind me that I do make mistakes and that it is perfectly fine for someone to correct me.

I had to realize that God uses anything or anyone to build my character. I needed to put my pride away and to be more patient with others. With this in mind, and sporting a clean heart and a new spirit, I thought of that coworker as I wrote another document. I sent the document to my coworker, who willingly edited it. I gained a new editor, I discarded some of my pride, and now I'm free to make mistakes. Additionally, I am no longer annoyed when other people make spelling mistakes.

Rose Joseph Thomas

Knowing God

Be still and know that I am God.
Ps. 46:10, NKJV.

I'VE DECIDED that whatever I do, I want it to be useful. I'm a grand-mother and do not have much time to waste. If there's something in life that I have failed to do or learn, now is the moment to do it or learn it. Therefore, while I take care of my little granddaughter Julie, I also want to do something useful.

While I watch her, I read a book, but I barely read two paragraphs before my attention is distracted. She's learning to stand up, and recently she learned to sit up by herself. She also turns and swivels fearlessly. I try to embroider some Christmas presents, but after a few stitches I have to stop and help her. I cannot leave her alone with her toys. A month ago she would play quietly with her hands and her stuffed toys. Now she can crawl anywhere in the house. And so I can read, I can embroider, or I can watch Julie.

I'm afraid that she will hurt herself. She totally disregards danger. She throws herself from her stroller to retrieve whatever fell out. I use the seat belt, but she slides around, and suddenly I notice she's dangling half out, kicking and laugh-ing. How much will I get done this morning? I finally realize it—nothing, nothing except to be with Julie.

So what is it that I can learn from this? There is no experience in our lives that is meaningless in the eyes of God. Today I can give love, caresses, and hugs. *Thank You, Lord. There are many who do not have that.* There's nothing like the joy of rocking Julie so that she sleeps trustingly in my arms; nothing like the pleasure of guiding her first steps and reliving the beautiful moments with my own children as I care for my grandchild.

Patience is an important lesson I must continue learning, and lessons of quiet-ness of spirit. Today I will remain calm, without turmoil. I will find quietness for my soul, and I will know God. I also have learned God's love and care toward me as I care for Julie. This is the greatest privilege and the best lesson—to understand what God does for me and for each of us every day. I have learned much through this experience.

Consider your challenges today, no matter what they are. What lesson do you think God is trying to teach you?

Leni Uría de Zamorano

God Supplies

Once I was young, and now I am old. Yet I have never seen the godly abandoned or their children begging for bread. The godly always give generous loans to others, and their children are a blessing. Ps. 37:25, 26, NLT.

AS I WRITE THIS, my family and I are going through a very lean patch. I have just used the last money vouchers that I had to get some things for breakfast, and, well, lunch is going to have to take care of itself.

As I stand in the kitchen dividing the last of the bread and pouring some cereal in a bowl, I am reminded of a promise, today's text: "I was young and now I am old, yet I have never seen the righteous forsaken or their children begging bread" (NIV). It rings through so loudly that I am driven to sing and give God praise in my heart. I hasten to pen these words as a testimony of His faithfulness. I know that it is He who has put this in my remembrance and has given me this song to sing.

I think back on every lean season that we've experienced, every moment of near panic and stress, and on this time in particular. I recognize that my family has never gone hungry for even one day, nor did the car not have gas to take us to work, nor did a bill go unpaid. We are sheltered and warm while the rains beat down on the roof and the winds howl. Most of all, we have the love of Christ within us and our love and respect for each other. This gives us the assurance that we will come through this desert just as we have all the others, and we will come through praising our Father, Jehovah Jireh (God is provider). We will come through with a song.

Hard times will come to test and to tempt us to distrust God and believe that He has abandoned us, but let us hold fast to His promises. He has promised, "So be strong and courageous! Do not be afraid and do not panic before them. For the Lord your God will personally go ahead of you. He will neither fail you nor abandon you" (Deut. 31:6, NLT). He has also promised to supply all our needs according to His glorious riches (see Phil. 4:19). So rejoice in adversity because when things seem at their lowest and gloomiest, that's when you can be sure that God is making a way for you and me to stand and see His deliverance. What's more, it means we have a testimony to share, a song He will give us to sing.

Greta M. Joachim-Fox-Dyett

"Hi, There"

The soothing tongue is a tree of life.
Prov. 15:4, NIV.

I WAS BORN IN A little village in Ghana, West Africa. There, everybody is everybody's keeper, and everyone knows everybody. Thus, you have to say hi to everyone you meet wherever you go. Otherwise your parents or guardians will be told and you will be reprimanded. If that continues, you will be punished.

Hence, my first day out and about in England, I said hi to everyone I met—but no one took notice of me. Then my friend advised me to stop, because here is not like our village, where it is a must to speak to everyone. It took me time to get used to walking past people without greeting them.

Suppose I should walk past someone without saying hi and then I trip or fall. Would he, should she, help me? I think they could refuse to help as I passed by them without any recognition. But what do you think? Unfortunately, that is the way life is in most cosmopolitan areas. People say hello only to those they know or love, forgetting that there are others who need their love, help, attention, and care. Some people are loners, yet depressed that they have no one to talk to. Others have problems and wish that someone would just say something to show some concern or listen to them. Sadly, we just walk past them without noticing them.

Why don't we speak to those we meet in a corner shop, near the ATM, at the laundry, in the elevator, at the doctor's waiting room, or at the bus stop? That is how I met a woman who was desperate to locate my church. She had been in New Jersey for more than seven months. She was so grateful that I said hello when we met at a doctor's waiting room.

By speaking to strangers we can make new friends with the lonely and needy, and give hope to the depressed—all to God's glory. That's what Christ said we should do instead of staying attached only to old friends and loved ones, and exchanging gifts with those who are not in need. Luke 6:33 asks us why we do good to those who do good to us, instead of for the needy.

Let us recognize others. Then we may find ourselves on the righthand side of the heavenly King, and one day He will say to us, "Come and share your master's happiness!" (Matt. 25:23, NIV). *Yes!* Just for saying hi to strangers.

Mabel Kwei

My Picture

You are precious in My sight . . .
and I love you. Isa. 43:4, NASB.

ONE AFTERNOON I browsed in a resale shop. I saw quite a variety of "junk," but nothing I couldn't live without. Then against a back wall, I spotted a scenic picture. Pulling out the cardboard I gazed upon the artistry and immediately related to the symbolism in the painting. However, the large picture had no frame and seemed a bit pricy. Slowly I put it back, even after the clerk told me I could have it for half price. *I'll look for a frame and think about it,* I decided.

That night in bed I couldn't get the picture off my mind. I hadn't found a frame, but I still wanted it. Jesus whispered, "It is My gift to you." *Why didn't I realize earlier that this picture was especially just for me?* Before dozing off, I made the decision that next time I went to Trenton I would purchase my picture. If Jesus wanted me to have it He would keep it for me.

A couple days later I drove down the mountain to the resale shop. Retrieving my gift from the back wall, I informed the young clerk, "I came back to get my picture. God wants me to have this."

"A woman looked at that picture yesterday," she told me, "but I knew you'd be back."

Handing her the money, I smiled. "This picture holds meaning for me."

As I drove home I felt so loved. Maybe someday I can find a frame and hang the picture, but for now it sits on top of my piano. My picture is an ocean scene with a lighthouse, probably on the coast of Maine. Dark clouds fill the sky, and in their midst a rainbow arches downward. Two eagles fly over the surf below. Serenity pervades the calm after a storm. The symbolism speaks to my heart. Jesus is the Lighthouse of my life. For years rainbows have been God's personal reminders to me of His loving care. This past year has been difficult with several family deaths and tragic situations. The rainbow, which is central in the picture, is God's promise to bring good out of evil, to give me hope and a future beyond the sorrows and storms of the present. He also assures me, "You can soar like the eagles."

Jesus led me to that picture—and convinced me to buy it as a visual message. He is personally interested in me and understands my heartaches and longings. I am precious to Jesus. His picture gift is very special.

Barbara Ann Kay

New Life

I have been crucified with Christ; and it is no longer I who live, but Christ lives in me; and the life which I now live in the flesh I live by faith in the Son of God, who loved me and gave Himself up for me. Gal. 2:20, NASB.

SOMETIME EARLY IN 2005 I dreamed that I would die in the seventh month of that year. I shared that information with only one friend, because she was to be with me during the summer, and I thought she should know. Ironically, the seventh month, July, is my birth month.

I left Trinidad for Canada fully aware of that dream, and honestly never expecting to return home again. Daily, when I stood in the Sheridan Mall in the west Toronto area selling religious materials and kept hearing of the "shady" activities that commonly took place there, I thought I would get shot or harmed in another way. My girlfriend was not comfortable when I reminded her of the dream, since most of my dreams have had significance and I thought that this one would be no different.

I know with God there is no coincidence, so I believe it was by divine order that the program I was with chose Galatians 2:20 as the summer's theme. I taught them the song "I Am Crucified With Christ," made popular by Phillips, Craig, and Dean. It talks about Christ living in me; that even if I am crucified with Christ, I still live. Every day for devotions, we repeated the day's text and sang that song.

Dying to self seems foolish. Because I have to walk by faith and not sight, I have to trust God even where I cannot trace Him. I have to live one day at a time, trusting Him because surely God has not revealed His plans except in His Word. I am sure they are to prosper and not harm me, "plans for welfare and not for calamity to give you a future and a hope" (Jer. 29:11, NASB).

As I thought through the issues, I realized that sometimes I want to do my own thing, and then I have to reconsider because of His will revealed in His Word. My thoughts, feelings, and actions should not just be submitted to Him, but be dead. Whatever I do should be done not by my will, but through Christ living in me.

It was not until the summer ended that I realized what death took place—the beginning of the death of me to self!

Nadine A. Joseph

Anticipation

And then shall appear the sign of the Son of man in heaven: and then shall all the tribes of the earth mourn, and they shall see the Son of man coming in the clouds of heaven with power and great glory. Matt. 24:30.

ON A COLD EVENING in late February I went to a supermarket to pick up a few things. At first I couldn't figure out why there were no shopping carts lined up outside. As I tried to enter the supermarket, the realization dawned on me that people were buying groceries in preparation for a predicted storm. The store was wall to wall with people, and it was even hard to move. Everyone's face displayed anxiety and intensity. The checkout lines started at the counters and extended down each aisle to the back of the store. As I was under a very serious time constraint, I decided to go to another supermarket.

As I pulled into the parking lot of the other supermarket I quickly scanned the area for signs of shopping carts. To my relief, I saw some lined up against the outside wall. There weren't many, but at least there were some. This store was crowded too, but not nearly as much as the first. There was room to walk around, and the lines were significantly shorter than in the previous one. I collected my items and then settled in the line, prepared for the long wait. I spent most of my time in the line rehearsing the principles about patience reviewed in the previous week's Bible study.

The weather reporters had predicted a snowstorm, and thousands of people simply took them at their word and started to make extensive preparations to weather the storm. This experience caused me to think about the coming of Christ. Starting with Christ's disciples, believers have declared that Jesus is coming soon, and we need to be prepared. Why is it so easy to believe the weather reports, but so difficult to believe the Word of God? How many times have the meteorologists been wrong? Have God's words ever failed? He promised to return to take His people home. "For the Lord himself will come down from heaven, with a loud command, with the voice of the archangel and with the trumpet call of God, and the dead in Christ will rise first" (1 Thess. 4:16, NIV). Are we preparing with the same urgency and intensity with which the shoppers prepared for the storm?

Beverly P. Gordon

My $36 House

Delight thyself also in the Lord; and he shall give thee the desires of thine heart. Commit thy way unto the Lord; trust also in him; and he shall bring it to pass. Ps. 37:4, 5.

A YEAR BEFORE I earnestly began to look for a house, I noticed that apartments and homes for rent were very expensive. In frustration I said, "Lord, everything is so high I can't afford them. I don't know what to do!" Then I heard the Lord say, "Wait." I didn't want to wait. But nevertheless, I tearfully submitted to the Lord, prayed, and waited.

In February I felt impressed to resume my search. Through a friend the Lord put me in contact with a pleasant Christian real estate agent, and our search began. My real estate agent then put me in touch with a Christian loan agent. The fact that they were Christians made it easier for me to trust them. While we were house hunting, my loan agent called and told me that my credit score was 701. "What did you say my score was?" I asked. He repeated it. I was stunned, excited, and scared all at the same time. Now there was nothing to stop me from moving forward, getting a loan, and buying a house.

Then I heard about a company that built houses, and with only $100 down I could buy one. My real estate agent went to check it out. While I tried to decide what model I wanted, the agent called to say she had found a house that was on inventory for $89,900 with the same company, and they would pay 6 percent of the closing costs. Immediately we rushed to see the house, because someone else was coming too, and we wanted to get there first. The people were inside when we arrived, and the woman wanted the house. There was nothing I could do, since it was first come, first served. However, if she could not qualify, that would put me next in line. So after looking over the house, we began the paperwork. Before we even finished, the other real estate agent called and said her client did not qualify.

While processing the loan papers, my loan agent waived the appraisal fee ($350) that the buyer usually pays. Then on closing day I received a call asking me to bring $64.04 to closing. When I got there, the woman apologized. She had made a mistake, and they were to give *me* $64.04 instead. So I moved into a brand-new house that started at $124,000 for $36. Only God could have done that!

Elaine Gray

Who Has Seen the Wind?

The wind bloweth where it listeth, and thou hearest the sound thereof, but canst not tell whence it cometh, and whither it goeth: so is every one that is born of the Spirit. John 3:8.

FROM THE BEGINNING of Creation the wind has been blowing. One cold March day I found myself reminiscing about windy days I experienced during my childhood. I recalled the fun of windy days when my brother, sister, and I flew our colorful kites. With each gust of wind it was exciting to watch our kites soar higher and higher into the bright, beautiful sky.

Though many years have passed and my flying-kite-days are over, I continue to enjoy watching others fly their kites. On any given windy day, I take pleasure in watching the wind send objects in its path sailing here and there in the streets, yards, and on housetops. One morning, from my front door, I watched a white plastic bag sailing in the wind. It landed in a tree in front of the house, swinging, sometimes slowly, whichever way the wind would have it go. Watching this sight brought to mind one of my favorite poems by Christina Rossetti: "Who has seen the wind? Neither I nor you: but when the leaves hang trembling, the wind is passing through." God, our Creator, controls the gusting winds. One can only hear, feel, or see the results as they blow. When Jesus' disciples experienced the angry storm at sea, the billowy waves and fierce winds, then saw their Master calm the wind and waves, they were amazed. In unison they asked, "Who can this be? For He commands even the winds and water, and they obey Him" (Luke 8:25, NKJV).

I recall another windy day. I had parked my car at the shopping mall and was walking toward the entrance when I was pushed by the wind. Suddenly the wind snatched off my hat, and I helplessly watched it blown over and around the cars. Luckily a woman was sitting in her car watching my ordeal. She got out, retrieved my hat, and returned it with a smile. Thanking her, I informed her that God had destined her as my angel on this windy day.

I thank dear Jesus for His presence with me when the windy storms of life blow. He alone can help me in the stormy days of my life. I want to trust His promises in His Holy Word. My wish for you is that you too may feel His presence when you face any stormy winds.

Annie B. Best

A Treasure, Where?

Beloved, I wish above all things that thou mayest prosper and be in health, even as thy soul prospereth. 3 John 2.

HAVE YOU EVER been on a treasure hunt? How far would you travel to find treasure? What would you do if you found a treasure? Would you be willing to go to extreme measures to safeguard it? I'm sure that when it comes to a treasure you'd rather be safe than sorry, right?

But not many people realize the treasure they already own, and therefore don't take measures to safeguard it. Many realize it too late in their life to do much about it.

Are you on a treasure hunt? Search no more. You and I have been given a treasure by our Creator. The treasure chest is our own body. The treasure is our health. It is our duty to safeguard it, following the instructions of our Creator, that we may live happy, prosperous, and productive lives, lives that will cause others to glorify our heavenly Father.

Why do so many treat their treasure so carelessly? We know there are certain things we should avoid, such as some meats, animal fats, too many refined carbohydrates, too much salt and sugar. We also know important things we should do, such as drinking more water, exercising regularly, eating lots of fruits and vegetables, avoiding smoking and alcohol—and the list goes on. What are we waiting for?

Do you need some encouragement? Just visit any hospital. I guarantee it's not a pretty sight unless you're visiting the maternity ward. The rest is mind-boggling. Are we just taking our health for granted? Once we lose this incomparable treasure, our life will never be the same.

Do you still need additional encouragement? Look at the huge hospital bills just for spending a few hours in the emergency room! Surely there's something you'd rather spend your money on!

Our Creator is more than willing to help us stick to a plan that will ensure our health and happiness. He longs to see us in good health, both physically and spiritually. We have a God who tells us in today's text that He truly cares all about us in every way.

Have you been sick lately? Consider it a wake-up call. Start safeguarding the precious treasure of your health. Better safe than sorry, right? Your treasure is well worth it!

Rhodi Alers de López

The Forgotten Exam

Trust in the Lord with all thine heart;
and lean not unto thine own understanding. Prov. 3:5.

IT WAS ALMOST the end of my first semester at Monroe College, and the workload was pretty heavy: assignments to hand in, term exams, and the final exam just around the corner. March 3 is still crystal clear in my mind—the day of my final entrepreneurship exam.

We had been given at least two weeks' notice for that exam. We'd received a case study and were told that the exam would be based on it. But I was so busy preparing for exams in other courses and trying to finish my term projects that the two weeks went by much faster than I realized. To make matters worse, a week before the exam I had given my notebook to my lecturer as I wanted a second opinion on my term project. I'd forgotten that I'd written the date of this exam in the notebook.

The day I got my notebook back—was the day of my exam! To my astonishment, I had forgotten that fact. I could not believe this was happening. I was petrified, disappointed, and so upset that I had completely forgotten it. The first thing which came to mind was *I am going to fail!* However, after calming down a bit I also realized that I had forgotten that there was Someone even bigger than the exam looking down on me.

Before the exam started, I quickly said a prayer, claiming God's promise that "faith is the substance of things hoped for, the evidence of things not seen" (Heb. 11:1, NKJV). The first answer to my short, earnest prayer was that we were able to use the case study as we took the exam. I wrote the exam, trusting in God to give me wisdom and understanding to do my best. I also did it believing that my God is always on time and able to perform miracles once we depend on Him wholeheartedly.

I walked out of the exam room with a smile, certain I had passed my entrepreneurship exam. I must say that the God I serve is a loving God, and He is always listening to the petitions of His children. I say this because I passed the exam with an outstanding 96 percent! *Thank You, Jesus!*

I asked myself, Did I really deserve such a meritorious grade? I give my God all the praise. He has promised to provide the needs of His children in accordance with His will. And He did just that for me.

Amanda Amy Isles

Miracles—They Still Happen!

God is our refuge and strength,
a very present help in trouble. Ps. 46:1.

ONE EVENING I was feeling exhausted because some teachers and I had recently returned from a workshop. My husband and I prayed together, and then he went to bed. I lay on the sofa trying to relax by listening to a weather report. The last I heard was the warning of a severe storm before I fell asleep. It seemed just a moment later that I jerked awake at the sound of a terribly loud noise. A wall was coming toward me! In my confusion I thought the storm had ripped a tree from the yard and thrown it into the house. The Lord is so merciful, because when I awoke I ran into the kitchen, screaming for my husband. He awoke and ran to me, thinking that someone was breaking into our home. But no. "Look!" I cried. "Look!"

To our shock, a car was in our family room, stuck on the brick foundation of the house. Some of the shrubs were inside the house too, and furniture was thrown across the room.

The woman driving the car had been drinking. She was also driving with a learner's permit and had no insurance. She tried to run away as soon as she got out of the car, but by this time our neighbors were outside investigating the noise, and they called the police. We then called some of our family to let them know what had happened, so that they would not first hear about it on the news.

When my mother entered the house, her attention was drawn to the sofa. She said to me, "But you weren't on there!"

I looked at her and said, "That is exactly where I was." The Lord had shielded me from the flying debris of bricks, mortar, and glass that now covered the sofa. "It was a miracle that I was not hurt."

Our neighbors helped us put plastic over the car and the hole to keep the rain from coming into the house. Then they told me and my husband, "You must be Christians." We asked why they thought so, and they replied, "Because you didn't beat the woman up!" The next day she and her family came to our house. She was very apologetic. I told her that I was glad and thankful to God that we were both alive, and I hugged her. Hopefully it let her know that she was forgiven. Praise the Lord for His mercy and forgiveness—and His miracles!

Bertha Hall

Miracles Happen in Praises

I am the Lord, that is My name; and My glory I will not give to another.
Isa. 42:8, NKJV.

IT IS 19 YEARS LATER, and my mother-in-law, Comfort, is still alive!

One Wednesday in February 1994, Comfort was troubled by a slight headache. She immediately took some pills to help it, but things got worse. We heard nothing about this until Friday night around 9:00 p.m. We quickly got ready and hurried to her side. Her team of medical doctors said that her nerves were bad, her brain was not functioning normally, and her spinal cord was already damaged. If she survived, she would live a "vegetative life."

Here comes faith! Here comes trial, trust, belief! With such news came fervent prayer and a fixed focus on the Author and Finisher of our faith, Jesus.

Friends and family started praising God in prayer and fasting for days. They quoted Scriptures and claimed each line of the promises: "Comfort, you will not die, but live to declare the goodness of God. Dry bones lived in Ezekiel's days, and you are still living. Comfort, this sickness is not unto death, but that the glory of God might be revealed as professed by Jesus unto Lazarus. Yes, you shall be permanently cured; you will not lead a vegetative life; you will walk, talk, see, hear, and praise God at a thanksgiving service."

Twenty-seven grandchildren were not left out, and relatives far and near came to assist in their own ways and understanding. Some tried to use other powers, but we refused bluntly and told them that our God in heaven would not share His glory with anyone! That didn't go down well with them, but we insisted on the action and stayed focused on the Christian God.

On the twenty-fifth day of the coma, Mama spoke! It was sensible talk, too, not muttering. It was then that the medical team leader said, "We were just giving 'blind therapy.'" He claimed and identified with the Christian God of our family. Today Mama is still hale and hearty! Who is like unto our Lord? Trust in Him, and He will perfect your ways.

In April I gave birth to a baby girl whom Comfort named Oluwatoyin, which means "God alone be praised." And as part of a fulfillment of our vows to the Lord if He healed Mama completely, my husband and I became evangelists in our church district and conference. The prayers of the saints avail much.

Falade Dorcas Modupe

Where Is Your Heart?

For where your treasure is,
there your heart will be also. Matt. 6:21, NIV.

THE BACKYARD of our home is in front of a country house. Though we live in a city, we have the privilege of enjoying a farm environment. We like this place very much, for it brings us a sensation of calm and tranquillity.

One morning I opened the window at the back of the house and felt great joy when I saw the infinity of birds filling the yard. The tyrant fly-catchers, with their bonny yellow chests, embellished the trees. The rufous hornero was searching for material to build its house. The hummingbirds were flying from flower to flower to collect nectar. It was beautiful to see the ballet of doves and turtle doves singing happily and tranquilly.

As I watched, I meditated on how happiness is in little things: contemplating nature, cultivating a flower, and seeing it blossom; planting a tree and seeing it germinate; and listening to the songs of birds. But there are so many things that pass unnoticed in the rush of daily life. Maybe we are letting what would really bring us happiness pass unnoticed.

Every day we run blindly after the things that we think will bring us true happiness—such as money or fame. Are we looking for happiness in the wrong places? Are we wasting precious moments of our lives *not* watching our children grow, *not* enjoying friends or family, and most important, *not* spending moments with our God? Am I taking enough time for what is really important?

When we get to work, do we take time to say good morning to our colleagues? Do we have time to notice that someone by our side needs some help? Maybe this person is waiting for a friend's word or someone who will just listen to her. Sometimes the selfish search for our own welfare blinds us to what is happening around us.

What is occupying our minds, our hearts? I remember Jesus' important words regarding this subject in Matthew 6:19, 20: "Do not store up for yourselves treasures on earth, where moths and vermin destroy, and where thieves break in and steal. But store up for yourselves treasures in heaven, where moths and vermin do not destroy, and where thieves do not break in and steal" (NIV).

Where is my heart? Where is yours?

Darlen Cibeli Martelo Bach

Tori's Birth

Be still, and know that I am God.
Ps. 46:10.

I HAD A FEELING of apprehension that evening as my husband drove me to the hospital in our little rural town. The feeling was uncalled for as this was my third pregnancy and my first two deliveries had been uncomplicated. My labor pains were not that bad—why my fears?

We arrived at the hospital, and I spent the night in light labor. Around 4:00 a.m. the contractions started getting harder, and by 5:00 a.m. I was in full labor. Unfortunately, the baby was breech. When the young doctor attempted to turn the baby, it caused the most excruciating pain I have ever felt. Each time he tried to turn the baby, I screamed.

But through the pain I kept repeating the scripture, "Be still, and know that I am God." Even though I was in extreme pain, I kept repeating that scripture and had a surreal peace. It was totally unreal. When I had a contraction, the baby's heartbeat slowed way down, indicating that the baby was in distress. The young doctor finally called in the other doctor, one who had been in our area for 30 years or so and had delivered numerous babies. He determined that a C-section was needed immediately.

At our hospital at that time, all of the nurses were volunteers, and the one surgical nurse—who was needed for my C-section—lived about 50 miles out of town. It was March, and the roads were snowpacked and slick. So we had to wait until she arrived, got scrubbed, and ready before the surgery could take place.

Meanwhile hard labor pains continued to slam my body. With each contraction the baby's heartbeat slowed way down. Even though I was in extreme pain, "my" scripture kept running through my mind and I had peace about everything that was going on. I knew that the Lord was in control and whatever the outcome, it would be OK because He was in charge.

At last they could do the surgery. I had full anesthesia, and when I woke up the peace was still with me. I "knew" that my baby had died, and that it had been a boy (my husband had wanted a boy), but that was OK. I waited for my husband. He was crying when he came, tears of joy and relief. "We have a little girl," he said, "and she's fine!"

Oh, my God is so good! We named her Victoria—she is truly victorious! She is our miracle baby. "Be still, and know that I am God."

Gayle A. Kildal

Friendship Week

There are friends who pretend to be friends, but there is a friend who sticks closer than a brother. Prov. 18:24, RSV.

SEVERAL TIMES each year I receive an e-mail that states that this week is designated Friendship Week. I often wonder when exactly this week is, and who designates it. You see, every week is Friendship Week for me as I have been blessed all my life with great friends. They are from different geographical locations, of various ages, qualities, and functions.

I have friendships of more than 50 years. I have friends in Jamaica and friends on the other side of the globe in Australia. Some are my extended family, so we share each other's joys and sorrows. One friend, gifted with her hands and benevolence, has beautified my home with pillowcases and cushions. I have two friends gifted with encouragement. One sends spiritually power-packed e-mails when I am going through a bad spell, and the other calls me every day until the crisis passes. Then there are my young friends. I give them advice and counsel from my years of vast experience, acquired knowledge, and exposure to life, and they update me on current trends and their language—sometimes leaving me in minor shock—but being better able to communicate with them.

However, I have one Friend who is the greatest! Actually, He is my Brother by rebirth. His age is timeless. He knew me long before I was conceived and loved me long before I knew Him. He gave His life for me, and although He lives far away, He is by my side even before I call. His benevolence supersedes all others, for He supplies all my needs. What's amazing is that He does not overlook the small stuff, as He even makes parking spaces materialize for me!

He sends me text messages for every occasion. When I am sad, He texts, "Joy comes in the morning" (Ps. 30:5, RSV). When I am low in cash, He texts, "Consider the lilies" (Luke 12:27, RSV). When I face trials: "When you pass through the waters I will be with you" (Isa. 43:2, RSV). When I am tempted: "He will not let you be tempted beyond your strength" (1 Cor. 10:13, RSV). When I am afraid, He texts, "I will never fail you nor forsake you" (Heb. 13:5, RSV).

Every week is Friendship Week as we enjoy sweet fellowship together. Accept Him today as your friend. I don't mind sharing Him with you.

Cecelia Grant

The Art of Pulling Rank

And if I go and prepare a place for you, I will come again, and receive you unto myself; that where I am, there ye may be also. John 14:3.

THERE IS AN ART and a protocol for conducting meetings, such as Robert's Rules of Order, etiquette for e-mail and written communication, and even for table settings. There is also an art to giving and receiving. These skills must not only be taught, but reinforced with every given opportunity. I have a natural inclination toward tea etiquette, which is reinforced and broadened with every event I am enlisted to organize: teaspoons on the saucers, knives to the right of the plate, forks to the left—all a part of this orchestration.

Never could I have imagined in all my years that a day would come that a 7-year-old would introduce The Art of Pulling Rank. My older sister works diligently with my nieces to keep the art of letter writing alive and well. She and the girls spend hours searching for just the right stationery that will rightly represent each of them, their style, and their personality. On this carefully chosen paper, they are taught greetings, salutations, structure, and even punctuation. One particular Sunday they devoted time to the art of letter writing. It was then that my 7-year-old niece penned a letter to her great aunt in Bermuda, expressing her thoughts. She started the letter with the appropriate greetings. But then, without missing a note, she moved onto the content by expressing her position as "the favorite niece." Then she sealed the deal with a divine seal, writing, "Now, that's between God, you, and I." While I found myself laughing at this new art introduced by my niece, I relished the thought that I still held a position of importance and love.

It seems that not too far in my distant past I recall reading about a mother pulling rank to place her two sons at Jesus' right and left hand. I thought also about the fact that when you're in a foreign town or city and you attempt to locate a destination with a GPS, positioning is important. However, in the kingdom of God position is not relevant. And Jesus states: "Many that are first shall be last; and the last shall be first" (Matt. 19:30). Surely we should be more concerned about serving than about the rank that we hold, for God's greatest desire is that we make it to the kingdom where we can all enjoy our positions as sons and daughters. No pulling rank there.

Lady Dana Austin

The Book That Spoke

For you have been my refuge, a place of safety when I am in distress.
Ps. 59:16, NLT.

NEARLY TWO YEARS AGO, fresh out of my teen years, God inspired me to make drastic changes in my Christian life. I decided to revamp my entire Christian experience. I began to pray more often and to read all the spiritual books I could find to buy at a nearby Christian book center. My life was changing. God began to move in my life.

But these changes came with dire trials. The devil decided that he would not let me rest, since I'd determined to be closer to God. Slowly everything seemed to be going terribly wrong. Close friends of mine started turning against me. I began having problems with some of our church members. I questioned myself. Surely something was wrong with me. Even in my family things were going wrong. I became extremely depressed.

I remembered reading that all who live a godly life will suffer persecution. A close friend comforted me saying that it was because I was endeavoring to live right that the devil was out to get me. I concluded that if I am to meet heaven's requirements I must understand that it comes with its struggles.

I began to have sleepless nights as evil spirits started to attack. At times I had to sleep with the light on as a means of deterring their attacks. As I wrestled with spirits through the hours of darkness I discovered that when I called upon the name of Jesus I found relief.

One night the devil devised a double portion of distress, but God had a double portion of blessing. I woke up in the dead of the night as my bed began to shake— and I wasn't the one shaking it. I knew that evil spirits were around because I had the same uneasy feeling I'd experienced for weeks. I became extremely afraid, and like a child in need of her mother I cried out to the Lord. Suddenly the room went silent. I sat up, trembling. As I looked over the side of the bed I saw my devotional book, and I opened it. My eyes almost automatically skipped over paragraphs and went straight to the caption that said in bold letters, "Don't Be Afraid, God Is With You." At that, my tears flowed profusely as peace fell over my heart. In that moment God revealed Himself to me—He spoke to my troubles through a book. We just have to cry out to Him in our trials and let Him speak peace to our hearts.

Junet S. Jackson

Be Kind

Meekness, temperance: against such there is no law. And they that are Christ's have crucified the flesh with the affections and lusts. Gal. 5:23, 24.

HOW MANY THINGS has God taught me over the years? I would say there have been hundreds. One of the most important is kindness. He has asked me to look and listen to those around me and to ask Him to show me those who need help. Is it the older woman who is crossing the street with a heavy bag? I can help her carry that bag. Sometimes I am prompted to give up my seat on the bus for a child or old man. I need to be open to God's promptings.

In college I worked very hard to pay for the college fees. Sometimes I felt that I wasn't going to get the next bill paid. I remember one Sabbath when someone asked why I wore the same two dresses to church and Sabbath school week after week. My quiet answer was "That is all I have." I felt sorry for myself even though, as always, God was already helping me. He was helping in two ways: I was learning to trust Him, and He was giving me a friend who listened to Him.

One day this girlfriend knocked on my dorm room door. When I opened the door I saw her standing there with a very big box. She seemed a little shy and that seemed strange to me, because she was a sweet and wonderful person. All of us were glad she was our friend. Quietly she asked, "Would you like the clothes in this box? I'm getting new clothes. My grandma wants to buy me some new outfits, so I don't need these. Do you want them?"

Did I! I was excited and thanked her for her gift. We hugged, and she went on her way.

Now I had more than enough clothes for the next year and beyond. More than two dresses to wear to church! This friend is still a very special person to me, and I pray that she knows what a great and kind thing she did that day.

I want to be faithful to what God asks me to do. He usually gets my attention in a clear small voice, and I pray that I do not miss helping others and seeing others with God's eyes. Another Bible version translates today's thought as this: "God's Spirit makes us loving, happy, peaceful, patient, kind, good, faithful, gentle, and self-controlled. There is no law against behaving in any of these ways. And because we belong to Christ Jesus, we have killed our selfish feelings and desires" (Gal. 5:22-24, CEV). Isn't that what we all want?

Susen Mattison Molé

Crossed by an Angel

God will command his angels to protect you wherever you go. They will carry you in their arms, and you won't hurt your feet on the stones. Ps. 91:11, 12, CEV.

IT WAS EARLY 1970. I was only in my midteens, but I had already begun my teaching career. My first assignment was in the Belizean outback in Belize, Central America. Getting to the small school meant walking eight miles or 18 if I missed the sole means of transportation for the first 10 miles. Getting a ride in the back of that truck was as good as being in a luxury car.

On one particular Sunday my 9-year-old brother and I missed the ride. We sighed deeply as we faced 18 miles by foot with little hope of hitching a ride. The scorching sun made the journey more daunting. Even the trees on the roadside seemed wilted.

It was late evening when we reached the river. Usually the kind church members who live nearest to the river would leave a small canoe for the teacher to use to get across. But there was no canoe that Sunday. A mild-tempered horse, however, was waiting for us on the other side. Admiral, my favorite horse to this day, was only a few hundred yards away—so near and yet so far. Would I have to swim across? I could—and that seemed my best option—but I did not want my little brother to do that. So there on the bank of the river, as the shadows began to lengthen, I took my little brother's hand and spoke to the only One I knew could help us.

I had no idea how the answer would come, but it came in seconds. A gentleman who looked much like the people who lived farther up the tributary appeared in a small canoe similar to the one we usually took across. He offered to take us across the river. When we alighted from the boat and I turned to say thanks, he was no longer there. He had disappeared just as he had appeared. *Strange,* I thought. Up to this point it had seemed quite ordinary.

We mounted the horse and began the final leg of our journey. The people that lived nearest to the river were astonished to see us. "How did you get across?" they questioned us, apologizing for not leaving the boat on time. No one knew of the gentleman we described. God's promise in today's text had been fulfilled before our very eyes. My little brother's faith, like mine, was strengthened.

I cannot wait to meet that angel and hear the rest of the story.

Claudette Garbutt-Harding

Before the Judgment

For we shall all stand before the judgment seat of Christ.
Rom. 14:10.

I CAN NEVER FORGET the day I had to appear in court for a trial against a man who had attacked me while I was on duty in the hospital. The incident happened in 2006. However, it took five years for the case to come to a hearing.

My husband and I went to the court and met the policeman who handled my case. He was a Christian too. He asked me, "Do you wish to punish that man who harmed you, or do you want to forgive him?" According to my decision, I would be prepared to speak to the judge.

"I don't know," I finally answered. I remembered the physical pain and mental agony that I suffered from the attack. Depression had caused me to become diabetic and hypertensive—from which I still suffer. The whole experience passed in front of me like a vision. I couldn't make an immediate decision. I wanted to punish him as well as forgive him. Then I prayed for God to help me, and remembered our Lord Jesus saying on the cross, "Father, forgive them, for they do not know what they are doing" (Luke 23:34, NIV). As God forgave all my sins, I decided to forgive that man as well.

Even though I had not been the one in the wrong, I trembled to stand in front of the judge. But I answered all his questions, and before the end of the trial I was able to say, "Judge, I want to forgive the man."

On returning home, I sat down and thought about the final judgment when everyone will stand before the greatest and mightiest Judge, Jesus Christ. How will we answer Him? What will be the final result? Will He reward us or punish us? And how will we prepare for the final judgment? Are we sure our sins are washed away by the blood of Jesus? How is our life now? Are we a witness for others? Do others see Jesus in us? So many questions to ask ourselves.

Earthly judgment may depend on the person's wealth, position, money, name, or fame. We may escape from the earthly judgment but not the heavenly judgment. Our Lord Jesus is not a man to change His mind, nor does He tell lies. So it is not too late to change our attitude. God gives us many opportunities to repent. Let us prepare ourselves to stand before the throne of our Lord. By His grace let us study His Word prayerfully and get ready for His coming.

Victoria Selvaraj

In Faithlessness

"For I know the plans I have for you," declares the Lord, "plans to prosper you . . . plans to give you hope and a future." Jer. 29:11, NIV.

I AM SURE YOU KNOW the story of the Israelites told in the Old Testament. They were a faithless crew who served God and then served the gods around them. They went with Moses into the desert and had to spend an extra 38 years because they kept making poor choices. They just kept repeating the same mistakes again and again. When they finally got to Canaan they still didn't obey God's command, and chose to keep their enemies as their friends. For hundreds of years they went their own way, were made slaves, cried out to God—who saved them—and went right back to the same sins that got them into trouble the last time. Finally, God had had enough, and He brought a conquering nation to remove them from the Promised Land. They were taken to Babylon, and Jerusalem and the Temple were destroyed. In the midst of losing all they held dear, God told them that this was not all—He promised them 70 years of slavery, and oh, by the way, this is because "I have good plans for you and your future."

It is easy for me to see God when I am surrounded by His saints, those bright stars who seem to glow with His presence. Unfortunately, those precious saints aren't there day in and day out. They are not who I work with, or who I shop with, and I get lonely out there in the world. More often than not I feel alone in the dark. I stumble between wanting to please God and wanting to fit in with those around me. Some days I get so tired of always being different, of being the girl who isn't asked to lunch because they know I won't have a drink or slip of the tongue. To them, that makes me a prude or no fun. So my heart is like an Israelite. It longs for God's grace and beauty to fill it. The moments I bask in His glory are like none other, but when twilight comes I get distracted by the fireflies until I am lost in the dark. I cry out against my faithlessness and wonder why I can't be true to the God who loves me no matter what. Then in the darkness come the storms that push me back into the light. In my darkest storm, when my heart is so battered and bruised I can hardly breathe, He says, "Hold on. The storm isn't at its worst yet. You have a long battle ahead of you—but hold on. I have chosen you even in your faithlessness. I still know what you can be. I see your future."

Selena Blackburn

Baby Proof

The Lord is not slack concerning his promise, as some men count slackness;
but is longsuffering to us-ward, not willing that any should perish,
but that all should come to repentance. 2 Peter 3:9.

MY BABY DAUGHTER, Lily, is at that stage in which her curiosity has surpassed her discernment. I follow her around the house, pulling her hand out of the dog food bowl, picking up the tipped over recycling bin, listening to her giggles of pleasure when the paper towel roll comes undone at her command, and assuaging her dismay when I pry my phone away from her.

I had underestimated the meaning of the words "baby proofing." I plugged the outlets, put the chemicals in a high cupboard, and brushed off my hands in satisfaction at being a terrific mom. Ha! Since then I've also had to retrain myself to be mindful of loose change, to train my husband to watch out for the occasional screw or nail that might drop from his pocket, to reinforce the wobbly bookcase, and put the scissors out of reach. I still haven't figured out what to do with the dog food.

A thought occurred to me: my efforts at infant-injury prevention are similar to the way in which God treats us. When we are spiritual babies, inexperienced and unable to tell what is good for us, He protects us from spiritual danger. I kept mulling over that idea before realizing it wasn't really true. Although God directs our spiritual growth, He doesn't baby-proof the world for us. Those who are barely getting to know the character of God come into contact with spiritual harm: church members who misrepresent Him, systems that fail to meet their needs, prayers that seem to go unanswered and even unheard. Why doesn't God take better care of His babies?

One thing we see in the stories of Abraham, David, and Job, as well as in the lives of people we know, is that God allows people to become disillusioned. Even when we are just learning to trust God, He allows our religiosity to be injured, our faith to wane, and our morals to stray. However, He never leaves us at that point! God trusts that in time we will be able to see and respond to His amazing love for us. Just as I always pull Lily out of the dog food bowl and set her on a path in a better direction, so our great and loving God will do for us. His longsuffering character is not willing that any of us should perish.

Denise Tonn

The Wrinkled Washcloth

Create in me a clean heart, O God; and renew a right spirit within me.
Ps. 51:10.

IT WAS AN EARLY Monday morning, the first day of another workweek. I was intensely engaged in the daily and automatic routine of getting ready for work when a washcloth that had fallen to the floor caught my attention. As I stooped to pick it up and rehang it on the rack, I noticed its condition: dry, wrinkled, stiff, and difficult to straighten out. The only way to restore the washcloth to a condition of wrinkle-free softness so that it would hang in a smooth way was to wash it.

That's it! This is our condition. Our need for washing and restoration! How do we allow ourselves to become so wrinkled with sin, hardened and stiffened to the patient wooing of our heavenly Father? After all, He gave His only Son to die for our sins that we might be saved if we would just believe. We forget the way that God has led us up to the present moment. We put self before God in our daily living. We deceive ourselves into believing that we can manage our own lives. Can we really handle the joys, accomplishments, temptations, trials, and tribulations? We become proud in our own deceit and unwilling to acknowledge our helplessness. Surrendering all to God becomes either an afterthought or no thought at all. Meanwhile God, who gave us His all, patiently stands knocking at the doors to our hearts, wanting to come in and help us, wanting to be an integral part of our lives, because He loves us. Only when we fall—as did the washcloth—onto Christ, our rock and salvation, our refuge in the time of storm, can we avail ourselves of the redemptive washing/cleansing power of His blood and become renewed and restored. Hebrews 10:22 says, "Having our hearts sprinkled to cleanse us from a guilty conscience and having our bodies washed with pure water" (NIV).

It is this process that enables us to be willing to hear His word behind our ear calling us by name and saying, "This is the way, walk ye in it, when ye turn to the right hand, and when ye turn to the left" (Isa. 30:21). Oh, what an awesome heavenly Father we serve! He's all about saving us because He loves us. Let us pour out our hearts to God as did David, the psalmist, and say, "Wash me thoroughly from my iniquity, and cleanse me from my sin." "Create in me a clean heart, O God, and renew a steadfast spirit within me" (Ps. 51:2, 10, NKJV).

Cynthia Best-Goring

Angels Unawares

Do not forget to show hospitality to strangers, for by so doing some people have shown hospitality to angels without knowing it. Heb. 13:2, NIV.

AS A LITTLE GIRL I was always excited when it was time to take a trip to Montego Bay with my parents. Even though most of the trips were for meetings, I still enjoyed the ride and the entire idea of getting out. I must have been about 6 years old on this particular day. As soon as we reached the main intersection heading into the busy town, our car stopped in the middle of the road. Horns started to blare, and loud voices echoed annoyance toward us as we were now obstructing traffic.

At the time, my mother didn't drive and knew little about cars, and I simply sat in the back seat, pretty much helpless in this situation. My dad was on his own. I grew a little anxious as he looked at the engine to see what he could do. He tried this and that and my mother turned the ignition, but nothing happened.

And then, out of nowhere, a man appeared. He wore tattered clothes, broken shoes, and looked as though he probably even smelled. My palpitations increased as I thought he looked harmful, and the look on my mother's face confirmed my feelings. And he proceeded toward my dad. I was scared. Dad seemed hesitant about him too, but the man kept walking toward us as though he was going to do something to the engine.

"Don't let him!" my mother shouted from inside the car. But it all happened so fast my dad was unable to stop him. After touching a wire or two, the man said to my dad, "Tell her to start it now." Reluctantly Dad beckoned to my mom, and she turned the key. The car started! Our eyes must have seemed to pop out of our heads. It was unbelievable. In less than one minute a stranger had fixed our car.

My dad snapped out of his astonishment and lifted his stare from my mom to turn and thank the stranger, but he was gone. The man had disappeared, and none of us could tell where he had gone. My dad got back into the car and drove off to find him, but he was nowhere to be seen.

Today's text speaks of "angels unawares." There and then we pulled over and thanked God for sending us an angel. With His help we were able to complete our journey successfully.

Avia Rochester-Solomon

He Hears My Cry

The Lord hath heard my supplication;
the Lord will receive my prayer. Ps. 6:9.

MY DAUGHTER LOOKED like her father, and they were very close. When he died a few weeks after her second birthday, she was devastated. She cried, clung to me, and never wanted to be alone. It was as though she feared I would vanish like her father had. Children cry for a lot of things—it could be for food, comfort, or attention. My daughter cried a lot for my attention. Whenever she cried, she expected me to say, "Sorry." After I said it, she would stop crying.

One day she went to play with other children in the compound. I was happy that she was getting over the trauma. She was gone for more than an hour, but she came home weeping and was not able to say what happened. I thought she would soon stop crying, but it was not so. I tried to hold her. Several times I said the magic word, "Sorry," but it did not work. I pressed and felt all over her body to find out if she was cut or had broken a bone. I could find nothing that would make her cry. My neighbors came to help me comfort her. They brought toys, biscuits, chocolates. Still, she cried. Soon they left and I was alone with my crying daughter. Desperate, I gave her a pain relief medicine. By nightfall she was exhausted from all the crying and fell asleep, but I saw that she was uncomfortable even in her sleep. She frequently turned from one side to another with a sob. This was very unusual. I had tried all the mother-care tricks and skills I knew, to no avail, so I got up and knelt down to pray. I had no husband to give me the support needed at this time, so I cried to the Husband of all widows. I cried to the Lord for help, because I had exhausted all the maternal options I knew.

God heard my prayer. I could not sleep after praying, so I closely watched my daughter's face. Suddenly something in me told me to look even more closely. Then my attention was drawn to her tiny nose, and I saw a little object inside of it. I couldn't imagine what it could be. It was almost midnight and I could not afford to call the doctor, so I decided to remove it myself. It was a piece of chalk. I applied some ointment and she slept like an angel for the rest of the night.

It is a wonderful thing to know that God, who gave us so many great and precious promises, really cares for us. He will never forsake us.

Taiwo Adenekan

All Expenses Paid

*He which testifieth these things saith, Surely I come quickly. Amen.
Even so, come, Lord Jesus. Rev. 22:20.*

IF YOU WERE OFFERED an all-expense-paid trip to anywhere in the world, where would you want to go? That thought came to mind one morning as I was getting ready to go to church. I tried to think of places I'd like to see. Alaska? Switzerland? England? Florida? Not being much of a traveler, I couldn't think of any place I really wanted to go. Just being home sounded good to me.

Home! That's when the thought came to me.

I already have an all-expense-paid trip to go to a place I've never been. There is no brochure. Instead, it has so many features that a whole Book was written about it. The perks for this trip are wonderful! I can invite anyone to go with me: family, friends, neighbors. Anyone! It is going to be the best trip I've ever been on. Definitely not a trip I want to miss. And what's amazing is that though the cost is very high, it's already been paid. The only thing I have to do is be ready to go. No packing. Clothing will be provided. We will be given robes and crowns. Treated like royalty. No reservations to make either. That, too, is taken care of. The Book says that we'll stay in beautiful mansions. No worries about meals either, or where to eat—and no tipping needed. Everywhere you go there you will find fresh fruit and vegetables.

A King reigns at this destination. We can visit with Him, walk and talk with Him. We can ask Him questions. I'm sure we'll all have a lot of questions.

I don't know the time of departure. But the Book says the only thing I have to do is to be ready when the time comes so I don't miss the flight. I understand that friends I haven't seen in a long time will be going, and even family members who've been away for years. My anticipation is growing all the time. I can't wait! Oh, I read of the joy and excitement we'll have when we get there, for this beautiful, happy place will be our home forever.

Since I can invite others to go with me, I'm inviting you. You, then, can invite your family, friends, and neighbors to come too. It's almost time to go home. It's time for Jesus to come. Don't miss the flight. Is everybody ready? Are you?

Donna Sherrill

Even There,
Your Hand Will Guide

When I called, you answered me; you greatly emboldened me. Ps. 138:3, NIV.

WILLOWS ARE OFTEN THE FIRST TREES to leaf out in the spring. I learned that in Chengde, in northeast China, when I visited our oldest daughter who was teaching in a college there. It had been wonderful to visit Robyn, to see where she lived, the streets she cycled, the vendors who sold her ice cream. On my globe at home Chengde was just opposite Maryland, U.S.A.—about 7,000 miles (11,300 kilometers) away. It was so far that when I tried to picture it, all I could see was darkness. But now I was there, and the city was flooded with sunshine. Much, much too soon, it was time for me to return home.

A man from the college took me to the Beijing airport. It was one of the hardest things I'd ever done to leave my daughter and the driver as they returned to her town.

This was in 1993. The Beijing airport was small, dark, and gray. After checking in, I spent about three hours in a dim, crowded no-man's-land, standing by my luggage, unable to go farther until a door was opened to let me and 200 other travelers through. Later that evening I landed in Hong Kong and was picked up by missionaries who took me to their home for the night. They lived in a small, efficient high-rise apartment. Nice people. A good supper. A comfortable bed. And yet I was desolate. Robyn was beginning her second year of teaching at the Chinese college. She had already seen and experienced many wonderful things, and I felt much better having lived for a week in the city where she lived. But now I was so lonely. My heart was breaking. So I opened my Bible to Psalm 139, wanting to read the promise "If I settle on the far side of the sea, even there your hand will guide me" (verses 9 and 10, NIV).

Instead my eyes fell on the opposite page, Psalm 138. "I will praise you, Lord, with all my heart. . . . When I called, you answered me; you greatly emboldened me" (verses 1-3, NIV).

That was exactly what I needed. If I needed anything at all it was for God to make me bold and stouthearted—stouthearted as I left my daughter, bold to make the 14-hour flight to Los Angeles, brave as I spent the night in a hotel there, and finally flew to Virginia. Somehow my spirits lifted. God would take care of my daughter and the young woman she taught with. God would bless their work and the people they touched. God would bring me safely home. And them, too. And He did.

Penny Estes Wheeler

Blizzard Times Two

He giveth snow like wool:
he scattereth the hoarfrost like ashes. Ps. 147:16.

MY FUTURE HUSBAND and I had been dating for a few months when I suggested that we plan a weekend trip to Iowa where he could meet some of my relatives. I rationalized that it would be a pleasant way to celebrate my birthday in March. He agreed and borrowed his dad's new Ford for the trip.

We arrived in Iowa, picked up my two aunts, and off we went to Uncle Jim's farm to visit more family. We enjoyed a wonderful dinner and visit. All too quickly night approached. As the four of us left the farm, it began snowing lightly. Yet soon the few miles connecting the country road to the highway were almost impossible to navigate, for within minutes the light snow had turned into an Iowa blizzard. It was an eerie feeling: like heavy, white drapery being pulled all around us. My friend, driving, shook from anxiety. Not only was he unfamiliar with the road, but the road was all but obliterated by the swirling snow.

My aunt knew the road, and when we saw a faint flicker of light from a nearby farmhouse she insisted that we pull into its driveway. It turned out to be the farm of my former schoolteacher and her husband; my very first teacher in country school. They were gracious hosts and made us feel welcome to wait out the storm through the night. We awoke the next morning to the wonderful aroma of a country breakfast and the news that her husband had gotten up early and plowed the country road, opening a pathway to the highway. He announced that the highway was already plowed and ready for travel! They were so cordial to four desperate travelers in need of shelter from the storm.

Ten years later we faced another blizzard, this time as a married couple with two children, in the state of Kansas. My husband was the principal of a school in a small town. We had just transported my aunt back to Kansas City during the Christmas holiday and were traveling home when the blizzard hit. We were in our own Ford car this time. In addition to the danger of the blizzard surrounding us, the heater had suddenly stopped working. My husband's eyes strained to see the road as I prayed, "Lord, part this curtain of white for us to see." We experienced God's protection once again through another blizzard.

Retha McCarty

Love: Your Enemies?

But I say unto you, Love your enemies, bless them that curse you, do good to them that hate you, and pray for them which despitefully use you, and persecute you. Matt. 5:44.

LOVE YOUR ENEMIES. I think this is one of the hardest things to do, to love those who talk about you, those who abuse your kindness, those who stab you in the back, and those who are jealous of you because you are a child of the most high God.

Within the past few months I have experienced a very difficult time at work. I asked God to help me get along with a coworker. I resented conversations with her and knew that this should not be the character of a Christian. I asked God to heal me and change me, to build a hedge of protection around me when in her presence. I prayed that God would help me to walk in His steps and have the mind of Christ, to smile, and accept the task appointed. But it seemed that nothing helped.

One Saturday evening I was watching a religious TV station when the speaker talked about forgiveness. He spoke of a young woman at his church who had stopped talking to him for reasons unknown. She avoided him at every opportunity. He was troubled by this, and decided to get to the bottom of it. So as he drove to church he decided to stop by her house. When she answered the door, he asked, "Have I offended you in any way? If I have, I ask your forgiveness." The young woman said to him, "You have done nothing. It is I who should be asking forgiveness."

Right then, I knew I had to ask forgiveness of my coworker, even if I felt I had done nothing wrong. God, however, revealed to me things that warranted my asking forgiveness of her. I fought against it, yet I knew this was the will of God. Upon returning to work, with a sincere heart, I went to her office and said, "If I have disrespected you in any way, I ask your forgiveness." Instantly I was relieved, renewed, and refreshed. I felt like a burden had been lifted from me, and that God was pleased with my decision.

I continue to pray for my coworker, and I ask God to help me love my enemies and pray for those who despitefully use me. At the end of the day, love does hold the key to eternal life.

Sylvia Giles Bennett

Healing Words to a Broken Heart

For your Maker is your husband—the Lord Almighty is his name—the Holy One of Israel is your Redeemer; he is called the God of all the earth. Isa. 54:5, NIV.

WE HAD BEEN MARRIED for 15 years when my husband told me he wanted a divorce. I was devastated, but had been expecting it for some time, as we had grown apart much earlier in our marriage. I had prayed to the Lord for guidance and comfort, and His word came back to me to persevere and endure. So for three more years I tried to work at my marriage. The fact that we had two teenage children only made matters more challenging, but I clung to the promises of my Savior. Unfortunately, the inevitable happened, and there was nothing more I could do to save a relationship that was lost barely after it had formed.

I was angry with myself and with God. I felt let down by the One in whom I had trusted, and was disappointed in the hopes and dreams I had cherished.

I cried out to my Redeemer, begging for forgiveness, encouragement, and wisdom. God had not failed me even though I felt like a failure and a loser. And every day His word came to me to reassure me of His love and faithfulness. I asked Him for His blessings and to take care of my children who chose to live with their father. God told me that He does not condemn me and that I need not fear. He told me of His unfailing love that will not be shaken, nor will His covenant of peace be removed from me. He promised that my children would be taught by the Lord and great will be their peace. He reassured me that I would have nothing to fear and that I will refute every tongue that accuses me. He would vindicate me (see Isa. 54).

Nothing would separate me from His love (Rom. 8:35). He told me that His plans are to prosper me, to give me hope and a better future (Jer. 29:11).

He reminds me that I am precious and honored in His sight. He loves me. He has called me by name, and I am His! He told me that He is doing a new thing for me (see Isa. 43). He promises that I will see His glory, the splendor of my God. Gladness and joy will overtake me!

He compliments me and tells me that I am beautiful to Him, my voice is sweet and my face is lovely. He tells me that He loves me with an everlasting love. I say, "Thank You, my Husband, for speaking words of healing to my broken heart."

Juliette Rose

Honor and Honesty

Finally, brethren, whatever things are true, whatever things are noble, whatever things are just, whatever things are pure, whatever things are lovely, whatever things are of good report, if there is any virtue and if there is anything praiseworthy—meditate on these things. Phil. 4:8, NKJV.

THERE ARE STILL many honest and honorable people in the world. It doesn't matter what people say about our society, I can still proclaim that honest people are still here on Planet Earth. I can testify of many good and honorable people who can be praised and thanked.

I just returned home from my church's 10-day camp meeting retreat. While there I began talking with a dear elderly woman who was very distressed, as she had lost all the money she'd brought with her. She told me that her bundle of money must have dropped out when she pulled a tissue from her handbag, and only when she went to her cabin did she realize it was gone. I encouraged and prayed for her, and for the person who had found it. And after her loss was announced in the main meeting, the money was returned to that dear woman.

A few days after our coming back home I went to a grocery store to buy some fruit and vegetables. I have a habit of checking my receipts before I leave the counter, and on this particular day I saw that the clerk had overcharged me for the oranges. The medium-sized oranges were only 49 cents a pound, but I'd been charged $1.38 per pound. When I called it to her attention, she returned more than $3.00. I was glad I didn't have to overpay for those oranges.

On my way home I stopped by an Asian store to pick up some tropical vegetables. It was a good thing I had stuck the three dollars in my handbag instead of in my wallet, because I discovered I didn't have my wallet. I searched the car, my handbag, and the piles of vegetables, but couldn't find it anywhere. I rushed back to the grocery store where I had bought the fruit. My first thought was *How could I have been so very careless!* I had prayed—I always pray before shopping so that I won't spend carelessly. Would whoever found that wallet return it to customer service? I prayed for an honest person and asked God to forgive my carelessness.

I didn't want to lose money, even if it was only $35. I rushed to customer service. My wallet was there. On my way to the car I thanked God for honest people who return what doesn't belong to them!

Ofelia A. Pangan

Burden Bearers

Carry each other's burdens, and in this way you will fulfill the law of Christ.
Gal. 6:2, NIV.

IT WAS A SAD DAY when Chuck, our neighbor at the bottom of the hill, moved away. We had enjoyed watching him transform the vacant lot on the corner by building a little white house on the land. We looked forward to his wave as we passed there on our way to town. But he could no longer make the monthly payments so had to give up all his hard work. Now we wondered who our new neighbors would be.

Soon we noticed activity around the house. Our new neighbors had moved in. One day as we drove by, a young man came out and waved us down. He introduced himself as Zane, the new neighbor. We chatted a bit, and I decided that a young couple had bought the house. Then we discovered that Mark and June, the people who lived there, were Zane's parents. Mark suffered from a rare kind of cancer, and Zane had come back home to help take care of him.

When our daughter-in-law invited them and us to lunch one day, we had a chance to get better acquainted. They had another son, still in high school, and we were impressed how polite and well-mannered both young men were. Mark hadn't felt well enough to join us for lunch, but we enjoyed visiting with June. A few days later I stopped by their house and left some freshly baked cookies, which the boys especially appreciated. I didn't want June to feel that she had to do something in return, so I told her this was a "welcome to the neighborhood" gift.

Our busy life moved on. A few weeks later when my husband went to offer Zane a tree he could cut up for firewood, he came back with the news that Mark had died. What a shock that was! June had told us about a new treatment she was using for her husband, but we simply didn't realize he was so ill. We also felt bad that we hadn't even met him. I knew that I must go right down and see June, but since I had never been in her position, what could I say?

When I drove into the yard, June came out to meet me. I didn't have any words to say so I just put my arms out and hugged her for a long time. My tears mingled with hers, and that seemed to be enough. I knew that she understood my feelings for her. Our visits always begin and end with hugs—something more important than words. They don't cost a penny, but they do help to bear others' burdens.

Betty J. Adams

Going Home

Do not let your hearts be troubled. You believe in God; believe also in me. My Father's house has many rooms; if that were not so, would I have told you that I am going there to prepare a place for you? . . . I will come back and take you to be with me that you also may be where I am. You know the way to the place where I am going. John 14:1-4, NIV.

ON ARRIVAL AT THE Sydney airport from Fiji, I discovered that my daughter Sala wasn't there to meet me because my younger daughter, Terri, who was holidaying in the Solomon Islands, had not contacted her about my arrival. I had heavy luggage, and traveling by train to where Sala lives was not an option. I quickly searched my travel bag to find her phone numbers, but to my dismay I could not locate them. I checked for inexpensive hotel accommodations, but the agent informed me that it was peak season and hotel prices were high. I sat there and thought, puzzled over my situation. *What will I do if Sala is not in the country?* Then breathing a prayer of thanks for my safe arrival, I allowed the Lord to take over my situation.

Soon I felt impressed to check my travel bag once more. Surprisingly, I discovered the address and phone number of a Papua New Guinea friend, Roseline Baker. She lives and works in Sydney with her Australian husband, Shaner. I was overjoyed, and thanked the Lord for this, then bought a cheap mobile phone and called Roseline. She was in Victoria, a different state, but gave me contact information for close friends and relatives Jeff and Jo Hansen. Yet I felt unsure about calling them. Putting them on the spot for help was embarrassing. I had planned to visit them a while later to discuss the possibility of working with them on community projects in Papua New Guinea. *Lord, is this a better time You've opened for me?* So I called the number. Jeff was immediately on the line. I told him my situation and he happily assured me that everything would be fine. And Jo told me they would help me get to Sala's.

Soon Jeff and Jo met me at the airport arrivals, and we prepared to leave for my daughter's home. I knew where we were going, but needed help getting there. Jeff had a GPS, so with the help of this magic machine it took only half an hour.

We all look forward to going home to glory. Today we have television, radio, and the Internet to help us share the good news about our heavenly home. It won't be long until we journey home. And thank God for friends who help us on our way.

Fulori Sususewa Bola

The Unprepared

For you yourselves know perfectly that the day of the Lord
so comes as a thief in the night. 1 Thess. 5:2, NKJV.

WHEN RETURNING from a trip to Georgia, my husband and I stopped in Miami to visit some relatives. In the midst of those happy days, I prepared to go to the airport with a friend to meet a couple coming from New York. They would arrive close to midnight. My husband would take us and drop us off, and we would return with them in a rental car.

They arrived, and after hugs and greetings the car was rented and filled with luggage, leaving only enough room for us to sit. I put my purse behind me, close to my head, between the luggage and bags. Our friend had never driven on the fast highways of the United States, so went along hesitantly, trusting in the instructions given him. After some time we discovered that we were lost in one of the most dangerous neighborhoods of the city.

I didn't know we were surrounded by such dangers, but I felt safe in the car, chatting with my friends. People were still roaming the streets, even at that late hour.

Suddenly the traffic light in front of us turned red. Only drivers who were naive and ignorant of the dangers of the area would stop at a red light at that hour—but we didn't know. Suddenly a very tall young man opened the back door of the car exactly where I was sitting, and began running his hands at my feet, looking for my purse.

The terror, the panic, and my indescribable fear empowered me, giving me strength to yell. At that moment of surprise and anguish, I asked God to not let him pull me out of the car. Perhaps surprised by the many shouts, the young man slowly backed toward the sidewalk without taking anything. Providentially my purse was above me among the bags.

Upon arriving home, we praised God the Father who always cares for us. I reflected, *So will be the return of the Son of man. Many will be found unaware, caught off guard. Jesus will come as a thief in the night, at a time no one is expecting.* I decided right there to be more attentive and to better prepare myself for the great event soon to occur. May it not be, for you or for me, a day of fright and horror, but one of joy and pleasure!

Zuila V. N. Rodrigues

Communion

For as often as ye eat this bread, and drink this cup,
ye do shew the Lord's death till he come. 1 Cor. 11:26.

AS A BAPTIZED church member since I was 7 years old, I've taken part in many Communion services. I've always known what this service means: it is about Jesus dying on the cross for our sins. The services were very traditional: a sermon, the ordinance of humility (foot washing), prayers for the bread and wine, serving, an ending thought, song, and dismissal.

Since moving to our new residence, we have had Communion on Friday nights and on Sabbath afternoons. Though these services had the same traditional elements, they included illustrations that brought home to me the awesomeness of Christ's sacrifice.

At one Friday night service the pastor gave a short sermon about how God forgives us no matter what we have done. All we have to do is confess our sins and leave them at the cross. The scene in the front of the church was of a bare, cruel cross. The ushers were asked to pass out a small piece of red ribbon to each person there. At the appropriate time, deacons stood at that cross with a hammer and nails. We were asked to think of that ribbon as our sins. Using the hammer, and taking a nail, one by one we went and nailed our ribbons (sins) to the cross. As the musicians played and sang, "They are nailed to the cross," I could not help visualizing the magnitude of pain that Jesus had to have felt as He hung on the cross at Golgotha for sins He did not commit. Because of love, He did it just for me. That was the greatest exhibition of love! He did it just for you.

I was not there when they nailed Him to the cross. But experiencing this particular Communion caused me to tremble with a deeper realization of how Jesus died. As I remember the words to a popular gospel song, it says, "They hung Him high, they stretched Him wide, He hung His head and for me He died. That's love."

If we confess, all our sins are forgiven. Though our sins may be as red as those ribbons, Christ has promised to make our hearts white as snow. I pray that as we continue to participate in Communion services, we will concentrate deeply on the cross and its awesome meaning—all just for you and me.

Marie H. Seard

Do You Know Jesus?

I want to know Christ and experience the mighty power that raised him from the dead. I want to suffer with him, sharing in his death, so that one way or another I will experience the resurrection from the dead! Phil. 3:10, 11, NLT.

NOT LONG AGO I had an unusual experience that profoundly impacted me. I had returned from my early morning walk with my husband and decided to remove unsightly grass on the street in front of our house. I had almost completed my task when my neighbor exited his house and greeted me with a "Hello there, neighbor. You all travel a lot, and when you come home you work hard."

It isn't too often that I see my neighbor all dressed up in a black suit with Bible in hand, so jokingly I said, "You look like a pastor. Are you going to preach today?" His response caught me off guard: "I will if they'll let me." I didn't expect this answer, so I asked what he would preach about. To my surprise, he said, "The first thing I would ask them is this: Do you know Jesus?" Walking across his lawn, he continued, "You see, a lot of people come to church all dressed up, looking good with fancy clothes, driving big expensive cars, and some with Bibles in hand. But the important thing is, do they know Jesus."

He continued, "Look at the disciples. They followed Jesus around for three years and they didn't know Him. Peter was with Him all the time, but in the end he said he didn't know Jesus. There was Thomas. He walked with Him too, but He didn't believe Him. When Jesus told them that He would die, they didn't believe Him, because they had another agenda. And that fellow called Judas—he came right up in Jesus' face and gave him a kiss so the soldiers would know which one to take. Yes, I would ask the people if they know Jesus."

"Wow! Carl, I am touched by your profound message. You have given me something to think about" was my response. I wished him a happy Sunday, and he went on to church and I completed my task. Carl's heart-searching words reverberated in my mind: "Do you know Jesus?" I found myself asking, "Shirley, do you know Jesus, or are you like the people Carl talked about, all dressed up with everything matching and smelling good but can't honestly say that you truly know Jesus as your Lord and Savior?"

Friend, let me ask you too: Do *you* know Jesus?

Shirley C. Iheanacho

A Holy Land Experience

For God so loved the world that he gave his one and only Son, that whoever believes in him shall not perish but have eternal life. John 3:16, NIV.

I RECENTLY WENT on a tour of the Holy Land and was blessed to see the places where Jesus had been while He was on this earth. We visited the Church of the Nativity, the place where it's believed that Jesus was born, and saw the stable where the animals witnessed His holy birth. I was humbled to see the church that is supposed to have been built on the correct location to commemorate this important event in history.

We had the privilege of going on a boat ride across the Sea of Galilee. We could just imagine Jesus preaching from one of the fishing boats to the crowds gathered on the hills along the shore. We could visualize Christ sleeping on the bottom of the boat while a storm raged, and could almost hear His voice commanding the waves and the winds to be still. We wanted to be bold like Peter, walking on the water to meet his Lord! We rode up to the mountain where Jesus spoke the Beatitudes and admired the beautiful gardens that abound. We visited the Jordan River where Jesus was baptized, and we watched 19 people renew their baptismal vows that Sabbath afternoon. I could hear heaven rejoice with us as we witnessed God's children recommit their lives to Him.

As we visited the Mount of Olives, I could almost see Jesus' tear-stained face asking His Father to take away the bitter cup He was about to receive. Though He knew He was sinless, He chose to sacrifice His all for our redemption. I had the privilege of visiting an upper room where He may have spent those last moments with His disciples before the Crucifixion. Walking through the Via Dolorosa and seeing Golgotha where Christ was crucified made me more grateful of the great sacrifice Jesus made for us all. His death on the cross has given us the promise of eternal life. The empty tomb is a reminder that He has risen from the dead and is representing us before His Father.

This experience has increased my desire to serve God and share His love with others. It has strengthened my faith in Him and renewed my commitment to follow Him all the days of my life. He truly is the Lord of love who chose to die on the cross to give us the gift of salvation.

Rhona Grace Magpayo

Thoughts From Above

Through him you believe in God, who raised him from the dead and glorified him, and so your faith and hope are in God. 1 Peter 1:21, NIV.

THE LITTLE AIRPLANE gained speed and lifted off the runway at Los Angeles International Airport. Because it was a small shuttle plane, I had a good view. It was amazing how quickly the people, then the cars, and then the buildings shrank in size. As we turned south along the coast I could see beautiful big homes clinging to the cliffs above the ocean, but they soon gave way to small dots of homes, rows and rows of them looking just alike from the air. The people and even the cars were now too small to see. Whole towns could be seen in one glance.

How is it that we became so important that God, way up in heaven, pays any attention to us? We are so insignificant. And there are so many of us—more than 7 billion! How is it that He hears my prayers, that He has a plan for my life, that He cares about anything at all concerning my life? How is it that this great God, who sees, hears, knows, and controls all things in the entire universe was willing to come as a baby to this insignificant blue ball we call home? That He was willing to live in the midst of the squalor of this world is amazing in itself, but the sickness, the hurt, the abuse, the sin, must have been so painful. And He did all this so that He could die a humiliating and painful death on the cross. Amazing, isn't it!

But praise God, the story does not end there. He rose from the grave, a victor over death. And that is what gives you and me meaning, worth, and hope. He did it for you and me—and for all those billions of other people who live in all those mansions, suburban homes, those huge apartment buildings, tenant housing, little hovels, and mud huts.

It is His resurrection that gives us hope, that gives us a future. As Paul wrote, "And if Christ has not been raised, then all our preaching is useless, and your faith is useless. . . . And if there is no resurrection of the dead, then Christ has not been raised. And if Christ has not been raised, then your faith is useless and you are still guilty of your sins" (1 Cor. 15:14-17, NLT). But Christ *is* risen! We know that. Now, let us go out and live for Him as well, accepting the worth He has given us and extending that worth to those around us. There are still millions and millions who don't know any good news. Today is the day to tell them: "Christ is risen!"

Ardis Dick Stenbakken

Putting a "Chord" in Discordant

Whatever your hand finds to do,
do it with all your might. Eccl. 9:10, NIV.

I'VE BEEN A CHURCH organist for many years, not so much because I have a talent as that my church has a desperate need. My kids used to sit on the front pew each week, not from piety, as I at first hoped, but in keen anticipation of what creative treatment I might give the opening hymn. And those times when they thought I might try a modulation into a different key before the last stanza left them limp with anticipation as they considered the wide range of disastrous scenarios that always resulted when I tried that.

I wish I *could* play a Bach fugue like E. Power Biggs and transport my listeners to the very gates of heaven. Sadly, I can't—the logistics of maneuvering hands and feet to keep three different melodies going simultaneously is beyond me. Nevertheless, there are times I almost ache to play "big" music, to let the chords crash around my ears and explode in my heart. So once a year—in July—I satisfy this longing by playing "The Lost Chord" as a prelude for church. The piece manages to get properly thunderous in places and reaches deep into my soul.

This doesn't seem to bother the congregation as much as you might think. By now they're used to a good many of my chords being lost, and this *has* been going on for years now. But one year was different, because after my usual annual rendition I got a note from Judye Estes. She wrote: "Whenever I hear you play 'The Lost Chord' I close my eyes and feel as if I'm sitting in the Mormon Tabernacle, listening to their beautiful organ music. Thanks to you and your talents I don't have to go all the way to Salt Lake City to be blessed!"

Wow. Not since the loaves and the fishes had the Lord so miraculously transformed so little into so much. Clearly an example of how He can take whatever we offer and generously translate it into useful service.

And in the hearts of each of Adam's children since that day in Eden has beat the aching longing for Divinity's reassuring touch. The longing to know that the great God of the universe sees and cares about the circumstances of each one of us. The longing to know that He still bends low and touches hearts . . .

Divinity touching humanity, including us in His work.

Jeannette Busby Johnson

Apples of Gold

A word fitly spoken is like apples of gold in settings of silver.
Prov. 25:11, NKJV.

FOUR O'CLOCK in the morning wasn't usually the busiest hour for this coastal restaurant. But that changed when my marine biology class, out on a field trip, filed through their doors. The only server there, a girl probably in her late teens, looked at us wide-eyed as one by one chairs and tables began filling up with college students. I secretly wondered how she would handle this unexpected influx of business.

I watched with interest as she went to each table, taking orders and answering questions. Then she came to my table. She displayed a pleasant demeanor while doing an excellent job of handling such a group, and I told her so.

She looked at me and with hope in her voice, exclaimed, "Oh, would you please tell that to my boss? I've been trying to get on the day shift, and that would really help." I assured her I'd be happy to do that.

When I went to pay my bill, I mentioned to the cashier the fine work the server did in serving so many people. She yanked a paper towel from the nearby dispenser, grabbed a pencil, and slapped both on the counter in front of me. "Please," she begged, her hands shaking with excitement, "would you write that down for our boss to see? I'd appreciate it so much!" That lowly paper towel almost took on a life of its own as I recorded every complimentary thing I noticed about this young server.

Jesus tells us about the importance of appreciation in the Bible story about 10 lepers. These men came to Jesus asking for mercy. When He saw them, Jesus told them to go and show themselves to the priests. On the way they were cleansed, but only one leper came back to thank Him. The Lord showed disappointment that the other nine didn't do the same. The leper who returned to offer thanks glorified God by acknowledging that the gift of healing came from Him.

In this fast-paced world, where technology often bypasses face-to-face communication, it's easy to take for granted the little things that people do to help us. One kind word or act, no matter how small, may be just what is needed to change a person's outlook, circumstance, or life.

God gives us many blessings daily. We glorify God when we thank Him for the privilege of sharing these blessings.

Marcia Mollenkopf

Trust

Trust in the Lord with all your heart and lean not on your own understanding.
Prov. 3:5, NIV.

TRUST IS A COMMODITY we can't live without. We must trust that other drivers are sane and sober. Or perhaps we keep a safe distance if we aren't too trusting. We trust the bank to take good care of our money, or we hide it under the mattress and trust the house will not burn down. In the frozen North we trust the gas company to provide fuel for our furnaces. Or perhaps we cut our own wood to burn in the stove that we trusted someone else to install correctly.

We can't live this life without trusting someone, somewhere. Even a hermit has to have some trust. And as we associate with others over time, our trust either disintegrates and we push people away, or it grows and we learn to trust even more. Trust begets trust.

Marriage is built upon mutual trust. I strive to trust my husband completely. And I mostly succeed. But there are exceptions.

One day after returning home from town, hubby hopped out to open the garage door so I could drive the truck inside. I was rather unsure of the perimeters of this vehicle, so he always guided me through the door opening. I had to maneuver a 90-degree swing as I approached, and this time he just kept waving his arms, urging me to keep coming. The right post of the doorway seemed a little too close for my comfort, but being a trusting wife I kept moving, albeit at a snail's pace.

And that was fortunate, for there was a bang. The truck promptly stopped, and the engine died. I had hit the brand-new molding on our brand-new garage.

What explanation was forthcoming from my upset husband? "I thought you'd keep turning the wheel as you came and there'd be plenty of clearance."

"The wheel was turned as far as it would go," I replied, a tad too testily.

"I didn't know that" was his meek and frustrated reply.

But it's only a garage, and the marks are small. Hubby's favorite expression is "Trust me, dear!" And I'm trying. It may take some time.

The neat thing about trusting God is that He is perfect and will never let us down. It's safe to trust Him, always. And as we step out in faith, our trust in Him will grow and become complete.

Dawna Beausoleil

The Mind of a Child

Anyone who welcomes one child like this for my sake is welcoming me.
But if anyone leads astray one of these little children who believe in me
he would be better off thrown into the depths of the sea
with a mill-stone hung round his neck! Matt. 18:5, 6, Phillips.

THE TODDLERS CLUNG to their mothers' legs as the mothers talked about their babies. Then one said, "We're going out to have some fun tonight—but only after we put baby to bed. If he knows, he will fuss." That reminded me of two youngsters who briefly entered my life.

When we were missionaries in Sarawak, my husband regularly flew sick people in from remote villages for hospitalization. I would take them to the hospital and stay close until they were on the ward. Far from families, they appreciated my frequent visits. One time Dick brought in a 1-year-old girl and a 5-year-old boy. He didn't know much about the boy, except that the local pastor had found him in the longhouse, sick, listless, and expressionless. During my visits, both the children came to me eagerly and played happily with me.

After they got well, the hospital would not release the boy until the father came to get care instructions. When I took the father in, the boy took one look and screamed—and would not stop! The father turned to me saying, "He has forgotten me." I thought, *On the contrary—he remembers you all too well.* Obviously he did not want to go home to neglect and mistreatment.

We took the little girl home ourselves, since we were taking supplies to her village. During the long trip, she clung to me. We stopped at the top of the hill overlooking her village to check the brakes and our load. In the distance I saw her father running up the hill. When she saw him, she immediately stretched out her chubby arms, and I was forgotten. She knew her father and his love.

What a difference in the response of those two young children to their fathers! Their minds had been imprinted so differently by the treatment they had received, and thus the young mother's remark haunted me. Children learn quickly, and can learn distrust as easily as trust. And once learned, distrust is difficult to reverse. God entrusts these precious little ones to us. He trusts us to impart love and trust, to be gentle with their feelings.

Jean Hall

God's Tithe

Bring ye all the tithes into the storehouse.
Mal. 3:10.

"VINCE! HAVE YOU SEEN my tithe?" Panic set in. "I can't find it!"

OK, Dana, I tell myself, *stop and pray.* We were on our way out the door for Sabbath school, and I had a problem: I could not find God's tithe. Solution: pray. With a long face I got in the car. My husband reminded me that I had already prayed about it and one thing we knew for sure was that it was in the house.

When we arrived home from church, I began helping my mother in her home with the food. Among the several trips that I took back to my house, I kept looking for the tithe, but still could not find it. It was on one of these trips into the kitchen that a voice said to me, "Look in the garbage bag under the sink." My immediate thought was *Why would the tithe be in the trash?* Still, I obeyed and opened the cabinet door. To my amazement, there lay my tithe near the top of the trash. It was then that I realized what must have happened.

Amid the hustle and bustle of the morning, I remembered resting my tithe on my bed. Then I got my dress from my closet. After taking the dress out of the dry cleaning wrapping I put the wrapping on the bed. When I put the dry cleaning wrapping on the bed, I put it on top of the tithe. After putting on my dress, I began making my way to the kitchen and out the door. As I left the bedroom, I picked up the dry cleaning bag—tithe included—and put it in the trash.

I was so thankful that God answered my prayer. Friends, there are several lessons that I learned from this situation. Some of them are:

When worried, pray.

Keep doing your part to solve the situation.

God will always protect His tithe.

God always answers prayer.

It is natural to worry when we lose things, but we can turn to God for help. Everything is important to Him, and He will always hear and answer our prayers. When we receive these wonderful answers, we need to share them with others as it can help strengthen their faith as well.

Dana M. Bassett Bean

The Midnight Cry

And at midnight a cry was heard: "Behold, the bridegroom is coming; go out to meet him!" Matt. 25:6, NKJV.

IT WAS MY DAUGHTER'S spring break from school, and we were heading to Jamaica to celebrate my mother's eighty-third birthday. I had the perfect gift—an intricate silver brooch I knew she would just love. At our hotel I requested a 4:00 a.m. wake-up call, since we had to be at the airport two hours in advance for the international flight.

While I was sleeping, the phone rang. *Can it be time to wake up already?*

"Cheryl?" It was my brother calling from Canada. "I have some sad news. Mom died in her sleep." I was suddenly wide awake! What was my brother talking about? Mom died! How could that be? I had just talked to her the day before, confirming my flight, and she had sounded fine. I was in shock. Tears flowed down my cheeks.

Later I was told that on her last day my mom had prepared my favorite foods, visited a sick woman, and had evening worship, singing the hymn "Sweet Hour of Prayer." She died at midnight in her sleep, smiling.

Months later I saw a comparison with the parable of the 10 virgins. Like my mom preparing for my arrival, the first five virgins prepared for the groom to arrive. The other five were unprepared, thinking that they were ready or that they had plenty of time to get ready. "And the foolish said to the wise, 'Give us some of your oil, for our lamps are going out.' But the wise answered, saying, 'No, lest there should not be enough for us and you'" (Matt. 25:8, 9, NKJV).

Now I spend my time preparing and waiting for Jesus to return. I want to live my life as if it is just a couple of hours before His flight arrives to take me "home." I want my final destination to be heaven. What are you doing—sleeping like the five virgins who thought they had sufficient oil, or preparing, like the other five?

I want to see my precious mom, Leila McGill-Henry, again. I miss her so very much. But most of all, I want to see the face of Jesus. Let us continue to prepare for His return so that when He comes, rather than hearing Him say, "Depart from Me, I do not know you," we will hear Him say, "Well done, My good and faithful servant."

Cheryl Henry-Aguilar

Creeping Up

Be sober, be watchful. Your adversary the devil prowls around like a roaring lion, seeking some one to devour. 1 Peter 5:8, RSV.

WHEN I WAS A CHILD, I used to hear the expression "creeping up on someone" and didn't have a clue what it meant. But as I got older I began to understand as I considered how things slowly come about. Deadlines creep up on us when we have too much to do and aren't pacing ourselves well enough to get the job done. People creep up on us when we aren't paying attention or don't know they're nearby until they jump out and scare us half to death. Cats crouch low to the ground and stealthily make their way toward their prey, creeping ever so slowly, then pouncing when they're within reach. Ill health creeps up on us when we ignore the little signs telling us we have problems that need to be addressed, until one day we have major issues to cope with. Old age creeps up on us when we are so busy enjoying life that years slip by, and we are no longer young.

To me, there is nothing good about "creeping up." In creeping, something or someone is always intruding on our space or time—slowly or cautiously lurking nearby, and we eventually have to deal with the ramifications of our ignorance or inattention. Of course it's baffling—a surprise, even—when something creeps up on us. But had we been more aware, we'd have no reason to lament the result.

How true this is of Satan as he sneaks up on us—never with an in-your-face proposition—but inching his way closer and closer, working out in fine detail exactly what he's going to do when he does present himself. Meanwhile, unaware of his presence or his schemes to bring us down, we innocently go about living our lives. Then one day, as if we'd never known who he is or what he is capable of, he shows up, and we fall prey to his cunning ways. If he had jumped out at us instead of creeping up, we would have been aware of his devilish ploys to deceive us and send us down pathways that lead us into sin and ruin our lives. We would wisely have freed ourselves from the adversary's grip before this could have happened.

In today's text God tells us that the devil prowls around to devour someone. Don't let that someone be you!

Iris L. Kitching

A Place Prepared for You

My Father's house has many rooms; if that were not so,
would I have told you that I am going there to prepare a place for you?
And if I go and prepare a place for you, I will come back and take you
to be with me that you also may be where I am. John 14:2, 3, NIV.

ASIAN ELEPHANTS are on the endangered list. As their habitats dwindle, their numbers are falling at an alarming rate. To help assure the future of these fascinating and intelligent creatures, Australian zoos are not only contributing to habitat preservation, but also participating in a conservation breeding program. After extensive planning and at considerable cost, in 2006 a herd of one male and four female elephants was flown from Thailand and took up residence at Sydney's Taronga Zoo. Most of the elephants came from work camps where, ironically, some helped with the logging of the very forests essential to the survival of their species in the wild. However, one named Thong Dee (Golden) was a street elephant in Bangkok, where she roamed the city begging for food. Since elephants require many kilograms of food per day, it was a very precarious existence for her.

I like to think that for Thong Dee, coming to Taronga Zoo was something like reaching "elephant heaven," with the plentiful food, congenial companions, and specially prepared facilities—including a swimming hole, a mud wallow, and a comfortable barn. The keepers report that Thong Dee has a sweet nature and, once she realized that her food supply was assured, her friendly and playful personality emerged. Thong Dee has also bred successfully and is now the proud mother of Luk Chai (Son), the first elephant calf to be born in Australia. Luk Chai delights zoo visitors such as myself with his childlike antics as he splashes in the mud and plays with an elephant-size soccer ball.

The keepers have developed strong bonds with the elephants and have been accepted as part of their family group. The trust and affection that the elephants and their dedicated helpers have for each other is easy to see. Observing these fortunate elephants set me thinking: the disease of sin is rampant and the human race is in danger of extinction, but God had a plan. At great personal cost Jesus stepped in to ensure our survival. Now He is lovingly preparing a new home for us and is coming back soon to take us there. What a wonderful future we have to look forward to—praise God!

Jennifer M. Baldwin

Through a Kitten's Eyes

Consider the ravens: They do not sow or reap, they have no storeroom or barn; yet God feeds them. And how much more valuable you are than birds! Luke 12:24, NIV.

AFTER MY PASTOR-HUSBAND left for work, I busily began to pick up things scattered around the living room. As I did so, I talked to the Lord. We had moved to a new place, and I was not sure how life was going to be. For one thing, we were financially strapped. I also felt emotionally depleted. What kind of people would I have to deal with now? I was still young and trying to learn to cope with life as a pastor's wife.

Eunie, our year-old daughter, was in her crib facing the kitchen, noisily playing with her colorful favorite ball. Abruptly, in the middle of my reverie talking with the Lord, I realized that she was remarkably silent. I looked up at her. Her big eyes were fixed on something in the kitchen, and her face had a look of surprise and terror. I immediately went to investigate.

What I found was a strange cat on the table staring back at Eunie. Its paw was on the head of the fish that I intended for our lunch. I was horrified, because my husband was going to be gone several days, and he had left us with only one cup of rice to cook and the fried fish that was on the table. We had no food for the next day, so I needed that fish.

Eunie's look seemed to be saying, "Mommy, do something!" I quietly approached the table and managed to get a hold on the fish's tail to pull it away. The cat snarled and gave a horrible hiss as it grabbed the other end of the fish and tried to run. But my hand was quick too. I cut off a small piece of fish and gave it to the cat. It ran joyfully away with its portion.

The day passed. It was almost dark and I had planned to retire early when I heard an insistent knock at the door. Opening it, I was shocked to see a woman holding a big basket full of vegetables, rice, fruit, and fish. She came in, placed it on the table, and left. The following morning a lay preacher came to visit with a big hand of bananas and other root crops. The provisions continued flowing until my husband returned. But I never saw the kitty again.

Since then, when I am overwhelmed with doubts, I remember the kitten's eyes. God is ready to supply all our needs, whether material or emotional, whether nourishment for the body or for the soul. When we wholly trust God, our attitudes and desires become His.

Leah A. Salloman

Vulnerable as a Child

Behold, I send you out as sheep in the midst of wolves.
Therefore be wise as serpents and harmless as doves. Matt. 10:16, NKJV.

HAVING GRANDCHILDREN has made me frighteningly aware of how vulnerable kids are. When Silas was 6½ and Iris was 2, they were both very much at the mercy of adults and their environment. They knew no fear; adults had to fear for them. Once Iris could turn a doorknob, her parents had to take precautions. They did not know she could open the door until she had let herself out and wandered into a neighbor's yard. Thankfully, she wasn't drawn to the street.

The children were also psychologically vulnerable. One day Grandpa shouted angrily at Silas, and Silas fled to his room. Grandpa thought that shouting would make Silas more inclined to obey, but instead it made him wary of Grandpa. Silas and Iris have good parents who love and affirm them, but their mother works daily with children whose parents are far more concerned with their own welfare than that of their children. Whether they ignore the child's basic needs, or belittle and verbally abuse them, such parents chip—or hack—away at the child's fragile self-esteem, unaware of the terrible destruction they are causing. Such damage often goes unhealed and eventually leads to similar destruction in succeeding generations.

When Jesus sent His disciples out to spread the good news, He noted their vulnerability. Today's Christians are not only vulnerable to worldly wolves, but also to wolves clad in sheep's wool who abuse Christians by misusing Scripture. Some keep their followers in a continuous state of childishness, producing Christians who are afraid to think for themselves or to trust their own judgment for fear they will offend God by not being "as a child."

Insensitive and unspiritual Christians abuse others by harsh words of judgment, or actions such as gossip and betrayal. Such wounds are rarely brought to light, salved, and healed. They are left to cripple the victim or to fester with attendant poison.

"Be wise," Jesus counseled. Wisdom is a protection against false teachers. And He taught us to be careful in our relationships, treating others with kindness and love. When we allow God to place forgiveness in our hearts, when we bring healing care to the wounded, vulnerability is transformed into an opportunity for God to work in others' lives and our own.

Dolores Klinsky Walker

So Trust

Trust in the Lord with all thine heart;
and lean not unto thine own understanding. Prov. 3:5.

I VISITED MY SISTER, Lorinne, in Beaverton, Oregon, the second week of April. Spring had arrived and covered Oregon in a beautiful green. My husband and I fell in love with the place. We were traveling to California by road, going down through the mountains and coming back by the sea. The mountain drive was awesome; the mountaintops were still covered with snow. But driving by the sea was so breathtaking I cannot describe it in words.

Lorinne drove us to Loma Linda, where my husband was to attend his meetings. She and I would go sightseeing by ourselves. We left the San Bernardino area and drove toward Death Valley. This place is known to be the lowest, the driest, and the hottest place in the United States.

There was hardly anyone on the road, and if we had car trouble I didn't know how soon we would be able to get help. To be honest, I was a little anxious, because this was a new place for me, and both sides of the road looked barren and desolate. Besides that, we were the only people around for miles.

I reassured myself with the thought that Lorinne had been there before and knew the way. She had also planned the trip and prepared for it, so she knew how much time it would take us to get there and how much time we could spend in the area. Besides, her sport utility vehicle was in excellent condition. I really didn't need to worry, but part of Psalm 23 still kept going through my mind throughout my trip to Death Valley. And it wasn't the "I will fear no evil: for thou art with me" part of the psalm. It was "the valley of the shadow of death."

This is so typical of my attitude toward God. I should just trust Him, because He knows everything and can even help me get out of difficult situations when I ask Him. Sadly, I continue to worry about many things. How nice it is that God does not hold me to my worries. Instead, He lovingly (and sometimes firmly) steers me away from them.

We did reach our destination and finished sightseeing without any incident. So now my prayer is "Lord, please help me remember to trust You every day in everything that I do (without any exceptions)."

Rosenita Christo

God's Patchwork

"For I know the plans I have for you," declares the Lord, "plans to prosper you and not to harm you, plans to give you hope and a future." Jer. 29:11, NIV.

THE EXCITEMENT of moving into our new home frayed into reality as I walked through the crooked lanes between the ancient stone cottages of our little village. I suddenly felt very alone, hundreds of miles from friends and family. My husband's ministry had brought us to Scotland where there weren't any jobs for me, so I worked long hours as a freelance writer.

I wandered up and down the handful of gray, cobbled streets in the damp gray evening. The memorial monument was gray, the birds were gray, the sky was gray, and even my heart felt gray. How would I ever make friends in this tightly knit village where the same families had lived for generations? A shower of rain added grayness to grayness, and I sheltered in the local community center. The hallway was warm and bright. On the bulletin board were signs about the local toddler group, slimming clubs, cars for sale, and Lyme disease. And in the middle of this haphazard mosaic of village life was a small poster advertising "The Muchty Quilters."

Quilters in Auchtermuchty? In this tiny speck of a village? I'd lived in cities where there wasn't one quilting club, and here was a group five minutes' walk from my door!

The shower stopped and the evening sun sparkled on the wet-stone world as I wandered back to our home, warmly comforted. Quilting was the only hobby I had brought with me to Scotland. I wasn't particularly good at it, but I'd been interested in patchwork since I was a child.

God knew that one day I'd find myself all alone in a strange place. He knew I would need the warmth of shared friendship around the joy of a common interest. He knew I would need the creative and caring women who would share their quilting tips, pieces of fabric, local information, and the stories of their lives. I thought it was just an unimportant hobby, but God had been "piecing" quilting into my life all along, knowing that one day it would bring me color, warmth, comfort, and friendship in a lonely, gray place.

How is God piecing your life together? What are the shapes, patterns, and colors that He has placed into your life that help you to feel treasured by Him? And what about the pieces that don't seem to fit yet, or that seem unimportant? I wonder how He will use them to bless you.

Karen Holford

Always on Time

And we are confident that he hears us whenever we ask for anything that pleases him. And since we know he hears us when we make our requests, we also know that he will give us what we ask for. 1 John 5:14, 15, NLT.

DURING OUR 10 YEARS of mission service in Africa we constantly received requests from students or their parents for tuition assistance or sponsorships. As a result we were constantly soliciting funds from church members and friends to complement our own contributions.

We embraced every opportunity to present the needs of students during mission emphasis appeals and other events. One Sabbath after we presented one student's situation, a church member offered to pay the costs of the student's entire final year.

During a luncheon we presented the story of a Rwandese refugee and received a check from one family for $1,000. We cashed the check, put the cash away safely, and began preparations to leave the United States. The day before our travel, my husband and I looked everywhere for the cash but could not find it. Eventually we had to leave without it.

On arrival back in Africa, we used our own funds to assist the student, but felt confident that the money would be found to replenish our savings. We would often think about it and pray that God would show us just where to find the money.

Two years later while browsing a bookshelf, I suddenly became fixed on a nursing text. I was not sure I'd seen that title before, so I hastily retrieved the book, hoping to casually thumb through its contents. The book fell open, and I saw a small white envelope with our names on it. A voice within said, *Could this be the lost money we have been looking for?* Sure enough, when I opened the envelope I found 10 $100 bills.

I breathed a prayer of thanksgiving and with excitement ran to my husband, who was equally overjoyed. This money had shown up just in time. We were now sponsoring the student it was meant for, and one week earlier he had informed us that the laptop we'd purchased for him had been stolen. We were devastated, because it would be impossible for him to keep up with classes as a computer major. Finding the money then was a relief and comfort in knowing that God does not always come when we want Him, but He is always on time.

Lydia Andrews

Father Knows Best

People can make all kinds of plans, but only the Lord's plan will happen.
Prov. 19:21, NCV.

WHEN I WAS A LITTLE GIRL, every week I faithfully watched a television sitcom called *Father Knows Best*. Invariably, with each episode, Jim Anderson, the father, always had the right solution for his puzzled or erring children. Our heavenly Father also has the best solution when we carefully follow His plan.

Not long ago my daughter Alicia was looking for a condo to buy for herself and my granddaughter, Jordan. When she found a pristine unit, at the right price and in a good location, I was pleased with her selection. But because other first-time homebuyers were bidding for the same unit, Alicia's real estate agent advised her to bid $5,000 above the asking price. Alicia followed her instructions, and we prayed for God's intervention, but agreed that if it didn't happen God would have something better.

Two days later we learned that a higher bid had been accepted. We were disappointed. This seemed the perfect two-bedroom, two-bath unit for Alicia and Jordan.

Later that week Alicia asked me to go with her to see a three-bedroom unit with enhanced features, but she warned that it was priced way beyond her budget.

Hesitantly I agreed to go, certain that it would not work for her. But I was joyfully surprised at the beauty of the place and immediately felt that this was the right unit for her. The rooms were spacious. The walls were freshly painted, new carpet had been laid in each room, and a new heating unit occupied the hall closet. But there was one big problem: the price. "Bid low," I suggested. "If God wants you to have this place, the owners will accept your bid."

Alicia again submitted a bid, this time $30,000 below the asking price. We fervently prayed and waited. The following evening the real estate agent phoned and told her that the property was hers.

Often our view is limited, and we settle for what seems appropriate when God may have something entirely different and ultimately much better for us. We plan, assuming our selections are God's selections. Fortunately we serve a wonderful Father who always has our best interests at heart. Our job is a simple one: we have only to trust God, assured that our Father knows best.

Yvonne Curry Smallwood

The Silver Lining

And we know that all things work together for good to them that love God, to them who are the called according to his purpose. Rom. 8:28.

A FEW YEARS AGO I wrote a devotional about my sister Barbara. She had married, but five months later her husband, Peter, died of a heart attack. I remember my emotions at the time and thinking, *What good could come out of this?*

Before Peter died, I occasionally talked to my sister. I was always the one who sent gifts and cards and kept the lines of communication open. Six or more months could go by before I would get a return phone call. When she did return a call, we would have a nice conversation, and it wouldn't seem that months had gone by, when in reality they had. However, after Peter died it was a different story. My sister began calling several times a week. I enjoyed getting to know her better. If I left a message, I got a return phone call within a few hours or days.

One day when Barbara called she said that she felt funny; her feet itched, and she had spots all over her skin. I asked where she was. She told me she'd been running on the beach and was now in her car. She'd taken a Benadryl and was beginning to head home. I figured the crisis was over, and we started to talk about other things. During our conversation she mentioned that her eyes were swelling. I asked her how her throat was doing. "It feels as if there's something in there," she said. As calmly as I could say it, I told her to go to the nearest emergency room. She said one was five miles away. The sound of her voice was changing, getting thicker. I prayed silently. It seemed like an eternity, but she finally arrived. I was still on the phone when I heard the swoosh of opening doors as she entered the ER. I heard many different voices; then the line went dead. Hours passed before I was able to talk to my sister. She explained that she had had an allergic reaction to something. She said that one of the nurses told her she had almost died. The nurse then asked, "How did you know to come to the hospital?"

Barbara said, "My sister told me. She knew."

I will always be grateful to God for helping my sister and me stay connected and for keeping her safe. It is amazing how tragedy can turn into triumph. It's all about looking for the silver lining that's in every cloud.

Mary Wagoner-Angelin

The Greatest Rescue Mission

Then war broke out in heaven. Michael and his angels fought against the dragon, and the dragon and his angels fought back. But he was not strong enough, and they lost their place in heaven. Rev. 12:7, 8, NIV.

ON EASTER SUNDAY, April 2, 1972, in the northern part of South Vietnam, Lieutenant Colonel Iceal Hambleton was flying as navigator in an EB-66 electronic warfare aircraft when it was hit by a surface-to-air missile at 30,000 feet. He was the only one of a six-man crew to eject successfully, but he landed in an area that was reputedly teeming with 30,000 enemy troops near a highway junction on a Communist supply route. He was seriously wounded in the arm and back. Although he was rescued after 11 days on the ground, it was not before the loss of several aircraft and their crews. This was the longest one-man search-and-rescue operation in U.S. Air Force history.

Hambleton was rescued by American and South Vietnamese Navy SEALS Lieutenant Thomas R. Norris and Nguyen Van Kiet. Norris would later be awarded the Medal of Honor and Van Kiet the Navy Cross for their action. Hambleton won the Silver Star, the Distinguished Flying Cross, the Air Medal, the Meritorious Service Medal, and a Purple Heart for his effort.

A war was also fought in heaven. Michael and His angels won. Lucifer and his angels were cast out. Adam and Eve sinned and were cast out of their beautiful Eden home. They had fallen from grace and had to suffer toil and pain, sorrow, rejection, spiritual separation. They faced the prospect of eternal death.

But there was a rescue plan. God is fighting to rescue souls from eternal ruin. He sent His Son Jesus to redeem Adam's fallen race. Just as several men lost their lives in an effort to rescue one man, Jesus, paid a heavy price to save us.

He arose from the grave and returned to base to make preparations for His chosen children. One day soon this rescue mission will be complete. In the same way that military men receive honors, the saints of the ages who have worked, watched and waited for their Lord will live and reign with Him and drink of the river of life. "Look, I am coming soon! My reward is with me, and I will give to each person according to what they have done" (Rev. 22:12, NIV).

Bula Rose Haughton Thompson

More Money?

Woe to him that increaseth that which is not his! Hab. 2:6.

As the partridge sitteth on eggs, and hatcheth them not;
so he that getteth riches, and not by right, shall leave them
in the midst of his days, and at his end shall be a fool. Jer. 17:11.

I PRAISED THE LORD for safe journey mercies and looked forward to some rest. In this part of this city are many porters who wait to "help" arriving passengers with heavy luggage. I saw them through the vehicle window and predicted I would be a bit harassed. I pointed out my luggage to the van conductor, and in the twinkling of an eye I saw hands embrace my luggage. It was one of the porters, his cart strategically positioned in a "ready-to-go" direction. I was glad for some help, but I needed to make sure no one ripped me off.

"How much?" I asked. We agreed on the price. As we walked, and just a few meters from the house, I heard him murmuring. Asking what the problem was, he said that he expected me to pay him more! *But we finished this part and agreed on the price,* I thought. Now he wanted me to pay him four times what we had agreed upon! I was shocked. Then he began to make threats. I could not see anyone who could come to my rescue should the scene turn more dramatic. As we kept on walking and I remained silent, he threatened either to take off with my bag or to beat me up. I wouldn't choose either. No amount of calm speech helped the situation.

I knew my God would hear me, so I prayed, *Lord, save me from this ugly situation. You know I want to do what's right, and You know the heart of the porter. Save me—and save him, too.* The answer was instant. Right ahead were four men involved in a conversation. I bravely explained to them the demands of the porter, the latter listening intently. No sooner did the "four angels" understand my predicament than one of them pulled the bag off the porter. While the others ordered the porter to back off, I paid him what we had agreed on, and he left. I gasped and welcomed air back into my lungs. I thanked the men, who then carried my bag to our doorstep.

Greed and extortion can lead only to trouble and unhappiness. Habakkuk questioned God about Babylon. Jesus hates the sin of insatiable desire, pride, and greed—all of which did not end with Babylon's fall. May they not trap us as well.

Beryl Aseno Nyamwange

Never Alone

Yea, though I walk through the valley of the shadow of death, I will fear no evil: for thou art with me; thy rod and thy staff they comfort me. Ps. 23:4.

I AM NEVER ALONE, even when I feel lonely and when no one else is around. At times I feel intense loneliness, or I have feelings that there is no one who understands. Yet I know that I am not alone, for God's Spirit reassures me that He is with me always.

Many years ago I visited my grandmother in South America. She was very old and sick at the time we went to see her. While there, we took her to church, and during a lull in the service she yelled out "God!" It was very uncomfortable for me, because the people in the church did not understand. I did not understand either, as I was young. The members mumbled that "something is wrong with that old lady." In truth, something *was* wrong. She had Parkinson's disease and the dementia that goes along with that disease as it progresses toward the end.

However, she also had something else that I really didn't understand until 20 or more years after her death. She had God: God in her spirit, God in her mind, and God by her side. He was real to her, and He was someone she called out to even in her dementia.

This understanding has come to me because many times I am tempted to feel lonely. Since my children have matured and moved out of the house, there is much quietness here. But in the quiet I have found a new depth in my relationship with God. I have God, and I realize that He has me, even in the palm of His hand. God is with me, God is near, and God is here to talk to.

As a matter of fact, I find myself audibly talking to Him when I'm alone. It comforts me, and often I feel as though He is right here with me. I'm afraid that like my maternal grandmother before me, I will someday be heard yelling out "God" when the need to feel Him near is upon me. I want Him to draw me nearer and hold me tighter, especially when my earthly anchors fail me.

Whom or what do you call out to, or reach out to, when the cares of this life fall heavy upon you? I hope, my dear sister, that your anchor is God, because it is His will to keep us in all our ways and to bear us up, lest we dash our foot against a stone (see Ps. 91:12). In our deepest and darkest hours we must trust Him and reach out to Jesus. He is reaching out to you!

Wendy Wongk

Peace and Presence

But let the godly rejoice. Let them be glad in God's presence.
Let them be filled with joy. Ps. 68:3, NLT.

IT HAD BEEN A LONG DAY of traveling in the Cassie Hills in northeast India. We were now very close to our destination of Haflong, Assam. The day that started out with fog and dampness had given way to bright sunshine, and the hills through which we traveled were beautiful. This was my first trip through these hills, and I enjoyed the new vista at each curve in the road.

Because we had gone through some mud puddles, remnants of the recent rains, our vehicle had become very dirty. When a shallow river came into view, the driver thought it was a good opportunity to wash the mud and dirt from the vehicle. Of course he would not let me help. I had gotten used to this, so I wandered a short distance down the wide bank of the river and found a great rock where I could sit and watch. It wasn't long before a woman from the nearby village walked up and sat on another rock very close to me. We smiled at each other and said hello in our respective languages. We then turned our attention to the driver washing the car, the children playing in the water, and the dogs who enjoyed running after them.

This beautiful woman and I talked without words. She pointed to the children, then held up a number of fingers, indicating the number of children she had. I did the same. We continued our silent discussion for about 30 minutes. I was very much at peace. Then she stood, smiled, and bowed in the Indian tradition. She turned and walked toward the village.

I sat watching her go and realized that I had just had one of the most wonderful and interesting conversations I have ever had. Though we did not speak the same language, we had a great conversation. It included just sitting and enjoying the presence of each other.

Isn't that how our relationship with God should be? How much richer our relationship is when we are able to "be still in the presence of the Lord, and wait patiently for him to act" (Ps. 37:7, NLT). David must have spent much time sitting and enjoying the presence of God as he wrote a great deal about this. Following today's verse, he wrote, "Sing praises to God and to his name! . . . His name is the Lord—rejoice in his presence!" (Ps. 68:4, NLT). For when we are in His presence we can then "Be still, and know that [He is] God" (Ps. 46:10, NIV).

Candace Zook

With God, No Problem

The Lord is my shepherd;
I shall not want. Ps. 23:1.

ONE SUNNY, beautiful morning my husband, Wilson, and I decided to go to the city to buy some goods for the weekend. As Wilson drove our van, a sticker on the back of the car ahead of us caught our attention. It was the familiar verse Psalm 23:1, written this way: "The Lord Is My Shepherd, No Problem!" We both burst into laughter, but my memory took me back years before, to the early part of our ministry.

Wilson was among the young district pastors the day he came home from a monthly workers' meeting. He looked worried as he handed me an envelope containing his financial statement and only ₱81.50 (less than $2). In a soft voice, he said, "This is all we have for the whole month."

"What?" I asked, as tears started rolling down my cheeks. Within the hour the landlord expected us to pay our rent of ₱250. I went to our room quietly, and my husband followed without a word. Later he said, "Try to look at my statement. The deductions have been mostly from the materials. . . ." His voice trailed off as I remained quiet. "God will provide," he consoled me. Then he suggested that we go to see different churches for the month, visiting homes during daytime and conducting seminars evenings. We were sure that we would be fed by the members, and they too would be blessed by our visits and lectures. I said, "OK, let's pack our things, leave tomorrow, and be back just a day before another worker's meeting."

Just before our prayer ended, we heard a hard knock on our front door, and Wilson immediately went to see who it was. To our surprise, it was a church elder in one of the biggest churches nearby. "I won't stay long," he said. "I've just brought the full payment for the Bible lesson guides the church got." Then he handed us a big sum of money and left. My husband hugged me and exclaimed, "Definitely—God is good all the time!"

As we continued to follow that car, I had a smile on my face and a song in my heart. I started humming the song "His Eye Is on the Sparrow." We reached our destination where we bought the things we needed, but the encounter we had that morning reminded us that "The Lord Is My Shepherd, No Problem!"

Shirley Cadiz Aguinaldo

117

What Are You Reading?

Study to shew thyself approved unto God. 2 Tim. 2:15.

Blessed is the one who reads aloud the words of this prophecy,
and blessed are those who hear it. Rev. 1:3, NIV.

"WHERE DID YOU HEAR about this scholarship program?" I timidly asked a mom as I eased up to her.

"In the newspaper," she responded.

"What section of the paper?" I gingerly prodded. And our conversation continued.

We were attending a meeting for students who'd received a scholarship based on certain criteria. I'd found out about it via one of our son's high school teachers. She had been reading the newspaper when she saw the article and thought of our son. So she gave him the information, we followed up on it, and he became a recipient.

But in the back of my head I kept wondering, *Why didn't I see that article?* At the time, I was an avid reader of the newspaper. I'd become anxious if I didn't get to read it every day. Seeing the papers pile up when I was just too busy to catch up almost sent me into a panic, thinking that I'd missed out on something important. I thought it was vital to keep abreast of current events.

After that incident, I knew that I wasn't totally dependent on the newspaper for information that God wanted me to know. In fact, I began bragging to people that I didn't bother to read the newspaper anymore—until my husband chided me about the inappropriateness of my way of sharing that information. My aunt reads the paper religiously and inquired recently why I hadn't checked on her when her part of the country experienced some unusual deadly weather. You can guess the reason. I sheepishly admitted to no longer reading the newspaper, and felt bad that I wasn't aware of their problem. But God had taken care of her.

Well, I still seldom read the paper. And what news I don't hear about or see on the Internet when I'm using it for keeping in touch or for my job, I don't worry about anymore. I've discovered something better to read: the Bible. Now, if I miss a day of reading my Bible, I know I've missed something truly important. I've missed getting to know my Father better and His will for me. I thank God for His Word, the Word above all words.

Sharon M. Thomas

The Honeysuckle

Ointment and perfume delight the heart.
Prov. 27:9, NKJV.

WHEN I WAS GROWING UP, if I saw a honeysuckle I couldn't resist picking a flower, breaking off the bottom tip, and sucking the drop of sweet nectar waiting there.

The honeysuckle is a shrub or vine of family genus *Lonicera,* having tubular, very fragrant white, turning yellowish, flowers. My dictionary says the name is from Old English hunistice: *hunig*—honey, and *sican*—to suck.

Now many years later I'm married and living in my own home. After years of living in other provinces, I am now privileged to have a honeysuckle hedge. It doesn't need much attention to maintain—it just seems to thrive.

As you enter our premises and walk up the path to the door, even if you did not notice the hedge of honeysuckle behind the olive tree, you would definitely smell the delightful fragrance of those honeysuckle flowers wafting through the air.

One vine may hold hundreds of tiny flowers. Each flower resembles an open hand: four petals together like four fingers and one petal opposite like a thumb. This flower reminds me of giving, with the sweet influence of love.

This tiny, sweetly perfumed flower reminds me of Mary, the Mary who sacrificed all her years of savings to buy very costly perfume to anoint Jesus' feet. Oh, what a gift of love! Love isn't love till you give it away. Mary loved Jesus so very much, for He had saved her from the bonds of a sinful life. She had heard that Jesus would be in that home for supper, and she quietly slipped into the house. She did not want to be noticed, but as she opened that alabaster box the fragrance just filled the room. She couldn't hide now; all eyes were on her, and questions were asked (Mark 14:3-9; Luke 7:37, 38; John 12:3).

Like the sweet scent of the tiny honeysuckle flower, Mary could not hide as her fragrance of love spilled out and perfumed the air. How she loved to linger in Jesus' presence. Her love for Him was deep. No sacrifice was too great for her to give to Him.

Will you give your life over to Jesus today? Renew your love to Him. It will be a sweet fragrance. He loves you so much!

Priscilla E. Adonis

I Am a Sinner Saved by Grace

See, I have engraved you on the palms
of my hands. Isa. 49:16, NIV.

HOW DID THIS TRANSFORMATION happen inside me? When did the Holy Spirit start to transform me into a woman who cannot even imagine living without this deep faith in my Lord—a person who wants only to find out what talents God will be asking her to use?

Let's backtrack in time. Let's look at how many times God knocked at my door, and yet I chose to keep running away, pursuing my worldly life. God led me to the Adventist hospital in Hong Kong. I participated in courses they offered. I jogged through the Peak with them on Sundays. I took my kids to the Adventist hospital for medical care. Many people there spoke of God's love, but I was deaf! God led me also to select a Christian dentist in Hong Kong. I remained deaf.

Then, after 24 years of absence, God whispered in my ears to go back to my own country, Brazil. It was the one country I thought I'd never return to, as I was at the peak of my professional career. But for the first time, it seemed, I heard His voice! Maybe this was the beginning of my transformation. I will always remember that early morning in Hong Kong when I clearly heard a voice say, "Go back to Brazil." I obeyed without debating or questioning! Within five months I was in Brazil.

God continued leading me, even though I was not clearly aware of it. He led me to enroll my daughter in Pathfinders, an organization where children can learn about God and the Christian lifestyle. Slowly, bit by bit, I started observing my own transformation: changes in my eating and drinking habits, changes in my lifestyle, until the day came when I said, "I am ready to accept Bible studies." The Holy Spirit kept on transforming this sinner, giving me hope for salvation! The precious day came when I was ready to be transformed into a new being, and I walked into the waters to the sound of 150 youth choir members singing "The Power of Love"!

Now I finally understand the words of the song, "More Than Ever," by Bill Gaither, cherishing the cross more than ever as we sit at Jesus' feet. It ends with "All the miles of my journey have proved my Lord true!" That is why He is so precious to me, too! I am transformed by the power of His love! May you be transformed by His love also.

Joelcira F. Müller-Cavedon

We Only Have to Ask Him

I will instruct you and teach you
in the way you should go. Ps. 32:8, NIV.

MY FATHER, NOW RETIRING and closing his business, had hired me as a secretary one year before when I very much needed a job. Now I again needed work. Applying at a local hospital owned by a Christian organization, I was hired to work in patients' accounts. After only a couple hours' training, I was left on my own—confronted by a stack of folders with computerized face sheets that I could not comprehend. My task was to collect the money owed on these delinquent accounts. I struggled through the day and went home very discouraged. I decided that I must go to my supervisor the next morning and admit I was not smart enough to do this job. It was the only honest thing to do. Yet, being the only support for myself and two children, I desperately needed the work. I decided to plunge on, ask questions, learn procedures, and somehow perform well enough to keep it.

A few days later I learned that the hospital encouraged lunch-hour prayer groups in the chapel and decided to investigate. Joining three other people, we prayed over various challenges in our lives. I asked my friends to pray with me to be successful in my work. We claimed the promise in today's text. Slowly I regained my confidence and became proficient at my work. About a year later I was promoted to a supervisory position.

As our prayer group continued to meet, I brought another request to them. I was hesitant, thinking they would label me totally unrealistic, but I wanted to go back to college. I would have to work full-time while going to school full-time. Could I hold up to that? How would I pay for it? We began to pray, claiming Matthew 19:26: "With man this is impossible, but with God all things are possible" (NIV).

Doors began to open. I applied at a Christian college in another state. Government grants and a scholarship paid my way; a nearby hospital hired me and let me work around my classes. But most of all, my Lord enabled me to graduate in three years because, you see, all things are possible with Him!

Through the years I have thanked Him again and again. God is always ready to help us in whatever struggle we have in our lives. Why do we hesitate? We have only to ask.

Peggy Miles Snow

A Very Personal Psalm

God is our refuge and strength, a tested help in times of trouble.
And so we need not fear even if the world blows up, and the mountains
crumble into the sea. Ps. 46:1, 2, TLB.

INSTEAD OF A SERMON, our pastor announced that we would assist him and write a psalm. Ushers distributed paper and pencils. When our psalms were collected, the ushers gave us the psalms written by people on the other side of the aisle. We were instructed to read aloud the one we received if we felt it was noteworthy.

I could *not* believe the psalm I had been given: "I sorrow so much for the great evil in this world, for the beautiful Christian person who has suffered at the hands of another evil person. Maybe that evil person or person's pain is so great that they have to cause pain to someone else. Lord, please give her Your strength to endure. Won't You please come and end all the wickedness so those who love You—and all that You have created—will have fear no more. Come, Lord Jesus, come. We're waiting for You."

It would seem that the author who wrote this knew all about me. But this was a new church for me, and no one knew me well. I sat dazed. I did not read aloud "my" psalm. We were told to give our psalms to the ushers. I kept mine.

How could anyone in this church know what was troubling my heart? Was this a direct message from God for me? You see, on January 11, 1982, my whole world stopped when I was abducted at knifepoint, blindfolded, raped, and sodomized in an act of senseless, random violence. How could I forgive the perpetrator if I were ever to know who had done this to me? It just didn't seem fair to have to look at his pain! My pain was so intense. Every part of my body had been violated, and I was so afraid.

I had always found comfort in Psalm 46. I opened my Bible, but instead was drawn to Romans 12:17, 21. "Never pay back evil for evil." "Don't let evil get the upper hand but conquer evil by doing good" (TLB).

I became a volunteer counselor and court advocate at a rape crisis center and found my own peace by helping other women in their recovery process. That morning the Holy Spirit impressed someone to write what I desperately needed to hear—my very own personal psalm.

Patricia Hook Rhyndress Bodi

God Cares for Us

For the eyes of the Lord move to and fro throughout the earth that He may strongly support those whose heart is completely His. 2 Chron. 16:9, NASB.

THIS STORY TOOK PLACE when I was 8 years old. My mother, Omee, had passed away, and I remained with my father. When I started going to school, I noticed that the other children's mothers brought them their breakfast. They brought oranges and bananas and would sit with their children, hug them, and eat with them. But I always sat alone, watching the others. It wasn't pleasant at all! I felt very left out and awfully lonely; my heart ached. Sometimes I cried, remembering my own mother and watching how mothers love their children, but my mother was gone. I had no mother to bring me breakfast—or anything else. I missed her very much. Though she passed away 13 years ago, I still miss her.

When I was 9 years old, I began going to church and Sabbath school with the other children. The teachers encouraged us to love one another, to do good to others, and to share what we had with our friends. They also taught us that we should not feel envious when we see that others have something we don't have. From that time on I changed my attitude. Even though I still saw the other children's parents bringing things for them in school, I didn't feel lonely anymore. I had learned to know that Jesus was my friend. He helped take that loneliness away, and He gave me freedom and satisfaction inside my heart.

"Cast all your anxiety on him because he cares for you" (1 Peter 5:7, NIV) is a comforting promise. God is telling us that we are to leave all our worries with Him. Because Jesus accepts us as His own children, even if we are in trouble and sorrow, God will not leave us alone. For the eyes of the Lord moved to and fro throughout the earth, and He strongly supported this girl from Sudan who had lost her mother.

My dear sisters, God is looking over the earth today at you too, and He will take your anxiety away, because He cares for you. I know because this is what happened with me. You too can experience the love and support of God in your life. God has promised, "I will not leave you as orphans; I will come to you" (John 14:18, NASB). Let's continue praying for the children who face difficult situations in the world today.

Hanan Jacob Maniwa

God Has Better Plans

Call unto me, and I will answer thee, and shew thee great and mighty things, which thou knowest not. Jer. 33:3.

MANY READERS WILL relate to having to care for an elderly person who is no longer competent enough to manage her financial affairs, care for personal needs, or make wise decisions. My single friend of more than 40 years had led a successful teaching career. She was an organizer and decisive person. She planned for her later years long before most people consider they are getting old. She sold her home and moved into a triplex so she wouldn't have yard work to do. Her next move was into a senior lodge, where meals and other personal services were provided. She has now come to the place where she must move into long-term care.

A move to an assisted living facility was the hardest one of all, because it is "the end of the road." She had entrusted me to be her personal directive when she was declared incompetent by her physician to assume responsibilities for her well-being. Twice she refused to be assessed for a transfer to "the place across the road," as she called it. When the senior lodge made the third recommendation for an assessment, I was called to convince her that this was the next step she needed to take.

I did not look forward to having to explain why she had to move. I thought of the abnormal things she now did. The most recent sign of dementia was that she didn't always answer the phone because she didn't know which object in the room was the phone.

I have a habit of giving God suggestions as to how He can help me solve problems. The day I planned to have this difficult chat with my friend, I asked God to make sure she didn't answer the phone so I could give this as one reason she needed to move.

Unfortunately, she answered the phone—so that blew my speech! But God did something even greater. As we sat together in her overstuffed room, I asked her to look at her feet. She had put on a pair of yellow socks and added a blue sock over the top of the yellow one on the left foot. We both had a good laugh, and she agreed that maybe she needed to move.

Let's not be tempted to give God suggestions today. Trust Him. He has greater and mightier plans than we can ever imagine.

Edith Fitch

Don't Run, Write!

I will bless you with a future filled with hope—a future of success, not of suffering. Jer. 29:11, CEV.

IN MY SOPHOMORE YEAR of college I felt a peculiar twinge. It felt as though God was calling me to write devotionals, but I thought that couldn't possibly be true. Besides the fact that writing devotionals would never secure the success that many people were depending on me to attain, I mistakenly believed that people my age did not write devotionals! I dismissed the thought almost as quickly as it appeared. I pushed it to the back of my mind and left it there while I went on with my work, my school, and my life. But every now and then that little idea I'd pushed away would wave at me as if it were whispering, *I'm still here.*

The next five years found me rocked left and right with personal frustrations, devastations, and realizations. Eventually I found myself at a point where it was just me and God. I prayed earnestly, "Dear Lord, what do You want me to do?" Within days the little idea that I'd pushed to the back of my mind all of those years before made its way to the forefront.

Even though I asked God what to do, I was not very willing to move forward. "But Lord," I reasoned, "I don't have an adequate computer. How in the world can I write a devotional without a computer?" Perhaps I thought I was posing something difficult for God. But three months later a brand-new laptop and printer arrived at my front door. I had won a contest that I'd forgotten I'd entered some months before. Could I continue to deny that God was leading me to write a devotional? Maybe not, for someone else, but I needed more proof.

Reluctantly I began to write. After a few weeks I started feeling discouraged again. I began to ask, "Who's going to read this, Lord? Who will read what I wrote and feel encouraged? I'm reading it, and I'm not encouraged at all."

A few days later my sister asked me to write a word of encouragement for one of her coworkers. I was hesitant, but this time I didn't run—I wrote. The coworker was sincerely grateful, and from that point on she occasionally requested that I write pieces for her. She told me she was blessed by them, and often encouraged me to keep on writing.

When you ask God for something, be prepared for the answer.

Maxine Young

April 29

Balancing the Equation

Being confident of this very thing, that he which hath begun a good work in you will perform it until the day of Jesus Christ. Phil. 1:6.

AFTER SPENDING a full-time school year at Northern Caribbean University studying religion, my husband was unable to complete his course because of a lack of funds. Years went by—but going back to complete his course of study was never far from his thoughts. We had several discussions about it, but balancing the equation did not seem possible: on the one hand, there were tuition fees, books, transportation costs, and on the other hand, paying a mortgage, utility bills, food, and caring for two young children. How was it to balance? Impossible!

One day the Lord impressed me to fast and pray for my husband, particularly for him to go back to school full-time to complete his studies. I obeyed the Lord, but I didn't say a word to my husband about it. That same day he called and told me he had decided to go back to school and complete his studies. I never argued or complained; instead, a peace came over me.

My husband resigned from his job and spent the next two years completing his studies. You might be wondering: Did the equation balance? It did. How? The Lord provided family members, particularly my aunt, to assist; occasional promotions on my job; tuition loans; savings; and the other important source: divine providence. Our cupboards were never empty, and all the bills were paid. What a mighty God we serve!

Jeremiah 29:11 says, "For I know the thoughts that I think toward you, saith the Lord, thoughts of peace, and not of evil, to give you an expected end." Isn't it wonderful to know that God has a plan for each of us? I am extremely glad. I had an uncle who was an architect. As a child I watched as he meticulously drew plans for his clients. They took weeks to complete, but when it was done, how good it looked with everything in place. I learned that those plans cost a lot. But without a good construction team and the right materials in place, what use are plans? Like an architect, God has a plan for each of us. He also has the right materials (Christ's righteousness and trials) to ensure that the building (our character) is in line with His design. Cost? Paid by Jesus' blood. So why do we worry, complain, and doubt Him? God's love will not lead you where His grace cannot keep you. The equation does balance!

Thamer Cassandra Smikle

God's Perfect Timing

*In the day of my trouble I will call upon You,
for You will answer me. Ps. 86:7, NKJV.*

I WAS BOUND FOR South Africa. At the airport, after I had checked my baggage, I went outside to look for my sister and her daughters, who were waiting for me so we could say our last goodbyes. As I hurriedly walked to meet them, I did not notice that my passport had fallen to the ground. It was not until I was at the gate, needing to show my passport, that I looked in my bag and discovered it was gone.

I became frightened. I was in great trouble. Without the passport I could not leave the country. I would not only miss my flight—I might even lose my teaching post. It takes quite a long time to have another passport issued and for a work permit to be processed. The school administration could not wait for me that long. I had already had an extended vacation and missed one week of school. I urgently needed to find that passport!

Walking back and forth, I traced the path I'd taken from the counter to the gate, where my sister and her children were also searching for my passport. I kept praying that God would help me out of my dilemma. God's answer came in perfect time. As I approached the security guard at the gate entrance to ask if anyone had turned in a passport, a woman handed him a passport she had found lying on the ground. Fervently I prayed, "God, let it be mine!" I asked the security guard if I could see it and almost jumped with joy when I saw that it was mine.

I thanked the woman for her generosity in taking time to return the passport. In my excitement to get it back, I forgot to ask her name. The only words I could utter at that moment were words of gratitude and appreciation for her kind deed. She was an angel sent by God to rescue me in the day of my trouble.

Unfortunately, I have forgotten her face. I may forget, but I know that God never forgets the goodness she showed to me in my time of distress. I pray that God will bless her as much as He blesses me.

In the day of my trouble God answered my prayer. What a loving and caring God we serve. Truly He does not have deaf ears to our prayers and requests.

Minerva M. Alinaya

Somewhere to Lay My Head

Honour thy father and thy mother:
that thy days may be long upon the land. Ex 20:12.

WHEN I GOT MY FIRST JOB, I decided that I wanted to personally build an extension on our mother's house. Friends thought it rather strange that instead of getting a car, doing further studies, or getting an apartment I took to building—building with block, stone, and cement. I was 23 years old, a woman, and ignorant about construction. And many times Mom and I were taken for granted. Many times we spent what we didn't need to. It proved a most formidable mountain to complete the intended building, and I often cried out.

What strikes me most about this experience is that when I started to build, I did not intend to live at home. In fact, plans were afoot for something else. But God sees all things. Weeks before I was scheduled to officially leave home, that path permanently changed. Then even as we were still building, a family member had a challenge and it became critically necessary for the house to have more space. What if I had not been impressed to build? She and I would have had to use the same room. That extension, which was intended for my mother, now became my weekend refuge and harbor. Soon afterward I decided to go back to college. I had to relocate, and this house became my full-time home yet again.

Who builds an apartment for their mom within their first year of starting to work? Not many. Who but God could have so impressed me? Every time I go home, lie in that bed, or look at the roof, I think about God's goodness, providence, blessing, guidance, and impressions. He has strange ways of taking care of us. He has ways of putting things in place for tomorrow's need. Today, the extension still houses family, friends, and acquaintances as needed.

I daresay it pays to honor our parents, to trust God's promptings, and extend ourselves and means to bless others. What I thought I was doing for someone else ended up blessing me, too. I continue to see how amazingly God leads, although at times it seems like a meandering path. I pray to be sensitive, attentive, and responsive to what God may be trying to communicate. I still don't understand many things, nor can I explain the twists, turns, and seeming disappointments, pains, and heartaches. But I'm learning that God does provide for our needs in strange yet real ways.

Keisha D. Sterling

No Joy

God is our refuge and strength,
a very present help in trouble. Ps. 46:1.

MY LIFE HAS BEEN in turmoil recently. We have been going through a bad spot at church, and it has taken its toll on me. I usually sing, but I cannot find the joy that gives me the desire to sing. I am teaching a Bible class, and although they say I've been doing a good job, my heart has not been in it.

I started a new job, and I have been fighting to find my way—with very little success. We had two unexpectedly large expenditures that pushed our finances into disaster, and I do not see a way out. My brother-in-law died, my sister-in-law's mom died, and my mother got sick and was hospitalized for two weeks.

At home the air-conditioner is leaking and blowing hot air. I have not been focused, and my youngest child, for the first time, isn't doing her best in school. My oldest child senses the upheaval and has been clingy lately—a sure sign of stress.

Yesterday my husband walked in the door and announced that his car had died in the driveway. I wanted to curl up and cry, but of course I couldn't. I got the children to bed, called my dad, and asked to use Mom's car so we could get the girls to school and us to work.

I'm emotionally and physically exhausted. I can't take anymore. I slept last night but awoke with a stomachache, another sure sign of stress. As usual, I studied my Bible lesson guide, read my Bible, and then read the women's devotional book. Today's story was called "A Childlike Faith." It was just what I needed to read. It reminded me to trust God and have a childlike faith that He will take care of it all.

I finished getting ready for work and got in my mom's car. I like quiet first thing in the morning, but this morning I felt compelled to turn on the radio. Guess what God did for me? He played two songs that I needed to hear. The first stated, "Lift up your face. Salvation is calling." The second stated, "He has conquered." All I could do was cry.

I have never doubted that God loves me, but today He told me just what I needed to hear. He reminded me that He is still in control and that no matter how bad the situation, He is present, willing, and more than able! I gave it all to Him today. And guess what? I found my joy.

Tamara Marquez de Smith

And Then

And if I go and prepare a place for you, I will come again and receive you to Myself; that where I am, there you may be also. John 14:3, NKJV.

IN HIS BOOK *God Came Near* Max Lucado states: "The cross wasn't a tragic surprise. It was a calculated choice!" Guess what? Neither is the second advent of Christ a surprise. John 14:3 states Jesus' promise that He is coming back to earth again. No surprise or selfish intent! Just a pure and simple truth. He's coming back to take those who have overcome to a real place called heaven. And contrary to popular belief, it won't be secret. "Behold, He is coming with clouds, and *every* eye will see Him, and they also who pierced Him. And all the tribes of the earth will mourn because of Him" (Rev. 1:7, NKJV).

You ask, "How will it be?" First, Christ must finish His work as our advocate in the Most Holy of places, the heavenly courtroom. He stands as our defense lawyer, the best (and the only qualified) from the heavenly school of law. He boldly approaches the throne of God and covers our sinfulness by the blood He shed for us on the cross. At an appointed time God will declare, "It is finished!" "He who is unjust, let him be unjust still; he who is filthy, let him be filthy still; he who is righteous, let him be righteous still; he who is holy, let him be holy still" (Rev. 22:11, NKJV). The court is adjourned! He sighs, "I did all that I could for those who believed in Me, and all that I could for those who questioned Me. It's time to fulfill My promise."

And then . . .

The dark, desolate canyon of Orion's belt will widen and illuminate. Thousands upon thousands of angels will gather around Him with trumpets in hand to commence the celebration. They are excited! They can hardly wait! The brightness of His purity will pierce the eyes of the unexpecting, but the righteous will have their divine sunglasses ready. He sits on downy, cumulus clouds, a crown of glory embracing His head. Triumph is in one hand, and reward is in the other! Applause! Accolades! Divinity descends!

Jesus welcomes me—what indescribable joy! I'll have a new body that will never get sick or die. I'll have a beautiful mansion with no mortgage! My dinner reservations are confirmed at the banquet table; amazing! How can we not get excited? What a marvelous hope!

Evelyn Greenwade Boltwood

Remember the Jacaranda

They will be called oaks of righteousness, a planting of the Lord for the display of his splendor. Isa. 61:3, NIV.

THIS MORNING I looked out my window and saw the vibrant lavender beauty of our Jacaranda tree in full blossom. Extravagant frills of delicate lavender blue cascaded freely from the top of the tree's magnificent crown to the outermost tips of its branches. Every now and then flowers loosened and, soft as falling snowflakes, floated down and nestled on the grass below, making a lacy carpet of blue and green.

Behind the glorious Jacaranda danced a snowy drift of rain-induced crocus, dazzling white and fading to pink among the vivid green of storm-sprouted new grass. Such beauty! Rich in color against the stormy blue sky.

And you know what, dear daughters of God? That beauty reminds me of you, of your distinctive, set-apart-for-Christ life. You are that stately tall tree blossoming and resplendent in beauty. You are the one who stands out from the rest and radiates pleasure and joy to all who see you. The one planted by the Lord for the display of His splendor.

Gazing out my window, I am overwhelmed by the beauty I see and the spiritual lesson it teaches me. A Jacaranda tree in full blossom always stands out; neither crowd nor distance can hide its vibrant display. Its beauty conquers any surrounding landscape. Overlooked and unnoticed in winter while leafless and bare, its true beauty and value lie hidden within. But come springtime and voila! What went unnoticed before now commands the attention and admiration.

So it often is with the faithful daughters of God. You may feel you have been planted in dry ground or in an obscure corner. Or buried under nappies (diapers), lunches, and laundry. But you have been planted where you are by the Lord Himself for the displaying of His splendor. At the right time He will bring you forth dazzling with beauty for all to see, and to His glory.

Don't worry if it feels as though life's flowers are all falling. Fallen flowers under a Jacaranda are a part of the tree's unique beauty. They carpet the ground with a reflected loveliness. Everything they touch is somehow transformed.

Remember the Jacaranda!

Lynette Kenny

When God Held My Hand

For I am the Lord your God who takes hold of your right hand and says to you, Do not fear; I will help you. Isa. 41:13, NIV.

NERVOUSLY I WAITED with my mother-in-law in the hospital surgical waiting room. Just minutes before I had kissed my husband goodbye and said a last prayer with him before he disappeared through the doors for a surgical liver resection. Just two months before, at age 38, my dear husband had been diagnosed with stage-four colon cancer. He had already undergone an emergency colon resection 18 months before, and the stress of the situation was taking a toll on me. We had a 12-month-old son to love and care for, and I was deeply concerned and worried about my husband. Since the colon surgery the cancer had spread to two places in his liver, and his oncologist recommended that the cancer be surgically removed. It had been explained that the surgery should last five to seven hours.

Just then I heard my name on the hospital intercom. My mother-in-law and I hurried to the desk, where we were told that the doctor wanted to talk with us in the private conference room. I looked at my watch. It had been only about four hours! Then I remembered that the surgeon had told us if the cancer had spread to other parts of his abdominal area, it could not be surgically removed. The risk of spreading the disease would be too great. They would just have to sew him up and begin chemotherapy. Why were we called to a private conference room? I had seen other surgeons come and talk to the family right there in the waiting room. Surely something terrible must have happened. Why else would the surgery be so short?

Then the doctor's footsteps interrupted my depressing thoughts. The surgery had been successful. The cancer had not spread, and they were able to remove it all. My husband was in recovery and was doing very well!

A peace flooded my soul as tears of relief poured down my cheeks. God had been with me all along, holding my hand! He just wanted me to trust Him and be at peace even when I couldn't see and understand. He wanted me to trust Him and just rest in His arms of love. I knew that there were rough trials ahead, but I knew that God would be there holding my hand. "When I am afraid, I put my trust in you" (Ps. 56:3, NIV).

Tammy Sommer

Crocodiles and God

The Lord executes righteousness and justice for all who are oppressed.
Ps. 103:6, NKJV.

I LIVE IN AFRICA, and living in Africa provides lots of food for thought. Crocodiles and God is one conundrum to be explored. Did God make crocodiles? Can God use crocodiles for good or bad? Of what use are they? Some people might think they should not be on this earth, because they are so ugly and frightening, and they kill and swallow many people in the rivers and estuaries across this continent. But this true story, which happened in the country where I lived for so long, reveals to me that God is the great Creator and can make ugly things beautiful. God can do anything, and I can trust Him.

Close to a river in Chiredzi, in the southern part of Zimbabwe, an 11-year-old girl was walking to church when she realized she was being chased by an evil man, a man known to be a murderer and a rapist. She ran in terror, but soon came to a river separating her from the church meeting place and safety. All she could do was run across the logs floating on the river, hoping she could reach the safety of the church before the man, only about 100 feet (30 meters) behind, caught her. He followed in hot pursuit, jumping from log to log, but those angry logs suddenly churned the water. They opened wide their mouths and ripped his body apart as they dragged him under. Obviously those "logs" were crocodiles.

The terrified girl arrived at the church and told the people meeting there of her narrow escape, but the man was nowhere to be seen. The members wondered whether this story was true, so they all went to the river to look. And there in the river they saw 15 lazy crocodiles with eyes protruding and backs floating on top of the water, looking satisfied and peaceful in the sun. They could see the girl's footprints in the mud on both sides of the river. The man's footprints were only on one side and were not far behind the girl's.

This story reminds us of the children of Israel facing the Red Sea and safety. Moses spoke to them saying, "Do not be afraid. Stand firm and you will see the deliverance the Lord will bring you today" (Ex. 14:13, NIV). He will still deliver His children any place, any time.

The whole congregation renewed their commitment to Jesus Christ, and many were baptized.

Joy Butler

Special Delivery

Give thanks to the Lord, for he is good; his love endures forever.
1 Chron. 16:34, NIV.

I'M AN INFUSION NURSE, and I see clients of all ages, diagnoses, creeds, and ethnicities during my workweek. On Fridays, when I visit one particular client whom we'll call Tamika, I'm constantly amazed by her generosity. She goes on her scooter, complete with her oxygen tank, to pick up day-old bread to deliver to the needy. Even though she is on the food stamp program, she insists on giving me something every time I visit. If I bring her peppermint tea, for instance, she'll try to give me coffee. But what also impresses me is how she gives God praise.

One day I had the strong impression to fill a bag with the foodstuffs she needed most. Packing a bag with eggs, turkey bacon, potatoes, teas, and a host of other foods I knew she should have, I added another bag with things she'd once said she *wanted.* Then I discovered I had a problem. How could I deliver the bags without her knowing I was the giver?

We decided for my son, his friend, and my daughter to drive a car to Tamika's house and put the bags at her front door. I watched from the car as my accomplices delivered the bags, and heard Tamika exclaim, "Oh, this is just what I needed! Exactly what I prayed for!"

When I told my husband about our escapade, he had to join in the excitement. Knowing that Tamika needed a bus pass for her frequent visits to her doctors and the hospital, he drove all the way downtown to get her the pass. The next time I went to Tamika's house, as I listened to her speak of a recent example of God's goodness, I slipped the pass into her Bible. She had needed, she told me, $4 for a prescription but had absolutely no money. As she prayed for God's help she was interrupted by a visit from her neighbor. "I have an extra $5 that I want to give you," the neighbor said. Tamika could do nothing but praise the Lord.

When I saw Tamika the next Friday, she could hardly wait to tell me about the bags delivered to her doorstep and the pass she'd found in her Bible. Now she would be able to attend church, getting up early and taking four different buses to arrive for the church service. Listening to her praise the Lord, I was convinced that my plan had been God-breathed.

I enjoy serving as God's earthly angel and look forward to meeting my own guardian angel in that glorious mansion in the sky.

Kathy Walter

Commitment

Dear friends, don't be surprised by the fiery troubles that are coming in order to test you. Don't feel as though something strange is happening to you, but be happy as you share Christ's sufferings. Then you will also be full of joy when he appears again in his glory. 1 Peter 4:12, 13, GW.

I WAS 12 YEARS OLD when I was baptized and officially joined my church. It seemed that most of us were ready to make that commitment around that age, and I think it was a good decision for me. Later in the teen years many begin to question authority: the authority of parents, teachers, and others. Somehow, having made that commitment when I was 12 made it easier for me to stick with family (even though I also began to realize they weren't always perfect) and church (whose members weren't always perfect either).

When I was almost 19, I got married. That is a very young age for that major commitment. When you marry and make all those promises, you don't have any realization of what will be coming down the road of life. All kinds of things that can jeopardize the commitment of marriage can come into one's life. They can attack the very foundation of that institution. It takes a firm commitment to help us over the rough spots.

Of course, we're asked to make a commitment in many areas of life. This is why any commitment must be firm and nonwavering. It helps hold one in place during life's storms, the ups and downs, the ins and outs, of living life. Where there is no commitment to church, family, or marriage, what can hold a person steady?

Staying with a commitment helps you hold fast to the important things and to bear up under tragedies, as well as to step forward in faith to reach your ultimate goals. Thank God that through the life of Jesus we are shown the pattern for commitment!

If you find your commitment has wavered, I invite you to recommit now with God's help. He is there for you and can mend the broken places in your life. If our commitment to Him is firm, all other commitments will fall into their proper place. "You need to persevere so that when you have done the will of God, you will receive what he has promised" (Heb. 10:36, NIV). Lift your head and heart to Jesus, who suffered all for you. He is committed to you.

Peggy Harris

Where Is My Blessing, Lord?

The Lord make his face shine upon thee, and be gracious unto thee: . . . and give thee peace. Num. 6:25, 26.

AS I SWUNG OPEN the door to exit the ladies' room of our church, my usually noncombative self wanted to put a fist into the belly of the very pregnant woman coming in. Recently my caring mother had given me the book *The Wedded Un-mother.* That was me. For six years I'd been in a serene marriage to a loving husband—with no children. Now I was filled with anger because my lifelong dreams of being a "mommy" had come to nothing. *Why her? Why not me? Why is she pregnant and I'm not?*

My sister-in-law gave birth to her third blessing with the comment "We thought we weren't going to be able to have more, but the Lord blessed us." *Where is my blessing, Lord?* My sister had her second son, "an accident," she said. *Lord, it doesn't have to be a "blessing." An "accident" will do.*

An "accident" never happened. Instead, we got two miraculous blessings. Today I look at our grown son and daughter and am reminded of God's abundant and generous miracles. The Adoption Creed says, "Not flesh of my flesh nor bone of my bone, but still miraculously my own: Never forget for a single minute, you didn't grow under my heart but in it." We had all the markings of the perfectly fabulous family that would live happily ever after.

Praise God, we now live happily because of a God who never fails. The years were splotched with challenges in kindergarten, unpleasant visits with school principals, behavioral-modification schools, icy receptions to our visits at boarding school, misuse of the gift of a paid-in-full college education, sleepless nights praying for the young adult "out there." Living happily? God gave us these beautiful little people at the time of their births. He accepted us as His partners to raise two of His precious children. Sometimes the journey was intense. *Always* His grace was sufficient. Through tears and abundant joy, God's boundless love intertwined through all.

God didn't respond to my anger the way I asked, nor did God answer my prayer for *easy* children. All glory goes to Him for the frequent phone calls, surprise and scheduled visits, and many warm sharing times we now spend with our adult children.

Sandy Colburn

Three Words

But this I say, He that soweth sparingly shall reap also sparingly; and he that soweth bountifully shall reap also bountifully. 2 Cor. 9:6, ASV.

I HAVE BEEN ASKED a question, and I am sure others have been asked this too: "What three words do you want on your tombstone?" A few years ago I may not have known, but I've thought about it and now I do. My three words would be: "Made a difference." If I have made a difference in just one person's life I believe I have done what God has wanted me to.

One way we make a difference is by sowing seed. I do my best to sow seeds even though I know I may not see the results. I have heard people say, "You must sow seeds so that you will reap." I do hope one day I'll reap some, but even if I don't, I know that some seeds I sowed will provide fruit.

God calls us all to sow seeds, and that may be all we are called to do. Think about the story of John Chapman, known as Johnny Appleseed. He sowed thousands of apple seeds, and through his work many apple trees grew. But he didn't tend them and didn't always see the results of the seeds he planted. He may have prepared the ground and protected the seedlings while they were small, but the results weren't always seen. In the same way, we can't always tend the seeds, and we don't always see the results. Are you waiting to see your seeds bear fruit before you sow some more?

When I write something, I hope that the seeds that I sow will one day bear fruit. However, I may not be the one to reap it. I pray that people whom I have influenced just a little bit will be my neighbors in heaven. I will see that they were reaped for God from a seed I had sown. I have been asked, "Why do you write what you do?" My one desire is to make a difference in someone's life. If I see just one person come to a relationship with God, I will have fulfilled my purpose.

It can be a bit discouraging when a person in whom you are sowing seeds seems to reject God's message. But there is always a chance that your seed is just what is needed. It is waiting for the living water of Christ to come so it can bear fruit. So I ask you two questions: Are you sowing the seeds? and What three words do *you* want on your tombstone?

Melanie Carter Winkler

A Mother's Hope

He does not treat us as our sins deserve or repay us
according to our iniquities. Ps. 103:10, NIV.

MONICA KNEW SHE was too late, but still she sank to the floor at the foot of her son's bed. "Lord, forgive me for not praying enough as he was growing up. Forgive me for thinking I could influence him to choose You just by teaching him about Jesus. Forgive my self-sufficiency."

It was midnight, and her boy was locked in the slumber of youth.

As she rose from her knees her eyes focused on his sleeping form: the outline of his athletic frame, the thick blond hair wreathing his handsome face, and the even cadence of his breathing. She was amazed at how practical and helpful he was when there was a need, and she felt overjoyed at his warm, pleasant personality. She saw the kindness and care he showed to the elderly and the very young, and she loved him with all the devotion that a mother has.

But herein lay her misery: her son had no love for God. Years of family worship, Sabbath school, parochial school, and church youth events had resulted only in unbelief. *It must be my fault,* she reasoned. She reviewed the way she had reared him and concluded with sorrow that she hadn't involved God enough. She decided that if she could have her time over again she'd pray and be far more dependent on God for the conversion of her child. She'd demonstrate her connection with the Lord, and he would see how vital such a connection is.

Then she remembered the promises of Scripture and knew the Lord had not forsaken her. Even today God was walking with her and hearing her every prayer. At last Monica had learned how indispensable a living relationship with God really is. "Because I trust Him more now, I can see God's hand in our lives and especially in the life of my son," she confesses.

Monica's story is a work in progress. It has no miraculous outcome or spectacular ending—yet. But because she belongs to God, her story is also His story. Through prayer she is engaging the God who never sleeps. She is calling on the One whose power knows no limitation and whose wisdom knows no end. But is there anything she can still do for her boy? She *can* keep on—keep on praying, keep on loving, keep on believing, and keep on hoping. "May the God of hope fill you with all joy and peace as you trust in him, so that you may overflow with hope by the power of the Holy Spirit" (Rom. 15:13, NIV).

Carole Ferch-Johnson

Extraordinary Women

Likewise, teach the older women to be reverent in the way they live, not to be slanderers or addicted to much wine, but to teach what is good. Then they can urge the younger women to love their husbands and children, to be self-controlled and pure, to be busy at home, to be kind, and to be subject to their husbands, so that no one will malign the word of God. Titus 2:3-5, NIV.

THE BIBLE RECOUNTS the lives of many extraordinary women, women such as Ruth, Hannah, Elizabeth, and Mary, just to name a few. These women faced many difficulties but were determined to overcome. Do you have extraordinary women in your life? I surely do.

Extraordinary women can present themselves in many different ways and times. They are there when we're heartbroken. They listen to our woes, wipe our tears, provide a shoulder to lean on, give us priceless advice, good friendship, and even financial help when possible.

These women present themselves in the form of good friends, mothers, cousins, nieces, aunts, grandmothers, mothers-in-law, and sisters. We can find them in our homes, at work, at church, and over the telephone when distance divides us.

Thank God for these wonderful women. Mother's Day is the perfect occasion to take time to tell these women how much they mean to us, and that we are thankful that God placed them in our lives.

The support such extraordinary women provide proves to be so helpful. They teach us how to be godly, self-controlled women. They help us to develop motherly skills, to prepare nutritious and delicious meals, to care for ourselves and for others. Extraordinary women look out for each other and are there for each other no matter what. These women always give a listening ear without being judgmental, but they are honest enough to tell us when we are wrong—with love. And because we love and respect them, we heed their godly counsels. Titus admonishes us in today's text, as older women (and everyone is older than someone) to be reverent in the way we live. As we become older women we must become good examples and extraordinary women for others to follow. Let us teach what is good. Let us be pure and kind so that we may not malign the word of God. Won't you be an extraordinary woman for Christ?

Taniesha Robertson-Brown

Never Alone Are We

Are they not all ministering spirits, sent forth to minister for them who shall be heirs of salvation? Heb. 1:14.

 "GOOD NIGHT, Grandma and Grandpa Loshack," we said as we left their home after supper. We began to walk down the Dore River Road to our place. It was a very dark night. The moon was not shining, and we had no flashlight. What a predicament to be in! But there was no alternative, so we kept walking.

"Snap!" went something in the bushes beside the narrow dirt road.

"Mother, what was that?" whispered a small voice from a very little boy.

"Probably a deer stepped on a fallen twig," I replied as casually as I could. We then continued to walk along in silence, when right above us on an overhanging branch we were startled to hear, "Whoo, Whoo, Whoo-ooo!"

"Mother, what was *that?*" asked my son in a shaky voice.

"Just Mr. Owl calling for Mrs. Owl," I answered. I knew that was an owl for sure, no guessing. We were nearing our driveway when through the still night we heard an unmistakable scream—loud and clear—of a mountain lion.

"Mother, what was that?" quavered a truly frightened little one now.

"That was a mountain lion screaming, but he is on the other side of the river," I answered. I truly hoped he *was* on the far side of the river and not in the field below our house. Clutching his hand even tighter, I hurried him up our long driveway. Only when the door was closed and locked and the lights were on did I heave a huge sigh of relief.

Mark had never realized our danger. He knew only that mother was with him, holding his hand, and he was safe—just as I knew that our guardian angels had walked with us down that lonely, darkened road. Often when we are in an unusual, frightening position we almost panic. But how blessed we are to know our guardian angels, although unseen, are always present with us. Never alone are we, never! "For he shall give his angels charge over thee, to keep thee in all thy ways" (Ps. 91:11, KJV). What a prayer of praise and thanksgiving I gave to our heavenly Father. We were home and safe. We were never alone—never!

Muriel Heppel

Safe in His Arms

They shall bear thee up in their hands,
lest thou dash thy foot against a stone. Ps. 91:12.

I WOULD LIKE TO share two separate incidents that have happened to me. In each, I was saved miraculously. One happened when I was a child, and the other after my marriage.

When I was 7 years old, there was a great famine in my village, as there had been no rain for three consecutive years. It was dry everywhere. One day I went to a nearby well with my dad to wash our clothes. It was a deep well with a little water at the bottom on one side; the other side was dry. Steep steps led down into the well. My dad was washing the clothes at the bottom of the well. I was standing on the steps approximately 80 feet (25 meters) above, grabbing the clothes that were thrown up to me by my dad. I was to take them to dry. All of a sudden I slipped and, screaming, fell into the well. Instantly my dad stretched out his arms and caught me before I touched the water. When I opened my eyes, I was safe in his arms. All this happened in a fraction of a second. If I had fallen on the other side where there was no water, I would certainly have died on the spot.

The next incident was an accident involving my husband and me. My husband was riding a bicycle, with me sitting behind him. When he failed to see the speed bump on the road and bumped over it, I fell from the bike, and my shoulder hit the ground. In that instant my dress got hooked onto an auto-rickshaw, which came from behind. It drove on, dragging me about 65 feet (20 meters) farther. By God's amazing grace, not only did I sustain no serious injuries, but God made sure I was not run over by any vehicle from behind.

In today's text God says that angels will hold you up with their hands so you won't even hurt your foot on a stone. But the Bible holds other promises as well that are true for us. Proverbs 1:33 says, "But whoever listens to me will live in safety and be at ease, without fear of harm" (NIV). I found that was true. A long time ago God told Israel, "See, I am sending an angel ahead of you to guard you along the way and to bring you to the place I have prepared (Ex. 23:20, NIV). He is still keeping that promise.

Let us praise and thank our powerful God for the times known and unknown when He has kept us safe in His arms.

Jothi Gnanaprakasam

Two Dresses for the Wedding

Now to Him who is able to do exceedingly abundantly above all that we ask or think, according to the power that works in us, to Him be glory in the church by Christ Jesus throughout all ages, world without end. Amen. Eph. 3:20, 21, NKJV.

EXCITEMENT WAS IN THE AIR! My firstborn son was to be married in just a month. As the bridegroom's mother I had to look smart!

Preparations had turned out to be more expensive than I'd anticipated. Our country had just changed its functional currency to hard currency: United States dollars. The economy was still trying to pick up, and prices of items in the shops were exorbitant—especially clothes!

God performed many miracles for us as a family during the wedding preparations, and prices were reduced for some of the services. I took courage, strength, and faith that God, who had led us this far, would also make sure that I got the wedding dress that I desired. I had two sisters-in-law overseas, and I told them my need. They promised to bring a dress and shoes for me when they came for the wedding. However, they were not able to get airline tickets. Naturally I panicked. I had no money for a dress, and the date was drawing near.

Two weeks before the wedding I decided to walk into town to look for a dress. The Lord directed me to a boutique that had lovely dresses, and I found one I liked, but the price was a whopping $200! I decided I wanted it and trusted God to supply the needed money.

The next week as we finished our midweek prayers, which had been conducted at my house, one of the women remained behind. I thought she just wanted to chat and was surprised because under normal circumstances she would have hurried home to her family. She asked me if I'd bought my dress. I told her I had seen one in town, had no money to pay for it, but knew God would supply somehow. She asked how much it was. Then she told me that she didn't have the money at that moment, but she was going to buy the dress for me! An answer to prayer!

A few days before the wedding, I got a call from my sister-in-law saying that she had found someone coming to our country and had given my dress for the wedding to her. I now had a headache trying to choose which dress to wear! My God had supplied exceedingly abundantly more than I had asked for! Two lovely outfits! What a mighty God we serve.

Alice Mafanuke

Ask in Confidence, Believe, and Claim the Promises of God

And all things, whatever you ask in prayer, believing, you will receive.
Matt. 21:22, NKJV.

That whatever you ask the Father in My name He may give you. John 15:16, NKJV.

Now this is the confidence that we have in Him, that if we ask anything according to His will, He hears us. And if we know that He hears us, whatever we ask, we know that we have the petitions that we have asked of Him.
1 John 5:14, 15, NKJV.

SOME MONTHS AGO MISS LEE, a Buddhist, said her boss gave her one month to meet the sales quota, or else she would be fired. She asked me for help. I replied, "I can pray for you, asking God for His wisdom, mercy, and grace. I will also ask Him to bless you with more stationery orders." Soon God blessed her with many stationery orders. She says she now believes in God, and is very thankful to God for His providence. Many times she thanked me for praying for her, and said she was still receiving God's blessings. I told her, "Thank God and praise His name."

Sometime later Miss Lee said she was unable to cope with her sales order from a corporate company because it was so large. She gave the stationery order to her superior, as her superior had no orders, but she asked me for my advice. I told her she had made her decision. "It was your choice to give to whomever you wanted because God blessed you."

A few weeks ago Mabel told me that her husband, Phillip, had been hospitalized with a high fever. I said, "Let him be anointed." As I had the flu, I instructed her as to how to anoint her husband. I said, "When you do it yourself, you will see the wonders of God." That afternoon she and her two daughters visited her husband. She anointed her husband with oil and prayed according to God's will, and in Jesus' name. The next day she was happy to learn that he had opened his eyes. Mabel spoke to Phillip, and he responded. Later he had recovered enough to return to the nursing home.

"My mouth will speak in praise of the Lord. Let every creature praise his holy name for ever and ever" (Ps. 145:21, NIV). We asked, believed, and claimed God's promises.

Yan Siew Ghiang

Tempers

Be angry, and do not sin.
Eph. 4:26, NKJV.

"IT IS DIFFICULT to turn your passion into ministry if you are an angry person." When I read this statement I knew firsthand that it was true.

As a young bride in my 20s I had a terrible temper. I remember being so angry at my new husband that I often banged my pans so hard on the counter they would not sit straight on the burner. I even remember being so angry that I would bang my head against the wall. I'm sure my even-tempered husband had never seen anything like this! As you can imagine, I have prayed about my temper many, many times and asked God to take control of it.

People do crazy things when they lose their temper. I have seen toddlers throw temper tantrums, teenagers run their fist through glass doors, and young mothers treat their children with disrespect. I have seen a grown man embarrass his wife and friends by yelling at a server.

One of the first things that attracted me to my husband was the fact that I never saw him get angry. After 43 years of marriage it is still true today, and I am thankful.

Today's text states, "Be angry, and do not sin," so it is OK to be angry—in other words, to experience strong feelings of displeasure and indignation. Jesus was certainly angry when He threw the money changers out of the Temple. But it is not OK to manifest anger in behavior that is sinful and mad. It is not OK to throw tantrums, frying pans, or fists.

Proverbs says that a kindhearted woman gains respect and a gentle answer turns away wrath, but a harsh word stirs up anger (see Prov. 15). Mismanaged anger contributes to divorce. It makes others uncomfortable, and it transfers to our children.

I knew I had to stop the anger issue before we decided to start a family. I am thankful that when my daughter heard about my early years of throwing tantrums, banging my pans, and hitting my head, she was very surprised. She said she didn't know I had a temper.

If you're wondering if I still have that temper, the truth is yes. Every now and then I still feel anger creeping up my body. Praise the Lord, He has helped me manage the sinful effects of my anger.

Jesus knows about our anger and the other things that keep us from serving Him. Our only need is to be close to Him. My sisters, remember to stay close to Jesus every single day.

Nancy Buxton

He Is Faithful. Are You?

For He shall give His angels charge over you, to keep you in all your ways. In their hands they shall bear you up, lest you dash your foot against a stone. Ps. 91:11, 12, NKJV.

HOW DO YOU begin your day? Do you begin each day with the Lord? Is your time with God your very first appointment? Each morning before I start my tasks for the day, I have made it my habit to spend the best time of the day with the Lord. Sometimes it means getting up a little earlier in order to have my quiet time. This is the most important hour of the day for me. I am better prepared to face whatever the day may bring.

It was late afternoon. My grandson, Christopher, and I were driving home from his piano lesson and were partly across a four-lane intersection when the traffic light changed. A man driving toward us was in the turning lane and evidently in a hurry. I guess he thought if he stepped on his accelerator he could make his left turn before my car crossed the remaining lanes. It was one of those moments that an instant decision had to be made. Since no one was behind me, I braked quickly. However, I could hear his rear tire rub across the front passenger side of my car, and I pulled over to the side of the road. The other driver pulled over as well. Christopher and I were a little shaken, but not hurt. As I checked the front of my car, there were no dents, scratches, or broken lights, only some black marks from his rear tire. Later I was able to scrub off these marks.

I was thankful our guardian angels were with us and kept us safe. I was also thankful I didn't have to fill out an accident report or notify my insurance company. Just a few months before, I had changed insurance companies. Even though this accident wasn't my fault, reporting an accident would not look good on my record with a new insurance company.

There are so many times each day that God's protection keeps us safe. Do we remember to thank Him? Or do we take His protection for granted? For many years now, at the end of the day, I have written in my gratitude book five or six things that took place that day for which I am thankful. It is a blessed way to end the day.

So many times we are not aware of God's loving care, but one day our guardian angels will relate to us the many experiences during which God's hand kept us safe.

Patricia Mulraney Kovalski

An Act of Love

So if I, the Master and Teacher, washed your feet, you must now wash each other's feet. I've laid down a pattern for you. What I've done, you do. John 13:14-17, Message.

OF ALL THE WORDS the Lord Jesus spoke, the ones that reach most to my heart is His beckon to wash one another's feet. This humble act prepared His followers for His institution of the Lord's Supper or Communion. For me, it's like a minibaptism and a renewing of my vows to serve Him. However, for some, participation in the service of humility is not physically easy. Kneeling to serve may be problematic. A suggestion: keep a watch for those who need assistance and those who do not attend the services. Are they absent because they can't ably take part? Is your church building itself handicapped by lack of easy access for participants? Meeting these challenges may be the most profound act of love you'll ever perform.

I did not learn of Jesus at my mother's knee. In fact, she didn't commit her life to Jesus until after my marriage and motherhood. However, I did learn from her an act of compassion that she carried out when she started participating in the foot-washing services. She'd take a basin, drape a couple of towels across her arm, and disappear from the room where the other women of the church were gathered. She'd climb the stairs from the basement up to the anteroom of the women's restroom, where she knelt to serve a sister—or maybe more than one—who could not traverse the stairs to participate. Her simple ministry provided inclusion, easing neglect for these aging, shy, or otherwise challenged women.

In later years my mother suffered a stroke that left her unable to speak or to care for herself. While she was living in a nursing home, our pastor suggested we take these twin services to her. I explained that she couldn't swallow, and he said, "No problem, it's symbolic; I'll just touch her lips with the grape juice." As I knelt to wash her feet, her eyes brightened. The pastor also invited some teenage young people from the church to be a part of this service. He hoped that someday they might choose pastoral ministry. Mom couldn't speak, but I know that service provided her with joy. It brought all of us joy.

It is all about love. Is there such a ministry waiting for you? "Having loved his own who were in the world, he loved them to the end" (John 13:1, NIV).

Betty Kossick

We Have a Story

Tell them how much the Lord has done for you,
and how he has had mercy on you. Mark 5:19, NIV.

FROM THE TIME I agreed to tell the children's story in church to the time I told it was for me sheer misery. I accused myself of always agreeing to every request. I chided myself for not having enough backbone to sometimes say no.

I had told the children's story a number of times in my former church, as well as at Vacation Bible School. So what was the problem now? Perhaps it was that I was new to the congregation, but I think it was because I felt intimidated. Each week I had listened to others tell exciting stories of their childhood adventures or about intriguing family encounters in which the Lord did dramatic things. I had no such experience. At least that was what I told myself. I ransacked my brain for a fitting story and found nothing. I read several and rejected them. They were other people's stories. I wanted one of my own.

With time running out, it finally dawned on me that I did have a story—one about my visiting niece's lost cell phone that was found after I'd prayed, quietly but earnestly. I also remembered that having my prayer answered gave me a rush of spiritual joy. How exciting! God had actually listened to me and answered. Lesson: He watches out for sparrows and for lost cell phones. Surely He will look out for me.

I prepared my story along with appropriate demonstration—a pillow with a cell phone in its pillowcase—where the lost phone was found in the nick of time for my niece to leave on her trip back to New York. The story received an enthusiastic response, both from the children and from the appreciative adults. I was pleasantly surprised.

For some time afterward I reflected on the event. I thought I didn't have a story of my own, but I did. How like us sometimes to downplay what should be a source of spiritual affirmation and delight. We all have a story. Each of God's small miracles in our lives from day to day is a story. Our salvation is a marvelous story, some of us having more drama and impressive occurrences than others. But if we have known God's saving grace, it's a wonderful story. And we should be willing and ready to share it with His children.

Judith P. Nembhard

Silencing the Gremlins

But Jesus said, "Let her alone; why do you bother her?
She has done a good deed to Me." Mark 14:6, NASB.

I'VE WRITTEN 10 books. With one or two exceptions, they've sold poorly. The temptation to give up after such a string of failures can wear on a person. Some days a little gremlin sits on my shoulder and says, "No one cares what you think! You make no difference at all. You're so pathetic. Put yourself out of your misery and just give up on this ministry business."

At such times I remember Mary Magdalene. She had a brilliant, creative idea. You see, the law of Moses forbade receiving offerings from prostitutes, so a cash donation was out of the question. But nothing said an ex-prostitute could not spend her money on precious ointment, fit for a king, and then lavish Jesus with that glorious stuff in preparation for His burial. "Maybe then He'll know how much I love Him!" she said to herself. Off she ran to the apothecary shop to spend about $40,000 of her life savings on an alabaster box of spikenard.

As she poured out her offering and many tears of gratitude, a room full of gremlins broke into a chorus: "Why this waste? She's wasting God's money. She can't do anything right!" Some translations say, "They were scolding her" (Mark 14:5, NASB). That word in the Greek, *embrimaomai,* means "to snort with anger." I can just hear, "Why doesn't she just *cook* like her sister, Martha? This is what happens when you allow this kind of woman in here."

Mary couldn't help feeling a jolt of shame. Glancing around the room full of glowering eyes, she planned her retreat. For a moment the gremlins seemed triumphant, all fat and happy in their cruelty. Broken, trembling, sniffling, Mary gathered her robes around her and . . .

A voice shook the air. That voice had shaken mountains, and now it shook mountains of prejudice. That voice said three of the most beautiful words in the entire Bible: "Leave her alone." Jesus went on: "Wherever this gospel is preached, tell what she's done." The room boiled with emotion. Not only is He silencing us— He's amplifying her! No one dared challenge Him.

Today Jesus tells your personal gremlins to "Leave her alone." He promises to use your poured-out life. He loves your reckless giving. Let them snort with anger. It's all they have. You, woman, have a future in eternity.

Jennifer Jill Schwirzer

When You Miss Someone

And they said one to another, Did not our heart burn within us, while he talked with us by the way, and while he opened to us the scriptures? Luke 24:32.

SOME PEOPLE you know so well that you can hear their voices, even when they are not talking. You can hear them in an e-mail, a personal birthday card, or a scribbled comment on a sticky note. I have a couple of those kinds of friends.

Shaunda, a good friend from college, recently left after a year of service at Gimbie Hospital. Our goodbye was short, and the moment of farewell was relatively painless. After the loaded Land Cruiser drove out of sight, I headed home to the house we had shared. I found a note with my name printed on it in familiar handwriting. It was from Shaunda. While reading her reminiscing and encouraging words, I heard her voice.

As I went about my morning routine, my mind drifted back to scrubbing walls with Shaunda at Green Lake Clinic, to our rhythmic breathing during early-morning runs, and human-wheelbarrow stress-relief exercises. The reality of Shaunda's absence hit at various moments throughout the day—while choosing clothes from the half-empty closet, when I went to check the time on Shaunda's missing alarm clock, and while sitting in the office we once shared. There was a hole, yet I had hope that we will cross paths in the States.

I wondered if Jesus' disciples felt the same mix of emotions after He ascended to heaven. Did they walk along a certain path "remembering when," or attend synagogue only to replay one of Jesus' sermons in their head? "Then they worshiped him and returned to Jerusalem with great joy" (Luke 24:52, NIV).

I wondered if reading Matthew's account of Jesus' life triggered a mental sound clip of his Teacher's voice. Wouldn't it be great if miraculously an MP3 of Jesus giving the Sermon on the Mount were available? What if we could hear each pause, or when His voice got shaky because of His passion, or hear the spontaneous joy in a conversation? Although the inflection is unknown, we still have His powerful words. Like Shaunda's note, the meaning of the Gospels amplifies in a relationship. So explore nature, meditate on holy lyrics, read the Gospels, and remember the cadences of His words and the value of His message.

Renee Baumgartner

The Widow of Zarephath

But my God shall supply all your need according to his riches in glory by Christ Jesus. Phil. 4:19.

RECENTLY I WAS intrigued reading the story of the widow of Zarephath. This poor woman was down to her last. She knew this was it. After eating their last meal she and her son would die. Perhaps, if she knew the God of Israel, she had claimed all the promises about asking and receiving, about casting her cares on the Lord. She claimed them all, and still no supplies came to her door during the night; no raven brought food for her as it did for Elijah; manna did not fall from heaven as it did for the children of Israel. Surely she was not lying down in green pastures as David did. God had promised to supply her need, and hers was a desperate need. She was about to eat her last supper, like Jesus' last supper.

I try to imagine her feelings, whether they were of fear, doubt, torment, trust, hope, contentment, unbelief, complaining, or total dependence on the will of God. Jesus knew what lay ahead of Him after the Last Supper. He agonized with His Father, but left the outcome to Him. Although He had His Father's assurance, He still had torture and agony of soul. Just like God, the widow of Zarephath could have felt the same agony over the death of her son.

I believe she came to grips with her situation and totally submitted to the will of God. Only when Elijah asked for bread did she confess her real situation. Her miracle began to happen when she was willing to obey by preparing the cake and offering it to Elijah first. She put Elijah, who represented God, first. Do we, in our difficulties, seek God first?

When faced with trials, Daniel and the three Hebrew boys did not care what the outcome for their lives would be. They made sure they placed God first and let the chips fall where they may. Putting God first changed the widow's circumstances from death to life, not only for herself, but also for her family. As Christians, we might be the one God can use to save our family if we put Him first as the widow did.

The miracle of the flour and oil flowed until God changed her circumstance by sending rain. God always has a better plan than the one we see or even envision. It's wise to depend on Him and put Him first. Our miracle comes when we do!

Maureen Pierre

The Court of the Queen's Bench

And you yourself must be an example to them by doing good works of every kind. Let everything you do reflect the integrity and seriousness of your teaching. Titus 2:7, NLT.

SONNY'S SISTER AND I went to Starbucks to finish up the paperwork regarding Sonny's legal guardianship review before the Court of the Queen's Bench in Alberta. Over a cup of hot chocolate we worked and talked for three hours. I mentioned to Andee that this was a very special day for me, because exactly 40 years before I had entered Canada.

Tears welled up in Andee's eyes and mine. "Mom, back then you could have never imagined that you'd be doing this paperwork in order to take care of Sonny. I'm so proud of you and Daddy and Sonny. Congratulations for receiving the Family Leadership Award for the Northwest Region. But I'm so sorry you didn't get the Provincial Award."

"Maybe next year," I said with a smile. Twenty of my past 40 years have been spent being Sonny's advocate as well as a voice for many others who have developmental disabilities and their families. I have no regrets.

"If the time comes when you must take on the role of legal guardianship for Sonny, remember this," I told Andee. "Whatever decisions you make on his behalf will be the right choices. At times you may find yourself in unpleasant situations, working with unpleasant people, and things can get downright ugly and messy. However, you can't make a mistake, because you are not in control—Jesus is! All things will eventually work out for good because we love the Lord. He lives in our hearts. Claim every promise in the Bible, and don't be afraid to speak your mind in Jesus' name."

About a month later Sonny and I were interviewed for a service provider's accreditation renewal. The surveyor asked, "Sonny, can you give me an example of your rights?"

Without hesitation Sonny blurted out, "Take a shower!"

"Yes, Sonny, you have every right to be kept clean," the kind woman responded.

It has all been in God's plan. In the light of the cross, I thanked Jesus for His peace of mind that is beyond human understanding. But how much better it will be to stand before the court of heaven with Jesus as our representative.

Deborah Sanders

When I'm Afraid

God is our refuge and strength, a very present help in trouble.
Therefore will not we fear, though the earth be removed, and though the
mountains be carried into the midst of the sea. Ps. 46:1, 2.

MOST OF THE PEOPLE I know love to listen to rain and thunderstorms. But I am not one of those people. I have never enjoyed the rumblings of thunder, nor do I favor the sharp electrical point of a lightning bolt. When I think of a thunderstorm two short stories come to mind.

The first happened when I was about 9 years old. My face is buried into the shoulder of my nanny (grandmother) as tears roll down my cheeks. "I don't like storms," I whine.

Patting my head, she soothes me with sweet words. "Jesus will take care of you," she murmurs. "He made the rain. He knows what He's doing." I knew that Jesus would never leave me, and I knew that He loved me. Why was I so afraid?

The second story that comes to mind is the one of Jesus sleeping among His friends in a fishing vessel as it bobs up and down on the Sea of Galilee. Of course, we know that after a while the gentle sway of the boat became violent as a storm approached. Panicked, and in fear for their lives, all the disciples were afraid. This is the part of the story that boggles my mind. They have the Son of God in the boat with them—and they still experience fear.

My husband once said, "God never intended for us to experience fear. It's a result of sin in this world." Although Jesus is in the boat with me (in my life), I still may experience moments of fear. That is until I put my eyes on Jesus and faith in God, and remember that He is there with me. For me the beautiful thing about this story is not that He can calm the storm, but that He is experiencing the storm right along with me. He's in the boat. He feels the gusts of the wind. He hears and sees the thunder and lightning. If we can just close our eyes and listen for His voice, we'll hear Him say, once again, "Peace, be still." We can have our own calm in the storm.

Here are some of the lyrics from a song that I believe God has gifted to me: "You promise to supply all of my needs. You know my dreams and my fears, but fear is not something you created. It's part of sin in this world. So I will stand true. I will be your faithful. I will be a Job for you. I will stand true" ("Stand True," from Joey Tolbert's CD *Parables*).

Joey Norwood Tolbert

Judgment Day

I believe in your commands; now teach me good judgment and knowledge.
Ps.119:66, NLT.

I LIVED WITH my adoptive parents in Gensen, a sleepy barrio in Mindanao, Philippines. It was a picture-perfect farming village where church, school, government, and sociocultural life were all wrapped in one. My father was the church elder, barrio leader, school board chairman, and farmer's association leader. Everyone I knew in Gensen belonged to the same church.

One evening after a dinner celebrating my sixth birthday, one of the guests, a church deacon, did not leave the house with the others. He and my parents talked all night, and I fell asleep without seeing him leave. They discussed a problem that could be solved only by my father holding a mini court trial in the church school auditorium.

Children were not allowed in the auditorium the day of the trial. However, we were playing outside and could hear voices in oratory tones testifying for or against someone. Earlier I saw the deacon who had talked all night with my parents walk into the auditorium with his two teenage boys. His wife walked behind them, accompanied by her frail mother and their 4-year-old daughter.

This was judgment day for the deacon's wife. She was accused of committing adultery. My father brought in a judge from the city, who appointed two learned persons in the law and church doctrine—one to represent the community and the other to be the wife's advocate. A church member testified that he witnessed the adulterous behavior. After his testimony the husband testified that he loved his wife and would forgive her if she would discontinue the affair.

Then the wife's advocate spoke for the accused. He asked that the church and the community forgive her for what she had done. He said that she admitted what she had done. However, he said, she was not sorry for it.

The judge's decision was final: the wife had made her own judgment and should not be compelled to do what she refused to do. She was guilty and would suffer the consequences. The trial was adjourned with all present stunned and some in tears.

We too have a choice to make before our judgment day. Have we prayed for good judgment and knowledge supplied through our Lord and Savior Jesus Christ?

Rose E. Constantino

Would You Believe?

I call to God; God will help me. At dusk, dawn, and noon I sigh deep sighs—he hears, he rescues. Ps. 55:16-19, Message.

AFTER WEEKS OF shopping I finally found the right size upright freezer for the space in my kitchen. On Saturday night I decided to ready the freezer for use. This entailed removing crating screws and discarding the wood base used in transportation. This meant placing the freezer on its side, definitely daunting to execute by myself, considering the weight of the freezer.

After studying the situation, and being very careful not to hurt my back, I was able to ease the freezer down low enough for the top end to rest on two chairs. That way I had easy access to the base from which the screws and two wood planks should be removed. Now, I am not mechanically inclined, and when the screws could not be loosened with a screwdriver I became worried. I didn't have a clue what to do, so I sat dejectedly and stared at the freezer.

It occurred to me to tell the Lord that this was a real problem, and ask for His help. After all, He knows my limitations in all things mechanical. I looked at the tool shelf in the kitchen cabinet and started rummaging around. Lo and behold, I saw a pair of pliers and realized that with pliers the bolts could be grasped and unscrewed. I set myself to the task and was very vocal in my gratitude to the Lord as two bolts with corresponding wood plank were successfully removed from the upper side of the bottom of the freezer.

Now to the opposite side of the freezer's bottom. Again, my earnest attempts to dislodge the screws proved unfruitful. It became clear that the freezer must be placed on its other side to make the screws more readily accessible. However, this required raising the freezer to the upright position and easing it down on the opposite side. All the while I had a running conversation in my mind that went something like this: *Lord, You know I am not overly strong, not young, and I'm alone in the house. My only recourse is Your strength.* Then I set to work, and everything was accomplished with no hitches.

Reflecting on this experience, I am amazed and grateful at how much God cares for us. He is interested in the most insignificant aspects of our lives, providing encouragement, insight, understanding, and whatever else is necessary for us to accomplish undertakings great and small.

Marion V. Clarke Martin

Plane Flight

Be strong and courageous; do not be afraid nor dismayed . . .
for there are more with us than with him. 2 Chron. 32:7, NKJV.

I SHALL ALWAYS remember the day I flew with the nuns.

My heart pounded as I readied for my first plane trip in several years. I harbored an intense fear of flying that originated with my inaugural flight in a private plane commandeered by a show-off young pilot. I vowed then never again to leave the ground. Now I faced an unknown future leaving California by plane to live on the East Coast. Everything stressed me! Then God worked one of His amazing coincidences that come as a result of desperate prayer.

Sister Ann and I had met at a seminar series in Pasadena, California. A nun from a strict order, she now basked in the light of Vatican II changes. "A real breath of air" she called it.

When I expressed my flying fear to Ann, she told me that she and the sisters at the convent would soon be attending a conference in Philadelphia. We discovered we had reservations on the same plane. It was an incredible coincidence. I would be flying not only with a friend but with more than a dozen nuns.

They prayed for me on the day of the flight, and surrounded me like an angelic army as we boarded the plane. Ann was the youngest of the group, while some of the nuns were quite elderly. I remember Sister Mary in particular. Her wrinkled face glowed with the love of Jesus as she took my arm and guided me to the plane's entrance. Ann sat next to me, but not long after we took off, Sister Mary told one of the flight attendants about my fear. She soon returned to tell me that one of the attendants had called in sick. Would I like to take her place? "You'll forget your fear, I promise," she said. So I spent the five-hour trip waiting on passengers and never once felt frightened. God answered our united prayers.

I still remember the calming presence of the happy faces of the nuns. They became my sisters that day. We Christians belong to a big family made up of many ethnicities, practices, traditions, and histories. But One bonds us together, and that is Christ. In interacting with other Christians, we want to avoid ecclesiastical egotism, for no religion owns God. We do not worship an organization, but Christ. He should be first in any contact with other Christians.

Ella Rydzewski

Our Down-to-Earth God

Delight thyself also in the Lord: and he shall give thee
the desires of thine heart. Ps. 37:4.

IN THE COURSE OF just one week God not only answered my prayer but also showed me that He loves and cares for me even in the minutest aspects of my life.

My 17-year-old son was getting ready for his high school banquet, and wanted to get a new shirt. He went shopping with his friends and in a very expensive store found a brand-name shirt that he liked very much. It cost $80, and he bought it. When he came home and showed me the shirt, telling me how much he'd paid for it, I was surprised. I explained that expensive stores sell high-priced items and told him that he would definitely get much more for his money in a less expensive store. So we decided to return the costly shirt and see if he could get one that he liked for less money.

The following day he asked me to go shopping with him. Habitually we pray before starting the car. That day we prayed that God would help us find an inexpensive shirt. In the very first store we met a friendly salesclerk who helped us find a shirt that was on sale. Since they were having a good sale, my son picked up another shirt and a couple of ties. When we went to the counter to pay for the things he'd selected, we were pleasantly surprised to see the salesclerk deduct an extra 15 percent off on each of the items. My son was elated when he found out that for $78 he got two shirts and two matching ties!

This incident strengthened our faith. When we trust in God, He blesses us much more than we can ever expect.

A few days later I went to a store. After paying for my items by credit card, I took my two bags and was about to leave when the woman standing next to me reminded me that I had left my credit card wallet on the candy rack. I was so thankful she told me this! If I'd forgotten it, it would have been easy for anyone to walk away with that wallet, which held all my credit cards, including my bank card. I would have been devastated. My God was so kind to make sure that an honest person was standing right next to me. I came home rejoicing with a grateful heart. I praise God every day for the many ways in which He shows His love for us.

Let us each rejoice as we think about the beautiful promise in today's text.

Stella Thomas

The Children Speak

Verily I say unto you, Inasmuch as ye have done it unto one of the least of these my brethren, ye have done it unto me. Matt. 25:40.

IT WAS THE LAST DAY of the school year, and my volunteer work with the first grade was finished too. Children were busy saying goodbye and were so proud of the letters they'd written to me with pictures drawn from stories and geography we had talked about. Kaitlen, sitting close to me, asked, "Will you come to second grade next year?" I calmly said no, I always stayed with the first grade. So she called to the teacher, "Mrs. Abramson, can I stay in first grade with Mrs. Hardin next year?" Then there was a murmur through the class of "Me too."

The teachers asked if I would be back. I thought to myself, *I am getting tired.* My daughter, Janna, had said to me, "Mother, you really do not have to do that if you don't want to." She was right. But then I remembered the new letters and especially one from Kimberly that said, "You have really made me feel special." Surely I could share my time with them again.

Now the new school year has started, and again I and my books are found back in my chair surrounded by children sitting on the floor. They are a delightful new class. Miss Jennifer introduced me to a little Russian boy who was adopted at age 3. He looked up at me and said solemnly, "I have to be a composer, because I am Russian." Always someone or something new.

One day as I presented a book from England to read to them, I talked a bit about that country. Showing them a picture of the queen, I asked, "And who is our ruler?" Therese said quietly, "God is our ruler." Sharon repeated this, and Thomas, sitting next to her, said, "I was going to say that." I quietly assured them that God is the ruler over us all. They had been told they could talk about religion, but this was not the place. Must children leave their God outside the public classroom? I was glad I was there to confirm their thoughts that day.

I can share my time, my information, my caring, and my love for them. Remember, Jesus proclaimed that as we do to one another it is as if it were for Jesus Himself. And these students are His own precious children. I pray that God will help me and bless me as I am here in the public school classroom with these little ones.

Dessa Weisz Hardin

Answered Prayers

In every thing by prayer and supplication with thanksgiving let your requests be made known unto God. Phil. 4:6.

I WAS IN MY SECOND year of the college teaching program when my sister went to the hospital, on my birthday, to have a baby. I had no way to go be with her. Besides, I had classes all day. The call came that night. A beautiful baby girl, Linda Karen, was born one hour and 19 minutes after my birthday. We were happy that all went well, and I could hardly wait to see her.

Nine days later I got to go to my sister and husband's home to see my new niece. I was just coming for the weekend, but when I arrived I discovered that Priscilla was very sick. She'd had bronchitis that went into pneumonia. I kept her and Linda separated, Priscilla in the bedroom and Linda in the living room. I changed clothes and took care of the baby.

It was hard on Priscilla because she wanted to breastfeed Linda, but couldn't do it now for the baby would get sick. My sister had the baby on a three-hour schedule, so I had to make formula—which I'd never done. Priscilla told me how, and Martin went to the store to get what I needed.

After I took care of Linda, I would change clothes and take care of Priscilla. If either of them wanted anything when I was busy with the other, they just had to wait. Martin helped with Baby Linda after he got home from work.

I took the next week off from school. I really prayed for my sister because she was so sick. I thought we were going to have to take her to the hospital, but then her fever broke. I was so thankful to the Lord.

One night while I was feeding Linda, she began to hiccup. I didn't know that babies sometimes have hiccups, and I didn't know what to do. When I was 15, I'd taken care of a 6-week-old baby but hadn't had this problem. Linda kept it up so long that I became very worried. At last I prayed that God would have her stop, and just like that, He did! She didn't have any more hiccups while I was there. I told God how very thankful I was to Him for stopping them.

I am so glad we have a loving Father to whom we can take our problems. As we were told long ago: "[Cast] all your care upon him; for he careth for you" (1 Peter 5:7).

Anne Elaine Nelson

My Mother's Garden

Therefore we do not lose heart. Though outwardly we are wasting away, yet inwardly we are being renewed day by day. For our light and momentary troubles are achieving for us an eternal glory that far outweighs them all. So we fix our eyes not on what is seen, but on what is unseen, since what is seen is temporary, but what is unseen is eternal. 2 Cor. 4:16-18, NIV.

For we know that if the earthly tent we live in is destroyed, we have a building from God, an eternal house in heaven, not built by human hands. 2 Cor. 5:1, NIV.

WHEN SHE WORKS IN THE GARDEN, the soul of a girl is at play. However, she is no longer a girl. And though Parkinson's disease has claimed her body, her soul remembers we were born in a garden. And through the Garden of Gethsemane we shall all once more return to the garden prepared for us.

Berries, flowers, dill, tomatoes—she slowly pulls the weeds between. Tending our spiritual garden, daily the Spirit of God grows the inner person even though the outer withers away. Somehow the problems that come today will achieve an eternal glory. Yesterday, today, all I can see and feel is the frustration and disappointment of something gone wrong. But we are invited to see what is invisible and enduring. It is paradoxical that what one sees, the here and now, is temporary. Sometimes the present seems like it is all there is and that it will last forever. But the tangible and very real experience of problems with money and relationships, the clutch of sickness and grief of death—all the ugly sores of sin are time-limited. They will end. They will disappear. The good that endures is yet to be seen. "Now we see only a reflection as in a mirror; then we shall see face to face. Now I know in part; then I shall know fully, even as I am fully known" (1 Cor. 13:12, NIV).

In the meantime, God's Spirit is busy growing fruit in our garden; to grow fruit, the Spirit must also pull weeds. The Spirit understands if we twinge or cry when a stubborn root is pulled. The same Spirit who is actively at work is a comfort whatever our case may be. Our challenges are not too big for God. Even if imperceptible now, God is tenaciously working out these passing troubles into a breathtaking, beautiful garden that will last forever. So be of good courage today.

Lisa M. Beardsley-Hardy

My Turn

They will call on My name, and I will answer them. I will say, "This is My people"; and each one will say, "The Lord is my God." Zech. 13:9, NKJV.

I STOOD AT THE kitchen sink murmuring to a close friend, "I'd love to help with that ministry, but what would I do with the boys?"

"Yes," she replied with her usual quick candor, "now our focus is our children, but someday our turn will come." Her prophetic words joined my catalog of memorable conversations. More than 20 years later, it's my turn.

"Do you remember David?" I ask the women in the shelter Bible study group.

"Yeah, didn't he get swallowed by a big fish?" I smile, explain, and return to the lesson.

"What's the Second Coming?" I direct them to a page number in the Bibles we bring.

Betsy interrupts, "Hey, is Jesus the same as Christ?" My mind stalls. How can these women have these questions? We live in a city filled with churches. We live in the Bible Belt!

I sit on a turquoise, institutional-style plastic chair flanked on my left by Cassie, my friend from church, and on my right by a young mother of two, seven months pregnant. She'll stay until her baby is born so she'll have access to the hospital and medical treatment.

Across the blond Formica-topped commercial table sit three women. Betsy grew up in foster homes, and the "mother" who treated her the most kindly was a sincere believer in Wicca. Betsy struggles as a single mom, and sometimes her 2-year-old son cowers when she moves quickly. Jessica had two children by a man she never married. When they had trouble, he took the children and moved nearly 1,000 miles away. Emotionally devastated, she seeks a court injunction for their return. Tracy is estranged from her husband, and her son just died from an overdose. These women are the ones who come voluntarily each week to study about the unknown God of love. Others do not come during their hour of free time.

Cassie and I enter the locked doors for our weekly Bible study only after the receptionist responds to our electronic request for entrance. The offices and the hallway cradle hardness: weary women, angered and oppressed. Yes, this is a shelter for homeless women. It is my turn.

No, really, it is Jesus' turn to say, "This is My people."

Verlyne Starr

The Avenger

Like as a father pitieth his children,
so the Lord pitieth them that fear him. Ps. 103:13.

IT WAS 18 MONTHS after Ashika died that we decided to get another dog. From the first time I saw Avenger—the name a little boy at the veterinarian's gave to our puppy—I discovered he was very playful. The little puppy was brought to my office in a cardboard carton. All day long, while waiting to be chauffeur-driven to his new home, he was very busy in and out of the box.

Ever since his arrival Avenger has kept *us* busy. Thinking that he needed a play-mate, we got another little puppy. As though he was jealous of the younger pup, Avenger would playfully bite the newcomer. Unfortunately, he was inflicting little wounds on the dog's head and face.

Avenger is guilty of little naughty deeds. The little containers in which we feed him are often bitten to pieces. I change a pair of hose almost every day as he play-fully jumps on me whenever I arrive home. The doormat and the washing machine cover were stripped to pieces. Yard slippers were chewed up. Plants were destroyed. Recently he has been pulling every piece of clothes within his reach from off the clothesline. He takes them to make his bed. At one time the same pieces of clothing had to be washed three times three days in succession. We resorted to punishing him whenever he pulled the clothes off the line with the hope that this bad habit would be curbed, but to no avail. Every time clothing is hung out on the clothesline for drying, they must be rewashed. Now whenever he sees me walking toward him, he curls up in a corner, anticipating a scolding.

Little Avenger reminds me of my repeated misdeeds, and the way Jesus is so patient with me. Through His Word He does scold me, yet I persist in my naughty ways. Much like my little puppy, I commit the same sins again and again. But my Jesus bears with me, and I am forgiven when I so request. But once again, I fall back into my old sinful way. "I do not understand what I do. For what I want to do I do not do, but what I hate I do. And if I do what I do not want to do, I agree that the law is good. As it is, it is no longer I myself who do it, but it is sin living in me" (Rom. 7:15-17, NIV). I am so glad that I am not beaten for every misdeed, but that my Jesus loves me unconditionally.

Ruby H. Enniss-Alleyne

From Unequally to Equally Yoked

Trust in the Lord with all thine heart; and lean not unto thine own understanding. In all thy ways acknowledge him, and he shall direct thy paths. Prov. 3:5, 6.

EACH TIME SOMETHING happened to our family I felt anew that God was trying to tell me something. Cheryl sensed that I was worried and held me tightly, afraid of losing her brother. "Mom, is Dad on his way?" she asked. I nodded. "Will Kenneth die because he's premature?" I hugged her, not knowing what to say. Carl arrived just in time to see the doctor emerge from the operating room to inform us that Baby Kenneth was doing fine but would be held over for observation. We breathed a collective sigh of relief. Was this a test from God?

The feeling that I was not living within God's will kept nagging at me. Although Carl never interfered with my raising the kids as Christians, it bothered me that he would not join us. Why had I agreed to his insistence on marrying me? Did I love him too much to act on my belief that a couple should be equally yoked? Love was powerful. It did not matter to me that Carl was uneducated, older than I was, a spoiled only child, and most of all religiously different. I ignored all that and married him anyway. And I kept praying for his conversion.

One day I headed out in torrential rain to pick up a vacuum cleaner. The roads were slippery, and visibility was poor. The last thing I remember was a crash and the steering wheel and dashboard crushed against my stomach. I drifted off and awoke in an emergency room to hear that my pancreas was smashed. My husband was needed to sign consent for immediate surgery.

Someone was sent to find him. It seemed like only seconds before Carl appeared at my side, holding my hands and telling me it would be OK. The doctor was ready to wheel me into surgery, but Carl insisted he had something to say. Carl declared that if I were saved, he would give his life to the Lord. He held on to the surgeon's hands and prayed for those hands.

The surgery went well. When the doctor visited me in recovery, the first thing he asked was "How is your husband?" Carl had had a great impact on him. I praised God. Carl began reading several of my Bible lessons and studying the Word. He attended baptismal classes, and was baptized on my birthday, immediately following my recovery. With steadfast prayer and good example, those around us can recognize the beauty of God and turn to the Lord.

Andrea Thompson

The Train to Nowhere

In your unfailing love you will lead the people you have redeemed. In your strength you will guide them to your holy dwelling. Ex. 15:13, NIV.

WE WERE ON THE second Pathfinder (a church-sponsored adolescent group) mission trip to New Orleans to help rebuild after Hurricane Katrina. We had two major projects to complete in one week, plus cleanup at the conference center. I was the team's "mom" for the trip. All too soon it was 5:45 a.m., the final wake-up call. A quick breakfast and devotional led to last-minute packing, cleanup, and loading the vehicles. Now off to the airport. We were going home.

Here the challenges began. If I'd known what the day would bring, I would have stayed in bed! Yet I knew my heavenly Father was taking care of all the details—so why was I worrying so much?

No matter what our tickets said or what we did, our whole group could not get on the same plane. Prayer was quickly said, asking that the leaders would know what to do. We decided to divide the group, for a young girl needed one of our seats to get home immediately or her father would be held in contempt of court. Our smaller group of seven remained intact. We would take the next plane. Parents were informed each step of the way, and about each problem.

After the first plane left, we approached the ticket counter. They said if we were willing to fly to Houston, Texas, we could catch a flight to Denver. But upon arrival at Houston we learned there were no direct flights available. The only way to Denver was to fly to Las Vegas.

We'd all hung tight until now. But now the plane had mechanical problems, and no departure time was posted. I reminded us all that our Father was in control. He sometimes helps us push the extent of our abilities so that we can exercise our faith. If we never push the envelope, how do we know what the package can hold? Each Pathfinder looked at me for a few moments then said, "I can handle this."

At that airport is a train that goes round and round, but basically nowhere. With nothing to do but wait, several of our group boarded the train. They went nowhere. And nowhere is where we will all go if we do not allow the Father to lead us. This world is on the track to nowhere. Let us each join the Father on the train that is going somewhere: heaven.

Cathy Kissner

Scars

Reach your finger here, and look at My hands; and reach your hand here, and put it into My side. John 20:27, NKJV.

SCARS ARE MARKS that last for a lifetime. I have many of them imprinted on my body—cuts, scrapes, surgeries, dog bites, and many others.

When I think about any one of my scars, almost instantly I remember the incident when it was acquired. However, if it were possible, I wouldn't have any of them, since none are on my body because of my own will. And some caused me discomfort, pain, tears, and suffering.

But . . . some scars are necessary.

In 2009 I underwent a kidney transplant. It's not a simple thing to receive an organ. The donor, in addition to being special, must be compatible with my blood and other matching characteristics. And they must be willing to donate one of their kidneys!

My sister, in an act of bravery and courage, willingly performed that sacrifice. And thanks to the grandioso love of Christ, the surgery was a success.

Today both my sister and I carry scars on our bodies. Mine reminds me that through the gesture of someone who loves me, I was liberated from spending the rest of my life on a hemodialysis machine. My sister's scar reminds her of her gesture of donation and surrender.

Christ, donor of life and liberty, offered Himself in an incomparably larger way. He did not give Himself partially, but gave Himself entirely, without reservation, showing unconditional love.

The Bible says that someone *may* give their life for a just and loving person of good character. But the fact is that Christ died for us while we were still sinners.

He gave Himself! His body is replete with scars caused by His love for both you and me. His surrender brought us life, liberating us forever from the machine of sin.

The scars upon Christ's body will prove forever the extent of His great and immeasurable love! It is my prayer that I may not only be touched by this gesture, but position myself always, confidently, and obediently, at His side. How do we say Thank You to our Father and others, such as my sister, who have done so much for us?

Jussara Alves

A Foretaste of Heaven

And every creature which is in heaven and on the earth and under the earth
and such as are in the sea, and all that are in them, I heard saying:
"Blessing and honor and glory and power be to Him who sits on the throne,
and to the Lamb, forever and ever!" Rev. 5:13, NKJV.

WE WERE SO EXCITED. My husband and I were flying to England for the high
school graduation of one of our granddaughters. I cooked for weeks, preparing
some of their favorite foods to take along. I shopped for days, finding some clothes
my grandson particularly wanted.

Finally the day came. We landed at Heathrow Airport, cleared customs, and
went to pick up our luggage. But my luggage was not there. Fortunately, the next
day the airport called, and my son went to get the "found" suitcase. Then our holiday really began.

My granddaughter's graduation was as beautiful as the roses growing in the
well-kept campus gardens. JJ received several awards, confirming something I already knew—JJ was brilliant. Tears came to my eyes when our 12-year-old grandson sang "You Raise Me Up." I knew what others didn't. Jordan had a high fever,
but he felt he had to sing for his older sister.

We visited Windsor Castle, one of the queen's many residences. The castle was
very close to my son's home, and one day we joined the crowds camped out on
both sides of the street to see the queen, who was in residence that week. We saw
the changing of the guards, and the queen—a petite woman in a smart green outfit.
She waved at us from her royal carriage.

Telling my friends and family about this special trip, I saw some comparisons
between it and another one we're planning: being in heaven with our heavenly family. I thought of the beauty of the heavenly grounds. They'll need no watering to
maintain their lushness. I remembered how distressed I felt when I lost my suitcase.
But that won't happen when I arrive in heaven, for the only thing I'll take with me is
my character. I long to hear the beautiful singing, and it will be even more glorious
when the angels join us. I thought of Jordan's illness, which could never happen in
heaven (see Rev. 21:4). I thought how wonderful it had been to see the queen, but
how much more magnificent it will be to live with our King forever.

Heaven is a wonderful place. I must be there. Will you?

Kay Sinclair

God Is Only a Prayer Away

Stand firm and you will see the deliverance
the Lord will bring you today. Ex. 14:13, NIV.

OUR FAMILY WILL NEVER forget June 8, 1988. I was a young mother of two, ages 3 and 5, and we were awaiting the return of their daddy and my husband, who had been attending church meetings in Bangalore. It was Friday evening. I was busy with Sabbath preparation. Time passed, and he had not arrived home. Finally about 9:00 p.m. we saw him at the door—in torn and wrinkled clothes. Stunned at the sight, I stood motionless, staring at him with mouth wide open. "Valsa, open the door!" he cried. It brought me back to myself, and I ran to do so.

He then told us of the terrifying train accident at Quilon, where Ashtamudi, the biggest of eight lakes, meet. My husband and the church section president were chatting in the train when they felt an unusual jerk. Then before they knew what was happening, they found themselves immersed in the water that had rushed through the train windows when it derailed and fell into the lake. People were trapped inside like rats. For 45 minutes my husband hung on to a fan yelling and praying for God to save him. How true is the saying "God is only a prayer away." At last some men fishing nearby ran to the rescue, broke the train window bars, and dragged him out.

He was wonder-struck to see the hundreds of dead on the shore. Most of those had drowned in the fully submerged cars. Among the very few survivors were my husband and the church section president. The hands of the omnipotent God held them safe while 1,500 died on that spot. Newspapers and television portrayed the horrible accident. As God said: "When thou passest through the waters, I will be with thee; and through the rivers, they shall not overflow thee" (Isaiah 43:2).

God preserved the life of my husband to live and work for Him. Twenty-four long years later I still recall that terrible day, and when I do I sing the song that portrays God as being so good and so strong and mighty that there is nothing He cannot do. That same God lives today and is able to save anywhere.

My friends, if He could do this miracle for us, don't you think He is kind enough to do that for you as well? Yes . . . yes . . . yes!

Valsa Edison

God, Sudoku, and Creation

Then God saw everything that He had made, and indeed it was very good. So the evening and the morning were the sixth day. Gen. 1:31, NKJV.

ONE OF MY HOBBIES is doing puzzles, especially Sudoku. When my husband was very ill, dying from cancer, I sometimes went without sleep for three to four days and nights. During those times, when possible, I spent the time doing Sudoku. I was never good in math; it was my poorest subject. But this puzzle is an enjoyable challenge to me. I have a pocket puzzle that I take whenever I have to wait: at a doctor's office, the hairdresser's, at any type of appointment where I must wait for my turn to come. In fact, I am happy to get the time to do these puzzles since there is no time otherwise. I now do all the work my husband used to do as well as the work I already did. It is impossible, but somehow, with the Lord's help, I manage.

One day while doing my puzzles, I thought about the enjoyment I get from them—especially when I get them almost right or even all right—once in a while. And then I began to think about how much fun God, Jesus, and the Holy Spirit must have had creating our world and all the creatures, as well as humans. I am sure Adam had fun naming the animals, but not as much fun as God and Jesus had making them, and the birds and fish, too. It's fun for us to see all the various creatures they made, but I would love to have been a little mouse in the corner while they were doing it. As I write, it's springtime, and looking out the window, I see lilacs, dogwoods, redbud trees, ornamental cherries, apple trees, forsythia—and I could go on and on. Anyone who has sewn, crocheted, painted pictures, or even taken pictures or made pottery or other crafts will acknowledge what I am saying. Creation is fun.

We all get our creativity from the Lord. All our talents come from Him, for us to develop and use for Him and for others. And we all enjoy learning and making something that we've never done before. We take pride in our work, and I know that God and Jesus took pride in their work. When we look at snowflakes and realize that all are original with no two alike, it is amazing to me how one could think they just happened without a master designer. That is beyond my imagination! Praise God for His love in providing such a marvelous creation!

Loraine F. Sweetland

The Bread That Came From Heaven

Then he looked, and there by his head was a cake baked on coals, and a jar of water. So he ate and drank, and lay down again. 1 Kings 19:6, NKJV.

WE WERE THE first residents of the Alvorada I neighborhood, in Manaus, Amazonas. My parents received land from the government, and my father built a shack on Eighth Street. He said, "It was a funny house. It didn't have walls or anything." We all lived together: my aunt Maria, my parents, and my four sisters. I was only 4 years old, but I still remember.

One day my father arrived home from work. It was Friday, the day of preparation, and we children had been anxiously waiting. You see, we had not had our usual meals that day, so our mother calmed us down by telling us that our father would soon arrive with a snack. Normally he also brought lunch and food for the next day. However, when Dad got home, he brought the news that the day had been bad. He was a boatman who helped people cross from one side of the Rio Negro to the other, and sold snacks to the passengers. But as it had rained a lot that day, he had not had any customers. He added that the snack he sold "swam," his way of saying it went bad. With no money and no lunch, we children became sad as well as hungry.

But Mom never lost faith and she gathered the family and held evening worship as usual. Shortly afterward was our bedtime. But as we were preparing to go to bed, someone knocked on the door. A car had stopped in front of the shack and someone got out, carrying a box. Without any explanation, the man left the box at our front door. It held enough food to feed our family for several days!

Our hearts overflowed with joy, and our entire family knelt down and thanked God for the miracle He had performed. Just as God fed Elijah in the desert, God had fed His children—literally. He sent us what we needed. In turn, all He desired is that we not lose our faith. Even before we ask, He is providing what we need because He knows us very well.

We children are grown now, but we have not forgotten the miracle that occurred in our childhood. Joel tells us, "Tell your children about it, let your children tell their children, and their children another generation" (Joel 1:3, NKJV). So today we all tell our children, who will tell other generations. And God's name will be exalted forever and ever.

Ester Figueiredo Araujo

Dream, College Test: Coincidence?

For God may speak in one way, or in another, yet man does not perceive it. In a dream, in a vision of the night, when deep sleep falls upon men, while slumbering on their beds, then He opens the ears of men, and seals their instruction. In order to turn man from his deed, and conceal pride from man. Job 33:14-17, NKJV.

IT WAS FINALS time at college where I was finishing my third year, and I had accumulated a lot of material to study. In addition, to pay for my studies and other expenses I worked eight hours a day as a public servant of the state judiciary. My parents supplied all my needs at home, but I was on my own for tuition. Thus, at this time of year, despite having studied diligently since the beginning of the semester, I was very tired and stressed.

I knew that one particular test would be very difficult as the professor was very strict. I'd not been able to get off work the day before that test (I took morning classes and worked until 7:00 p.m.), so I was exhausted and distressed. It was almost 8:00 when I got home that night, and I thought, *Only by God can I do this test.* Weakness and frustration invaded my soul because I had not been able to review all the content I knew would be on it.

I reviewed the material until after 11:00, then went to bed. I woke up at 4:00 a.m. to review some more, but was not able to study all of it. Still, God had given me a dream in which I saw a sheet of paper containing four questions; the last one caught my attention. I remembered that question (even today I remember it). When I woke up, I opened my notebook and found the material that answered that question.

When I arrived at the college I started talking with two classmates before the test began. We reviewed the material, and I told them about my dream. Soon after, we were handed the test. When I looked at my paper, I could not believe it: it had four questions, and the last question was exactly as I had dreamed. When I left the classroom, I was surprised by the two classmates who told me, "If you had not told us before going into the test, I never would have believed you or your dream." I did very well in the final, received an excellent grade, and, above all, could see the goodness and mercy of God acting in my life and making me testify of Him.

What do you think about handing everything over to Him now?

Marcela Bittencourt Brey

Children's Games

Then the kingdom of heaven shall be likened to ten virgins who took their lamps and went out to meet the bridegroom. Matt. 25:1, NKJV.

GOD HAS GIVEN ME the privilege of working with children. I recognize it as a great responsibility. Although it is sometimes stressful, it is also fun, as children express themselves spontaneously. I feel that I have already heard everything!

Among the many "pearls" the children have offered are some I will never forget. On one occasion three little boys, approximately 3 years old, were trading ideas, wanting to start a game. Suddenly one of them said, "I'm going to be the Father!"

The second quickly shouted, "I'm the Son!"

To my great surprise, the third instantly said, "I'm the Spirit!"

I confess that I get emotional, even today, when I think of the magnitude of that childlike conversation. So that a spiritual life may be victorious, the presence of God in His fullness is indispensable: Father, Son, and Holy Spirit. How many times we forget that He is triune! We pray to the Father in the name of the Son, but we almost always forget the Holy Spirit. Certainly this does not please God. When we do so, we are missing a part of the trinity, missing a part of God.

In the parable of the 10 virgins, five remained outside. When taking up their lamps, they did not take enough oil. Later, crying out, "Lord, Lord, open the door," they forgot the third part of the Trinity and received the harsh response, "I do not know you" (Matt. 25:12). This is because they lacked oil, which symbolizes the Holy Spirit. How will the Lord save those who do not know Him, those who ignore the Holy Spirit? The Spirit is the part of the Trinity that convicts us of sin, justice, and judgment in the last days.

I praise God for the privilege of knowing those three children, and for the moment that so simply taught me that the Holy Spirit must be present. The game would not have been right if it had lacked the Spirit. One child would be left out; or rather, the game would have lacked Someone. It would not have worked!

Today I always pray to the Father, in the name of the Son, so that the Holy Spirit of God may move in me. Dear sister, I hope that this will be your prayer from here on as well.

Gilsana Souza Condé

God Still Speaks to Us

After this, the word of the Lord came to Abram in a vision: "Do not be afraid, Abram. I am your shield, your very great reward." Gen. 15:1, NIV.

IT WAS A BEAUTIFUL Sunday morning. After I had my personal worship, I decided to go to the beach. I took a shower, ate something, and caught a bus to the beach. When I got there, I contemplated the beauty of God's creation. After some hours I began to feel uncomfortable and anxious, feeling as though I should go home. At first I ignored this feeling, but finally I decided to go.

When I got to the bus stop again, I felt propelled—this time to go to an ATM to take out some money. I did not understand the reason for any of this, but I went to a supermarket, got the money, and headed home.

When I got home, I had a shock. My grandmother had a bandage on her hand. I asked her what had happened, and she said, "I cut my hand while seasoning the meat." Removing the bandage, I saw that the cut had perforated her vein. This would demand some stitches. I cleaned her cut and took a quick shower.

Then with the money I had been prompted to withdraw, I took my grandmother in a cab and headed to the hospital. We had to change the bandages three times on the way, for the cut had not stopped bleeding. When we got there, I was informed that the hospital was without a surgeon, so we took another cab to another hospital. There I was told that its surgeon was on holiday. I prayed to God, asking what I should do and imploring Him to make the cut stop bleeding. I decided to go home, but on the way I prayed for God to enlighten me. And He did it! I called a friend who is a nurse and asked for some instructions as to what should be done. She kindly instructed me. When we got home, the cut had stopped bleeding, and I did what my friend had told me to do. Finally, my grandmother was OK.

After things settled down, I understood why God had asked me to go home and also to withdraw some money. If the Lord had not talked to me, my grandmother could have had a much more serious problem.

Isn't it marvelous when we allow God to be in control of our lives? He speaks to us, He tells us not to worry but just to turn to Him, and He will be our shield and our reward.

Carmen Virgínia dos Santos Paulo

The Lord Is Faithful

If thou turn away thy foot from the sabbath,
from doing thy pleasure on my holy day; and call the sabbath a delight . . . :
then shalt thou delight thyself in the Lord. Isa. 58:13, 14.

I HAD JUST GRADUATED from college and was faced with the challenge of starting my career in a highly competitive world. The odds of my joining the company I was most interested in were not reassuring, for 57,567 candidates were vying for 10 positions.

After six months of testing, I found myself among the remaining 15 candidates. I was left with only a personal interview with the director and a psychologist. Near the end of my interview the director said, "Congratulations! I think we are going to work together." The psychologist, however, had not finished. She asked, "What do your parents do?"

I replied, "My dad is a pastor, and my mom is a psychologist." She asked what church, and when I told her, she commented, "Isn't that the church that doesn't do anything on Saturdays?" I explained that the Sabbath is a different and special day in which to do God's work and do good for others. They looked at each other and said, "Let's wait for the results."

Three days later the psychologist called me and asked if I would participate in company meetings, maybe once a year, on a Saturday. I replied that I would be available at any time, including Sundays and holidays, but not on the Sabbath. The result came by e-mail: "Thank you for participating in this process. You did very well, but we had to choose another candidate."

I cried a lot and asked my dad, "Why did the Lord let me pursue this job for six months if He knew there would be this problem with the Sabbath?" My dad said, "Daughter, don't ask 'why.' Ask 'for what.' Your motive was very noble. You were not approved because you chose to be faithful in keeping the Sabbath—not for lack of capability. The Lord will provide."

Three months later I was invited for an interview with an American company. After this interview the vice president told me she had originally chosen another person for the position, but now felt I should be hired instead. I started off as a coordinator, was soon promoted to a manager, and soon after that to a director. Today I am successful and have worked in more than a dozen exciting countries; but most important, I have learned that the ways of the Lord are always better than ours—all we need is to trust. "Weeping may endure for a night, but joy cometh in the morning" (Ps. 30:5).

Liliane Calcidoni Kafler

And the Door Was Shut

Watch therefore, for you know neither the day nor the hour in which the Son of Man is coming. Matt. 25:13, NKJV.

I HAD WAITED for a long time for a public course for professors in my area and in my city, and finally the course opened, just as I had hoped.

I signed up, and the day of the theoretical exam arrived. I woke up early and drove to the university to take the test. Already knowing where it was located and where I should be at 7:45 a.m., I arrived with anticipation. A large group of us waited in the designated room.

The people responsible to randomly select the essay topic arrived. After the topic was chosen, we were told that we had an hour to study, and then must return to the classroom at 9:17. My friend, who was also taking the course, had brought an article that was related to the topic. It was in her notebook in her car, which was parked in front of the building, so we went to her car to get it. We stayed at the car, studying. After a little while I asked the time, since I had no watch. She told me that she had set the alarm on her watch.

Before the alarm went off, we walked back to the classroom. However, when we arrived at the door, the two people responsible for giving the test were leaving, and we were not allowed to go into the classroom. "We said to be here at 9:17, and by our watches, you are two minutes late!"

Immediately the parable of the 10 virgins came to my mind. I had been inside the classroom, I had arrived early, and now I could not take the course that I had wanted so much. I lost the chance to improve my salary and stability in my career as a professor in a public school.

However, I began to imagine how terrible it would be if Christ returned and I were not ready. I would lose far more than just a career and stability. Rather, my loss would be permanent, as I would lose the opportunity to see Jesus, my friends, or my daughter, who is already resting in the Lord. I would lose my eternal life.

I want to be alert and let nothing delay or impede me from being ready for the best and biggest event in the universe, Christ's second coming. Don't you want to be ready too?

Aucely Corrêa Fernandes Chagas

Promised to God

Wait on the Lord; be of good courage, and He shall strengthen your heart; wait, I say, on the Lord! Ps. 27:14, NKJV.

I HAD THE PRIVILEGE of being born into a Christian home. My father was faithful to God in everything. Even while facing financial difficulties to sustain the family, he sought always to maintain a life in communion with God. He preached and gave Bible studies, trusting in God's promises. But he never imagined that after two months of life I would be diagnosed with an incurable disease. So he knew that he would lose his little Débora before one year of life.

After many sleepless nights, and spending everything he had, he was left with no hope. The doctors said so. He waited only on God for a grand miracle.

Then a sister at church offered my father a particular tea to give me. She said that it would help me. That night Father decided that before giving me that tea, he would pray the following prayer: "O God, if it is according to Your will that my daughter grows and becomes God's servant, a messenger of Your Word, someone who pleases the heavenly Father and her earthly parents, then may this tea cure her. Otherwise may tonight be her last night alive."

Then he spent the longest night of his life, anxious to see his little girl the next day. At sunrise before going to check on me, he prayed, "O God, I thank You if my daughter is alive, because I know You have great plans and dreams for her life. And if she is dead, I also thank You, because You know what is best." Then he went to my room and saw that I was awake and smiling. He shouted for my mother, "God cured our daughter!" From that day on, I was not taken to the doctors again. God had cured me.

I grew up with the desire to be a great messenger of God. Today I achieve my dreams by working as a missionary for Jesus in the Amazon. As I go out with my pastor-husband, I seek to encourage the church members to maintain a life of communion with God. Everything I am and have I owe to my heavenly Father and my father who one day pleaded to God for my life.

My dear friend, most of us can know that our earthly fathers love us, but we all can know that our heavenly Father always loves us and will always do what is best for us. Just trust and surrender yourself into the arms of our loving heavenly Father.

Débora de Souza

Fragile Beginnings

I praise you because of the wonderful way you created me.
Everything you do is marvelous! Of this I have no doubt.
Nothing about me is hidden from you! Ps. 139:14, 15, CEV.

THE DAYS HAD become very anxious ones for our family, for my son, Daryl, and his wife, Julianne, were living with the fear of losing their unborn son. How my heart longed to ease their pain, but any comfort seemed futile as the reports shattered hopes. I pleaded with God for strength to support us all in this time of crisis; I embraced the words "Christ gives me the strength to face anything" (Phil. 4:13, CEV).

The hours dragged by that June 17, 2005. Decisions had been made to deliver the baby when the medication given would be most effective. But he was only at 26 weeks gestation.

The moment came when Julianne was taken from her hospital room, my son at her side. The two "nanas" remained. We stared into space, unable to express the thoughts in our hearts, but each with silent prayer to God above whose heart is touched by our every sorrow.

Kyle was delivered alive, but very fragile. We saw him for just a few moments. We were filled with emotion. Weighing only 20 ounces (570 grams), his tiny body was only the length of a pen. He was cared for within a humid crib, his life supported by machines. It was a critical and trying time, especially for his parents. There were anxious days and disturbing phone calls. Then the dreaded news came that Kyle's bowel had burst, and emergency surgery was needed. The surgeon gave only a 40 percent chance of survival.

The waiting was agonizing. However, he survived, only to have the same thing happen a week later. This time a colostomy bag was necessary, but once again his life was spared. We thanked God for guiding the hands of this surgeon and the skill to use such small instruments on such a tiny baby.

Many heard of our family ordeal, and prayer groups were formed in many places in Australia. "The earnest prayer of a righteous person has great power and produces wonderful results" (James 5:16, NLT). God answered the prayers of His people, and Kyle lived.

Kyle is now a normal, happy little boy bringing joy to us all. Praise God for a wonderful miracle.

Lyn Welk-Sandy

My New Face

In the day of my trouble I will call upon You, for You will answer me.
Ps. 86:7, NKJV.

I COULD ALREADY feel the blood dripping down my face when my mom ran to meet me to see what had happened. Quickly the wound was cared for by the delicate hands of one who loves her child.

It was a sunny morning, and my brother and I had decided to play in the backyard. While running, as all children do, I fell to the ground, cutting my face. We thought that with time it would heal like any other cut. But then a little sore developed into a skin disease called vitiligo.

I was taken to the best doctors of the city and region, and in each consultation the answer was the same: "Your daughter has an incurable disease called vitiligo. The disease will spread over all of her body, producing white patches that will never leave her skin. I'm sorry, but there is nothing we can do."

My mother could not sleep, but spent nights crying and crying out to God for her little daughter. She thought of how my adolescence and youth would be marked by patches on my face and body.

The churches in our city were already in prayer, crying out to God for my cure. My parents had already spent a lot of money; they held nothing back.

At that point, another patch appeared on my foot, increasing the concern all the more.

The only solution was God, and it was with prayer, fasting, and complete surrender that God cured His daughter. He gave her a new face when doctors had no hope for her problem.

Treatment was with sunlight, but the basis of all the cure was, and is, only God, the Doctor of doctors, whose love and care is greater than everything.

The patch gradually disappeared, and my skin returned to normal. And as God's cure is perfect and complete, today, if I hurt myself, my skin returns to its original pigmentation. What God does is perfect!

When we think that there is no solution for a problem that to our eyes seems impossible, we can look up. The same God of our parents still works marvels for His children today, and His love is immeasurable.

Minéia da Silva Constantino

Make Me a Blessing

For I was hungry and you gave Me food;
I was thirsty and you gave Me drink. Matt. 25:35, NKJV.

IT WAS A BEAUTIFUL day on the sunny island of Jamaica. My sister Dilyn had graciously allowed me to tag along with her family on one of their family vacations. I had always dreamed of visiting Jamaica, but never really made any plans to make it a reality.

We had spent the day sightseeing and enjoying the beach in Negril. After having fun all day, we decided to get something to eat. We found a fast-food place that sold delicious Jamaican patties, which my brother-in-law loves. But when Jangles, our driver, pulled into the parking lot, we were abruptly approached by a man who looked as though he was in need of money. He didn't have a friendly smile on his face. In fact, he looked kind of mean. I think he knew we were tourists, because he immediately started wiping our vehicle down with a rag.

"Don't you wipe the car," Jangles ordered, but he kept on anyhow. After we purchased the food, the man started asking us for money. Jangles told us, "Don't pay him any attention—let's go!" and quickly started the car. We jumped in, but when the man realized that we were about to drive off without honoring his request, he picked up a large stone and followed us as we slowly made our way through Negril's crowded streets. At one point, he stood in front of our car, the stone in his hand, as if he were going to smash our windshield. Jangles stormed out of the car and aggressively confronted him. After a few minutes of angry words, the man dropped the stone and disappeared into the crowd.

As I think back on that day that started out so beautifully, I ask myself, *Why didn't we just give him some money?* I believe it would have changed the ending for the poor man's day, and ours. So many times we pass by people who need our help, fearing that we'll get caught up in their problems, not wanting to get involved. Scripture tells us, "Blessed are those who have regard for the weak; the Lord delivers them in times of trouble. The Lord protects and preserves them—they are counted among the blessed in the land—he does not give them over to the desire of their foes" (Ps. 41:1, 2, NIV). So I ask God each day to help me be vigilant and always ready to help someone who may be in need. I want to be a blessing to someone today.

Marlyn L. DeAugust

Power to the Weak

He gives power to the weak, and to those who have no might
He increases strength. Isa. 40:29, NKJV.

IT WAS ONE of those days when you have far too many things to do, and it seems that time conspires against you. I was hurrying so fast down the street that my legs fairly flew. It was then that something interesting happened. In front of me shuffled two elderly women on their fragile, tired legs. I reached them, ready to pass like lightning, when instantly came the thought: *How good it is that I can walk so quickly. I know that in a few years I'll be like these women, walking with great effort. Already my legs are not as obedient as they once were to the command to hurry, sent by my brain.*

In that instant I sharpened my ears and slowed down my pace to hear one of the women sigh and say to the other, "Ah, when I was younger I had strong legs and could also walk so fast. But time has passed, and I cannot do that anymore."

"Yes, we both moved quickly once upon a time."

I thought about that simple event for several days, and finally concluded that in our spiritual lives exactly the opposite should happen. If today I feel like a failure; if today I lack the strength to run from sin; if today my legs are weak and I am almost falling, every day I can become stronger if I walk with Jesus. And with the passing of the years in this life's journey, I gain more energy and I gain more strength as I grow in my relationship with Jesus. It will progress to the point that I will be able to fly as high as eagles, to run and not grow weary, to walk and not be faint (see Isa. 40:31).

The apostle Paul tells us that we can "press on toward the goal to win the prize for which God has called [us] heavenward in Christ Jesus. All of us, then, who are mature should take such a view of things. And if on some point you think differently, that too God will make clear to you. Only let us live up to what we have already attained" (Phil. 3:14-16, NIV). Even if I become physically weakened by the race of life and the busy years spent here on earth, I know there is a better day ahead. That is why I continue trusting in God's promises to defeat sin and give me spiritual strength in the Christian walk.

Ellen Rezende Festa

Angels in My Life

The angel of the Lord encamps around those who fear him, and he delivers them. Taste and see that the Lord is good; blessed is the one who takes refuge in him. Ps. 34:7, 8, NIV.

FOR MANY YEARS I had nightmares in which I dreamed I had lost my children. When I awoke, bathed in sweat, I had to go to their bedrooms to make sure they were still there.

I am not surprised about this fear, because I really have lost my children a few times. Once in the market it was dark before I finally held my little girl in my arms again. I found her in a shop happily licking a candy cane. She hadn't even missed me! But close to this shop was a river, and I was sure she had fallen into it. It was dreadful. Another time I lost my other little girl in a supermarket in Italy. A man walked with her through the parking lot so she could show him our car. There were hundreds of cars, and none of us could speak Italian.

In the meantime my girls have grown up into adults. They have learned to have confidence and a basic trust. And I am so glad for this.

My daughters are all Pathfinder Guides. One had to lead a scout's weekend when she was about 18. She was to meet her charges after school somewhere in the mountains. The train connections were difficult. That evening the train was late, and she didn't meet her connection. Everything seemed to be against her. Finally she reached the little village to take the bus, but the last bus had left already. She didn't know what to do, but she was used to praying. So that is what she did. And she started walking, with a heavy rucksack, step by step. She felt lost.

Suddenly a car stopped beside her. A kind woman driver offered to take her to the final bus stop. When they arrived there, this angel helper asked my daughter where she had to go. She showed her on the map where the farmhouse was and where the children were waiting. It would have been an almost hourlong, steep, uphill hike. It was dark and there was a lot of snow.

The woman offered to take my daughter that last bit too. When my daughter saw where she would have had to pass, she was so happy for God's guidance! When she arrived at the group, there was so much happiness. The children shouted and made a lot of noise. They all then jumped thankfully into the straw and fell asleep.

Do you still believe there are no angels?

Denise Hochstrasser

Crossing Your Jordan

I have set the Lord always before me: because he is at my right hand, I shall not be moved. Ps. 16:8.

AT A CERTAIN TIME of the year the Jordan River is in flood stage; the banks overflow and there is no way across—it is impassable. But on one occasion during Israel's history the Israelites were instructed by God through Joshua, "Now therefore arise, go over this Jordan, thou, and all this people, unto the land which I do give to them, even to the children of Israel" (Joshua 1:2). I think that at the time of the instruction, the melting snow had made the river deeper and wider. The Israelites were in a difficult situation, and in front of them was the river Jordan. God however had spoken: "Arise, go over this Jordan."

They had received their instructions. Believing that God was with them, they put their trust in God. They lined up and marched toward the river, the priests leading the way. When they reached the edge of the Jordan, the priests stepped into the water, and the Lord God omnipotent created dry land for them to walk on. The waters parted, and they all crossed over.

Whatever your Jordan is today, whether an unexpected test, an unforeseen situation that demands a lot of you, a friend encouraging wrong, a male friend trying to lead you into sexual impropriety, a colleague encouraging you to compromise your principles and make some quick cash, or even bills you cannot pay, the Lord is saying, "Arise and go across."

Trust in the Lord. Believe in Him. He will carry you through. Trust in the Lord. He wants to do wonders for you. Trust in the Lord. He is always at your right hand. You do not have to cross your Jordan alone. God is beside you; He will never leave you nor forsake you. He has engraved your name in the palm of His hand—that is how precious you are to Him. He will do everything to keep you safe.

Allow Him to lead and take care of you. But it must be a conscious decision. You must make the choice to let God lead. The Israelites did it, and they safely crossed a previously raging river into the Promised Land.

God did it for them back then, and He will do it for you today. Only trust Him.

Sanjo Angella Jeffrey

"Sir, Who Are You?"

Be not forgetful to entertain strangers: for thereby
some have entertained angels unawares. Heb. 13:2.

MY HUSBAND AND I were planning a pleasure trip and trying to decide the best way to travel. Should we go by train, with an eight-hour layover, by plane, which was very expensive, or by bus, which would take a long 18 hours. We prayed and discussed it. Because my husband is legally sightless, the ultimate decision was his to make. A few days passed and he announced, "We should take the bus, and I'll be able to 'see' some of the countryside." We chose a schedule, and I started packing.

During a two-hour wait at the bus terminal I picked up our tickets and began observing my surroundings. I noticed a young man sitting with three other people. After a while I saw him escort a young man who appeared to be mentally challenged to the restroom. As we began boarding, he was in front of us and we exchanged a few pleasantries. We sat in our priority seats, and he sat almost across from us. At our second stop my husband wanted to use the restroom. I thought, *Lord, how should I do this? I don't want him going in there by himself, and I can't go in there with him.* Then I saw the same young man coming out of the door. He acknowledged us and in that instant something said to me, "Ask him."

I said, *No, he doesn't know us!* Then I heard again, "Ask him!" so I called out to him, "Excuse me, sir, could you please do me a favor?"

He said "Sure!" I asked if he would escort my husband to the restroom. He nodded yes, and took my husband's arm. My husband quickly asked, "Sir, who are you?"

"My name is Charles," he said, "and I'm going to escort you to the restroom."

From then on whenever we made a stop, Charles came and checked with my husband to see if he needed anything. He heard him say he was cold so he asked the driver to turn down the air. Charles was from our hometown, and he had attended the same high school as our children.

When we arrived at our destination, Charles made sure we retrieved our luggage and that someone was there to meet us. Now I know our trip had been carefully preplanned. Our angel was there waiting on us. God said He would take care of all our needs.

Elaine J. Johnson

The Stove Top

But I am the Lord your God,
who divided the sea. Isa. 51:15, NKJV.

MY HUSBAND AND I decided to get a new stove top. The main reason for the change was a one-eighth-inch chip and a noticeable crack from one side to the other. Heavy wear was obvious.

We contacted a company with whom we have been doing business for more than 40 years and with whom we have enjoyed a satisfactory relationship. We placed our order for a gray-speckled, stainless trim, no. 9114674591, ceramic glass stove top, just like the one we were using, but were told that that model was no longer available. Instead we would receive a white top. We agreed to this as the stove and all the other kitchen fixtures were white.

We were pleased when delivery took place in two days, and arrangements were made for the stove to be installed within another two days.

The installer arrived on time, but when he opened the package, we were greeted with a dark reddish-brown top, not the white stove top we had ordered. The installer hurriedly repackaged and whisked it out of the kitchen. He then directed UPS to pick it up, return it to the company, and collect the white stove top from the company. He also gave us his telephone number and told us to be sure to contact him as soon as the package arrived. We did this, but we received no reply. This was a bit disappointing, because he seemed to be such a nice man, so full of compassion and so concerned with our problem.

A different installer came next. He pointed out that what we really needed was someone to repair the top. He refused to touch the package, but he advised us to tell the company to send the proper worker. The company assured us that that person would arrive in the next two days. But the day passed and no worker showed up. The situation was now worsening, as burner space on the stove top was limited.

Finally, almost three months after the first order, a new stove top was installed. Churning with excitement, I observed the very one we had first ordered: not the dark reddish-brown top, not the white top, but the gray-speckled, stainless trim, ceramic glass stove top.

We praised the Lord. He was silently working for us before we called, and we rejoiced as we were able to share our joy by the gift of a *Happiness* booklet to the service installer.

Quilvie G. Mills

Protector God

He delivers and rescues, and He works signs and wonders in heaven and on earth, who has delivered Daniel from the power of the lions. Dan. 6:27, NKJV.

SINCE I WAS A CHILD I have always believed in God. My family did not attend any church, but my parents taught me to trust in our heavenly Father, and my sister and I had the opportunity to study in a Christian high school. There I learned more about God's care for His children.

When I was 16, I remained at school for an afternoon class. Class finished, I went to the bus stop to go home. I was waiting for the bus when I turned and reached for something in my purse and saw a man standing very close to me. Scared, I looked to see who it was. He did not look at me, but pretended to be distracted. We were the only ones there, and there was no reason for him to be so close! I was very frightened until a thought came to my mind: *There is an angel between this man and me.* Then I decided to get as far away as possible, so I went to the other side of the sidewalk. From there I saw another man, standing with a bicycle, watching me. Then suddenly he went to the man whom I'd just fled. They exchanged some words. Then seemingly scared, the man on the bicycle made the sign of the cross, rode down the street, and quickly turned at the first corner. The other man hurried up the street, almost running, looking back several times. He seemed frightened by something.

Now I stood alone at the bus stop, very confused about what had happened. The bus came and I got on, sitting down with relief. I now understood that my angel had truly been there. I could not have done anything, a defenseless girl, alone with those two men. I do not know what they were planning, but I was sure of God's protection. I think that perhaps an angel had appeared to them. That is why they looked at me with fear and left running.

After that day I knew that there is no reason to fear anything in this world, because we have an all-powerful God by our side in every situation. He does incredible things before our eyes! This experience strengthened my faith. As a Christian, I hope to always trust in God.

My desire is for you to also feel the presence of your Father, the Creator of the universe, who is always very close to you. Wherever you are today, remember, "For He shall give His angels charge over you, to keep you in all your ways" (Ps. 91:11, NKJV).

Yara Bersot Pellim

Led All Along

The Lord will guide you always; he will satisfy your needs in a sun-scorched land and will strengthen your frame. You will be like a well-watered garden, like a spring whose waters never fail. Isa. 58:11, NIV.

THE MORNING SUN had already begun to light the eastern sky. I had slept a little later than usual, as I'd returned late the night before from a music ministry in an adjacent state. I propped myself up on pillows, reluctant to make the full commitment to rising and shining. My mind wandered back over the years.

Years before, I had an adequately paying job. But then through a turn of events, I found myself in this small town where jobs were scarce and the pay didn't cover basic living expenses. In 10 years I'd had three of those short-lived jobs. I had taken classes at a community college to keep my job skills up-to-date, thinking I would surely find another job, but to no avail. But with a fair amount of creative skills I earned some money through commissions. As fulfilling as this was, the money wasn't enough.

When my savings were depleted, I began drawing from my retirement account to keep up my mortgage payments. Then, as my retirement account drained, I put my house up for sale. I had never been late or missed a payment, for I felt that God's reputation was at stake before my non-Christian neighbors. Silly me! I needed to learn that God is more than competent to look after His own reputation.

The month after my retirement account closed I began to pick up odd jobs and more commissions. By the end of the month I had earned enough to pay the bills. And so it has gone for a couple of years, leaving time for music ministry, always a deep desire of mine.

So sitting there watching the dawn, with a heart full of gratitude for God's leading, I was suddenly struck with how my life had mirrored His plan of salvation. No matter how I may struggle to "work," to "make it," my feeble attempts to earn God's favor are worthless. It is only as I give up the focus on my own attempts to attain the true desire of my heart that blessings for this life are strewn in my path, and the blessing of life to come. I needed only to give up the struggle and lay it all down at His feet. He is more than able, and His promises are sure!

Sylvia Stark

The Revolving Stone

Let the one who has never sinned
throw the first stone! John 8:7, NLT.

FOR MANY OF US, perfection is what we do or what happens in our own little circle. Everything else falls into less than perfect, waiting to be fixed, or better yet, in need of our fixing. We look at others with a feeling of superiority. But this is not a new behavior. We find many instances in both the Bible and life around us. And still we fail to learn what Jesus taught.

One biblical story that I truly enjoy is found in John 8. There she was, an adulterous woman cringing in the dirt, thrown there after being pushed, ridiculed, and abused by those perfect individuals with their chins in the air and stones in their hands, ready to eradicate the sin in others. As they looked at her the verdict was clear: guilty.

As parents, one of our greatest fears is to have one of our children in the middle of an accusing crowd such as the one in the story. The sin could vary, but the accusing behavior would probably be the same. Yet in spite of our fear, we forget to bestow on others the same mercy and love we would enjoy. So we go on making more mistakes and sinning even more just because we are afraid of the accusing treatment and the angry stone thrown at us and our loved ones.

Oh, but what a God we serve! As we continue reading this story we discover one of the finest wordless sermons ever preached. Jesus conducted the greatest evangelistic meeting, one that brought liberation to sinners, for neither the accused nor the accusers are condemned. What a lesson! You and I are in the same category. We are sinners who can become perfect only through the grace of God. Whatever good is happening in our lives today is not because of what we have done, but because of the love and mercy that we receive. Yet we fall short in grace to others.

As Jesus' followers, we need to be like Him. "Always live as God's holy people should, because God is the one who chose you, and he is holy" (1 Peter 1:15, CEV). He is telling us what is expected of us, but He also tells us how to conquer our sinful behavior. "Come near to God, and he will come near to you. Clean up your lives, you sinners. Purify your hearts, you people who can't make up your mind. Be sad and sorry and weep" (James 4:8, 9, CEV).

Let's take a moment to ask God to change our ways. Let us put down our accusing stones, and help us to bestow on others the same grace and love He bestows so graciously on us.

Dinorah M. Rivera

Angels in Human Form

Don't forget to be kind to strangers, for some who have done this have entertained angels without realizing it! Heb. 13:2, TLB.

ONE MOMENT I was walking to the car, feeling more energy than I'd felt for months, and anticipating going home. The next moment I was falling on the blacktop parking area. With both hands, both knees, and my head, I slammed into the pavement, jarring my whole body. I found myself flat on the pavement, staring at the hubcap on the rear tire of the car. I weakly cried out for help and prayed silently for God's help, too. I was concerned that I had reinjured my right knee that had been surgically replaced six weeks before. How could I explain to my doctor that I really was trying to be careful? Sometimes accidents just happen; we surely don't plan them!

A large group gathered and tried to help me. Someone brought a pillow, someone called 911, and one nice woman said she would stay with me as long as I needed her. She held my hand and spoke softly to comfort me. An ambulance arrived, and the paramedics took charge. My answers to their many questions showed that I had no concussion, and I didn't need to be hospitalized. They agreed, but said I couldn't drive. The kind woman offered to drive me home in her car. She transferred my groceries to her car. She made sure I got into the house safely and after putting some things into the freezer and the refrigerator, she had me sit down and put my feet up. She insisted that I should not be home alone and that she would stay with me until my husband got home. She called her family, and they understood why she would be late. We learned more about each other and our families. My husband was so glad to hear of her caring actions and thanked her for her concern and kindness. She declined any payment or reward.

While telling my sister about my adventure, she asked if I felt that my benefactor could have been an angel. Yes, the thought had crossed my mind several times during and after the experience. I had prayed for help, and it was sent to me.

We never know when we might be entertaining angels unaware.

God knows exactly where to find human angels and often puts them in the right place at the right time. We thank Him for the love and care He shows every instant. Where would we be without Him and His human angels?

Lillian Musgrave

Why Is Trust So Hard?

Trust in the Lord with all your heart . . . and He shall direct your paths.
Prov. 3:5, 6, NKJV.

WE SING "TRUST AND OBEY." We talk about how important it is to trust God. "In God We Trust" is printed on United States' money. But do we *really* trust God?

What does trusting in God look like? Have you ever become anxious over your next meal? Will you be able to buy school or church shoes and clothes for your children? Maybe it's a dependable car that you need. Did you just lose your job? Trust God.

In personal relationships, is it a mother or father who let you down? Are you single, looking for the perfect someone? married to someone who turned out to be not what you were hoping for in a companion? Is a family member chronically ill and nothing seems to help? Are your prayers being answered? Did your spouse, parent, or child die? Trust God.

Lost! We were going to a resort near Mount Hood, Oregon, and the all-day drive had been great. We stopped to buy fruit at a farm along the way. After we'd parked, our car now faced back the way we'd come. We turned on the GPS and were given different directions than we had printed with MapQuest. We were told to go back the way we had come and turn west.

After we traveled along tree-lined narrow roads through a beautiful lush, green forest, the road came to an end, with no sight of our resort. It was evening, and we were very low on fuel. Now I was anxious! We retraced our route and stopped at the gas station we'd thought was too pricey when we'd passed it earlier. Now we gladly paid the price. Getting back on the original road, we arrived at our destination safely. Trust God.

When I was stressed and worried over our situation, I asked myself, *Why am I not trusting God with this? He knows where I am and where I want to be. If we run out of gas, He'll help us. He's with us.* But then the other voice would say, "Yeah, but will you be out here all night on the road before that help comes?"

Trusting God with every aspect of my life has always been a challenge for me. It's easy to trust God when things are going smoothly, but real faith and trust come in when life isn't smooth. "As for God, His way is perfect; the word of the Lord is proven; He is a shield to all who trust in Him" (2 Sam. 22:31, NKJV).

Louise Driver

Goatheads

And we all, who with unveiled faces contemplate the Lord's glory,
are being transformed into his image with ever-increasing glory,
which comes from the Lord, who is the Spirit. 2 Cor. 3:18, NIV.

I THOROUGHLY ENJOY gardening, although I do not always allow enough time for it in my busy life. There are myriad lessons to be learned by digging in the dirt, planting a seed in faith, tending to a plant's needs, and being witness to the miracle of life and growth. But one aspect of gardening that I do not particularly appreciate is weeding. It is time-consuming, strenuous, and sometimes painful. However, if it is done often enough, it is much easier the next time.

One weed found in our region is nicknamed the "goathead" because of the sharp stickers that resemble a goat's head. At first glance the goathead plant is deceivingly lovely. Lacy green foliage and delicate yellow flowers camouflage the stickers underneath. The plants grow abundantly and take over virtually anything in their path. Once a person realizes that the pretty-looking plants are actually insidious and pose a threat to their yard, they are difficult to remove. Not only have they laid down firm roots in the soil, but their stickers make removal a tedious and time-consuming process. Even after the plants have been removed, any stickers left during removal can hide in the soil and produce new plants for up to seven years.

Every time I see a goathead plant, I am reminded of the devil. Not only do the stickers themselves resemble the archetypical devil's head and horns, but their presence in a yard is similar to the devil and the sin he brings into our lives. The devil disguises sin in the initial, deceitful beauty it presents and the fun it appears to afford. By the time danger is revealed, the devil has already put down his roots and crowded out other properties essential to health and life. He has no plans of leaving without a fight. Fortunately for us, our heavenly Father is eagerly ready and willing to pluck the wiles of the devil out of our hearts, although the poisonous barbs of sin often hurt as they are removed. We must be ever on guard, because once a sin has entered a heart, it can easily sprout up again for years to come. Every day we must rely on our heavenly Gardener, our Savior, to tend to our hearts and keep them weed-free.

Roxie L. Graham-Marski

Only a Bill

Thou shalt not.
Ex. 20:17.

AS I WALKED in with the mail I tossed it on the table near the trash can. You know how it goes—advertising for things you don't want, catalogs for things you don't buy, political propaganda. Of course there's an occasional personal letter, or a bill, and then every month there's the bank statement. I recognized that envelope, so I put the bank statement in a safe place where I could come back to it.

A few days later when I had some quiet time I pulled out the bank statement and my checkbook to reconcile the figures. There were the usual things: the check to the church, a check to the hairdresser, payment to Children's Place, ATM withdrawal, and Discovetr Card payment. My eyes blinked as I looked over that last entry again. Yes, it said Discovetr Card—*discovetr*. I chuckled out loud as I thought of some data-entry person hitting the wrong keys as I've done so many times. Then the word in the middle, *covet,* kept jumping out at me. It certainly gave me a lot to think about.

Could there be any relationship between my credit card and the act of coveting? Oh, surely not! However, I must truthfully say that I do love to shop. My husband says it's my therapy. And I must admit that it's pretty handy to shop when I have a credit card in my purse. But does any of that count as coveting?

I knew the Bible verse that says, "Thou shalt not covet." I checked the dictionary. It gives the definition of covet as to wish for excessively, crave, desire. Then it was time for self-evaluation. Having a credit card handy when I shop does make it easier to do more than just desire things I see. But I do want to be a good steward of God's money. After all, it's not mine to begin with. However, my standard response for carrying a credit card is that it makes it possible for me to take advantage of a sale I might happen upon unexpectedly.

My bank statement came with that startling typo two months in a row. Perhaps someone (i.e., the Holy Spirit) was trying to get my attention.

Maybe what I need to do when the mail comes is to quickly get the attractive advertising and alluring catalogs in the trash before excessive desire and craving have time to take root!

Roxy Hoehn

Water Damage

Behold, I make all things new.
Rev. 21:5.

WE ALL LOVE THE gentle rain on a hot summer day. The temperature seems to drop, the air smells cleaner, and we're thankful that we don't have to water the tomatoes that day. But rain is not always gentle and refreshing. Sometimes we experience downpours that damage or destroy life and property. Here is an example of what I mean.

Our newly renovated home had one little problem: a leaky roof. It had embraced storm after storm until the water had blackened the walls, damaged ceilings, and discolored the cabinets and walls of my brand-new all-white kitchen. An expensive roof job finally took care of the leak, but the water damage remained. Painters scraped and refinished the ceiling. Then came my part. I set to work to repair the damage that water had caused. Somewhere beneath the grime and blackness lay my sparkling white cabinets and walls. With the picture of "what was" in my head, I scrubbed and washed, changing pail after pail of water. Gradually my true kitchen began to emerge. And there I saw myself and reflected on God's work in me.

God's picture of me is the original, the one He created. How His heart must grieve as He witnesses the ravages of water damage in my life, the destruction of the sin storms that have blown over my soul. It's not a pretty picture. But He does not give up on me. He's working to restore the image of His spotless child. After my baptism my God continues to cleanse my soul at the Communion service and through the foot-washing ceremony. Slowly the true picture emerges and I can say, *Lord, I am beginning to see a glimmer of what You want me to be. This gives me hope that one day You will complete the job and I'll be new without and within.*

You too may have suffered water damage. Your body and soul may bear the scars of physical or sexual abuse. Or you may have been scarred by psychological abuse. You may have suffered illness or other physical challenges.

First, permit Jesus to heal the leaks, so the problem does not recur. Then give yourself over to Him, body and soul. There's a sparkling new you beneath the dark, gloomy picture. As Christ works to heal the water damage to your soul, oh, the glorious unfolding of what you were meant to be!

Annette Walwyn Michael

Love So Amazing

For God so loved the world, that he gave his only begotten Son, that whosoever believeth in him should not perish, but have everlasting life. John 3:16.

WE WERE LIVING IN Karmatar, a mission station far removed from civilization. All of us who worked in the church's offices lived close together in a colony, like a joint family system. As a result, we regularly got together for potlucks—especially on Sabbaths. It was almost like heaven on earth. Very seldom did guests visit us from outside, but whenever we had guests we would get together again. Sabbath sundown worships were very special for all of us.

Next to our home lived a Canadian family. In a short time the wife and I became very close friends. We both had older children studying in boarding schools. Their two little boys and our youngest son played together almost every day. Then one afternoon when I returned to the office after lunch (I didn't usually lock my office door during the lunch hour) I was taken aback. Brightly colored hibiscus flowers were everywhere—on my desk, on my chair, on the typewriter, and on the window sill. I had not the slightest idea who could have done this. I walked over to my friend's office and there, too, were three or four hibiscus blossoms. "So you, too, have flowers," I said. "Do you know who brought them?"

"Who else but Kevin?" she said. Kevin is her son.

"If it were Kevin," I countered, "why did he give you only three or four hibiscuses but covered my room with them? Surely he would have given you more because you're his mother."

"Yes, I'm sure it was Kevin," she said. She then came to my office and was surprised to see the flowers everywhere. "Kevin must love you very much," she told me. She was not hurt that he'd given me more flowers, because she too was fond of me. However, it touched my heart deeply for a 7-year-old to show so much love to me. That expression was so amazing.

When I saw Kevin, I hugged him tightly and thanked him for the flowers. It reminded me of God and His great love; not just for the human race, but for each of us individually. He emptied heaven when He sent Jesus for us as a ransom, and Jesus so willingly laid down His life so we could have eternal life in Him. And when God shows me His love in countless personal ways, I cannot help exclaiming, "What love, what wondrous love, so amazing and so divine!"

Birol Charlotte Christo

Soaked and Soggy, Wet and Weeping— Waiting for the Rainbow

Weeping may endure for a night, but joy comes in the morning.
Ps. 30:5, NKJV.

AS WE PORED OVER THE MAPS, our excitement grew. This would be our greatest adventure yet! My husband and I had decided to take a long bicycle trip. We'd be pedaling 1,400 miles across one third of the United States. Usually summer meant continuing education classes, but this summer we opted for a different education. We biked all day and camped most nights, though occasionally we stayed at a hostel or an inexpensive motel that would allow us to take our bikes and gear into the room. We saw our country up close and personal, and gained a new appreciation for the people who call it home.

For me, the Fourth of July, the U.S. Independence Day, is a very special holiday. Our family enjoys patriotic celebrations, picnics, and the all-important nighttime firework show. Wildly patriotic, I am over-the-top with excitement when it comes to fireworks! I look forward to them all year. So the morning of the Fourth we planned to start early and ride long. We wanted to reach a large city where we would enjoy a magnificent fireworks display that night. But sadly, as the "dawn's early light" broke, we were greeted by nothing but rain.

We pedaled in the rain all day long. Everything, and I do mean *everything*, was completely, 100 percent soaked. I was just sure that the rain would stop in time for the fireworks, but I was wrong! Disappointment spilled over into tears as the event I'd been anticipating for months was drowned by a rainstorm. Happily, the next morning the storm moved on, and a beautiful rainbow eased the disappointment of the soggy holiday.

I've enjoyed many other firework celebrations since that rain-soaked night, but I've had other disappointments that lasted longer and hurt more deeply than missing fireworks. I'm sure that you've met with many disappointments of your own. Today, if rain clouds dampen the joy you should be experiencing, if your plans threaten to fall apart, remember this: it takes both sunshine *and* rain to make a rainbow! The hardships we face may be the very things Jesus uses to make something beautiful out of what at first appears hopeless. He specializes in that, you know. So today, wherever you live, celebrate! Step into the "Son" shine! Then watch Him change your disappointments into dazzling rainbows.

DeeAnn Bragaw

The Wallet Witnessed to Us

Turn us again, O God, and cause thy face to shine; and we shall be saved.
Ps. 80:3.

I WAS PRIVILEGED to attend my church's worldwide fifty-ninth General Conference session in Atlanta, Georgia, the summer of 2010. It was a beautiful experience. God's presence was definitely with us. We could feel Him.

Three of my church sisters and I booked a room at a lovely hotel, only a 10-minute walk from the Georgia Dome, where the meetings were held. Sometimes, however, when we were running late for a session, we would take a taxi to the dome.

Three days into the session I got a call from my sister in Jamaica. My brother had suffered a serious stroke and was being transferred to a nursing home. I went to a cousin's house to share my sadness and have her help me arrange travel to Jamaica. When I went to get my credit card to pay for the ticket, I made a surprising discovery. My wallet was not there!

I was not terribly disturbed. I had asked God to guide me, and I knew He was in control. But my credit card, debit card, driver's license, and other important documents had been missing for two days, and I had to find them. Prayerfully, I retraced my steps to search for the wallet. I went to the Lost and Found Department in the display area where I'd spent a lot of time. My wallet was not there. I went back to the hotel. I asked at all the grocery stores and restaurants in between, but no one had seen my wallet.

Later I asked at my hotel again. The receptionist looked surprised when she saw me. "You're the one that the taxi driver has been looking for!" she said. She explained that because my name was not on the guest registry, they could not find me. Then she reached for the cab driver's card, dialed his number, and handed the phone to me.

Soon the taxi driver was in the lobby. He had my wallet. "You must have dropped it in the car," he said, handing it to me. I couldn't help praising the Lord. I witnessed to him, telling of God's glorious goodness. I didn't tip him at that time, but I urged my friends to use his service when we left for the airport. We tipped him heartily then, adding a health book to show our gratitude. As the old hymn says: "All the way my Savior leads me; what have I to ask beside?"

Hazel Roole

Of Mint and Prayer

Rejoice always, pray without ceasing, give thanks in all circumstances; for this is the will of God in Christ Jesus for you. 1 Thess. 5:16-18, ESV.

THE YARD OF OUR retirement home is intended to make things easy—little watering and less mowing. The back yard is gravel, but at the foot of the block wall that surrounds it we have about 18 inches of dirt where I've planted flowering vines and ivy.

Before leaving on a five-week trip, we made arrangements for someone to mow the handkerchief-size front lawn. The plants in the back yard had to take care of themselves. We made sure the automatic irrigation was just so and left home. On our return, everything was fine—except for the overgrown mint.

I knew there could be a problem with mint spreading uninvited along the wall, but I was not prepared for mint plants four feet tall. I love mint tea on a cool evening and I often make pots of iced mint tea for summer use. But I had no intention of preparing mint tea for the whole neighborhood!

As I pulled mint and trimmed the ivy, I remembered that somewhere in the back corner I had planted a lantana, because I wanted some color, and a lemon balm bush, my very favorite herb tea. Where were they? Carefully I pulled mint until I found the two plants—totally overpowered by the mint. Without sun, both plants were limp and trailing.

The mint episode got me to thinking. What keeps me too busy for my personal devotions doesn't need to be bad, just as mint isn't bad. Sometimes I get so busy with good things—even visiting neighbors and taking sick people to the doctor—that I don't have or take the time for my own personal study and prayer time.

So, mint is good—but not growing wild! Likewise, my good deeds cannot be allowed to take so much time and energy that I have no room for the quiet time so needed to enable me to grow and blossom. I want to remember the mint and keep the clutter of life from interfering with my relationship with God. If He needed whole nights of prayer, I certainly need a regular schedule of communication with my God! May my heart be continually lifted up in joyful prayer for all His benefits.

Nancy Vyhmeister

Angel From Heaven

*Thou hast given him his heart's desire,
and has not withholden the request of his lips. Ps. 21:2.*

FOR THE PAST 10 YEARS we have taken our German shepherd, Buddy, on our annual family camping trip. Then one morning I went to Buddy's crate to take him out for a walk, but he was unable to stand. Buddy was bright-eyed and ate well, but could not use his back legs. I phoned the vet, and he sadly told me we would need to make a decision upon our return home. I was sad the remainder of the vacation.

At home we unloaded the camper with Buddy watching us. Each time we moved he tried his best to get up. I knew in my heart what we were facing. The next day I packed my pockets with trests and Kleenex and we took Buddy to the vet's office. The vet told us that Buddy was not going to walk again, and we reluctantly made the decision to put him to sleep. Tearfully I told him goodbye, gave him the treats, and left my husband to stay with him. We buried dear Buddy in the back-yard, where he loved to play.

His bright eyes were no longer there, and I missed him terribly, so my husband and I agreed that in the spring we'd look for a new pet. I prayed that the Lord would send me a young but adult dog who was leash-trained and would enjoy being outside in our yard. On the morning I announced that I was going to start looking for a dog, my husband came with me. At the shelter we said we were looking for a shepherd mix. The next day we received a call from a woman who runs a shepherd placement service. I told her of our prayers. She paused and said, "This is funny. I got a call yesterday from a couple who must give up their young shepherd for adop-tion. Could you see her tomorrow?" I was overjoyed! The next day an SUV drove up bearing the logo "One Shep at a Time." The door was opened, and a beautiful shepherd jumped out. Soon my husband and I were petting Angel and playing fetch with her. Tears came to the woman's eyes, and she said, "I believe this was a divine appointment."

The Lord answered my prayers. Angel was everything we had prayed for. We loved her immediately, signed adoption papers, and she became a family member.

If the Lord cares about the little sparrow, He is willing to divinely connect a lonely master and a dog who needed each other too. He cares about everything that touches us.

Rose Neff Sikora

The Bee

Though now for a season, if need be, ye are in heaviness through manifold temptations: that the trial of your faith, being much more precious than of gold that perisheth, though it be tried with fire, might be found unto praise and honour and glory at the appearing of Jesus Christ. 1 Peter 1:6, 7.

MY MOTHER SUFFERED from constant headaches. Then those constant headaches changed to what she described as someone stabbing her in the top of her head with a knife and extreme burning in her face. This horrifying pain came every hour, day and night. Throughout the house I, who cared for her, could hear her stomping and crying. In three years we saw 13 physicians, she was admitted in five different hospitals, and had two brain surgeries, but the pain continued.

During this time I was going through a lot of stress and frustration because no doctor could figure out Mom's terrible pain. I was also in a state of bewilderment and anger because my Lord did not seem to hear or answer our prayers. He seemed to have left us in a time when we needed Him most. But He was there. He sent messages every now and then through song, sermon, or devotional reading. One particular Sabbath morning He used a bee. Yes, a bee.

Starting my car, I suddenly saw a bee walking about on my windshield. At 30 miles per hour I watched my passenger intently, waiting to see when it was going to be blown away. When my speed reached 50 miles per hour, the bee no longer faced the wind. He'd turned his body against the wind so that it was hitting his backside. I figured it would be blown away when I reached 65 to 70 miles per hour, but to my shock the bee turned and gripped even more firmly to the windshield. When I parked the car at church, my passenger flew away. I sat there stunned.

God was teaching me a lesson. The bee represents you and me. The wind represents the strife and trials that come our way. The bee's response to the trial he was going through was to turn his body around so that the wind would hit his backside. This should be our reaction to trials and to him who sends them our way.

Though my trial with my mother still goes on, I reflect on my special passenger. If you are going through a difficult time, be like the bee! If you are going through some trial in your life, I pray this experience will be an encouragement and strength to you.

Chynsia Morse

Waving Him In

Offer hospitality to one another without grumbling. 1 Peter 4:9, NIV.

THE WIND BEGAN TO RISE, and looking out my window, I saw a hanging plant whipped back and forth, so I hurried outside to bring it in. The gigantic willow trees that line our driveway swayed violently, creaking as they strained to stay upright. Then, above the roar of the wind, I heard the sound of a motor as a man rode down the driveway on a beautiful new Harley-Davidson motorcycle, seeking shelter under the willows from the approaching storm. I knew that one stall in our garage was empty, so without a thought I waved to him to come on in. Opening the garage door, I watched as one thankful man drove into the garage.

I invited him into our house, and my husband joined us as we sat down to visit. Through the windows we watched the full force of the storm. Rain and hail pelted the ground. Needless to say our unexpected guest was happy to have his motocycle protected from the elements.

I'd been baking that afternoon, and the house was filled with the aroma of freshly baked buns. The scent was enticing, so I prepared and served several buttered buns. As we talked, we learned that our visitor lived in a nearby town and was on his way home from work. We invited him to use the phone to call home and let his family know he was OK, then we continued to chat until the storm was spent. Feeling that we had made a new friend, it was with a sense of joy that we sent him on his way.

This experience reminded me of the many times we have opened our home to friends, family, neighbors, and yes, strangers. Our life has been enriched by these experiences. Whether it has been a weary traveler in need of help or a happy family gathering, the hospitality we have been able to extend has been a blessing to us. We frequently tell friends and acquaintances that "the motel is always open." The extra effort it takes to volunteer bed and breakfast to guests has given us many precious memories and lots of new friends.

Inviting the Lord into our home brings more blessings than we can count. I don't even have to wave Him in—I just need to open my heart and invite Him to take up residence. He is not a once-in-a-while guest but is ever-present. His love shelters us from the storms and keeps us safe.

Evelyn Glass

Through It All

Oh, taste and see that the Lord is good; blessed is the man who trusts in Him! Ps. 34:8, NKJV.

 EXCITEMENT WAS IN THE AIR. I was about seven months pregnant with our first child when my husband was given an opportunity to study at a university in another African country. We made all the preparations any anticipating couple would make. When we got to the new country, it became evident in many ways that God had gone on ahead of us.

At a visit to the gynecologist, we were told the baby was in the wrong position. I was terrified of having to deliver through Cesarean section. About the same time, we received a phone call notifying us that thieves had broken into our home in Zimbabwe. That was not news we needed to hear at such a time. We found assurance only in presenting our situation to the Lord, surrendering all to Him, casting all our cares upon Him.

The delivery date arrived. Recalling the experiences of others seemed to multiply my fears. A short prayer, "Lord, do not forsake me now!" seemed to keep me going as I tightly held my husband's hand. Miraculously, after four to five hours of labor, our baby girl, Joelah, healthy and without complications, lay on my chest as I wondered at the miracle of life.

We were joyously adjusting to the presence of the third member of the family when we faced the biggest challenge of our lives. Ten days after Joelah's birth I began having terrible headaches. A doctor examined me and thought they were caused by stress. He prescribed rest and painkillers. But the headaches persisted, and before I knew it, the left side of my body was completely paralyzed. I had suffered a hemorrhagic stroke and lay in the hospital for weeks. The doctors could not ascertain the cause. Considering the extent of the hemorrhage, they wondered how I was still alive. My husband was told that the chances of my fully using my arm and leg again were very slim. In the midst of this storm, we clung to God's promise to never forsake us.

Often I would just break down emotionally and cry to God. Amazingly, God has led me in a step-by-step process of healing. Five months after that ordeal, the arm and leg that had been written off are fully functional.

Each of us has a path to tread. When currents threaten to sweep you away, stand on Jesus Christ, the Rock of our salvation. Through it all, I have learned to trust in Him.

Nanzelelo Motsi

Reunion

And I heard a loud voice from the throne saying "Look! God's dwelling place is now among the people, and he will dwell with them. They will be his people, and God himself will be with them and be their God." Rev. 21:3, NIV.

IN JULY 2010 our church held a worldwide convention in Atlanta, Georgia. This conference is held every five years in different locations, and church members from all over the world (including delegates representing different areas) attend. For months my husband and I looked forward to going, and truly it was everything we anticipated. I counted down the days on the calendar. We'd planned for it, made preparations for it, saved up money, and prayed about it almost every day. It was exciting, and brought us so much joy. We'd made contact with some old friends, arranging to stay together in a rented house. (We had a small reunion at that time, too.)

We were blessed spiritually, our faith was strengthened by the different speakers, and the music was outstanding indeed! We met friends from long ago, more than we expected—even one of my high school friends. It was exciting to meet people from so many different countries; it was interesting to see many wearing their colorful national attire. The last Sabbath was the climax—thousands of Christians from "every tongue and nation" gathered to worship our Creator, Lord, and Savior. We sang together and prayed in the name of our God. I had goose bumps as I looked around and saw the thousands worshipping in the huge Georgia Dome.

I needed to think of the heavenly reunion that will take place soon. It will be a joyful and wonderful one. And we won't need to say goodbyes to friends, as we did in Atlanta. No more saving of money, no more application for visas or travel documents. The marvelous events that will take place in heaven include meeting most of our loved ones, family, and friends. There will be no more despair, no crying, no more separation, no more sickness. I'll be able to eat all the fruit I like and not need to worry about allergic reactions.

Would you like to visit other planets and galaxies? Wow! It's all free. If you plan to be there in the grand reunion in the heavenly kingdom start preparing now. We can do this only while here on this earth. Remember, your character is the only possession you can take. But it's all you'll need. Jesus will provide everything else.

Loida Gulaja Lehmann

Tuxie

*Yea, I have loved thee with an everlasting love:
therefore with lovingkindness have I drawn thee. Jer. 31:3.*

HE WAS DRESSED in a black suit, white collar, and gloves. He was a family member for half as long as our children had been. Sadly, we laid him to rest this summer.

As a child I loved my pets, especially the ones that would cuddle with me. As an adult, I feed, protect, clean up after, and pay the "after fight medical bills." His love consisted of following me around. Hugs were short. Love was on his terms, for he'd wiggle and squirm until I released him. I often wondered why we put up with his self-centered attitude.

Tuxie's relationship with me reflected my relationship with God. God created us, loves us, and supplies our needs for air, water, food, good health, clothes, shelter, and transportation. He even supplies many of our wants: cars, computers, lovely clothes, pie with ice cream, and vacations. He thrills to give us good gifts. He wants to hold us close and communicate with us, which will lead us to true, heartfelt worship, love, and cheerful obedience. But how often we act like Tuxie, following at a distance and not giving Him our whole heart? Do we act standoffish till the door closes, then fuss about getting in, squirming and wiggling until we get our own way?

We say we love God, but like Tuxie, it's on our terms, and we expect that it won't affect our relationship with Him. We decide how to celebrate the Sabbath, set our own dress standards or work ethics. Even in worship we forget to praise Him for His holiness and His blessings. We forget to ask Him what He would have us do, or how to do it. We go to Him with a list of needs and wants, and get right down to the business of asking Him to heal our friends, work out a business deal, or to keep us safe as we rush off to conquer our world.

God made us perfect, beautiful, and intelligent. Jesus left heaven for 33 years to love us and show us how to love back. We are the creatures; we depend on God's care for survival. Yet like Tuxie, we are difficult and hard to love. But in spite of that, He promises to draw us with kindness and everlasting love!

We loved the kitty God put into our life, and I thank Him for using that relationship to show me God's unconditional love. I want to become more lovable today.

Elizabeth Versteegh Odiyar

Preservation Plus

The Lord shall preserve thee from all evil: he shall preserve thy soul.
The Lord shall preserve thy going out and thy coming in from this time forth,
and even for evermore. Ps. 121:7, 8.

A LARGE GROUP of excited students set out to hike from Maracas Valley, going over the mountains to the beach beyond. Despite having deep misgivings, I had let myself be talked into going too. "Don't worry," my friends said. "We have guides who know the way. We won't go too fast, and we'll wait for you if you tire."

I was fine for most of the journey, but finally, overweight and not as fit as the rest of the group, I began to fall behind. Excited about spending the day away from campus and eager to get to the beach before it grew too late, promises were forgotten and the group got farther away.

Finally only one person was left walking with me. After a while we could not even hear the group ahead of us. We came to a fork in the path and took what looked like the well-trodden option only to come to a sheer descent covered with foliage and vines. There was no sign of the group. Shouting brought no response, and we realized we'd gone the wrong way. We turned back but became disoriented. Despondent, exhausted, and filled with visions of being lost on the mountain, I burst into tears. My friend comforted me, and when we reached a clearing she convinced me to sit and rest while she scouted around for signs of the group. It seemed to me that the clearing had a strange smell, but I was too tired to make a fuss about it, so sat down to rest. As I waited I recited psalms and comforting Bible verses to myself.

After what seemed like hours my friend returned with the search party, who'd come back to look for us when the group reached the beach and realized we were missing. It was too late to go another way, so we descended the treacherous slope. I held on to vines, was given piggyback rides, and slid some of the way down on my bottom!

We were taken to the campus by minibus and arrived after nightfall to find sobbing students and prayer vigils being held on our behalf. Only on our return did a guide tell me that the clearing where I'd waited was probably the lair of a mountain lion or one of the other wild animals known to inhabit that area. I thanked God for preserving my life and resolved to be more careful to listen to the promptings of the Holy Spirit. What a wonderful God we serve!

Ardis Sichangwa

Do You Play the Piano?

We are bound to thank God always for you, brethren, as it is meet, because that your faith groweth exceedingly, and the charity of every one of you all toward each other aboundeth. 2 Thess. 1:3.

THE 20-MINUTE drive to the little church in Genoa was a little surprising. Except for the previous three years in Memphis while my husband was in school, I had lived in Nebraska all my life. But the beautiful rolling hills were not like other areas of Nebraska in which I'd lived.

The town of Genoa was very small, and we easily found the little white church on the corner. From its open windows flowed the music of Del Delker as we walked to the door with our two children, ages 1 and only 1 month. The elder met us at the door with a smile, a handshake, and the question: "Do you play the piano?"

I stuttered a little as my mind tried to evaluate if a year of piano lessons in the eighth grade counted as "playing the piano" for a church service. So I finally said, "Just a little." He smiled and said, "That's enough." The Del Delker music was turned off, and they hurried my 1-year-old downstairs to a Sabbath school class and welcomed us to the Genoa church.

The membership was small—only two older couples and one or two families. We were accustomed to the churches in Memphis and those at the colleges where we'd lived, so we thought we'd prefer a larger church. But the Genoa church soon became our church too.

After a few years the church's state headquarters sent someone to hold evangelistic meetings in Columbus, where we actually lived. Then a decision was made to move the church from Genoa to Columbus. Our church in Columbus is still small, but it has grown to 70 members with a church-sponsored elementary school. And yes, I still play the piano now and then. However, one member donated an organ, so that's what I try to play now.

As we greet the visitors to our churches, let's make them welcome by giving them a smile and a firm handshake. Help their children to their classrooms, and ask them if they sing or play piano. As it says in Psalm 150:3, we can "praise him with the sounding of the trumpet, praise him with the harp and lyre" (NIV), or the piano or organ, however expert we may or may not be. We can never have too much music!

Judy Gray Seeger Cherry

Disabled? Not on Your Life!

For as we have many members in one body, and all members have not
the same office: so we, being many, are one body in Christ, and every one
members one of another. Having then gifts differing according to the grace
that is given to us, whether prophecy, let us prophesy according to the
proportion of faith; or ministry, let us wait on our ministering: or he that
teacheth, on teaching; or he that exhorteth, on exhortation: he that giveth,
let him do it with simplicity; he that ruleth, with diligence;
he that sheweth mercy, with cheerfulness. Rom. 12:4-8.

UPON LEAVING THE marketplace in Nairobi, Kenya, my friend and I were besieged on every side by beggars of all ages and needs. As we navigated our way through this maze, we were thankful that our missionary friends had arranged for a local person to escort us.

Suddenly I saw an unusual sight; a tall, well-built man carrying a smaller, apparently crippled man on his back. The smaller man's legs were wrapped around the tall man's waist. They wove in and out of traffic with such agility that there was no time to assess their situation. I lost sight of them, but several times that day I wondered about them. Safely back at the school in Nairobi, we breathed a sigh of relief for surviving the trip through such traffic. That night at the fireplace as we recounted our experiences of the day, my friends Lydia and Newton asked, "By the way, did you see a tall, well-built man carrying a crippled man on his back?"

"As a matter of fact, I did!"

My friends informed me, "The 'hitchhiker' can see—he navigates the tall blind man through traffic, directing him to likely places to receive alms."

For a while I could not respond, pondering the ingenuity of these two persons with disabilities who had figured out a way to pool their resources, talents, and blessings for the benefit of them both. The blind man could not have lasted five minutes in the Nairobi traffic swirling out from the airport. Neither would have the crippled man been able to move more than a few feet on his own, soon dying of starvation, given the competition.

The Bible says "two are better than one, because they have a good reward for their labor" (Eccl. 4:9, NKJV). In the body of Christ we are all members although we are not given the same gifts and talents. Let us use the talents God has given us for the edifying of the whole body.

Vashti Hinds-Vanier

Tendrils

I have shewed you all things, how that so labouring ye ought to support the weak, and to remember the words of the Lord Jesus, how he said, It is more blessed to give than to receive. Acts 20:35.

ONE SPECIAL LITTLE flower garden is entwined around my heart. Like the tenacious tendrils on her brilliant-blue morning glories, Mom Bird reached out and lifted me up at a precarious time in my physical and spiritual development. Her garden was nestled in the red clay of Colorado. By midsummer the broken wagon wheel at the front gate was almost hidden by an extravaganza of blue glory.

Mom Bird's life was not uncomplicated, but like her morning glory, she seemed to gain strength by reaching out. Those of us who lived in her student home achieved a higher level of spiritual, academic, and medical wisdom through her influence.

When I was confined to the sanitarium with a high fever, it was Mom Bird who applied or supervised my hydrotherapy treatments twice a day for a week, starting me on the healing journey from the chronic lung weakness that had plagued me since birth. She was there to lend nutritional and spiritual support as I gained enough strength to resume my regular workload.

Mom Bird's night shift as a registered nurse at the sanitarium sometimes challenged her regular mealtimes, but it never affected her spirit of devotion to her "children." And Mom Bird's tendrils were not confined to America; they reached clear across the ocean. Mountains of clothing, cleaned and mended by her own hands, were shipped to Africa.

In her last letter to me Mom Bird enclosed a recent photo (smiling as always) and a little folder entitled "Talk Courage! Talk Faith! Talk Hope!" and told me how much she appreciated the stories I sent her about the spiritual lessons I was learning in my greenhouse. Though she was no longer on active nursing duty, she still prepared fresh vegetables for health guests. "I still do salads for everybody! I praise my heavenly Friend for good health! No pain!"

There will be no more brokenness to hide over yonder, as represented by Mom Bird's broken wagon wheel, but when I think of heaven I can't help picturing a little blue morning glory entwined around a majestic white column at one particular mansion, ever reaching toward the Light.

Linda Franklin

Standing Up for God

In all your ways acknowledge Him, and He shall direct your paths.
Prov. 3:6, NKJV.

BECOMING A NURSE anesthetist had been my lifelong dream and passion, and my prayer for years. Since leaving Northern Caribbean University in 1998, I had made my request known to God and worked diligently toward that goal.

In 2010 I was granted an interview for acceptance into the program at a prestigious school. Each applicant had to sit through two different interviewer panels. After completing the first interview I was directed to the second room. The last interviewer who spoke to me was the program director. She said, "Cleopatra, I see that you took a class this summer and made a B in it. If you can take only one class and still earn just a B, how are you going to take four classes and makes A's? Don't you know that A's are important? I really don't think you're a good fit for such a strenuous program." My heart sank when I heard that. I tried to explain myself, but most of all I trusted in God.

For the particular class she had referred to, all the exams were online, and the instructor told us that we should do the exam alone. Some of my classmates were surprised that I was actually doing it alone and encouraged me to write the exam with them. I was tempted, but decided to do the right thing even if it meant failing. At least I would do it honestly.

After leaving the interview, I continued to pray, and I also asked for prayer. I have always believed in "much prayer, much power." You can only imagine how elated I was when I received the call the next day that I had been accepted into the program. Indeed, when you stand up for God, He will stand up for you.

God hears our deepest desires, utterances, and cries. He knows our hearts, and He will withhold nothing good from His children. Why don't we trust Him today? I have had many failures and heartaches working toward my goal, but all things do work for good when you serve Him. I am just starting my journey—which will be a tedious one—but I know that God is mighty and just to grant me the desires of my heart. "Take delight in the Lord, and he will give you your heart's desires" (Ps. 37:4, NLT).

Cleopatra Wallace

Come to Me First

Turn your worries over to the Lord. He will keep you going.
He will never let godly people fall. Ps. 55:22, NIrV.

I FELL TO THE FLOOR, a literal pain in my heart and the pit of my stomach. It seemed as if someone had punched me in the chest, stolen my air, and knocked my legs out from under me. I couldn't stand, or think—or stop the tears from falling. It had hurt so bad when he'd said, "I'm in love with someone else. I can't see you anymore."

The breakup had come out of nowhere and seemed to do just what its name implied: it broke my heart. I didn't think I'd ever be able to pick up the pieces and move on. As if the wound wasn't deep enough, I was often faced with my ex and his new love. The wound opened afresh every time I saw either of them, and I thought I could physically die from emotional pain.

Every place we had been, and every space we'd ever shared became a memorial of our perished relationship. Constantly walking among the graves put me under a cloud, but all the while I felt I had to pretend everything was just fine. I felt as though I would never get over the devastating blow of trusting someone only to find that they were untrustworthy. I went into isolation and depression.

One day after seeing my ex unexpectedly and subsequently crumbling into a torrent of tears, I saw a book. As I browsed through it, I came upon a poem entitled "Come to Me First." Here God reminded me that He knew what it felt like to be a jilted lover. He jogged my memory of the millions of times I had set Him aside for someone or something else. *I* had stood *Him* up, and scorned *His* love for another's. I heard Him plead, "Come to Me first, and I will never let you down. Even when the one you love walks away or does something hurtful, your life will not crumble because you will have built your life on Me, not him. Come to Me first," He begged.

Those words changed my life. I realized that the one I spent the bulk of my time and energy on was truly the one I loved the most. I began building a *real* relationship with Jesus. I would build my life on Him, so my life would never fall apart again. And here I am, 11 years later, married with children and as busy as ever, but still going to Him first. I love Him more than anyone.

Shari Loveday

He Rescues Them

The Messenger of Yahweh camps around those who fear him,
and he rescues them. Ps. 34:7, GW.

ON A RECENT TRIP to Hawaii a girlfriend and I took the opportunity to swim with wild dolphins. We were excited, boarding the boat that would take us along the coast of Oahu. The day was beautiful; we saw the occasional whale breaching in the distance and at one point saw some large sea turtles swimming below. We were told that the dolphins are found in coves near the shore in the early morning, but later in the day they head for deeper waters to feed.

We were on one of the later trips and had been on board the boat for quite some time when our captain pointed out a distant pod of dolphins coming our way. Once the boat had us in line with their travels, we were to slip into the water with mask and snorkel, but no flippers. We were instructed to just lie there quietly while the boat maneuvered away from us. We hadn't been there long when we were literally surrounded. The dolphins were surfacing between us and diving below us. I just looked in awe at their size, beauty, and gracefulness. Despite their speed and strength, not one of them touched any of us.

We were let off the boat twice for this marvelous experience. We then headed back down the coast. We had not gone far when some of us noticed a small group of dolphins slowly circling in the water not far behind us.

When we asked the captain about them, she said that they were likely waiting for a sick or injured dolphin to join them. They would escort it safely to deeper waters. Earlier she had told us about a baby dolphin they'd seen a few days before that had been bitten by a shark and was being "guarded" by adults in a cove. Just then we saw the mom and a baby coming through the water, and watched as the other dolphins swam with them, forming a flank on either side to protect them. The baby had a distinct piece missing at the front of its dorsal fin.

The scene brought tears to my eyes. I was reminded that our loving Father not only cares for these beautiful creatures and created them with the instinct to care for one another, but that He cares for us, too, and will send legions of His angels to camp around those of us who trust Him, and when we are in need He will rescue us.

Beverly D. Hazzard

Tossed and Cleaned

Wash me thoroughly from my iniquity, and cleanse me from my sin.
Ps. 51:2, NKJV.

I WAS VISITING BEIRA, Mozambique, for leadership training. My hotel was a five-minute walk from the beach. I made it a point to go for a walk early every morning, and on my way back I would walk along the sandy beach and pick up seashells.

While picking seashells, I discovered that the waves deposited a lot of other things onto the shore: sticks, plastic, papers, bottles, food stuffs, dead fish, clothing, and anything else that might have been thrown into the ocean. I also observed that after noon the tide rose, and the waves got higher and higher. In the process, the ocean was shaken vigorously, bringing all the dead/dirty and unwanted articles to the shore.

One day as I walked, today's text came into my mind. I then asked myself a question: *Could it be that during my life storms and trials, God is actually cleansing me from all impurities? Should I then complain when my life is being shaken vigorously?*

I then realized that it is God's duty to clean up His creation from all impurities. He cleans up the waters through the waves every day. No one goes into the ocean to purify the waters. The process is almost automatic. He cleans up the earth through vultures, pigs, maggots, and even rain. He cleans the atmosphere through trees that release oxygen so we can breathe fresh air. The earth, the water, and the atmosphere pass through this process willingly on a daily basis.

It is also God's duty to keep His children from spiritual impurities. He is ever ready to start the process in our lives if only we allow Him to. The question is how much we are willing to be tossed up and about for the cleansing process. Many times we are quick to complain when we face a storm in our lives. It seems the cleansing process becomes so painful to us that we fail to realize that it is for our own good.

I want to be willing to thank the Lord for the shaking that goes on in my life, for it is designed to purify me and make me as white as snow. Today I surrender my heart and say, "Investigate my life, O God, find out everything about me; cross-examine and test me, get a clear picture of what I'm about; see for yourself whether I've done anything wrong—then guide me on the road to eternal life" (Ps. 139:23, 24, Message).

Caroline Chola

The Trophy

But seek first the kingdom of God and His righteousness,
and all these things shall be added to you. Matt. 6:33, NKJV.

My 7-year-old son entered the car beaming. After his last period class he had in his hands a "trophy." Trophy? To me it was nothing more than a birthday party invitation.

But he explained it better to me. One of his little classmates was having a birthday party. It was to be a special event in an important children's party center. And the birthday girl was choosing who would celebrate with her.

My son then, in his childlike cunning, thought of a way he could be among the lucky chosen. So he told his birthday-girl classmate that if he were invited, he would give her a unique doll from his father's store. The doll walked, moved its head, and even blew bubbles. It was almost a living being. The invitation in his hands left it very clear that he had succeeded with his plan.

I could not stop smiling. But I also could not keep from showing him the implications of his act. I talked to him about sincerity, about true and disinterested friendships. And afterward I asked him two things: "Son, will you be able to complete the promise you made? And if she invited you only for self-interest, is the friendship worth it?"

He had not thought about those two implications, and after reflecting, he did not seem as excited as he had before.

It seems that the same thing happens to us as well. In our relationship with God, many times we want to bargain with Him. We get ourselves into situations, and we make such offers as "Lord, if You give me this, I will do that" or "If You grant me this thing, I will be able to be faithful to You." However, we often fail to deposit our full confidence and let Him decide if what we request is truly useful and reasonable or would lead us to situations that would divert us from His path.

Like my young son, it is necessary to reflect and perhaps "lose interest" in things that we value too much and that can be a stumbling block for us. And as Jesus told His Father, "Your will be done" (Matt. 26:42, NKJV).

Suely Luppi Novais

Hovering Over the Rock

For He shall give His angels charge over you, to keep you in all your ways. They shall bear you up in their hands, lest you dash your foot against a stone. Ps. 91:11, 12, NKJV.

It felt really good to wake up. Confronting suffering with courage, and knowing that God cared about me, was enough. I had been driving to church to be a godmother for a baptism, when my car had been hit. Now I lay in a hospital bed.

Feeling fragile and extremely worried about my 1-year-old son who was home with my quite elderly mother-in-law, I was told that part of my right leg had been crushed. *And now, how will I raise my son?* I worried. *How will I be able to be a good wife and mother with this problem in my body?*

I fell asleep and had a dream. I was walking on a street lined with stones. It was extremely difficult to walk with my injury. That was when I saw an angel in human form who said, "Come!" Frightened and unsure, I heard him say, "Do not fear!" I took his hands and continued walking. When we arrived at the end of the road, he looked at me and said, "Go in peace." Then he disappeared. Oh! How good it was to hear that soft voice.

When I woke up, I remembered Psalm 91, especially verses 11 and 12, which had been recommended to me for reflection. Reading them, I received the encouragement necessary for me to face that traumatic situation. I felt strengthened and ready to continue with my life, though from here on out it would be radically changed because of my injury.

What was most surprising after my dream was discovering that the angel who appeared and spoke with me was someone I would later meet. One day I was at home and turned on the radio. As I tuned in to a program called *A Voz da Profecia* (Voice of Prophecy), they made an invitation to receive Bible studies. I accepted the invitation, contacting the radio station to request someone to guide me in the studies. And what a surprise I had to see the Bible instructor who knocked on my door! He was the angel who had appeared in my dream. I could see that God had sent him and that He has very impressive ways of reaching us and completing the work that He started in us.

Today with much gratitude and joy, I serve this same merciful God.

Euclídea Assis Rabelo

The Widow's Joy

To appoint unto them that mourn in Zion, to give unto them beauty
for ashes, the oil of joy for mourning, the garment of praise for the spirit
of heaviness; that they might be called trees of righteousness,
the planting of the Lord, that he might be glorified. Isa. 61:3.

SITTING IN CHURCH that day found me inwardly overwhelmed as a myriad of emotions flooded my soul. As I sought to worship God, for the last several years my life and its events and circumstances had propelled me out of "drive" to "automatic pilot." My hands had been taken off the wheel as God led me to a station in my life that I had neither experienced nor dreamed of. I was now at the station of widowhood.

It had been a tried-and-tested marriage of 40 years, and now God in His infinite wisdom had called my husband to sleep, to rest in His loving arms, now awaiting the resurrection morning. So here I was, battled-scarred and worn, without a clear manual for this stage so unexpectedly thrust upon me. I had no doubt that the God who had navigated me through my entire life would surely continue to hold my hand in this new and strange position of widowhood, a place I had not imagined, studied, or prepared for.

As I mused and pondered, the church members transitioned to the foot-washing stage of the Communion service. Because I had received the holy sacrament the previous Sabbath, I was not participating. With my eyes closed I petitioned God not for the manual, directions, or reassurance, but for the three-letter word that I needed most: joy. *Lord, give me Your joy.*

Spirit-led, I opened my Bible to the concordance, pulled out a scrap of paper and pen, and decided to list the Scripture texts for the word "joy." I would later highlight them in my Bible. *No, I thought, not this Bible. It already has a rainbow of highlights. I will buy a special Bible, a joy Bible, and highlight all the texts in purple.* My excitement grew, for I suspected that God was up to something. Hastily copying the few verses from the small concordance, my eyes stopped on Job 29:13. What could be in Job about joy? I turned quickly to the text and God, as usual, had given me more than I had asked. The last portion of that verse stated, "I caused the widow's heart to sing for joy." God had not just given me joy, but a specialty joy—the widow's joy. *This will be my theme for the rest of my life,* I vowed. I closed my eyes and smiled at God.

Donnell Powell

The Cleared Path

He putteth forth his hand upon the rock;
he overturneth the mountains by the roots. Job 28:9.

IT HAPPENED ONE Tuesday morning. I was driving on a road that had once been familiar, but which I had not traveled for a while. Usually, as I drove by I would glance up and notice the mountains covered with green grass, watching until they were out of sight. I would admire their immensity and their stoutness as the car continued ahead on the road.

But this particular Tuesday as I looked up, instead of green I saw a large brown area. Someone was about to build a house on the top of the mountain, and in just a few hours a bulldozer, with all its force and power, had pushed through the mountain, and had cleared a pathway for trucks and cars.

Suddenly, as I slowed down, a thought came to me: *If human beings can make a path through a mountain that from a distance looked so high and inaccessible, how much more would God do for me?* When the children of Israel had before them the giant "water mountain," God parted the Red Sea right before their eyes, providing dry land to walk on. As they stood before the Jordan River at flood stage, and the feet of the priests that bore the ark of the Lord stood in the waters, God performed the same miracle. Later the walls of the strongly fortified city of Jericho were broken down flat by God, as if they were straw, as the Israelites obeyed and exercised faith in Him.

There are so many instances of the manifestation of the awesome power of the mighty right hand of God for me to think about and ponder. He has said, "And I will make all my mountains a way, and my highways shall be exalted" (Isa. 49:11). Then I said, *Thank You, Jesus, for bringing these thoughts to my mind. Thank You for reminding me that no matter what the situation, no matter what the circumstance, once I bring it to You, You can take care of it.*

I drove on and the mountain was left behind, but the thoughts stayed with me. In my heart I knew that when tough situations rise up before me like a humongous mass, as I pull up the picture in my mind of the mountain with a clear path through it, I can pray and be confident that the all-powerful, all-wise God, who can overthrow mountains by the roots, is in control.

Violeta Mack-Donovan

Would I Be Willing?

Give me back the joy that comes from being saved by you.
Give me a spirit that obeys you. That will keep me going. Ps. 51:12, NIrV.

AS THE COORDINATOR for my church's Homebound Ministry I have found how needy the aged, particularly those confined to their homes or assisted living facilities, have become, but I enjoy being with them. This special group longs for the individual touch even if it's only 30 minutes a week. Within that time frame my team helps those dear people deal with loneliness, anxiety, and grief. We often have to reassure them that no matter how dreary it seems, God has promised that He will never leave them nor forsake them (see Deut. 31:6).

I remember working with Virginia. When I first started visiting her, she lived in her son's home, and because she was alone during the day, my visits were frequent. We enjoyed wonderful fellowship, and she displayed great faith as we exchanged stories of how God had watched over us all through the years. My faith was always strengthened each time I visited her.

Sometime later, however, her failing health required her to be in a facility where people are there to assist her 24/7. I thought I could reduce the frequency of my visits and concentrate more on those who were alone in their homes. But I missed Virginia, so one day I made the 36-mile round-trip to the center to see her.

As I stood at the open door of Virginia's simple room, I knocked hesitantly. Virginia raised her head, stretched out her hand, and called, "Marian! Marian!" I greeted her with a joyful hug. We talked, and I told her she looked beautiful. I clipped her nails, quietly sang a few hymns, and had Communion with her. Our visit ended with prayer. It was truly difficult for me to leave her, and I know she felt the same.

Driving home, I examined my own life. Was my life cluttered with "necessary" activities: meetings, the Internet, TV—things I feel I cannot live without? Then my questions became more spiritual. *What will I do when Jesus comes? Will I willingly leave these material disruptions and run to kneel at His feet? Will I recognize His voice and His inviting smile and shout, "Jesus, Jesus, I've been waiting so long for You"?* Will I? I pray that I will.

Marian C. Holder

With God All Things Are Possible

With men this is impossible; but with God all things are possible. Matt. 19:26.

DOCTORS AND NURSES ran frantically in and out of the operating room, trying to save both my mother's and my lives during my birth. The agony of losing a beloved wife or his firstborn was incomprehensible. "Whom do you want us to save, your wife or your daughter?" my father was asked. With trembling lips and God's assurance in his heart, he said, "Please try to save them both." With unceasing prayers they pulled my tiny head out using forceps.

It was difficult for visitors to overlook the deep wound marks the tongs had left around my forehead. However, everybody assured my parents that daily massages would help alleviate the impressions, which eventually proved to be true.

"Your child is going to have difficulty understanding mathematical concepts," the doctors warned my parents. This led to their being typically overprotective of me. As a result, I did not actively attend school. My father was the pastor and my mother the school principal, and all the teachers had strict warning to allow me to visit any class at any time. Today when I browse through old pictures I usually chuckle with embarrassment as I see photos of me holding trophies for events in which I had not even participated. Although nobody felt it was a fair deal, no one said a word.

Then one day my parents realized I was using my "learning difficulty" to my advantage. They realized that the "innocent" sweet kid who was supposed to be bad at math was actually extremely calculative, smart, and manipulative. Things started changing.

"How was your score on your math and physics exam?" asked my dad.

"Oh, Daddy, everybody did badly. We all averaged only 35 percent."

"Well, did even one student score above 90 percent?" he asked.

When I admitted they had, he said. "OK, then even you can do it."

Today I have two master's degrees and a doctorate. The four simple words, "You can do it" have been the core of my success. It is my goal today to motivate children to believe in themselves; parents not to make excuses for children; teachers to be that guiding light to each.

Let no one tell you, "It is impossible." With God, "all things are possible."

Suhana Benny Prasad Chikatla

The Present Husband

Delight yourself also in the Lord, and He shall give you the desires of your heart. Ps. 37:4, NKJV.

WHEN WE GIVE OUR lives over to God and ask Him to transform us, we can be surprised by the path our lives will take. I was at my parents' house watching fireworks on TV. I was single, 26 years old, and had concluded that it was not an easy task to find an ideal husband by myself. I felt the immense desire to ask God to help me find a good companion. I asked that my future husband would be one who loved God, be a Christian who shared my same faith, and, if it were possible, to be a vegetarian, as I was.

I spent a little more than a year praying about it. A friend had suggested a friendship Web site set up by people in our church, and I decided to visit it. I found a handsome, delightful guy, and we began to correspond electronically. We traded information and prayed together almost every day by phone. We always asked God to give direction in our lives, and in our virtual "overseas" relationship, which lasted about two years.

During that time he visited my family in my country, and I went to his country and visited him. Following many prayers, we decided to unite for God's honor and glory. We got married, and in 2008 I moved to my husband's birth country.

If it were not for our beautiful and dear Father, I would have never found my companion. Of course, I did my part as well. First, I put my life in God's hands, and second, I signed up for classes in a new language because I'd asked God for a husband from another country.

We have already been married 18 months and are very happy. Nothing would have been possible without our powerful Father. God is wonderful, and there is nothing impossible for Him. He is a true Father who will never forsake us, and He always wants the best for His children. He is also your Father and can do incredible things. He can perform miracles and carry out unbelievable events to human eyes. It is enough to turn yourself over to God and ask Him to guide your life as well.

What do you desire to ask of God today? You need to ask something, because He wants to do something for you right now.

Carla Pietruska

Just the Right Size

And we know that all things work together for good. Rom. 8:28.

WE WERE ON VACATION at the beach, and as usual we visited the outlet malls in a nearby town before leaving for home. I needed a new pair of walking shoes, and since my favorite brand is a little expensive, I hoped to find a pair like my nearly worn-out ones.

But unfortunately I could not find any shoes like the ones I wanted to replace, even though I searched in the store that carried that brand. All the styles had changed, and try as I might, I could find nothing even similar to what I wanted.

When the clerk finally got around to helping me she suggested a certain style, and it looked fine. I told her what size I always wear, she brought out a pair, and I bought them without even trying them on. It was only after we returned home that I took them from the box and saw with a sinking feeling that she'd brought me an 8½ wide instead of medium. I decided I'd have to try to make an exchange at the outlet mall a little closer to home.

Then I broke my ankle! Surgery put it back together with all sorts of plates and pins. After being in a cast for six weeks and then a walking boot, I was finally allowed to wear shoes again, but none of my favorite shoes fit my broken-ankle foot. Even though I felt foolish doing it, I wore a slipper on the injured foot everywhere I went.

One morning, it dawned on me that I should try those new, wide shoes. So I did. They were a little bit big on my good foot, but I could lace them very tightly, and they felt OK. Then I slid my swollen foot into the other shoe, and by lacing it loosely, it fit perfectly. I was so happy to be able to wear two shoes around the house and even take walks in them. No, I did not wear them to church, I still wore a nice shoe and a slipper, but for all other walking, those became a perfect pair for me.

There had been no mistake in the size of those shoes after all. God knew all the time that I was going to need that very pair of shoes after I broke my ankle, and He took care of it in advance. The *Message* paraphrase states today's text this way: "He knows us far better than we know ourselves, knows our pregnant condition, and keeps us present before God. That's why we can be so sure that every detail in our lives of love for God is worked into something good."

Anna May Radke Waters

I Believe in Miracles

Jesus said to her, "I am the resurrection and the life. He who believes in Me, though he may die, he shall live." John 11:25, NKJV.

I AM 71 YEARS OLD, and had the privilege of being born into a Christian household. I thank God I have remained firm.

My fight for life began on Christmas Day, 1999, when I was the victim of a bad fall. Days afterward I began to feel pain in my chest, shortness of breath, and the taste of blood in my mouth. I went to the doctor, and after several tests a tomography found that my left lung had been injured in my fall. It then burst, and the cells were dying. I was transferred immediately to surgery to have a high-risk surgical procedure.

It is now 12 years since I was reborn during the surgery. Because of a medical error, a needle was diverted and punctured my heart. My heartbeat slowed until it stopped completely. Even though I was anesthetized I heard the doctors saying that my blood pressure was crashing, vital signs were falling, and I was near death. Right then I thought about the third verse of an old hymn, which says: "And when at last the time comes, in which I face death, I will not fear since Christ is alive, I will live since He will give me new life." And then I knew nothing more. For two minutes and 27 seconds my heart did not beat. But by the power of God, whom I love and serve with all my heart, and the resources for resuscitation, my heart began beating again. However, I already had internal hemorrhaging, and it was necessary to break the pericardium to remove the blood that was covering my heart. Nevertheless, our God sustained me. For six days I was intubated and in a deep coma, breathing only by machines. Then God woke me up. He still had a plan. I needed to live to continue training and caring for my grandchildren and great-granddaughter, my son-in-law and daughter-in-law. After almost three months of intensive treatment, I was cured, thank God. I believe in miracles, because I am a daughter of God who was dead and was brought back to life.

My dear sister, if you are passing through the valley of the shadow of death or facing any problem that seems hopeless, do not be discouraged. Our God is the God of the impossible, and He is the same yesterday, today, and forever.

Maria Vicência Salviano Pereira

Celestial Sphere

*Commit your way to the Lord, trust also in Him, and He shall bring it to pass.
Ps. 37:5, NKJV.*

WE ARRIVED EARLY at the Air Force Command, in Rio de Janeiro, for an 8:00 appointment, not knowing that it had been rescheduled to 1:00 p.m. We identified ourselves and waited inside. Both my husband and I had brought a book with us, so we read as we waited. At one point I looked up and saw a familiar sergeant coming over to speak with us. When we told him what we needed, which was to first talk with the colonel in the treasury, he said it was not worth waiting, since the colonel would not receive anyone. I responded that since we were already there, I would try. I looked at my husband and said, "The colonel will not see me? I am going to pray!" Then I left the human sphere and entered into the celestial sphere. I finished talking to God, and we continued reading. God had begun to act.

We were called at 11:00. At the third counter to which we were referred, a man in civilian clothes began asking me questions. I spoke with the soldier, and patiently responded to the man at the same time. Then the gentleman asked us to accompany him, so we did. I, thinking he was a civil servant, talked enthusiastically as we walked. My husband, who is a member of the military, tried whispering something to inform me about the man's rank, but I did not understand him. We entered an office, and the man started the procedure to solve the error in my paycheck. When finished, I asked permission to see his name on his badge, since he had been so helpful. I was stunned! The man God had sent to help me was not a treasurer's assistant but the second-most important person within the organization—the deputy director. I had to wait a little longer in another room, where I thanked God with great emotion and witnessed to my husband about the God whom I love and obey. This God of miracles, this God in the celestial sphere, remains the same. Just believe!

Our appointment had been rescheduled for 1:00, but we left the Air Force Command at noon with the desired solution.

And you? How about starting to experience God's power right now? Do not give up!

Eliana Nunes Peixoto

Four Armed Burglars

The angel of the Lord encampeth round about them that fear him, and delivereth them. Ps. 34:7.

IT WAS THE EARLY MORNING of the last day of July 2007, when I was abruptly awakened by four burglars armed with long knives. They had already bound and gagged my husband so that he could not move or make a sound. They told him that if he moved, they would kill him.

I was terrified as I realized it was a holdup and robbery. They'd cut the phone lines and had already packed up all the electrical appliances they could find. They were ready to go except for one thing: they demanded money, our cellular phone, and the car keys.

I started to pray and told those two who held me about the God I serve. I asked one of them about church. We had a conversation, but all his answers were negative. However, after receiving the car keys, one of the burglars said that he would return the car. (He did do so, but not where he said he'd leave it.) He further showed us some rope, saying he would use it to tie us both, but he didn't do this, either. However, he did lock us in the bathroom after I gave him the bathroom door keys. They then left with their loot. After our arguing with one of them for a few minutes, his closing remark was "Pray for me."

We could not get out of the bathroom without a key, and the thieves had taken the key with them, along with my car keys and our mobile phones. Fortunately, I kept the grand piano key in the walk-in to the bathroom, so I tried this in the lock in the door. To my surprise, the key worked—we were free! Again provision was made for us to escape, and although we thought that all the phone lines had been severed, we discovered that one phone line remained intact. From this phone line, which God had preserved, I was able to call the police and my pastor. Both came promptly.

Trust God. He hears and answers prayers. While we are speaking, He is answering.

The robbers left without hurting us. Eventually I did get the car back, but not the many electrical appliances. But praise God, our lives were spared. This had to have been an intervention by angels, and we thank God. It is a good thing to keep in contact with Him!

Ethlyn Thompson

The Dog Bay

For he will command his angels concerning you to guard you in all your ways.
Ps. 91:11, NIV.

WE SPENT OUR VACATION in Spain enjoying the wonderful warm weather, the sunshine, and the fresh air that welcomed us every day. From our quarters it was only a short distance to the beach, where there was a small bay. Another larger part of the beach was a little farther away and could be accessed by only a small, rocky path. On that farther part of the beach walking was very enjoyable, and one could find wonderful shells that had washed ashore.

One day my daughter Selina and I got up shortly after sunrise and prepared to walk the rocky path to the beach. We planned to collect shells, thinking that very few people would be out there that early competing for the nicest finds.

Even at this early hour the sun was warm, which made the walk a delight. At times the rocky path was really steep and strenuous but still refreshing and enjoyable—until we arrived at a bay where two people were walking their three dogs. Upon our arrival, those wolflike dogs ran toward us, barking and snarling. Selina and I were terrified and couldn't help screaming. Thank God, the beasts were called off, but as we continued on the path we were now no longer cheerful, but trembling from tip to toe.

We found some shells on the beach and saw the rising sun reflected on the sea. However, we could not enjoy any of it, because our thoughts kept returning to the rocky path that crossed the terrifying "dog bay."

My silent prayer was *Please, God, protect us.*

An elderly man came toward us. In retrospect, I believe he was an angel. He identified himself as a German emigrant, so communication was no problem. I told him we were afraid because of the dogs that might still be on the path, and he was nice enough to accompany us to the dog bay. When we got there, we thanked God that the people with the dogs were gone.

For the rest of the way we were still a bit anxious but nevertheless happy, because we knew that for a part of the way an angel had been with us.

Sandra Widulle

The Power of Our Words

Like apples of gold in settings of silver is a ruling rightly given.
Prov. 25:11, NIV.

THROUGH THE YEARS I read today's text many times and always thought it painted such a pretty picture. But the full impact of our words did not impress me until I worked for Mrs. Wade.

Mrs. Wade, a very wealthy, elderly widow, needed help with household chores and yard work. She employed a number of workers to keep both her large home and yard well kept. Unfortunately, she was not a happy woman, and her disagreeable attitude was quite evident to all who worked for her. As time went on, I noticed that fewer and fewer people were still working for her. She had employed several gardeners to care for the landscaped, terraced yard, but eventually only an occasional man remained to mow the grass. Soon she had me planting flowers and raking leaves. Then after several weeks the other person who worked in the house no longer came. Now I was the only one doing household tasks.

Many times I drove home in tears as it seemed I could never quite please her. No matter how hard or how carefully I worked, she either found something to criticize—or simply said nothing. Then my pastor-husband received the news that we would be moving to a new district. I went to work quite eager to inform Mrs. Wade that I would not be working for her any longer. I thoroughly intended to deliver my message and never return.

After telling her the news, I braced myself for what I was certain would be a quick, unkind retort. But there was silence. Finally she said, "Well, I'm an old lady, and I've seen a lot of workers come and go in my day, but you are the best worker I've ever had. I'll write you a letter of recommendation."

Just a few kind words, but suddenly I was no longer so eager to quit. Now I wanted to work for her! And I did—until the very day we moved away. Solomon, the wisest man who ever lived, had a number of things to say about our words. In Proverbs 12:25 he wrote, "Anxiety weighs down the heart, but a kind word cheers it up" (NIV). And in Proverbs 16:24 he said, "Gracious words are a honeycomb, sweet to the soul and healing to the bones" (NIV). Our words have the power to heal or to destroy. How careful we should be with our words!

Sharon Oster

My Miracle

How precious is your steadfast love, O God! All people may take refuge in the shadow of your wings. Ps. 36:7, NRSV.

I WAS IN SAN FRANCISCO after teaching a seminar. My friend Martha and I were full of plans about what to see and do the following day. The weather was perfect. First we went to the top of the Mark Hotel, where we viewed the city and bay from 18 stories up. We toured the famous Grace Cathedral. Next we took a fun ride down Lombard Street, which has the distinction of being the crookedest, most winding street in the world with eight hairpin switchbacks in one block. Then on to Fisherman's Wharf and Pier 39. After lunch on the pier, we took a ferry ride that provided an unobstructed view of the city's skyline, sailed under the Golden Gate Bridge, and circled Alcatraz for a close-up of the infamous federal penitentiary from which no one ever successfully escaped.

Our day was drawing to a close, but not before we visited the Japanese Tea Gardens. After leaving the gardens, I noticed a slight problem with our car when backing up, but thought little of it since it drove fine. We entered the heavy traffic and began our three-hour drive back to Fresno. After stopping for supper, I encountered a much bigger problem when backing up the car. But again it drove forward perfectly, and we sailed home at 70 miles an hour all the way.

Because of the backing-up problem, I parked in front of the house. As I slowly pulled up I plowed into something with force. Since there was nothing to hit, I got out to find the problem. Then I saw that the right front wheel had hit the curb while the left front wheel pointed straight ahead. The two front wheels were pointed in different directions! The car was towed to the shop the following day, and it was determined that a broken tie rod had caused the problem.

I reviewed in my mind where I had traveled: the steep and crooked streets and the freeways at 70 miles per hour. A broken tie rod at that speed could have sent me hurling off the road or into another car—either way it could have caused a major accident. I bowed my head and thanked God for His loving protection. It is exciting to read stories of miracles that happen to other people. It is even more exciting when it happens to you—proof positive of God's loving care and protection on a daily basis.

Nancy Van Pelt

The Grapevine

So think clearly and exercise self-control. Look forward to the gracious salvation that will come to you when Jesus Christ is revealed to the world.
1 Peter 1:13, NLT.

I LIVE IN A GRAPE-GROWING AREA, and most farmers take good care of their vines. However, the grapevine unattended grows wild, its tendrils reaching out and grasping in every direction. Plants and weeds entwine with one another and end up in an unsightly, unproductive mess.

In a similar way my life without direction and well-formed plans—with no control on thoughts, no aims or objectives—left to drift, will end up a tangled mess. I have had such experiences in my life.

I've since discovered that my thoughts and plans need to be under the control of God as He directs. Without Him I move unwisely and without thoughtful consideration, taking one direction and then turning again in another, grasping at what I can as I go. Like the untrained tendrils of the vine, my life can fasten to unhelpful ideas and take wrong directions.

Before I knew God, my life had no real purpose. I would drift from one idea to another, and I had an emptiness in my heart that I could not fill. I'd had some contact with Christianity as a child, and somehow I felt that this was where I would find the answers I was looking for. So my search began. It wasn't an easy road, as there were so many roads. But the principle of lining up all your Bible texts on a subject helped me discover what the Bible taught, and led me in my search in finding God. I found things in my life that needed to change.

Before the out-of-control vine can be of any use, the tendrils must be cut off from the things they have been grasping, and then the vine must be trained to entwine about that which will allow it to grow in a well-formed manner. This then brings about a healthy and productive plant.

So I also had to break away from unproductive ideas and thoughts, and align my life with the highest standards as given to me by God through His Word. I must be ever learning and striving as a student of the Word, finding new light, new ideas, and new gems of truth to apply to my life, and so allow my life to grow into something beautiful and useful.

Dawn Hargrave

"Let Not Your Heart Be Troubled"

"Do not be worried and upset," Jesus told them.
"Believe in God and believe also in me." John 14:1, TEV.

ON THE DAYS JUST PRIOR TO August 9, 2010, I can truthfully say that I did not always feel like a courageous Christian. At times I may have appeared to be a beaten-down believer. It began with the mammogram I had that spring. I was asked to return, as the doctor had viewed a suspicious mass and they felt I should undergo a biopsy. I had managed to escape the procedure a few years earlier when it was concluded a biopsy was not needed. In neither case did I feel I had total control. I leaned upon the doctors for guidance and management, just as I should have done. However, ultimately and beyond a shadow of doubt, it was clear that my all-out faith had to be in our Lord Jesus Christ. I needed His leading.

The day before the biopsy I was asked to sing at a memorial service to assist the family of a former church member with celebrating the life of their patriarch. I chose "His Eye Is on the Sparrow," by C. D. Martin, and I recall that the words really spoke to me as I sang.

When I entered the hospital the next morning, the first doctor who saw me checked my vitals. I told him that I had slept surprisingly well considering the course of the day's events. His reply was "Oh, let not your heart be troubled!" Wow! This doctor had spoken the very same scripture that was in the song. Then I realized that even in the lyrics of a song that I myself would vocalize, God would bring my worries to a standstill and help me be at peace. I just needed a "faith lift," and God used a healer to help me. And all did go fine. I am grateful for the reassurance and care from the medical personnel.

Jesus did not tell us that we should keep on worrying after praying to Him. He wants us to have faith in Him. Worrying only makes things more complicated. It is not always possible to control the circumstances in our lives, but we can be masters of our thoughts regarding what occurs. The Lord has promised to never leave us or forsake us (Heb. 13:5). It is a matter of simple and childlike faith. Hallelujah!

Patrice Hill Taylor

Birthday Surprise

How precious also are thy thoughts unto me,
O God! how great is the sum of them! Ps. 139:17.

MY BIRTHDAY WAS coming up in August. At age 50 I was reaching a real milestone. My plans weren't big—simply to get outdoors to hike and enjoy nature. Usually my husband, Cal, takes the day of my birthday off from work, and we spend it together doing outdoor activities. I was looking forward to doing the same this year. It's nice to feel pampered once in a while, and especially on birthdays. Receiving the many cards and calls from family and friends creates a warm feeling inside of being loved and cared for.

Well, this birthday turned out even more special than I ever dreamed. Lately Cal had been doing extra things around the house. He had cleaned the carpet on the outside porch—a big job that took him way past midnight to complete. I also saw him doing a lot of yard work, but I just thought, *He's doing this just because it needs to be done.* Even our youngest son, Dmitri, vacuumed the living room, and when I asked him why, he said, "Dad told me to do it." Again I thought, *How nice—getting help with the many chores around here.*

Late Sunday afternoon, Cal called to me, saying, "Someone is coming up the drive." I turned around and saw a big SUV roll into our yard. My family had made the 13-hour trip from New York for my birthday! I watched them get out of the vehicle—my mom, my sister, and my brother-in-law—but I couldn't believe my eyes. They were actually standing in front of me! I had no clue they were coming. Never in my wildest dreams had I thought they would. All I could think of was that they had come for *me.* They had come to be with *me.* An overwhelming feeling of joy filled me inside. We spent time together, connecting in a closer way. What my family did for me is etched in my mind and heart. Just thinking about it makes me cry.

Yes, my birthday arrived with many gifts and surprises, but the most precious was that we were together. One day Jesus is going to surprise us, isn't He? One day He's coming from heaven to this earth just for you and just for me, and that is a day we will never forget. We will be together with our forever family for eternity. What a time that will be when He comes again! Just thinking about it makes me cry.

Rosemarie Clardy

Rebecca:
"That Which Binds"

Blessed is the man who endures temptation; for when he
has been proved, he will receive the crown of life which
the Lord has promised to those who love Him. James 1:12, NKJV.

ON A FRIDAY EVENING, August 7, 2009, my dear daughter was born: Rebecca—the promised daughter! Beautiful and bright, but with two congenital problems. She had a cyst in her gums and an aortal heart canal that should have closed at 8 weeks but had not. Thus she needed surgery for both issues. The first, when she was 2 months old, went quickly and calmly. We returned home the same day. However, the cardiac correction, when she was 4 months old, was a true trial by fire for my husband and me.

What was at first a simple correction turned into various complications, beginning with severe laryngitis because of intubation, which evolved into respiratory arrest, as well as four days intubation, urinary infection, persistent high blood pressure, anemia, gastrointestinal bleeding, withdrawal from the use of sedatives, and intubation for the third time because of a general infection.

My daughter was literally passing through the valley of the shadow of death, and my physical and mental strength were at their limit. My body no longer reacted. No hunger. No thirst. I prayed without ceasing, and many prayed together with me. Rebecca spent 20 days in the hospital, 13 of those in the pediatric NICU.

It was a period of terrible affliction for me. Never had I experienced such feelings. However, the Lord freed my baby from all illness and sustained me with His strength. Several times I asked why this was happening. God, in His infinite goodness, placed in my heart not the "why" but the "what for." Rebecca came to unite me with God, so I could develop the fruit of the spirit, for which I had cried out in the last few years; so that I could learn to place all of my anxiety before the Lord; so that I could learn to praise Him in times of calm and times of distress; to break arrogance and pride and to recreate me into Himself. Above all, to prepare me for the second coming of Jesus.

Now I can thank the Lord for carrying me through His refining fire. How much He loves us! Blessed be the God of Israel, the God of miracles, the God of our salvation!

Suzi David Arandas

Saved by a Thorny Thicket

In every thing give thanks: for this is the will of God
in Christ Jesus concerning you. 1 Thess. 5:18.

IN JANUARY 2001 I was appointed acting principal of Matandani Secondary School. At that time I was eight months pregnant with our fifth child, Chimwemwe. As head of the institution I often traveled on official trips to Blantyre, a commercial city in Malawi. It is more than 65 miles (100 kilometers) from Matandani. I rode in the school vehicle, and staff members who had business in Blantyre usually traveled with us because transportation between Matandani and Blantyre is a challenge. The first part of the road from Blantyre is very rough, with many slippery spots during the rainy season.

Chimwemwe was born February 27. After only one month maternity leave I resumed work, and since he was still so young, I took him with me on my business trips. Then something happened. It was night, and more than five of us rode in the vehicle. I was sitting beside the driver with the baby on my lap. We were ascending a certain rough part of the road when suddenly the car stalled and started rolling backward.

"Apply the brakes!" I shouted.

"They're not working," the driver replied. It was clear that something was terribly wrong. Everybody grew deathly quiet. The car continued to roll backward with increasing speed until it suddenly stopped. Nobody knew why. We all rushed to get out as quickly as possible.

With my baby son in my arms, I quickly opened the door and got out, only to be caught in a thicket of thorny shrubs. I tried to free myself from the entanglement, but all my efforts proved futile. At last I was able to get back into the car and used the driver's door for exit. We spent the night there.

At daybreak we walked around the place while waiting for some help. That was when we discovered that a few inches from where my baby and I were caught by the thicket there was a very deep drain. God had protected us from falling into the drain. We praised God.

Whatever situation you may find yourself in, give thanks to God, for there is a reason for everything.

Margaret Masamba

"Lord, Remove This Thorn From My Flesh"

Concerning this thing I pleaded with the Lord three times that it might depart from me. And He said to me, "My grace is sufficient for you, for My strength is made perfect in weakness." 2 Cor. 12:8, 9, NKJV.

I ALWAYS QUESTIONED what the thorn in Paul's flesh was and why the Lord did not listen to his request. Then one day, when I had my leg in a cast, I accidentally let a pen cap get inside the cast. It was torment, for the more I tried to get it out, the farther down it went.

I despaired. I tried everything, but nothing worked. Then I decided to pray to God and like Paul, beg God, *Lord, take out this pen cap from my leg, please. I know You can.* And I, in my desperation, thought that as soon as I finished praying God would do what I asked, but that is not what happened. And once more I tried in vain to get out the cap. It sank farther.

To my dismay and pain, the cap lodged in a place that caused a lot of pain if I moved my leg at all. In tears, I cried out once more to God but nothing happened. So I told the Lord, *Only You can get me out of this situation,* and in that moment the cap stopped bothering me and I was able to fall asleep.

The next morning I again prayed to God and tried to get the cap out of the cast, but could not do so. I began my worship and there, alone in the room, the Lord spoke to me through a book by Ellen G. White. "Every temptation resisted, every trial bravely borne," I read, "gives us a new experience and advances us in the work of character building. The soul that through divine power resists temptation reveals to the world and to the heavenly universe the efficiency of the grace of Christ" (*Thoughts From the Mount of Blessing,* p. 117).

That is how I came to understand why Paul had to live with his thorn, and I learned to live with the pen cap in my cast. I learned to endure the trial by faith and perseverance. When I finally learned my lesson, the Lord Jesus enlightened me, and with the help of my friend I was able to get it out from my cast. But this happened only when I learned to live by grace.

May we take advantage of temptations and trials, not as incentive to sin, but as motivation to overcome by the power of God granted to our lives. We live by the Lord's grace and cultivate unshakable faith that moves and conquers mountains.

Carmen Virgínia dos Santos Paulo

Really, How Is Your Faith?

To have faith is to be sure of the things we hope for, to be certain of the things we cannot see. Heb 11:1, TEV.

TALKING AND PREACHING about faith is easy, especially when everything is going well, the sky is blue, and no crisis is in sight. But meet a crisis head-on, and the preacher of faith finds a need to search deeply regarding his or her degree of trust in the Lord.

My mother was dying in Penang, Malaysia, and when the news came for me to go home at once, I worked frantically to book a ticket to fly from Seoul, Korea, to Singapore and then on to Penang. The first leg of my flight, from Seoul to Singapore, was confirmed, but I was on the waiting list from Singapore to Penang. That morning, when I arrived at the Seoul Airport, I used every persuasive power to convince the duty manager to give me a seat from Singapore to Penang, but his hands were tied. "Try your luck in Singapore," he told me.

For the next seven hours there was nothing I could do. Yet, the human response was to worry about what would happen in Singapore. Could I get the connection?

It was interesting how I talked to myself regarding my own faith in the Lord. Sitting on the plane that left Seoul, I kept repeating Bible promises to myself and mentally surrendered to God. After my meal the Lord sent me such peace that He would take care of every detail that I fell fast asleep. The last few months had been stressful. Mom's illness had weighed heavily on my mind. But the Lord gave me peace and confidence in His leading.

We were deplaning when I awoke. The Lord brought the plane into the terminal where my connecting flight departed. At the transfer counter I shared with the ticketing agent that my mother was critically ill and that I *had* to get on the flight. She was compassionate and assured me that she would give me special consideration. It took an hour, but I occupied myself talking faith on the phone to my daughter. We even made some alternative plans in case it was not God's will for me to take that flight. Again I recalled how Mary and Martha thought Jesus was four days too late to heal Lazarus, but praise God, He is always on time.

When time came for me to check back with the ticketing agent, I was elated. My faith was renewed in a God who cares. God is surely good!

Sally Lam-Phoon

Forgetting the Past

I press on toward the goal to win the prize for which God has called me heavenward in Christ Jesus. Phil. 3:14, NIV.

GOD WANTS TO DO so many spectacular things for His people, if we would just surrender our will to His will. Most of us have our own agenda, but we know that what we really need is God's agenda. Many of us go from day to day doing what we want, when we want, and how we want. We don't even think twice about whether what we're doing is what God wants for our lives. We don't consider if what we are doing is glorifying God or if it is glorifying self. God said in His Word that He would give all of us the desires of our hearts if we would seek Him first and His kingdom of righteousness.

God has great plans for each of us. Some of us know early in life what God's plans and purposes are for us, and some of us find out later. Many of us know what God's will is for our lives, but we still do what we want to do before we do what God wants us to do. Our plans will only lead to destruction, but God's plans always lead to eternal life.

In order for us to be successful for God, we must not let our past or present hinder our future. We must let go of everything that stands in the way of God's purpose for us. If we have a problem with a brother or sister, then we need to resolve it. We must face adversity so we can create success. Friends may forsake us during the transformation process. We may need to go through darkness so we can produce light. We must endure heartache and sorrow before we receive joy. We may not be able to understand everything there is to know in this life, but what we can know and do is to forget what is behind us and reach forward to the things that are set right in front of us.

Mediocrity is not good enough when it comes to doing the will of Christ. We must put our best foot forward at all times so that we won't be a stumbling block to others. We should allow the Holy Spirit to work in us, giving us a passion for Christ and sharing God's Word with others. Some women have been mistreated most of their lives and don't recognize their gifts until God reveals the gifts to them. But with God, we can each let our light shine in a dark world. We need to live our lives for God, not for ourselves.

Sheila Webster

His Thousand Ways

Commit thy works unto the Lord, and thy thoughts shall be established.
Prov. 16:3.

MY FAMILY AND I were staying in our mission staff quarters, which were attached to a gas station. Because I was an administrative officer, I had the opportunity to move into the house where the previous treasurer had lived. But my husband and I discussed it and decided the new staff should occupy the house, not us. Just recently that house had been remodeled and updated. If I were to move into it, I could be blamed for fixing up the house just so I could move there.

But we had a problem. There was an ongoing disturbance next to our apartment. It was a huge, noisy generator operated by our gas station neighbor. Many times we prayed, asking the Lord how to get rid of it. We were really tired of the noise day and night.

Suddenly the mission administration decided to add another staff member to our team. Being the treasurer, I considered how to accommodate this new family, as there was no empty staff house. Then our president (a foreigner) proposed we change one of the two foreign guest quarters into staff housing. I knew the rooms were not earning as much as they should, so turning them into staff quarters would be more profitable, and everybody agreed to that idea. Now the question was who would move into the new house, as it was quite a bit smaller than the regular houses.

The president first requested that the executive secretary move there, but he declined. Then the president told me to move there. I said, "Let me talk to my husband." We talked it over, but saw the same problem as before. If we moved into the new house we could be blamed for being selfish. So I told the president, "If anybody else wants the house, it's no problem for us."

The president became a little angry and replied, "People always talk about you, how you sacrifice and are good to everybody else. I told you to move!" Without further discussion we moved. And we thanked the Lord for not having to suffer with the generator noise anymore. We had no idea how God was going to solve the noise problem, but our Lord knows how to solve any problem. Test Him. He has a thousand ways to satisfy you. But seek His guidance first.

Sweetie Ritchil

The Garden

Except the Lord build the house, they labour in vain that build it: except the Lord keep the city, the watchman waketh but in vain. Ps. 127:1.

IF YOU LOVE GARDENING, how would you feel if you discovered that your vegetables started to wither shortly after they matured? You would be worried and unhappy, right? My situation was different.

For more than a year I had been tending a small garden in front of my house. In it were different kinds of vegetables. The spinach, okra, tomatoes, and such were doing fine. Everyone around my neighborhood admired them and even came by in times of emergency to have some for themselves. The tomatoes were big and ripe for consumption, and the other vegetables were leafy and attractive to neighbors passing by. I was happy because all I had been laboring for—watering in dry season and weeding—wasn't in vain. I also sent some home to my parents as my mother loved fresh garden produce, and she was proud of my garden.

On August 13 I left work and headed home with the thought of picking some vegetables from my garden to prepare a balanced meal. But my plans were dashed when I got to the front of my house and saw a clean, cleared garden. All the vegetables were gone! The leaves still dangling from the stalks had dried up in the sun, and some plants were even uprooted. There was no hope of the garden reviving again.

The gardener, a new employee, had been told to clear the bushes around the garden, but assumed it all to be weeds and cleared everything! I felt very distressed and downhearted, but not discouraged. I prayed for God to help me control my anger and tried to see if there was any hope for the vegetables that still had roots to the ground. As God would have it, many started to revive again!

And I thought, *This is exactly what we do to the Lord. He plants us and tries to tend us right, but we destroy ourselves by our sins, thereby making Him unhappy and allowing the devil to gloat.*

This has helped me to appreciate God's work in my life and helped me determine not to destroy the life He has built for me. I want to grow a beautiful garden with God in heaven.

Temitope Joyce Lawal

My Story

How gracious he will be when you cry for help! As soon as he hears, he will answer you. Isa. 30:19, NIV.

WHEN I WAS LITTLE, we lived in a two-story house in McDonald, Tennessee. My younger brother, John,* shared a room with me while my youngest brother, Rick, slept in his crib in my parents' room. Another family lived next door, but the only person's name I can remember now was Erin, one of the daughters.

One day Dad went to the store, and Mom put me down for a nap. But I was restless, so as soon as Mom had fallen asleep, I got up and started wandering around looking for something to do. Suddenly I spied Mom's wallet, and just as suddenly I had an idea. To my 2-year-old mind it sounded brilliant. I would take some money, go to the house of one of the neighbors, and secretly leave them the money—an anonymous gift. So I took a quarter (which seemed like a fortune that anyone would love to have) out of the wallet and left—barefoot. Needless to say, I didn't get very far before my foot was poked by a stick, so I turned around and headed home. But I had already gone a pretty good distance, and I was lost. I was so scared that I ran—in the wrong direction. Of course I didn't know it was the wrong direction, but I was even more lost.

Finally, I stopped running and started thinking. Strangely enough, the first thing that came to mind was a story Mom had read to me about a little girl and her sister who had gotten lost. In the story, they prayed, and then found the way back. So I figured, *If God would answer them, then surely He would answer me.* So right there, in the middle of the trees in our neighborhood, I knelt down and asked God to take me home.

Almost immediately I heard a car. Turning around, I ran to it. It turned out to be a police car, and the officer took me home right away. Apparently Mom had awakened and not seeing me, had called the cops. God heard my prayer and was answering it before I even thought to pray. Matthew 6:8 says, "For your Father knows what you need before you ask him" (NIV). He certainly proved that true in my life.

Marielena (Mary) Burdick

*Names have been changed.

Follow the Leader

Follow me.
Matt. 4:19.

AFTER I FINISHED my devotions one morning, I lay in bed meditating, and the words "follow the leader" popped into my mind. It took me back to my school days when we played the game Follow the Leader. We chose a number of kids and then chose a leader. The leader would do certain actions, such as hopping around on one leg. Everyone else would have to do the same. The leader would change and do something else, such as walking backward or running sideways. The object of the game was to see who could follow the leader the longest. As soon as anyone made a mistake, they were out of the game. No one wanted to be out, so even when the leader did things we did not want to do, we would do it anyway in order to stay in the game.

In this game you had to concentrate and keep your eyes on the leader to make sure you followed all the changes that were made. As I think about those days, I wonder what I would have done if the leader had told us to jump off a high wall. Would I have done it?

Many people have ended in trouble and ruined their lives because of following the wrong leader. At school Follow the Leader was a game of fun, but in real life when we do the same it does not always end up well. Many drug addicts and criminals became that way because of following the wrong leader.

Christ commands us not to put our confidence in people. Psalm 118:8, similar to today's text, says, "It is better to take refuge in the Lord than to trust in humans" (NIV). In today's text God says, "Follow me." God will never ask us to do anything that is not right. He is our true Leader. He made us; He redeemed us. He is our example, and He will lead us in the way of righteousness. Neither will He ask us to do things we are not able to do.

To follow Jesus, we must keep our eyes on Him and go where He leads. "Whether you turn to the right or to the left, your ears will hear a voice behind you, saying, 'This is the way; walk in it'" (Isa. 30:21, NIV). Let us all endeavor to follow Jesus, our divine leader. If we follow close enough, He will lead us eventually to the kingdom of heaven.

May we all be true followers of Jesus.

Ena Thorpe

God's Compassionate Care

*I will be your God through all your lifetime, yes, even when your hair
is white with age. I made you and I will care for you.
I will carry you along and be your Savior. Isa. 46:4, TLB.*

INTENSE PAIN FROM previous injuries coursed through my body one morning as I tried to get out of bed. *Please, Father God,* I begged through tears as severe pain wracked my frame and depleted my energy, *I feel like staying in bed with the covers over my head, but it's Sabbath. My place is in church.*

Still feeling horrible, I dressed, got into the car, and drove the 35 minutes to church. Once there, however, I found that I had to talk myself into getting out of the car. I must go in.

It was a day of prayer and praise. Knowing this before I left home, I took three books from my stack of books on prayer. Pulling one of the books from my bag, I returned it without even opening it and took up another. In retrospect, I can see that my God knew exactly what I needed at that moment.

The booklet opened to where a small photo of a younger version of myself lay between the pages. I was not even aware that I still had that picture, but what was even more surprising was the title of the page: Old Age. Settling into the pew, I began reading: "No matter how old I live to be, you want me to bear fruit, Father God. Thank you for a promise that encourages me when aches and pains annoy me, and fears for the future fill my mind. . . . Let even my last days glorify your faithfulness" (Andrew Murray, *The Everyday Guide to Prayer,* p. 112). The passage also talked about our serving God through worship and obedience, and that I should not wither or faint. We are advised to thank God for the fruit He has given us: children, friends, and spiritual blessings.

I could not keep back the tears as I read the prayer. I felt unworthy and broken as I thought of our great God, the Creator of the vast universe, who thought of me—little me. I could not help scribbling this testimony of praise and service to Him: "When I consider God's tenderness and nurturing thoughts toward me, I praise Him for putting me together and then lifting me up when I fall apart. Great is God's faithfulness to me. I love You, Lord Jesus. My desire is to serve You for the rest of my life."

Madge S. May

Beware of the Adversary

Stay alert! Watch out for your great enemy, the devil.
He prowls around like a roaring lion, looking for someone to devour.
1 Peter 5:8, NLT.

MY HUSBAND AND I are bird lovers. Watching the antics of the birds through our sliding glass doors entertains us at every meal. Needless to say, we do not enjoy seeing our neighbor's orange tabby cat hanging around under our four feeders.

Recently I was reading near this glass door when I looked out and saw our feline prowler. I knew by the quivering tail something sinister was going on. On closer investigation, I watched an exciting mini-drama. A beautiful Eurasian collared-dove was on the fence gazing intently at the cat, seemingly undisturbed by the dangerous situation it was facing. It looked to me like the two animals were playing games with each other. The dove was daring the cat to try to catch it, knowing it could fly away at any moment. While one was lackadaisical in its grave situation, the other was ready for the thrill of the kill. Every muscle in the cat's body was on high alert. Its eyes were glued on the bird.

The dove was aware the cat was coming closer, so it casually moved down the fence away from its enemy. At one point it even turned its back on the cat. I was fighting with myself to keep from shooing the cat away, but I just couldn't. I was helplessly transfixed by the drama of the moment. Finally the cat made another move closer to the bird, and the dove flew away.

How often do we find ourselves rationalizing with our pet sins? We think we can fly away from the temptation at any time, not realizing how deadly is our foe; and how subtly he can convince us to ignore our conscience. So we play games with this cat (lion/devil). We don't realize how swiftly he can strike. When he does strike, we forget to earnestly pray to our ally and precious friend, Jesus, for heavenly strength to vanquish this deadly foe.

We recognize the very dangerous world we live in. We are grateful to God who has brought us courage and hope by dying on the cross for us. He tells us, "So humble yourselves before God. Resist the devil, and he will flee from you" (James 4:7, NLT). Today we need to surrender all to God. It's the only way we can escape this deadly adversary.

Donna Lee Sharp

The Ball

If ye then, being evil, know how to give good gifts unto your children, how much more shall your Father which is in heaven give good things to them that ask him? Matt. 7:11.

ONE AUGUST THE school where my son studied planned a party in honor of the students' fathers. There would be different activities and games, but unfortunately my husband had a work appointment that conflicted with the program. He'd never missed any school event before, but this time he had to be somewhere else. So I volunteered to go, though I feared that the event would not be the same for our son without his dad. When we arrived at school and my son saw his friends coming with their fathers, in tears he decided not to go in. Thus, my husband took us home and went on to his workplace.

After some time we decided to go back to the school and participate in the program. When we arrived, we were welcomed and saw other children whose dads could not be present.

When it was time for the drawing we noticed that the prizes were balls: volleyballs, basketballs, and soccer balls. My son became enthusiastic when he saw the prizes and said that if our number was drawn, he would want a soccer ball. Then I, who have hardly ever won anything, began to worry and pray. Each number called was an affliction. My son held tightly to me as I clutched the number 82 and prayed. Remembering how he had cried because of the absence of his father, I began to cry out to God, relying on His concern about even little things, knowing that the ball would be some consolation.

Then the person who was doing the drawing stopped for a moment, shook the envelope, and, as if in slow motion, announced, "Number 82!" Our hearts raced with joy, and my son and I ran and received the last soccer ball.

The shine in my son's eyes was intense. He was very happy and showed his ball to everybody. I told him how much I had prayed for our number to be drawn, and he was radiant with joy. We had a wonderful Sunday!

God does listen to our simplest and most insignificant requests. What we judge to be even of little importance is important to God because He loves us very much!

Érica Cristina Pinheiro de Souza

To God Who Hears—My Gratitude

The eyes of the Lord are on the righteous, and His ears are open to their cry. Ps. 34:15, NKJV.

I LIKE TO STOP and think about how God sees me. Before the greatness of God, Creator of the universe, who am I to deserve His attention, love, affection, care, and protection? Yes, I am His daughter, and I know with certainty that He loves and cares for me affectionately!

What else can I say when I read Jeremiah 29:11-13? "For I know the thoughts that I think toward you, says the Lord, thoughts of peace and not of evil, to give you a future and a hope. Then you will call upon Me and go and pray to Me, and I will listen to you. And you will seek Me and find Me, when you search for Me with all your heart" (NKJV).

I'd always been healthy until I began to feel ill with abnormal blood pressure. In the hospital I was given a wrong injection, and that is when real trouble began. I had two convulsions that caused me to break both arms, two ribs, and three thoracic vertebrae. As if that was not enough, I suffered a stroke.

For two weeks I remained in a coma. People who visited me said that I would not survive. My family expected the worst. The doctors and nurses said that only a miracle could bring me back to life. It was at that moment that prayers began ascending toward heaven on my behalf. I was anointed by my dear pastor. I was not conscious of what was happening, but today I know that so many people were praying for me that a miracle happened.

I stayed in the hospital 27 days and then used a wheelchair for four months. But today I am well and have no bad aftereffects. We held a beautiful service of gratitude, and my heart remains grateful to our all-powerful God and to my loved ones who prayed for me. Everyone who accompanied me witnessed the miracle that took place and recognizes that when we pray, things happen—God hears us and answers us.

"Each is tenderly watched by the heavenly Father. No tears are shed that God does not notice. There is no smile that He does not mark. If we would but fully believe this, all undue anxieties would be dismissed" (*Steps to Christ*, p. 86).

God can do everything, including care for me and you. He has proved it to me.

Hilda José dos Santos

Protected by an Angel

God is our refuge and strength, a very present help in trouble.
Therefore will not we fear, though the earth be removed, and though
the mountains be carried into the midst of the sea. Ps. 46:1, 2.

BECAUSE I HAVE A problem with claustrophobia, I will not ride in an elevator by myself or be contained or locked in any closed area from which I cannot extricate myself by myself.

About five months ago I accompanied my husband to the AAA office in town. While waiting, I needed to go to the restroom. I examined the door and the lock and noticed that the lock was bent. I proceeded into the cubicle and locked the door, hoping that I would be able to undo it when I got ready to get out.

I realized that I was in deep trouble when I attempted to unlock the door and was unsuccessful. Fear gripped me and I panicked! I began screaming for help, banging on the door, and climbing onto the commode in an effort to get out. Just then I heard the toilet in the adjoining cubicle flush. I immediately seized the opportunity and yelled to the person next to me to help me get out.

This gracious lady told me that she'd go and fetch someone to unlock the door, but I implored her not to leave me alone—for I would die! She said that her name was Sue and that she would not leave me. Because Sue, "my angel," was of small stature, she was able to crawl under the door, come into the cubicle, help me to calm down, pray with me, and rebuke the phobia which is from the devil. She claimed a promise in 2 Timothy 1:7 for me: "For God has not given us a spirit of fear, but of power and of love and of a sound mind" (NKJV).

Sue examined the lock and was able to undo it. Needless to say we were both happy and praised God for His help. We had prayer together before rejoining our spouses.

It is so easy to forget that God is a ready help in trouble and that all we need to do is calm down, think, and ask Him to come to our rescue. That day I allowed fear to get the better of me, but I know that the Lord is gracious and full of compassion, and He has forgiven me for this moment of weakness.

Kollis Salmon-Fairweather

100 Carrots

Store your treasures in heaven.
Matt. 6:20, NLT.

MANY YEARS AGO when our children were small we would often go for a Sabbath afternoon walk to the beach of the mighty Skeena River, where we made lots of happy memories. One day on our way to the river we passed a sawmill that was next to a market garden where they grew delicious carrots.

There were several stacks of lumber. One end of each stack was all perfectly flat and flush, but the other end was like stair steps, all uneven, depending on the length of each piece of lumber.

We noticed a carrot on the end of one of the boards, and when we were closer we saw another, and yet another carrot, on the end of almost every single piece of wood. Then we saw not just one carrot but five or more on some boards. We turned around to look at another stack of lumber and sure enough, more carrots were precariously stacked there also! We just stood and looked at this most peculiar, funny sight. Apparently the local squirrel had discovered the delicious, sweet carrots and decided that he—or she—would hide carrots for yummy winter snacks. Imagine the hard work it was for this little fellow.

Always ready to catch a "Kodak moment," thankfully I had my camera with me and we got a picture that still makes us smile as we remember the humorous sight we saw that day. (Actually I just now looked at the picture, and about 100 carrots are visible!)

So this busy little squirrel was no doubt storing up his treasure for the winter. Little did he know that it was probably in vain because the carrots would all too soon freeze and shrivel up. Maybe he should have chosen the hazelnuts that were in the area.

It makes me wonder what "treasures" we spend time storing up that one day will be worthless. Let's make sure that we are storing up heavenly treasures, such as doing kind deeds for those who can't repay us, or random acts of kindness and investing in people. Years ago I read a couplet that I like: "Only one life, 'twill soon be past, only what's done for Christ will last."

Gay Mentes

From Darkness to Light

In returning and rest you shall be saved;
in quietness and confidence shall be your strength. Isa. 30:15, NKJV.

I HAD TO LEAVE MY husband with two small babies and one 8-year-old boy. As if this were not enough, I began to hear voices. These voices ordered me to do things, and as I was very fragile, I ended up doing them. I reached the point of being admitted to a home for mental illness, suffering from bipolar disorder.

I had seven horrible crises. The voice had told me that I was cured, so I stopped taking my medication. That brought on another crisis. In the seventh crisis I attempted to take my own life, so I thought, *I need to find this Savior or this thing is going to kill me.*

I had already gone to some churches, and I had not found Him.

Then I decided to search in the Bible. When I read today's verse my heart filled with hope, since this verse said that I would have strength in quietness and confidence.

When the voice spoke with me, I recited the verse quoted above, breathed deeply, calmed down, and trusted in God, or imagined that He was by my side, and the voice disappeared. I did this exercise several times, until the voice ceased completely. Today I am free.

I also read about God's commandments and of the importance of keeping them, but there was no church in my city that kept all God's commandments. I felt like I belonged to a different flock. Then God guided me to the New Time radio. I discovered that at 8:00 there was very good preaching. But I was always very busy working around the kitchen at that time and always missed it. That made me sad, because I needed to hear the preaching. One day, to my surprise, my alarm went off at 8:00 without my having set it. I saw this as the work of God so I could listen to His message. My watch alarm continued to go off for a month, and eventually I'd become so used to turning on the radio at that time that I no longer waited for the alarm. Then one day the alarm stopped going off on its own.

God showed the great love that He has for each of us on the cross of Calvary, and when we desire the truth, He will guide us to it.

Eva Matos Rodrigues

Silence

Be still, and know that
I am God. Ps. 46:10.

MY JOURNEY WITH silence and my relationship to God began with two profound experiences. I was living in Bavaria in 1978 when my father came to visit so he could trace his roots. His parents had emigrated from Slovakia to what is now Croatia in the late 1800s. But Daddy wanted to trace his roots to the homeland. We went to Bratislava, now the capital of the republic of Slovakia, but then under Communist rule. As part of our visit, we went into a Catholic church, the only open church. The interior was pre-World War I and probably more like mid-nineteenth century. As we sat in a pew, a few older folk, mainly women, came, knelt, and prayed. The feeling of devotion was profound. This was indeed a holy space, and these people came to commune with God—in silence and reverence.

The second was when I went to Tenebrae, which means "darkness" or "shadow," and has for centuries applied to the ancient monastic night and early-morning services of the last three days before the Resurrection. The service starts with lighted candles, each of which is extinguished after a meditative anthem and a period of silence. Finally, the large candle, representing Christ, is carried out; and the church is in total darkness.

The reverence I experienced in the dark, silent church was palpable. At first, during the silences, I started to pray, but then I realized that words were superfluous. I needed to let God speak and envelop me in the dark silence.

After the last anthem the organ played a loud noise representing the stone being rolled to seal Christ's grave. Subdued lighting came on, and we left in silence. When I got into my car to drive home, I felt that my time with God wasn't finished. I drove home in silence, wrapped in God's presence. God speaks to us through the eloquence of silence.

Mother Teresa said, "We need to find God, and He cannot be found in noise and restlessness. God is the friend of silence. See how nature—trees, flowers, grass grows in silence; see the stars, the moon and the sun, how they move in silence. We need silence to be able to touch souls" (www.quotegarden.com/silence.html).

Gloria Durichek Gyure

Happy Birthday!

Jesus replied, "Very truly I tell you, no one can see the kingdom of God unless they are born again.". . . Jesus answered, "Very truly I tell you, no one can enter the kingdom of God unless they are born of water and the Spirit." John 3:3-5, NIV.

ONE DAY WHILE sorting though some papers, I came upon my baptismal certificate. While I did remember that I was baptized some 30 years before, I could not remember the exact day. Then I started to think back on birthdays past. We all remember our birthday (even though sometimes we don't want to remember). I remember as a child the excitement of an upcoming birthday. I reminded my mother months before, as if she would forget. The anticipation of that impending birthday could hardly be contained in my small body. I'm sure that we all remember the birthday parties, the gifts, the cards, the cakes, and all the loved ones who shared in our special day. I particularly remember my fourteenth birthday.

My mom was a divorced mother of three, so times were often hard. Money was always tight. So this particular year I did not expect anything more than a "Happy Birthday and many more." But, in fact, my mother gave me a big party. All of my friends and family members came bearing gifts. I was surprised, overwhelmed, and happy. In my childish mind I felt as if I were in heaven. Nothing could have been better. Even now more than some 30 years later, the thought of that day brings such fond memories.

I wonder how much more we should celebrate the day that we died to sin and were buried in that watery grave to come forth in the newness of life in our Lord Jesus Christ. It was the day our lives were completely transformed, ensuring that we would never be the same. What a celebration that should be! Imagine that birthday celebration with the Holy Trinity and angels all in joyful celebration with and for us. Each year we need to celebrate the day of our baptism—not with cakes and gifts and lavish parties—but in rededication, to give our lives anew to Christ, determined that the old person of sin stay buried. It is a time to spread the gospel of our Savior so that others may experience that unforgettable birthday. So let us celebrate our day of rebirth with such zeal and anticipation that it can hardly be contained within us, a day that points to the coming of our Lord. Happy Birthday!

Venessa Stinvil Gutierrez

Thunderstorms of Life

The Lord is my shepherd; I shall not want. He makes me to lie down in green pastures; he leads me beside the still waters. Ps. 23:1, 2, NKJV.

IT WAS A WILD, windy evening in August when a fierce thunderstorm came through Kingston, Jamaica. The day had been very warm and humid, with short periods of wind and drizzle. People could be seen looking toward the skies, watching for storm clouds. Animal farmers made sure their flocks were all in safe houses in case the storm came during the night. Some people set pots and pans to catch rainwater to be stored so there would be clean water during and after the storm. Vegetable farmers harvested crops to avoid complete loss. On this particular night many pounds of vegetables and other food were stored in large barns in order to accommodate families who might not have food during and after the storm.

Suddenly, at 7:00 p.m. the lightning started flashing! The thunder began rolling! People ran in all directions trying to get home. Rose, a 10-year-old, who had planted seeds for a science project, covered them with a very heavy tub before running to her grandma's room. She covered her head with pillows because she was scared of the lightning and thunder. And everyone in town bolted doors and made sure latches were secure. The little girl did not know it, but the heavy tub protecting the seeds also gave them the warmth they needed to grow.

So it is with us as Christians when we are covered by the warmth of prayer and devotion. The Lord, our Shepherd, will lead us into green pastures after the thunderstorms pass, and He will restore us and give us new courage. He will lead us where the pastures are green and our little seeds of kindness can grow into beautiful gardens of love. Our gardens of life will be watered, and after the thunderstorms of life have passed, our troubled souls will be led in paths of righteousness. Even if our petals fade and we die, we will rise again in the newness of life to live forever in the presence of the good Shepherd. We will be comforted by His rod and staff. There will be no thunderstorms of destruction; we will not need to store vegetables and other foods because a lavish table will be spread before us, and in the presence of our enemies our cups will overflow. We will never be thirsty or hungry, because the goodness of the Lord will be with us forever and ever, forever and ever.

Edna Ashmeade

Jumping to Compassion

But a certain Samaritan, as he journeyed, came where he was: and when he saw him, he had compassion on him. Luke 10:33.

MY HUSBAND, RIC, and I like to travel. We have had the opportunity to visit many countries stretching from North America to Asia. One of the most meaningful trips was when we vacationed in London with my parents. Having never been to England before, we were eager to see as much as time allowed. I planned a moderately active itinerary that focused on a different sight each day. It began the morning we arrived in London when we excitedly boarded a bright-red double-decker sightseeing bus to tour the city. One day we visited landmarks, such as the Tower of London, and marveled at the architecture of the Houses of Parliament with its famous feature, Big Ben. Other days we journeyed to the mysterious monoliths at Stonehenge and to the ancient Roman temple in Bath. Each evening we relived what we had seen over a leisurely dinner or quick supper before settling in for the night.

One evening, as we exited a restaurant just around the corner from our hotel, we looked down and saw a scruffy young man sitting on the sidewalk begging for money from the passersby. Most people, who may have thought he looked healthy enough to work, speculated on the circumstances that brought him to his current situation. My husband, however, stopped and gave him the untouched sandwich that he was carrying in a doggie bag from the evening's meal. The young man's loud thanks followed my husband and me as we continued down the street. Expecting to see the beggar toss the sandwich aside and continue to ask for money, I looked back in time to see him ravenously devouring the sandwich where he sat.

Like the compassionate Samaritan in Luke 10, my husband had seen the man as a person, not a beggar, and used what he had at the moment to meet the immediate need of a fellow human being. We'll never know what circumstances led the young man to such a desperate situation. Perhaps he was a backpacker who had been robbed during his adventure. Instead of jumping to conclusions, I learned the benefit of "jumping to compassion." That evening, as the young man looked up into Ric's face, I'm sure he saw the eyes of Jesus.

Sherma Webbe Clarke

The Perfume of Your Garment

Behold, what manner of love the Father hath bestowed upon us,
that we should be called the sons of God. 1 John 3:1.

OH, OH, OH! I was ecstatic about the revelation You gave me as I read this morning. You gave me the comfort of Your love that I had been desperate for. You answered my prayer that I would comprehend with my heart the extent of Your love for me; that I would know by experience how comprehensive it is, and be filled and flooded with God Himself as You promised in Ephesians 3:19. You gave me the experience of coming to You, and You opened Your arms wide and let me hug You around Your waist as if I were a child. You let me smell Your clothing, the perfume of Your garment. Then You wrapped the warmth of Your cape around me like Boaz did for Ruth. You told me again that You would never leave or forsake me as You promised in Joshua 1:5. You told me that I would never have to leave You, either. You said I could stay here enfolded in Your cape as long as I want to. And since You, the all-powerful God, say I never have to leave, I know that is true.

You let me feel the same joy as Mary Magdalene must have felt when she worshipped You by anointing Your feet with perfume and pouring out her love and appreciation from the bottom of her heart. There in Gethsemane You purchased the right to forgive her sins, which were many. I feel like Mary too.

You, the great God, who just let me experience Your love by being wrapped in Your righteousness, Your white cape, are the same Man who was abandoned by all Your best friends. The same Man whose heart broke there in the Garden of Gethsemane as You purchased the right to let me hug You. You purchased the right to wrap me in the garment of Your righteousness and Your love and faith and purity. "Behold, what manner of love the Father hath bestowed upon us!"

Today as I read, I realize what You have done. The cape, cloak, garment, the robe that You put around me is the robe of Your righteousness. *Oh, Jesus, and to think that I never have to be anywhere but here with You, abiding under Your warm white raiment.* The price is "simply for the self-surrender" required to accept such a gift! (Isa. 55:1, Amplified).

Elizabeth Boyd

Put God to the Test

"Bring all the tithes into the storehouse, that there may be food in My house,
and prove Me now in this," says the Lord of hosts,
"if I will not open for you the windows of heaven and pour out for you such
blessing that there will not be room enough to receive it." Mal. 3:10, NKJV.

THE WORDS "You shall not steal" (Ex. 20:15, NKJV) and "Will a man rob God?
Yet you have robbed Me! . . . In tithes and offerings" (Mal. 3:8, NKJV) stung like
hail bullets each time I received my meager paycheck. In addition a small voice,
like a continuous drip on a rainy day, kept nagging at me until the drops slowed,
became less, and eventually stopped. I became comfortable with my dishonesty.

I had not returned my tithe for a while. How could I share my paltry paycheck
with the church? Not only did I work for minimum wage, but my employer reminded me that the job I held would be discontinued. I lived in a small town, and
the prospect of further employment there was limited. My income barely covered
very basic needs. Tithe was not in my budget.

Frustration overwhelmed me. What were my alternatives? Perhaps I could return to school. But that would require tuition. After serious pondering and prayer,
I decided to take the risk. I enrolled at a state university. The Lord is longsuffering
and stretched my check to include the tuition. Challenges were many, but God was
with me.

Then one Sabbath a visiting minister at my church preached on stewardship.
Those hail bullets stung again, but this time the voice was loud and clear: "You
have robbed me in tithes and offerings." When a call for commitment was made, I
responded, and returning to my apartment I struggled on my knees. I opened my
Bible to Malachi 3:8-11, the verses the minister had read. My decision was final. I
would put God to the test. There was no shifting. I began returning tithe and remained faithful to my promise. And the "cruse of oil" was never exhausted. There
was always just enough to "fill the vessel" (1 Kings 17:16, NKJV).

At the end of my course, I started job hunting. Two days after my last interview, the director called me and offered me the job. God had reserved the perfect
job—really a ministry—for me. Put God to the test. See how His blessings shower
on those who trust Him!

Beulah E. Andrews

A Second Chance

[The Lord's compassions] are new every morning; great is your faithfulness. Lam. 3:23, NIV.

IT'S NOT OFTEN that we get to live the same day twice. Recently my husband, Bob, and I left Cairns, Australia, at 8:00 a.m. and arrived home in Michigan at midnight 31 hours later. Over the Pacific, we crossed the date line and started that Sunday all over again. We viewed two sunrises, one over the Coral Sea, and one over the Pacific. We ate breakfast in the Cairns hotel, lunch between Cairns and Auckland, New Zealand, dinner just out of Auckland, and breakfast again just before San Francisco. I spent the night in an upright posture, which didn't improve my second "go" at the day, but I pondered the opportunity of a second chance to live that day well.

Sitting there, I had time to pray for family, friends, church, and personal issues. I had time to contemplate the many tasks awaiting me at home after five weeks away. I began listing them on paper and checking the most urgent—unpacking, laundry, watering houseplants, hundreds of e-mails, boxes of snail mail from the post office.

I also had time to reflect on our wonderful trip—first to New Zealand for my husband to baptize a 12-year-old granddaughter living there and an 11-year-old grandson visiting from Oklahoma. Later we went to Australia to visit friends and sightsee. I recalled the warm support of the church members who attended the baptism, the sightseeing, hiking, and fun with our two daughters' families. Then my thoughts turned to God's goodness in sparing one daughter from blindness in a freak eye emergency, the hospitality of friends who hosted us in Australia, and the new bird species I could add to my life list. I smiled, thinking of the kangaroos, the koala we had fed and petted, the pelican feed we saw up close, the boat trip to the Great Barrier Reef, a train ride up into the rain forest, the friendly welcome of the church in Cairns, and much more.

If I could have a second chance at a normal day, without sleep deprivation, how would I spend it? Would I spend more time in prayer? Would I plan my life more strategically? Would I reflect on blessings and happy memories?

Before long we plan to move to a homeland with no night. Will we know how to spend 1,000 years there? We can communicate with Him face to face, we can plan trips around the universe, and enjoy endless learning. We can forever recount the blessings of God.

Madeline Steele Johnston

Another Kind of Fertility

My flesh and my heart may fail, but God is the strength of my heart and my portion forever. Ps. 73:26, NIV.

MARCEL, A PHOTOGRAPHER colleague of mine, had an assignment near my office and came over for a chat. I always like our conversations, so I dropped my papers and out came the usual "How are you?" A real question. Both ways.

I mentioned having a hysterectomy a month before, and he was surprised to see me smiling. He knew I didn't have children. To lessen his uneasiness I told him that I believed in God, I was sure that He had somehow prepared me for this, and I knew He was helping me get through the little blues I was having.

We hadn't gone much further in our conversation when he had to leave to begin his shoot. As he rushed out he quietly said, "I'm also a believer." And he was gone.

A couple of weeks later Marcel stopped back by my office. This time he had no assignment nearby. Instead, this was a time to continue our conversation with no interruptions. He handed me a little gift and said, "Lorena, I wish for you another kind of fertility. True, you won't have the chance to bear children, but you can bear another kind of children. You can do all sorts of things that can benefit others. You can give birth to things that will have a positive influence on people."

After he left, I grabbed my diary and wrote his words: "another kind of fertility." I knew this was a moment I would always remember. And I am now convinced this was also a message from my heavenly Father. It was a way to cheer me on. After all, He is the God who said, "Sing, barren woman, you who never bore a child; burst into song, shout for joy, you who were never in labor (Isa. 54:1, NIV).

That evening my husband and I were very moved as we pondered these wise, healing words. Even for a man, this was a particularly encouraging message.

So I invite you to take these simple words, ponder them, and make them fit in your own life story. It's our Father cheering us on. He can make our smiles bigger, our tears smaller, and our service for others extraordinarily rewarding: another kind of fertility.

Lorena Mayer

After Deliverance, a Choice

But God sent me ahead of you to preserve for you a remnant on earth and to save your lives by a great deliverance. Gen. 45:7, NIV.

"EWWWW! WHAT IS IT?" my husband exclaimed as he looked at the blob of vomit our large German Shepherd, Max, had just thrown up on the floor. I looked closer and saw the gelatos blob of goo move. I wasn't at all sure what it was, but I knew it was alive. I picked up the goo and took it to the sink and turned on some warm water and started washing off the contents of Max's stomach. To my surprise it was some kind of baby squirrel or chipmunk—I couldn't tell for sure. It was alive, but cold. Being a natural born mom, I stuck the babe in the warmest place I could think of, under my shirt in my bra. My husband just couldn't believe it! I went about my housework, and as the hours passed he would ask, "Is it still alive?" I would answer, "Yes," and laugh.

Well, Chip, as we named our little ground squirrel, had a bad front paw. We fed him cooked oatmeal with nuts and things mixed in because he couldn't hold regular food. When he went to church with me for the children's story, the whole congregation had to pet him. He was a regular ham and loved the attention. From his cage he spent hours longingly looking out the window at the great outdoors, and you could see he wanted freedom. I prayed, asking for guidance, knowing I couldn't release him to the wild with that bad foot. I had tried splinting it with various things, but nothing worked. Then we had the idea of just putting a bandage on it. The bandage stayed on only three days, but it enabled the foot to heal. When Chip finally chewed it off, he could use his foot again. We kept him for another week, making sure he could use it to hold all kinds of food. Then we took him down the road to a nice woodpile where he'd be safe, and turned him loose. I took him food for about a week, and he came out to see me for a couple days. But after that he didn't come out to my voice anymore.

Chip's story always reminds me that Jesus paid the ultimate price for us to have our freedom and the right to choose where we want to live for eternity. Jesus does so much for us, and if we choose to go live with Him, all our imperfections will be made perfect forever. Oh, to hear the voice of Jesus calling me home. What a glorious day that will be!

Mona Fellers

Paid in Full

For ye know the grace of our Lord Jesus Christ, that, though he was rich, yet for your sakes he became poor, that ye through his poverty might be rich. 2 Cor. 8:9.

IT SEEMS THAT MY daughter and I are always before the Lord asking Him for something, and thanking Him for past blessings. The year 2009 was no exception.

Just a couple of years earlier, my daughter Loretta had been diagnosed with multiple sclerosis. Previously she passionately homeschooled her two sons and worked on a doctorate in education. She had passed her comprehensive exams on the first attempt and looked forward to completing her degree in record time. Never did we imagine that that year, instead of writing her dissertation, she would spend the next 12 months in search of an answer. You see, her family operated on one income, and they had no medical insurance at the time of diagnosis. Loretta could no longer afford to attend school, and finishing her Ph.D. seemed more and more hopeless.

The university's policy was that doctoral students could not take off more than a year from the program. If that happened, the student must begin the program all over again. As her mother, I encouraged Loretta through prayer, and my husband and I also gave some financial assistance, but it was not enough. We trusted God to open the windows of heaven and shower us with a financial blessing. One day, as we beseeched the Lord, a text came to Loretta's mind. She was impressed to write letters to influential people around the world—ranging from movie celebrities to the president of the United States. Needless to say, the deadline to enroll in school was fast approaching. Magnificently, out of nowhere, a door opened. Loretta received a letter from the university stating that her tuition was *paid in full* for the remainder of her doctoral program. What a mighty God we serve!

This experience drew me closer to the Lord. You see, Jesus paid the ultimate sacrifice, saving me from my sins. God's desire is to save us, and He made it possible by giving up His only Son. I have learned that I do not need to worry or stress about the cares of this life. The debts are too high for me to pay. Jesus Christ has paid it all, and His blood has covered my sin. My debt is *paid in full.*

Vivian Brown

Dorothy's Testimony

Therefore we do not lose heart. Though outwardly we are wasting away, yet inwardly we are being renewed day by day. For our light and momentary troubles are achieving for us an eternal glory that far outweighs them all. 2 Cor. 4:16, 17, NIV.

WHEN MY SISTER Dorothy was diagnosed with HIV/AIDS, our family was more angry than saddened. Why had God allowed such a horrible thing to happen? Personally, I was extremely angry with her husband, blaming him for infecting her. To add insult to injury, he refused to give her money for medication. I threatened that if anything happened to my sister, I was holding him accountable. I was consumed with bitterness and anger toward him, and never did I think about the torment he might be going through. Despite Dorothy's pain and suffering, my beautiful sister never blamed her husband. She never begrudged him for deliberately withholding financial support, but instead thanked God for giving her a supportive family.

Our family solicited prayers from friends and fasted for days, believing that Christ in His boundless love would restore her health. Yet despite all this, Dorothy was not physically healed. In her last letter to me, which arrived two days before she began her rest in Jesus, she expressed her gratitude to God. "God has shown me so much love and miracles during this time," she wrote. "There is nothing I can ever do for Him, other than be waiting for Him on that beautiful morning when we will all gather at the sea of glass. My prayer is that we all will be there."

My sister explained that even if she did not receive the miracle of physical healing, she believed that God had healed her spiritually. She believed that God answered her greatest prayer request: saving her soul from eternal loss. She quoted Paul's words found in today's text.

I was told that everyone around Dorothy was crying during her last ride to Mulago Hospital in Uganda, but she was singing "To God be the glory, great things He has done." My mother and younger sister, strengthened by her courage and faith, started singing with her. Dorothy kept repeating the words, "My Redeemer liveth." Two days later she peacefully passed away in her sleep.

Instead of mourning, I started praising God for such a great testimony. I also forgave my brother-in-law, and at last I was filled with a great sense of calmness.

Edith Kiggundu

Encouragement Is a Positive

Like apples of gold in settings of silver is a ruling rightly given.
Prov. 25:11, NIV.

IT'S ABSOLUTELY marvelous, when looking back on one's life, to remember the different people we have met and the associations that we have had. Some have been inspirational and uplifting while others have been discouraging. I believe that in all situations God is trying to teach us lessons. We may never know until eternity what effect our words and actions have had on the people we associate with from day to day.

I think of the story of Russell and just what the encouraging words spoken by a sympathetic person did for this young man. It gave him the courage and confidence that God could speak through him to reach out to the young people in our church.

Russell attended a large suburban church in Adelaide, the capital of South Australia. When he was around 18 years old he felt the desire to preach God's Word. But Russell didn't have the confidence to preach in front of his peers, so he sought out a country church at Murray Bridge, approximately 50 miles (80 kilometers) from Adelaide. After much time in prayer and study, Russell was confident that he could deliver his maiden sermon. However, when the time came and he stood up to preach, words failed him. He lost his confidence and fled out of the church into the adjoining hall. There a middle-age woman caught up with him and spoke kind words of encouragement.

Later Russell moved with his family to Melbourne, the capital of Victoria, where he trained to become a schoolteacher. He has married and is now preaching fortnightly in a youth church. He also leads weekly Bible studies for a group of young men, and his wife leads Bible studies for young women.

We underestimate that powerful word "encouragement." God gives us words to speak and prompts us into action. "May our Lord Jesus Christ himself and God our Father, who loved us and by his grace gave us eternal encouragement and good hope, encourage your hearts and strengthen you in every good deed and word" (2 Thess. 2:16, 17, NIV). The wonderful thing is that God not only encourages us, but through the Holy Spirit He can help us to encourage others. We may never know the difference it can make in someone's life.

Joan D. L. Jaensch

Silver Sands

But for that very reason I was shown mercy so that in me, the worst of sinners, Christ Jesus might display his immense patience as an example for those who would believe in him and receive eternal life. 1 Tim. 1:16, NIV.

THE BUNGALOW that housed me and my husband, Milton, and several other couples on the faculty retreat was quiet. At 5:00 a.m. we crept silently past bedrooms, out the front door, and into the crisp, refreshing morning air. It really felt like a new day. As we walked along the winding trail toward the beach, a sliver of sun peeked over the eastern sky.

If the others knew what they were missing, they would have jumped up out of their beds and joined us. We listened to the quiet swashing of the waves and watched the sunrise, an orange glow in the sky. Like children, we hurriedly slipped our imprisoned feet out of our slippers to splash in the cool, tingling water. The silvery white sand felt like powder between my toes. Milton waded into the water up to his waist, and I up to my knees. My entire body felt immersed and refreshed by the clear, soothing water.

After a few minutes I noticed that Milton had walked a little distance away on the beach. Not wanting to miss a moment of our early morning escapade together, I headed after him. But walking in his footsteps in the sand was difficult. I needed two steps for his one. I called for him to wait, and immediately we reminisced on the popular poem "Footprints in the Sand."

On our way back to the bungalow, we reflected on the beautiful morning's experience, but I was overwhelmed with the thought of walking in another person's footsteps. As parents we expect our children to walk in our footsteps, but it's hard for them. As teachers we want our students to do and act exactly as we do. It's almost impossible. According to a popular Native American proverb: "Do not complain about others until you walk in their moccasins."

That morning the silver sands' experience jolted me into the realization that I should not expect others to be like me. I should point them to Christ, who is the perfect example. Show them how to develop a relationship with Him. When they emulate Him, He not only shows them what to do, but when they make a mistake He is willing to forgive them and cover them with His righteousness.

Gloria Gregory

Deliverance

And, ye fathers, provoke not your children to wrath: but bring them up in the nurture and admonition of the Lord. Eph. 6:4.

I NOTICED HE WAS always alone. He never spoke a word, not once, during a long period of time. *Who is this child?* I wondered. What was he doing in this jail among all these older men? There was a facility for adolescents. Why was he here? Why did he never attend the counseling sessions? I could not take my eyes off him.

One day one of the older men spoke to him, then, taking him by the hand, led him to one of the counseling groups. They boy went with him meekly and sat down. Not long after, he asked for a Bible. I gave him one, and he hugged it to his heart. Later I was told by many of the other men that he took it with him everywhere. When they went outside, while the others played ball he found a quiet spot and read his Bible. He spent many months behind those bars.

At last his case came before the judge. Of course, he must have been afraid. Early in the morning when the officer went to fetch him, he found him on his knees clutching his Bible and praying. The judge looked at him with compassion as he sat in the courtroom at his lawyer's side. Here was a child of 14. The counselor urged him to remove his shirt to show his back to the court. The judge's face grew pale, for the boy's back was so crisscrossed with scars that none of his natural skin was visible. When the judge regained his composure, he said, with tears in his voice, "Put your shirt back on and go home." I was told there was not a pair of dry eyes in that courtroom.

The story was that the boy's father was an alcoholic who came home drunk every Saturday night and beat him and his mother unmercifully. One night when his father was about to kill his mother with his brutality, the boy picked up a kitchen knife and stabbed his father to death. His mother ended up in the hospital, and he ended up in jail.

Lonely and frightened, he found himself incarcerated. He spoke to no one until he asked for the Bible which he read constantly. He and his mother were reunited, and he encouraged her to go with him to church. They are now faithful to the Lord who gave them deliverance.

Give thanks to the Lord, for He is good and His mercy endures forever.

Daisy Simpson

A God of Aesthetics

Whatever is true, whatever is noble, whatever is right, whatever is pure, whatever is lovely, whatever is admirable—if anything is excellent or praiseworthy—think about such things. Phil. 4:8, NIV.

SOME YEARS AGO I listened to a dissertation on my church and its values. The study focused on which values score highest among the church members and hypothesized why. The results were rather predictable. An unexpected twist, however, surprised us all. One of the examiners, a visiting professor from another denomination, said, "This is all very nice, but wouldn't it be interesting to look at the values that did not score very highly, for example, aesthetics? You preach about heaven, where everything is supposed to be so beautiful, but it seems that no one gives aesthetics any importance here on earth. How do you explain that?"

Whenever we read today's verse, we usually think about character, thoughts, et cetera, but seldom do we think that this verse could also be referring to sheer beauty.

A few days ago I read about the Israelites' exodus, particularly when God gave them instructions on how to live. God gave His people the Ten Commandments, explained their social responsibilities, then talked about Sabbath laws and festivals, and finally instructed them on how to build the Tabernacle. From Exodus 25 to the end of the book, 11 chapters out of the remaining 16 painstakingly describe an aesthetic creation! Could it be, perhaps, that beauty is important to God, even here on this imperfect earth? Perfumed fragrance, colorful curtains, dazzling stones, embroidered cherubs—could it get any more beautiful?

Exodus 35 clearly states that it is the Spirit of God that gives us "wisdom, with understanding, with knowledge and with all kinds of skills—to make artistic designs for work in gold, silver and bronze, to cut and set stones, to work in wood and to engage in all kinds of artistic crafts;" "to do all kinds of work as engravers, designers, embroiderers in blue, purple and scarlet yarn and fine linen, and weavers—all of them skilled workers and designers" (verses 31-33, 35, NIV).

Do you think that aesthetics rate high in God's value system and are part of His essence? I do. Why don't we make efforts to reflect that beauty and act upon "whatever is lovely" in our everyday lives? Today let us bring a little bit of God and heaven to this earth.

Cintia García Block

Labor Prompted by Love

We remember before our God and Father your work produced by faith, your labor prompted by love. 1 Thess. 1:3, NIV.

AT THE BEGINNING of every school year, in the midst of getting our new and used high school textbooks, we had to fill out a form about ourselves. The best part was not the form itself but its purpose. Prayer Patch Partners was beginning! Every student listed their birthday, family information, interests, and dislikes. Prayer Patch Partners then distributed the information to church members who wanted to pray for the students. The idea was that each student would have a prayer warrior praying especially for them.

For a teenager, something tangible like a little card or surprise went a long way in showing that someone cared and was praying for them. Unfortunately, most of the students never got anything. By the time Christmas rolled around, most had forgotten that they had Prayer Patch Partners or that anyone was praying for them.

From my freshman through senior year, I filled out the form. Each year passed without even a note from my prayer partner. I couldn't help but wonder if I had been forgotten.

When I was a senior, I came to my job one morning and saw a little African violet plant on my desk. Seeing the plant sitting there in its plastic pot, soft velvety leaves with purple blossoms waiting for me brought me tingles of happiness. I asked, "Who is this from? Is it for me?" My bosses said they couldn't tell me, but I knew it was from my Prayer Patch Partner.

Throughout that year I found little surprises sitting on my desk when I arrived at work. It was the best feeling to know someone was thinking of me and praying for me. I felt loved.

Some time after my high school graduation I was telling my cousin about the Prayer Patch Partners and how much it had meant to finally get something from mine. Suddenly I noticed that my cousin and aunt had funny looks on their faces. "What! Were you my Prayer Patch Partner?" I asked incredulously. My aunt said she wasn't but had felt badly that I and some of the other students never had anything that would acknowledge they had a prayer partner, so decided to take matters into her own hands. So all of my little surprises and gifts were from her!

My aunt saw the need, not only for prayer, but for action. As our text says, "your labor prompted by love." It is my prayer that your love will prompt you to labor for those around you.

Beth-Anne Nicole White

A Bucket of Joy

But to do justly, to love mercy, and to walk humbly with your God?
Micah 6:8, NKJV.

A CHURCH FAMILY came to my home to visit me during my illness, and brought along their small son. As they entered the door, I suddenly felt sad as I remembered that I had no toys in my home for him to play with. This, of course, made the stay challenging for the parents. But after exploring his surroundings, the child slowly found joy in playing alone with his only toy, a small car. Finally he fell asleep listening to the chime of the clock.

When our son was young he had so many toys that there were always enough for him and his friends to share. However, as he got older and moved out to attend college, we gave away or tossed most of those beloved treasures. About a week after the little boy's visit I began checking around the house, knowing we still had to have some toys somewhere. It was then that I came upon the puzzle. I was delighted, but found myself staring at it for a minute. It was yellow cork board with colorful orange, blue, green, and purple punch out numbers. It was an attractive, safe, easy, and interesting game for any child. But what intrigued me was the order of the numbers. The numbers were in order from 1 to 0. I had often wondered why the zero was at the end instead of the beginning. I am not an educator, so after checking the Internet, I learned that the 0 is one of the most important numbers. It plays a central role in physics, chemistry, computer sciences, and mathematics, denoting important elements, objects, degrees, values, logics and theories. But that still didn't explain the puzzle to me.

I thought about how we as adults focus so much on numbers. Each of these numbers has its own identity, shape, and color. Did it matter which one was the most important? The zero at the end looked just as good as any other number to a child. Like these numbers, sometimes, we try to put ourselves above another just so we look good. But at the end, it makes us no better than any other person. As my family used to say, we all have to put on our pants one leg at a time.

Caring how we treat one another is what we strive to teach our children, and yet we forget our own lessons. Don't we say to them, "Jesus wants us to love one another"?

Now I have a bucket of toys, including the puzzle, ready and waiting for a small visitor to come again. That should be a bucket of joy as well.

Catherine McIver

Talking to God

In peace I will lie down and sleep, for you alone, O Lord, will keep me safe.
Ps. 4:8, NLT.

IT WAS ONLY about two weeks after my husband, David, died and I was having one of my very serious chats with God.

We had not played the "Why me?" game. David was wonderful, and had faith that God would either cure him or let him sleep until Jesus came to get us. It wasn't easy living through the 12 to 14 months that the surgeon had said my husband would live. One minute a sporadic twitching right arm; the next, a death sentence. "A malignant brain tumor," they said. For the first few weeks we were run off our feet with hospital visits, radiotherapy, an operation to insert a small reservoir into his skull to extract fluid from the tumor, and returning the movement to David's right side.

Many things happened during those months, and our home was inundated by nurses, doctors, people changing our home for David's needs, and, most important to us, our "small group" from church. Every Thursday morning we would study Jesus, and every week our faith grew in the knowledge that our God loves and saves. The friendships grew around that table, and it was these friends who nurtured us and carried us through the darkest of days.

David celebrated his seventieth birthday, and that night, after all the visitors left, David fell asleep. The church was full for the celebration of his life. A few months earlier he had even written a song, and a choir sang it during the service. We laid him to rest on a sunny afternoon, and now on his headstone are the words of today's text, a prayer I remember daily.

The days after David's death were incredibly sad and very quiet compared to the previous months. I had shouted at God, cried at Him, and finally asked Him "Why?" When we had all asked for just one miracle, had He not heard us? The answer I got was amazing: "I gave you two miracles." Had I missed them? I hadn't seen anything.

"What two miracles?" I asked through my tears.

"Neither of you had any pain. I took that from you." You see, I suffer with rheumatoid arthritis and didn't have a single flare-up during David's illness, and I had lifted him from chairs, beds, and wheelchairs. Four days after the burial I woke up to find I couldn't move my hands.

When people ask me about God and His existence I say, "He exists. I have proof."

Wendy Bradley

Is This Jesus I'm Serving?

Whatever you did for [others]. Matt. 25:40, NIV.

My grace is sufficient. 2 Cor. 12:9, NIV.

I COULDN'T STOP thinking about what our son Paul said: "Is this Jesus I'm serving?" I've counted it a privilege and joy to serve others. In fact, it was exciting to think that I could be serving my best friend, Jesus, the one who created me! The one who has made it possible for me to be with Him eternally. Paul's question reminded me of Jesus' saying, Whatever you do for others, you do for Me. What a privilege is ours!

God loves us deeply. He is closer to us than we know. Just think, every breath He supplies, every heartbeat, is a gift from Him. He answers prayer. He cares about everything that concerns us. Inspired writings tell us that we will know Him by His voice! We hear God's voice in many ways, especially as we spend time reading His Word, His love letter to us.

I was given a phone number and asked to contact a young wife who was going through a stormy divorce. For many months she and I spent hours on the phone praying and sometimes weeping together. All that time, I had not met Carol, but I knew her voice each time she'd call.

At camp meeting one Sabbath morning I was searching for an empty seat under the huge tent. Then I heard a voice, and knew immediately that it was Carol. I could hardly wait to hurry to see her, to stand by her side with a warm, gentle hug for the first time.

It gave me a little glimpse of what it will be like when we see Jesus. We will know Him by His voice! To survive the storms of life, we're going to need to know Him. We get to know God not only through His Word but in nature, in providential leadings, in impressions of the Holy Spirit, through His friends—and there may be ways we haven't noticed.

Now as I go about my "daily dozens" I'm often thinking, *Is this Jesus I'm serving?* Serving Him as we serve others will be our pleasure. No sacrifice will be too much.

Prayer time is a wonderful time to reconnect, to listen for God's voice and to realize that prayer opens the door for Him to speak to our heart with peace, comfort, and love. What a glorious day it will be when we hear Jesus' voice with the message "My grace is sufficient for you."

Ione Richardson

Blessings x 4

We remember before our God and Father your work produced by faith, your labor prompted by love, and your endurance inspired by hope in our Lord Jesus Christ. 1 Thess. 1:3, NIV.

FOUR MULTITALENTED women have blessed our church. These women are Sister L, a Bible worker; Sister F, a housewife; Sister E, a retired schoolteacher; and Sister G, a retired professor and motivational speaker. Amazingly, all four women exhibit the same soft-spoken and prayerful qualities. Each of them worked for many untiring years in the Sabbath school and other ministries in our church. But now, because of illnesses, they are unable to continue teaching on a regular basis.

Several years ago many of our church family gathered together to pay tribute to them with "A Basket of Flowers" in the form of songs, poems, and signing. These tributes were performed by people of different ages, from young children to middle-age adults.

What a legacy these four women have given to women of all ages in the church! They saw the need and gave their all. To list what they've done would take up all the space allowed for this devotional. Through the years I've had the privilege of working with all of them in various capacities, in different ministries. They do not seem to have the word no in their vocabulary. When asked to help with a task, they are eager to do whatever they can, and they do it with such enthusiasm. Sister G, for instance, was always ready to assist, whether it was to give a speech in women's ministries or to teach a Bible class to the entire congregation.

These women remind me of the women who were involved in Jesus' ministries while He was here on earth. They always see the good in everyone. Their caring and loving attitude, uncomplaining spirit, and ever-encouraging words make them a joy to be around.

It is a blessing to have them among us. Now I am learning to follow their examples. I pray that with the grace of God I will get there, so I, too, will be able to be a good example for the younger generation. Paul admonishes us: "Whatever you do, do it heartily, as to the Lord" (Col. 3:23, NKJV).

May we each do all we can for the glory of God, as these women have done.

Gloria P. Hutchinson

261

Walking With Friends

But they that wait upon the Lord shall renew their strength;
they shall mount up with wings as eagles; they shall run, and not be weary;
and they shall walk, and not faint. Isa. 40:31.

THROUGH OUR jacaranda-and-bougainvillea-lined neighborhood in Nairobi, Kenya, my English neighbor, Lilian, and I walked in the fresh morning air. We solved world problems, organized potlucks, and discussed the choruses of the "Elijah" and "Messiah" in which we sang at the All Saints Cathedral. We climbed Mount Longonot and peered into its volcanic valley, and we walked through piney forests near Mount Kenya as mists cleared to show its snowy peaks.

The aroma of baking bread reminds me of the walks my next-door Canadian friend, Donna, and I took in the early mornings in Beirut, Lebanon, up the hill toward Middle East College. Distant brakes screeching, bursts of gunfire, and musical car horns all floated up from the city waking up next to the sparkling blue Mediterranean. Beyond the already-open neighborhood grocery, majestic gated villas, nooks of wild cyclamen and anemone, we gazed at the ships anchored in the harbor. We connected over school events, the wonder of living on the hill called "Septieh" (seven), and the beauty of a shared friendship in a biblical country.

These days my friend Janet and I meet on the curve between the cornstalks and the black-eyed Susans near Andrews University in Berrien Springs, Michigan, to walk more than three miles almost every day. Our time is spent picking up trash, trying to memorize Bible texts, identifying birdsongs, and marveling at changing seasons! Shared prayers include neighbors, chemotherapy, and volunteer projects. Our goal is to be able to keep walking together . . . into heaven.

Jesus knew how to multiply freshly baked bread. He came to clean the "trash" from people's lives. He walked and healed on the shores of the Sea of Galilee; He considered the sparrow and lily. He climbed mountains and loved children, knew tears and the results of sin.

And so around the world we can each walk with Him every day—past mountains peeking through clouds, through valleys of sadness, in the high notes of inspired music, through gardens of beautiful flowers, on the shores of the Mediterranean, the Indian Ocean, and Lake Michigan. "He walks with us, and He talks with us. . . . And the joy we share as we tarry there is like none other we've ever known" (author's paraphrase of C. Austin Miles, "In the Garden," 1912).

Beverly Campbell Pottle

He Really Does Know How We Feel

And the Word was made flesh, and dwelt among us. John 1:14.

ETHEL, MY DOWNSTAIRS NEIGHBOR, and I heard fire trucks roaring down our street that morning, and we rushed out to see whose house was on fire. As we followed the fire truck around the corner, we saw a crowd gathered in front of the burning home. You could hear the crackle of wood and see smoke belching out of every window. It was terrible to watch such destruction. I heard a woman next to us say aloud, "Just think, all of your lifelong belongings and memories going up in smoke." As women, we could easily sympathize with such a plight.

Ethel and I were standing next to a woman who was crying. We knew she was the owner because she kept repeating, "Lord, I just can't believe this is happening to me again." She told us that this was the second time she had a house destroyed by fire.

Ethel put her arms around her shoulders and said, "I know how you feel."

The woman wiped the tears from her eyes, looked at Ethel, and asked, "Has your house ever burned down?"

An obviously chastened Ethel quietly answered, "No."

Others cannot know the deep sense of loss, the emotional trauma, the utter frustration and helplessness that one experiences in the face of such a tragedy unless it has happened to them. Then, and only then, can they truly say, "I know how you feel."

This tragic incident brought vividly to my mind Christ's incarnation described in Hebrews 4:15: "For we have not a high priest that cannot be touched with the feeling of our infirmities" (ASV). In coming to earth as a baby, Christ learned firsthand what it felt like to be human. He was laid open to the good, the bad, and the ugly experiences of humanity.

Ethel meant well when she told the homeowner she knew how she felt, but it did nothing to assuage her grief. Had Ethel told her that she herself had lost a house to fire, then the woman might have felt some comfort from her words.

That is exactly why we, as Christian women, can have comfort in our adversities, trials and tribulations, because Christ took on humanity. He knew fatigue, hunger, thirst, abuse, rejection, betrayal, bereavement, as well as love, acceptance, and joy in service to His Father.

Therefore, He really does know how we feel.

Dorothy D. Saunders

September 14

The Thorn in My Flesh

Even though I have received such wonderful revelations from God.
So to keep me from becoming proud, I was given a thorn in my flesh,
a messenger from Satan to torment me and keep me from becoming proud.
2 Cor. 12:7, NLT.

THEY SAY CONFESSION is good for the soul, so let me confess. One of the things I've struggled with since I was a teenager is pride. I'm one of those multitalented people. God blessed me with many gifts. It took me many years to learn that I did not have to use all my gifts at the same time, but to use just those I needed at a specific time. But my pride always got the better of me. I was one who was happy to show off my talents even if it meant making someone else look bad. Truth is, I thought that it was a good learning experience for the person, so I would correct them and show them the right way to do things. How arrogant of me! I think of how God must have looked at me and just shook His head, knowing that one day I would learn. Well, one day I did.

It began with a series of health problems that came my way. Each one disabled me for a period of time, and even when I recovered I was not able to function as I had in the past. I found myself depending more and more on God to help me do what before had seemed so easy. I struggled with anger, self-pity, and impatience. And of course I told God that He was unfair for giving me so many gifts and then allowing me to be in a position where I struggled to use them.

Then one day as I read my Bible, I came across today's text from Paul. It was like a wake-up call, an "aha" moment. I understood what Paul was saying. You see, since I have to depend on God to give me the strength and joy I need each time I get up to speak, each trip I make, and each day at the office, I realize that it's not me—it's Jesus! All of my gifts that I was so proud about are not my gifts at all. They belong to God first. And now I find myself less proud and more inclined to give God all the glory and praise for everything I do. So I can truly say that it's not by my might, nor by my power, but by God's Spirit that I do what I do for Him (see Zech. 4:6). And I look forward to the day when Jesus comes, and my thorn will be removed.

Each of us has gifts, and each of us has challenges. The test is whether or not we try to do everything on our own and take the credit. It is in fact the Holy Spirit who empowers all we do.

Heather-Dawn Small

An Encounter With Kidnappers

The Lord also will be a refuge for the oppressed,
a refuge in times of trouble. Ps. 9:9.

IT WAS THURSDAY afternoon as I sat in my sitting room with friends who came to empathize with me on the death of my husband. My husband had passed away one week prior and was still in the mortuary. Suddenly two armed teenage boys rushed in, shooting and demanding that everyone lie on the floor. They pointed their guns at me, commanding that I follow them. They took me to a bus they had parked outside the gate of our house. After about an hour's drive, I was taken to the bush, where I met other men and women who were also kidnapped.

The kidnappers began demanding a large sum of money from me. I responded by asking them a few questions: Do you kidnap widows? Do you kidnap someone a second time? I do not have the money you want!

They took my cell phone, but several calls came through my phone from my children, friends, relatives, and ministry friends asking for my release. When their pleadings proved futile, I began to pray to my faithful Father, who sees all things.

Life holds no surprises for God. No path is unknown to Him, no circumstances unsettling. Because the future is perfectly clear to our God, His children have an assurance that we can follow where He leads, whether the way is marked by storm or calm.

It rained heavily on me throughout the night, and the Lord protected me and kept me healthy. The next morning I dried in the sun. After a few days in the bush and payment of a large sum of money, I was finally released!

Recently kidnapping has been a problem in my country. Much of this is a team approach, with the young men carrying out the kidnapping and some young women feeding them.

I have a great concern for the young people of my country—and yours! What can we do to help them lead useful lives? We can, of course, help see that they have a Christian upbringing; we can establish a warm relationship with adolescents, know who their friends are, visit and help out at their schools. As it says in the Bible: "Only be careful, and watch yourselves closely so that you do not forget the things your eyes have seen or let them fade from your heart as long as you live. Teach them to your children and to their children after them" (Deut. 4:9, NIV).

Sal Okwubunka

Lessons Learned in the Dentist's Office

If we confess our sins, He is faithful and just to forgive us our sins and to cleanse us from all unrighteousness. 1 John 1:9, NKJV.

I WAS AT THE DENTIST'S office. I hadn't been for a while, and I was paying for it. As I searched my mind for something to think about to distract myself from the pain, I realized the parallels between my dental office experience and sin in my life.

I know that the analogy goes only so far, but think about it: plaque is like sin. It builds up. If you don't do something about it, it only gets worse. Before I went to the dentist, I thought my teeth were pretty clean. After all, I had brushed and flossed only that morning. But my teeth weren't clean. Not really. Not compared to how clean they could be. I hadn't been to the dentist in a while, so I had forgotten what really clean teeth actually feel and look like. I thought I knew, but I needed a reminder. I'm the same way about sin. I can get pretty complacent, thinking that I'm a pretty good person. After all, I haven't killed anyone, or stolen, or lied. But "small" sins can creep into my life without my noticing them. Sins such as pride or resentment or anger. If I don't nip them in the bud, I come to think they're normal. I don't see the ugliness and pain they can cause.

To continue the analogy, I can faithfully brush and floss twice a day, but I still need to go in for my cleaning. Or said another way, I can read my Bible to learn how to be the type of Christian God wants me to be, and I can pray each day that He will help me, but when the sin is there, I need to go in for a cleaning. I need to confess my sin and ask God to forgive me, to remove the sin from my life. It may not be pleasant. It may even be painful, but the same as going to the dentist, it must be done. Putting it off only makes it worse. The more plaque there is to remove, the longer it takes, and the more painful the process. The longer you allow sin to grow in your life, the harder it can be to eradicate it, and the more painful the process can be.

A final parallel is this: as I have said, I hadn't been to the dentist in a while, and I was a little embarrassed about that. But the people there didn't blame me for staying away or refuse to help me because of that. Don't be ashamed to go to God with your sin and ask for forgiveness. He won't blame you or refuse to help you. He'll be glad you came to Him.

Julie Bocock-Bliss

Elizabeth and the Alligator

Trust in the Lord with all your heart, and lean not on your own understanding; in all your ways acknowledge Him, and He shall direct your paths.
Prov. 3:5, 6, NKJV.

THE 5:00 A.M. NEWS STORY was about Elizabeth, an adorable "Snoopy" dog, caught in the mouth of a six-foot-four-inch alligator. She had bite marks all over her. She looked so scared and pitiful. Elizabeth and her owner were walking along the Hillsborough River when the gator jumped up and grabbed the dog in its jaws, taking her underwater. The owner quickly grabbed his gun and, to save his best friend, began shooting into the water. The gator released the dog. The owner pulled her up to safety and gave her CPR. He wasn't sure if she would survive, but she was a fighter. Being underwater for two minutes was more harmful than the bites themselves. A gator trapper caught and killed the gator. The owner will now build a fence between his home and the river.

Isn't Elizabeth's situation like ours when we are outside of the will of God even though we may be walking with Him? The alligator (Satan) leaps up out of the river of our sins and grabs us! He pulls us under, making us feel guilty and unworthy to seek God's forgiveness.

God grabs His weapon, His power, and begins to shoot! There goes Satan on the run. Then comes the fatal shot. God rescues us, His best friends, and saves us from our sins. Christ has won the victory for us, and, like Elizabeth, we are released from the jaws of Satan. We are rescued. God gives us CPR too: His commitment and protection, His purpose for our lives, and His restoration—love, hope, and faith.

Christ is the fence of protection between the river, the gator, and us. Unlike the owner who built a physical man-made fence between the river and his house, God puts His fence of protection all around us—His promises and assurances. He will heal the bites, but the longer we stay "under," the harder it becomes for us to be rescued. Don't stay under too long.

Who's your gator trapper? Who will reach into the dangerous waters just to rescue you, His damsel, from the jaws of death?

The gator was caught (just as Satan has been caught), killed (just as Satan *will* die), and Elizabeth was saved (just as we are saved).

Edna Thomas Taylor

Rescued

*When you are in trouble, call out to me. I will answer and be there
to protect and honor you. You will live a long life and see my saving power.
Ps. 91:15, 16, CEV.*

GOD SPEAKS TO US in many ways: through His Word or the wonders of His hand in creation as we appreciate them. I believe we can learn valuable lessons from Him.

This has become more obvious to me over the past 10 years since we "re-homed" a dog from a rescue center. My daughter was 9 years old at the time and the first to see Chloe on the Web site of the dog rescue center. It didn't take much persuasion for me to agree to adopt her. Chloe, a cocker spaniel, had been kept by owners for the sole purpose of making money. She had been used to produce litter after litter of puppies. She lived in a concrete kennel, and was never walked or house trained. She had very minimal human contact and was not shown any affection. Those who love animals will understand that dogs are social creatures that enjoy contact with people. This experience in the first five years of her life had left Chloe untrusting of people. Because of lack of space in her kennel, all she knew was to pace round and round. She was unable to walk on a lead, and very anxious and nervous. It required loving patience to help Chloe learn to trust humans and to train her to be able to live happily in her new home. However, the results are amazing. She is now a loyal and loving pet who follows me everywhere and waits patiently by the door for me to return. Chloe shows pleasure at being by my side, and she trusts me totally, looking to me as the one who rescued her from her sad life and offered her a much better one with a bright future.

This is what God has done for us. He looked lovingly down on us in our sad situation. He did not need any persuading to rescue us and offer us a new life with Him. Do we respond to His wonderful love as Chloe has responded to me? Do we trust Him completely, follow Him loyally in love wherever He leads us, and are we waiting patiently for His return? As today's text reminds us, He is always there for us.

It is my prayer that we will show our wonderful Savior the gratitude and love He alone deserves for rescuing us when He gave His life on Calvary. May you follow Him today and every day, as we dedicate our lives to Him and look forward to His soon return with joy.

Karen Richards

Mender of a Broken Heart

Our soul waits for the Lord; He is our help and our shield. Ps. 33:20, NKJV.

I HAD SPOKEN with my younger brother twice that Sunday morning. We talked about everyday pleasantries that a brother and sister would talk about, and promised to call each other later that week. That same evening the phone rang. It was my sister-in-law to say that my brother was in the hospital. With much anxiety, I asked if he was seriously ill. She told me that he had had a heart attack and that the doctor was trying to stabilize his condition. I could not believe what I was hearing!

I cried to God day and night as I had never done before, begging Him to heal my brother. Days went by. When I heard that the doctor told him that he had to undergo a triple bypass surgery, I was frightened. I prayed with all my heart that God would bring him through safely. The surgery seemingly went well. Soon he was talking to everyone and seemed on the upward path to complete recovery. He claimed the healing that he believed God had given Him.

As the weeks went by, however, there was a reversal, and he finally succumbed to his illness. My heart was broken, but I felt that I had to be strong for my other siblings. However, when I saw my brother lying in the casket the day of his funeral, I knew my heart ached too badly for words. Between my sobs, I asked God to mend my aching, broken heart.

God reminded me of the rough-hewn cross where His only Son suffered and died at the age of 33. My brother was older than that. God reminded me through the sermon preached on that occasion that we are all just a step between life and death. He pointed me to the fact that my brother had surrendered his life to Him, and God was not going to leave him now. Many precious memories poured into my mind, and I felt the peace that only God can supply. I look forward to meeting my brother in the resurrection morning. My soul is mended.

My friend, you may or may not have had a similar experience, but we all need to know that there is a "friend who sticks closer than a brother" (Prov. 18:24, NKJV). He is the world's greatest comforter, guide, friend, and soon-coming king. In your time of need you can call on Him and be certain that He will be there for you. He will not leave you alone. He can mend every broken heart. Will you make Him your friend today?

Shirnet Wellington

Just as Much

There is one Lawgiver, who is able to save and to destroy.
Who are you to judge another? James 4:12, NKJV.

ONLY ONE OF THEM said thanks, I mused as I studied the story of the 10 lepers. Some people can be so ungrateful. A few weeks later I was about to go on a long road trip. Before setting out, I breathed a request for divine protection. No sooner had I returned from the trip, I busied myself with updating friends and even doing laundry. Hours later the boisterous waves of activity subsided, and I came to an awareness of myself. God had brought me home safely, but I had not even turned back to thank Him for His wonderful mercy. It was then that I realized how my thinking on the 10 lepers had descended into a dungeon of self-righteousness and judgment while I was under the illusion of being on a tower. Whatever I had thought about the lepers, I was that—just as much.

In Gethsemane they had come to take Jesus away. Peter drew his sword and whacked off Malchus' ear. Yet only a few hours after his swift and violent judgment, he himself denied Christ. Whatever he had felt about Judas and Malchus, he now was—just as much.

It is so easy to judge others and say "How could . . . ?" And "I could never . . ." Perhaps you have observed the loud amens that come from the righteous section during sermons on fashion or fornication. Often this is a symptom of the tell-it-to-them-not-to-me virus—a disease of the most vicious kind, because it gradually erodes our spiritual health. Romans 3:23 says, "For all have sinned and fall short of the glory of God" (NKJV). And Romans 8:33 informs us that it is only Jesus who has died, is risen, who justifies, and is qualified to judge or condemn.

Sadly, the easiest thing for us to do is to see the flaws of those around us. But if we applied the Word to our lives and reflected on its personal implications, we would realize that however disgraceful we think others' actions have been, however in need of prayers we think others are, so are we—just as much. I am grateful that the Holy Spirit was available to lead me out of this darkness and into His marvelous light. So now instead of thinking, People can be so ungrateful, I ask myself, In what ways have I been ungrateful? How can I show more gratitude?

I'm loved by God, and so are you—just as much.

Judelia Medard

The Retreat

*The Lord is my shepherd; I shall not want. He makes me to lie down in
green pastures; He leads me beside the still waters. He restores my soul;
He leads me in the paths of righteousness for His name's sake.
Yea, though I walk through the valley of the shadow of death,
I will fear no evil; for You are with me. Ps. 23:1-4, NKJV.*

AFTER THREE CHALLENGING years of juggling work, studies, and home responsibilities, I finally finished graduate school. One of my immediate plans following graduation was to go on a spiritual retreat. I wanted to spend some solitary time soul-searching in a retreat center up in the beautiful mountains of Malibu. Hesitant to be away from my family, I settled for a three-day weekend with them in Newport Beach. It was a family fun, prayer, and self-reflection time combined. With the weekend over, I thought, my spiritual retreat was through.

One week later I had a minor surgery that turned into a fight for life. For days I was weak and shivered with high fever and pain. During my sleepless nights at the hospital, I constantly prayed for strength and recovery. I asked God to heal every infected cell in my body. To prevent the intrusion of negative thoughts, I silently sang hymns of praise, prayed for the afflicted, and meditated on forgiveness, forgiving the medical team for probable negligence that led to 22 days of hospitalization, the most harrowing time of my life. Many times I surrendered to God. "Thy will be done" was my constant prayer. I cried at the thought of leaving my husband, 9-year-old daughter, and the rest of the family behind. Yet I found comfort in believing that in God's care, they would be fine. I watched a Christian TV channel, the only station that my weary senses could take. I believe this was God's way of speaking to me.

Amid all these, a voice told me that I was not alone. I had a feeling that someone strong and mighty was holding me up. This gave me ample strength to push to recovery. In one of my follow-up visits, my doctor commended me for the courage that she saw in getting through a very serious condition. Looking back, I decided *that* was my spiritual retreat. It was not in the mountains of Malibu, but within the confines of the hospital, and with God Himself. In the darkest hours I was able to touch His face, hear His voice, and hold His hand. Indeed, our relationship with God tends to deepen in the midst of our tribulations.

Clody Flores Dumaliang

Are You Connected?

*Remain in me, as I also remain in you. No branch can bear fruit by itself;
it must remain in the vine. Neither can you bear fruit unless you remain in me.
John 15:4, NIV.*

THE ALARM CLOCK BUZZED. It was 5:00 a.m. This was my usual time to wake up—especially on weekends. Slowly I got up from bed, had my personal morning devotions, headed to my laundry area and gathered all my soiled clothes. I separated the white and light clothes from the dark ones and gathered all my needed equipment. Thinking to accomplish more that early morning, I tried to move with speed. I turned on the washing machine; unfortunately, it made no sound. There was no electricity. I checked the line where it was connected to the extension wire; all was OK. I checked the wires under the machine, thinking they might have been cut or eaten by rats, but everything was in good condition. I checked the wiring connection; nothing was wrong. I became impatient. I was disappointed. I sat down and murmured to myself, *I woke up so early so I could finish many things, but I haven't started anything yet, and time is running out.* Thirty minutes had already passed. I really wanted to do my washing before going on to the other chores. I could not call a technician to have my washing machine checked or repaired because it was still very early, and I didn't want to disturb others that early. I began to think what to do. I then remembered something: *Is the wire connected to the main line or switch hidden in the corner?* I ran to check. Indeed, behind the cabinet where the main switch was, the line was not plugged to the main switch—the main source of power. I laughed to myself for being so dumb and impatient.

Are you connected to the main source? Yes, oftentimes we try to run our own lives by our own human effort. We do not even think or realize that there is a Power Source greater than ourselves. A power that can move us with speed and run our lives smoothly—power beyond human comprehension. That power comes from above, from our heavenly Father, our Creator and God. He is our source of strength and power. Unless you and I are connected with the power that comes from God, we can never function to our maximum. We can never attain what we are supposed to attain, even with the best of our ability. Be sure you are connected. Never detach yourself from that source of power: Jesus.

Ruby T. Campos

My Son's Eye Miracle

The eyes of the Lord are on the righteous, and His ears are open to their cry.
Ps. 34:15, NKJV.

MY SON, BEN, was helping his dad and his uncle Jerry work on Jerry's pickup. They were trying to remove a bearing when a piece of the bearing chipped off, flew up, and gashed Ben's eye. This flying chip was about two inches long and razor sharp on both ends. It cut through Ben's eyelid and into the eyeball above the iris. After I talked with the eye doctor who was on call that night, my mom and I hurried Ben down to the Grand Junction emergency room.

I believe it was God's hand to have Dr. Hanna on call. He is one of the best in his field. He stitched up Ben's eye: two stitches in the eyelid and 10 stitches in the eyeball sclera. And he kept Ben in the hospital for two nights, giving him strong intravenous antibiotics and eyedrops.

Two days later we took Ben to Dr. Waterhouse, a retina specialist. After carefully examining Ben's eye, he said that Ben needed surgery to clean out the eyeball and repair the retina. So the next Monday we took Ben back to Dr. Waterhouse for another eye exam, to see if the injured eye was ready for the surgery. He checked Ben's eye this way and that way, and finally said, "I'm not going to do surgery on that eye at this time. Not with 20/20 vision in it. Besides, it's healing nicely on its own!"

I wanted to cry and shout "Praise the Lord" all at the same time. The Lord was healing my son's eye! Both Dr. Hanna and Dr. Waterhouse asked Ben to return for weekly checkups, and then monthly checkups, to make sure the retina was still attached and everything else still doing well.

Each time both doctors were amazed. Dr. Waterhouse said to his assistant, "We've never seen this kind of thing before, have we?" And Dr. Hanna said, "In all the patients I've treated for this type of injury, none of them have healed up like this on their own."

I said, "It's a miracle from God." And it truly is a miracle. Both doctors said Ben could have lost his eye or his eyesight. Ben says his eyesight isn't as good in that eye as it used to be, but Dr. Hanna says it isn't bad enough to need glasses full-time. So, I just praise the Lord every time I think of His marvelous love and mercy and healing! I also thank God for all those others who prayed for Ben. God is truly still listening to hear our cries.

Reba Cook

God Knows Our Heart

You are the ones who justify yourselves in the eyes of others, but God knows your hearts. What people value highly is detestable in God's sight. Luke 16:15, TNIV.

I BELIEVE THAT we all have the desire to do what is best in God's eyes, but the truth is that sometimes we use that as an excuse to justify our actions.

My husband was the pastor of a church located at a major university. One night as our family was out celebrating his birthday we received a phone call from the university's girls' dean asking him to come and pick up a girl and her boyfriend. The girl was pregnant. So around 9:00 we drove to the school to get this young couple. The girl stayed with us, and her boyfriend went to the house of a friend. We called both sets of parents and explained the situation. The boy's mother came, and as difficult as the situation was, we helped her and the young couple as much as we could. They got married and went back to their hometown.

You might be asking, What does today's verse from Luke have to do with this situation? Well, six years earlier my family was in the process of moving from one state to another. The house we lived in then was going to become the home of the new pastor's family. We were leaving on vacation at the time, so I lent my keys to the new pastor's wife in case she wanted to check out the house she would soon call home.

We were still on vacation when a neighbor called me. She told me that the wife of the new pastor was painting the interior of our house with all our furniture still in place—and with no precautions. So I called the woman about my concern. She was quite rude, to say the least. She was in such a hurry to move in that she shipped our things through the worst moving company around. There was a lot of damage, and we lost a lot of our furniture and other things.

Little did she know that our paths would cross again. She was the mother of the young man who got his girlfriend pregnant. I helped her in that situation, but deep inside I was happy she was suffering. People complimented my support, but God knew that I wasn't being genuine with the "good deed" I was doing. That's why I chose this verse: "What people value highly is detestable by God's sight." Today I try to see and understand the reasons behind my actions. I want to act by the grace of God and not by my selfish heart. God knows what is inside our hearts.

Rozenia Cerqueira Marinho

Give It to God

*I love the Lord, because he hath heard my voice and my supplications.
Because he hath inclined his ear unto me,
therefore will I call upon him as long as I live. Ps. 116:1, 2.*

IT WAS LATE ONE Saturday night, and I had returned home from spending the evening with some friends. My life was going quite well, yet I found myself feeling sad and even crying a bit about my loneliness. Life as a single woman was not what I had pictured for myself from the time I was a young girl. I had always dreamed of being married and having a family. As the kind of person who always wants to "fix" everything for everyone, I had spent several years trying to fix that loneliness piece in my life. Needless to say, my efforts failed, and I found myself reasonably happy, yet lonely.

As an educator I had had the opportunity to learn some psychology, and deep down I knew that one of my problems was that I always tried to make things work out. While that can be a good thing, it is not always within one's capabilities to "fix" everything.

Finally, that evening as I lay in bed crying, I prayed to God and asked Him to help me be content with being single. That was the first time I had ever uttered those words. I followed those words up with "or bring someone into my life." Usually, I asked Him to bring someone into my life to make me happy. Sleep followed, and I awoke the next day with a bit of a new view of life.

On Monday evening I received a call from a man who said that we had a mutual friend and that he would like to meet me and go out for dinner. I agreed.

Tuesday was met with a bit of anxiety and skepticism about going on a blind date at my age. I convinced myself that one date couldn't hurt and that, likely, I wouldn't be interested in him anyway.

The evening of our first date arrived, and I answered the door to see the kindest, gentlest, most loving man I had ever met. He stood there with a dozen roses for me—and the rest is history. We've been married for 17 years, and I tell everyone that "God smiled on me when He brought my husband into my life."

I thank God every day for bringing me and my husband together. I just needed to give all to Jesus.

Karen J. Johnson

A Shower of Blessing

And I will cause the shower to come down in his season;
there shall be showers of blessing. Eze. 34:26.

HYMNS BRING BACK so many memories for me. It's not just the message in their words but things that happened at the time I heard them that remain fresh and alive in my heart.

When I was about 6 years old, my mother heard about a cooking school to be held nearby. Mother was just learning English, and she thought this would help her understand English better and teach her how to cook the food eaten by the people in our new country.

It was after the Depression, and a difficult time for my dad—who worked only part-time as a mechanic—to find permanent work. He earned only about $5 a month. He grumbled because we ate so much soup, but that was about all we could afford on his income.

Mother wanted to go to the cooking class. It cost 50 cents, which was a lot of money for us, and my dad didn't want her to go. But she was determined. This made Dad angry, and every day he brought up the fact she was wasting a solid 50 cents.

At the first class it was announced that there would be a drawing the following Friday when the class ended. Mother didn't understand what a drawing was and was afraid to ask, but sure enough, on Friday they had the drawing and Mom won the prize. She was told it would be delivered to our house. We had no idea what it would be, but we were very excited.

Right at 3:00 p.m. the doorbell rang. There stood two men with a huge basket full of groceries. When they left, Mom said, "We will wait until Dad comes home before we empty the basket." She continued, "He will see that the 50 cents wasn't wasted!"

When at last Dad came home we children ran to the door and drew him into the kitchen. His eyes grew big when he saw that basket. Mother took her time removing each item, all the time singing a new song she had learned: "Blessed Assurance, Jesus Is Mine."

There were bags of sugar, flour, nuts, raisins, yeast, powdered milk, spices, and five oranges—a very rare treat indeed. Around the top of the basket there were apples and bunches of grapes. Dad never mentioned the 50 cents again.

And, oh yes, we all learned to sing, "Blessed Assurance, Jesus Is Mine."

Margaret Fisher

A Love Story

Behold, what manner of love the Father hath bestowed upon us,
that we should be called the sons of God. 1 John 3:1.

EVERYBODY LOVES a love story, and I am no exception. One June I awoke to a sparkling Sabbath morning and watched my two daughters and stepson get dressed for church. The birds sang outside, the air was cool and crisp, and the joy of being alive filled my senses. It was a perfect day. The girls had been invited to sing at one of the churches in the Hamilton area, and my daughter, who would be driving, asked me for directions. My other daughter, having brushed her hair vigorously, asked me to help her brush the hair from her shirt, and my stepson asked my opinion on his outfit. It warmed my heart to feel the love that tightly wound itself around us.

I didn't think about the devastation my family had faced that past year: failed marriage, fragmented family, and reduced income. I didn't think about the times I had questioned God. That morning God gently reminded me of His love by opening my eyes to what I had. The healing had begun.

As the young folk left the house, I marveled at the great lesson in love that I had just learned. My children were almost oblivious to the dynamics playing out around them, and unaware that God was already busy directing and fashioning their day. And that is how God has designed things to fit into His perfect plan of redemption. He is constantly at work, doing everything to ensure our salvation.

So as I struggle with the cares of everyday living and the pain of past hurts, I thank God that He takes the time to send me messages of hope. They are like springs of living water from which I drink thirstily until I am thoroughly refreshed. My prayer is that I will continue to recognize His love signals, and that one day I will be able to completely return that love.

How great a love the Father has bestowed upon us, that we should be called the children of God; and that we are indeed. I thank God for the insight He awakens in me to recognize His great love for us—for me! My wish is that today you will also see and appreciate His great love in your life as well.

Joan Dougherty-Mornan

Give of Your Best to the Master

For even the Son of Man did not come to be served, but to serve.
Mark 10:45, NIV.

I RECENTLY CAME ACROSS a story of a woman who heard that a family that had just moved into her neighborhood needed clothes. Her heart was touched, and she immediately began looking for items to pack up and send over. Knowing there was a boy in the family close to her own son's age and size, she picked up a jacket from his closet floor.

Just as it landed in the box, she noticed there were two buttons missing and a little stain on the front pocket. What to do? Her son needed a ride to his game and they were late. So, should she work with the coat now and disappoint her son? Should she put the coat back and take only the girls' things she had found? *Well, she thought, if he's cold, he'll appreciate it even if it's not perfect.* The coat went in the box for her husband to drop off later.

You guessed it—at the next ball game she saw the boy wearing the coat, walking across the gym floor, stained and still missing buttons. Needless to say, she was embarrassed and fervently hoped the family would never find out who had donated it.

I think in situations like this, the best you can do is determine to "do better next time." Maybe that's why Jesus had to remind us so many times to take care of His little ones. But don't they deserve as good, or even better than what our own children wear, play with, read, and eat? Where I live we get calls from different charities: Amvets, Purple Heart, or just a local thrift store asking if we can have something ready for their next pickup. I'm no goody-goody, but I do like to share, so my immediate response is "I'm sure I can find something!" And, praise God, I have never had to be ashamed of what I place in the box. If it's broken, torn, stained, or obviously way behind today's fashion, then I find another use for it. We were getting rid of some bathroom shelves recently, and I didn't think they were good enough "for the box," so my husband made a really nice bird feeder for the backyard!

My sister Jane and our cousin Ramona supervise the Community Services center in their church. One rule my nephew made was "the underwear has to be new!" So they have stocked their center with new or "like-new" items. The community is happy and very complimentary.

Is your giving according to the Master's guidelines? *I'd like buttons on my coat, please!*

Carol Wiggins Gigante

Caught!

The Lord protects the unwary; when I was brought low, he saved me.
Ps. 116:6, NIV.

FLASHES OF RED and blue lights blazed in my rearview mirror, sending the message loud and clear: another ticket! I gritted my teeth, hissed, and managed a sickly smile as the officer approached my car to ask me for the license—which I didn't have. How could I have been so stupid? No sense complaining now. I knew that I was taking a chance.

Years before, my driving instructor had drilled me night and day that the penalty for driving without a license is $500, five points on your record, and/or a maximum of 60 days in jail. In my case, I had let stupidity take the wheel. Now I had to deal with the consequences. To relieve my stress, I clenched the wheel tightly and started to curse. I thought to myself, *Why didn't he catch me on some other day when I wasn't so busy?* Was this an inconvenience? Yes! Any possibility of escape? Fat chance!

H'mmm, I mused quietly to myself, *Suppose that officer were to let me off the hook? What would I do differently to avoid a next time? Oh, who cares?* Now it didn't matter anyway. The officer was softly tapping on the window. I rolled the window down and grabbed my work badge from his hand. "Have a good day, lady! Drive safely!"

"What?" The sarcasm on my face turned to surprise. Quickly I turned the ignition on, smiled, and headed for the road. He followed, but only as a guide. I didn't have to be concerned. I was blessed. This was my lucky day.

God allows us to live our lives however we want, without ever forcing us to make choices. Why? He wants us to do the right thing on our own, and to see the benefits of following Him. Just as I got worried when I realized I had been caught, so it is in our spiritual lives. We don't think about how a penalty could change our circumstances until it is too late and we're faced with the consequences! In fact, sometimes, in our fast-paced world, heaven doesn't even seem real, so blindly we continue taking wild risks as if we get to live forever without consequences. But someday payday is coming. Thank God for Jesus trading places with us, giving us a fresh start. Let us live prepared, loving, godly lives, so that when He comes, we won't be surprised. We'll be ready.

Hilary E. Daly

Emma's Prayer Text

When you pass through the waters I will be with you; and through the rivers, they shall not overwhelm you; when you walk through fire you shall not be burned, and the flame shall not consume you. Isa. 43:2, RSV.

AT TWILIGHT ON A fall day around 1972 my parents, Marvin and Emma Dick, realized that the storms up the creek were about to cause a flash flood in the creek near their home. The cattle grazing nearby were in danger, so they both rushed out to cut the fence wires to allow their cattle to escape.

The waters rose dangerously fast. Marvin, ahead of Emma, realized immediate peril and yelled for her to go back. The flood's roar caused misunderstanding, and she thought he told her to come closer. Just seconds later the waters became too swift. He climbed a nearby tree, but she hadn't yet reached the woods. Swift water swept her off her feet, and the only thing to grab was the top fence wire. Marvin watched her floating until darkness obscured his view. Sometimes Marvin saw her flashlight beam, but his heart sank when he saw a light go bobbing down the creek. Until morning he didn't know if she'd dropped the flashlight or been swept away.

Hours passed as cold, wet tiredness took over, and Emma could no longer hang on to the meager fence wire. Her hands let go, or maybe the wire broke. Wet winter garments would have made swimming difficult, but in this overpowering current it was impossible.

Prayer had already been a major part of this whole experience. Emma floated above and under water, while her prayer thoughts turned to Isaiah, today's text. Even though she had no power, panic did not control her because she knew God's capabilities. Against circling, strong currents, angels must have helped her climb into an Osage orange tree (a thorn tree), where she spent the rest of the night.

The next morning Duke's barking alerted neighbors to my parents' problem. They brought a fishing boat and saved them both. Because of wounds from the thorns, it took Emma weeks before she could button her own buttons. But she went through the raging water and did not drown. Many of the cattle survived. As a result, my parents witnessed to many.

We will have our own future trials. Will we each have the Word of God written in our hearts to keep us trusting and worshipping the Lord God?

Helen Dick Burton

A Crippled Hand

And we know that all things work together for good to those who love God, to those who are the called according to His purpose. Rom. 8:28, NKJV.

MY GRANDFATHER, Erich Max Höllein, was born in 1921. When he was 8 years old, he had an accident that led to the crippling of his left hand to the extent that he couldn't use it anymore. However, he learned to live with the disability. During World War II he was not drafted into the Army because of it. So while his older brother and thousands of other young men lost their lives in this terrible war, he went to the university and studied law. Later he married, and he and my grandmother had three children, and then four grandchildren. He had an excellent career, first with the local government and later as a board member of a German bank. So what appeared to be a childhood tragedy, in later life turned out to be a great blessing. After all, who knows if he would have survived the war had he been drafted?

Have you ever contemplated the impact of your own tragedies of the past? I remember that at one point in my life I dropped out of the university after three semesters and saw no prospect for my future. However, I ended up doing something different, which later opened up many doors for me. In fact, I'm still reaping the benefits. I think about when I was interested in a young man, and it didn't work out the way I had hoped. What heartbreak! Yet later on I realized how this particular person would have made my life a misery.

My grandfather passed away in 2008, at age 86, after a short illness. But even this tragedy brought about something good. I had to go to Germany from the United States for the funeral, and a friend from California happened to be in Germany for special cancer treatment at this time. So I was able to be with her and her husband and support them there.

Indeed, "all things work together for good to those who love God" (Rom. 8:28). He is the only one who has the big picture, who sees the end from the beginning. Our part is to continue trusting in Him, even when we face trials, tragedies, and unfulfilled desires. I have no doubt that the Lord also uses those opportunities for us to draw closer to Him. "I'm convinced that there is nothing that can happen to me in this life that is not precisely designed by a sovereign Lord to give me the opportunity to learn to know Him" (Elisabeth Elliot).

Daniela Weichhold

A Friend at All Times

A friend loves at all times, and a [sister] is born for a time of adversity.
Prov. 17:17, NIV.

GOOD FRIENDS ARE truly one of life's greatest treasures. To have a friend is to have someone to turn to no matter what, someone to confide in, someone to trust and rely on. Real friends are giving, not concerned with what they will get in return. They are not manipulative or two-faced. They are not judgmental or conditional. Real friends are indeed a treasure.

Do you have a friend who loves you and cares about you? Do you have someone who stands by you, carries you through when there is no one else? Do you have a friend who walks with you when you feel completely alone? Do you have a friend who covers you with prayers and always gives her best in order to lift you up? Do you have a friend like that?

Perhaps it is hard to find such a friend when people around us are always on the move. We may find no time for what is essential, no time to stop and listen in a healing way. But I hope you have such a friend. If you do, please let her know how important she is in your life.

Friends are precious, bringing health to body and soul. Studies show that if you have a close friend you are more able to cope with disease, and you are more positive in life. Researchers are now starting to pay attention to the impact of friendship on overall health. A 10-year Australian study found that older people with a large circle of friends were 22 percent less likely to die during the study period than those with fewer friends. And this past year Harvard researchers reported that strong social ties could promote brain health as we age.

I thank God for many friends in my life, especially one who has been encouraging me this past year. Her name is Carolyn. She came into my life by God's direction. God knew I needed someone to be a friend at all times. Today I am a better person because of her unique touch in my life and ministry. She not only prays for me, but is the one who gives me the courage to move forward. When I see Carolyn, I see God's love through her. I see God's kindness and mercy. I praise God for her life!

To think of Jesus as a friend means that we can also see in Jesus a model for what friendship at its best means. Good friends are truly a treasure, and in Jesus' friendship we have the greatest treasure of all.

Raquel Queiroz da Costa Arrais

This Too Shall Pass

Weeping may endure for a night, but joy cometh in the morning. Ps. 30:5.

THREE YEARS AGO I suffered a horrific fall at work. It required surgery, then two and a half months of nonweight-bearing on my right leg. The pain was excruciating—more than I knew I could bear. And the physical therapy, home care, and assistance I required were foreign to me. Handling this role reversal was indeed a challenge.

What had landed me in this place? Many people gave their take on why God had allowed me to suffer such a brutal fall. I felt like Job on the ash heap as they bellowed out their rationale. They meant well. However, they had no idea why God had allowed the tragedy. Like Job, I would have an audience with God when the time was right.

As I lay helplessly in the hospital, having to ring a buzzer for assistance, not being able to get to the restroom in time, and having someone to clean me up and dress me were more than I could ever have imagined. Me? Yes, Shirley, you! The thought brought tears to my eyes. I remember one night feeling especially depressed and helpless. My nurse sensed this and asked what was wrong. As I lamented how powerless I felt, she caringly responded, "This too shall pass."

At that moment I remembered that my son had brought my CD/DVD player to the hospital along with my favorite gospel CD. It had that very song on it: "This Too Shall Pass." I pulled it out and played the song again and again. This song, one I had always skipped to get to my favorite song, was now very precious to me. I needed to be reminded that the place where I was now was temporary. The day would come when I would walk again.

The Christian life is not without pain and suffering. The best-laid plans can go awry: the unexpected death of a loved one, children losing their footing, and the list goes on. But in the midst of life's situations and circumstances, God gives us His assurance that He is with us. That He will never leave us or forsake us. He is my strong tower, a very present help in trouble.

Life has its trials, but the Christian has the Spirit of the living God who hardens them to difficulty. "Weeping may endure for a night, but joy comes in the morning." We long for the day when these trials will be over; but until then, we will hold tight to Jesus' hand. We are children of the King of kings.

Shirley P. Scott

Only a Miracle

Casting all your care upon Him, for He cares for you. Be sober, be vigilant; because your adversary the devil walks about like a roaring lion, seeking whom he may devour. Resist him, steadfast in the faith, knowing that the same sufferings are experienced by your brotherhood in the world. 1 Peter 5:7-9, NKJV.

ONE OCTOBER, after some days of fever and sore throat, my daughter, Carollina, was admitted to the ward for infectious diseases. Placed in isolation, she had pneumonia and suspected swine flu (H1N1 influenza). We were in desperate shock. How could this be! Carollina was only 22, recently graduated, and had never been sick before. She was not in the at-risk group, and had not had contact with anyone with the disease. She was a girl full of dreams.

The next day doctors moved her to the intensive-care unit—as a precaution. But the following day she had to be intubated. What anguish! For several days her chart was stable, but her body was not responding to the medications. We talked with her doctors every single day. Some days the news was good, and we were hopeful. Other days she was worse.

Her case was critical. She could breathe with only 40 percent of her lungs, had a high fever, and was swollen to the point she had to have a tracheotomy. Also, she required blood transfusions because of anemia. Test results confirmed swine flu, and at last that was cured, but it left her lungs compromised. Her doctors said that only a miracle could save my Carollina's life.

We live in Bofete, a small city in Brazil where everyone knows each other. The city began to mobilize, gathering around us in prayer. We began to ask for a miracle, because only a miracle could save my daughter's life.

After 34 days in the ICU Carollina went to an infirmary, where she stayed for 22 more days. Fluid was drained from her lungs. She had to learn how to use her lungs to breathe, and how to walk and talk again. The doctors told us that her life is a miracle, that she was reborn to us, and we are certain of this. Today she is fully recovered, with no aftereffects.

Through all this we learned to trust more in the power of prayer and to wait on God, to depend on Him. Each day we love this God more, and as much as we cannot understand certain things, we see God's hand at work in the lives of those He loves.

Débora Maurlia Nascimento Leite

Put the Tears Away

And if I go and prepare a place for you, I will come back and take you to be with me that you also may be where I am. John 14:3, NIV.

"LET'S FEED Mr. Fishy, Kenny," I suggested to the 2-year-old one morning at nursery school. "Mr. Fishy needs his breakfast."

"Mr. Fishy needs his breakfast?" Kenny questioned, taking the fish in his tiny hand. Unfortunately the attempt to feed the two goldfish while his attention was still focused on his parents leaving for work in the city ended in chaos.

Tears flowed down Kenny's cheeks as I redirected him to a play table. "Help me, Gloria," he begged as he tried to roll the dough flat with his little red rolling pin.

"Gloria, Mommy come back? Daddy come back?" Kenny questioned as he looked into my eyes, seeking reassurance.

"Yes, Kenny," I answered. "Mommy and Daddy will hurry back after work because Mommy and Daddy love Kenny so much."

"Mommy and Daddy pick me up after work," Kenny repeated as he buried his face on my shoulder. I reassured him again as we cuddled and listened to the CD music playing in the background. "I put the tears away," Kenny assured me as he readied himself for the next task.

"See the new shovels in the cornmeal bin, Kenny? Please help me fill the buckets."

"Soon and very soon we are going to see the king." The words caught my attention as the CD continued to play. Suddenly an unexpected torrent of emotions overwhelmed me. Vivid memories of my final goodbyes to my own mother flooded my mind. The song continued, "No more crying there. We are going to see the king."

I pulled up a small chair and sat close to Kenny as unsolicited tears coursed down my cheeks. I quickly wiped them away, hoping Kenny would not notice. But in a flash Kenny dropped his shovel and climbed onto my knees. "It's OK, Gloria. Put the tears away. Mommy come back. Daddy come back."

Is your Daddy coming back to take you home? My Daddy said: "I will come back and take you to be with me that you also may be where I am." *Thank You, Daddy.* I will put the tears away.

Gloria Carby

Believing the Unbelievable

Seek ye the Lord while he may be found, call ye upon him while he is near: Let the wicked forsake his way, and the unrighteous man his thoughts: and let him return unto the Lord, and he will have mercy upon him; and to our God, for he will abundantly pardon. Isa. 55:6, 7.

And he said, The things which are impossible with men are possible with God. Luke 18:27.

THROUGH HIS INSPIRED WORD, His daily blessings, His created world, His personal communion, and various life experiences, our gracious God reveals all that we need to know about Him. Yet some things remain beyond our comprehension. That God's thoughts and ways are so much loftier than our own is one such unfathomable concept.

Despite the abundant evidence of God's gracious love for us, the enemy of souls frequently discourages many of us by continually impressing us with our past mistakes. God long ago forgave these sins. But Satan delights in haranguing us with an overwhelming sense of our guilt and wretchedness—which God never intended for us to bear.

Satan focuses our eyes on self instead of on our Savior. But Jesus' robe of righteousness cloaks us now, and whenever the enemy distracts, discourages, or otherwise deceives us in this manner, we should remember that God's thoughts, His ways, and His astounding, unconditional love have reclaimed us. Our Father sees Christ's perfection superimposed on our re-created self.

In addition to immediately calling upon Jesus, we have been given another wonderful defense against the waves of doubt that can cause us to fall prey to Satan's mind games. The Bible tells us that Christ deeply loves all who were longtime prisoners of Satan, for God labored tirelessly to convince us of His personal love. When we have come to Christ in genuine conviction and repentance, our most horrendous sins are erased. We dare not be persuaded that Christ's great, loving sacrifice was for everyone else but us, or that we have committed the unpardonable sin.

God's ways and His love indeed are far above our own, and we may never fully grasp them. With the utter trust of a child, we simply need to believe Him when He says that He has pardoned and renewed us through Christ. He gave Himself for every one of us, powerful evidence of His incomparable love and His comprehensive grace.

Heidi Vogt

The Land of Pure Delight

He carried me away in the Spirit to a mountain great and high, and showed me the Holy City, Jerusalem. . . . It shone with the glory of God, and its brilliance was like that of a very precious jewel. Rev. 21:10, 11, NIV.

I RARELY SIT by the airplane window, preferring instead an aisle seat where I can move more freely. But on a recent trip I had the entire row of three seats to myself! After we ascended, I put my feet up and stretched out to enjoy the flight. Leaning against the window, I gazed upon a scene that was absolutely breathtaking. Clouds covered the sky as far as I could see—billows of small white puffs evenly layered so that I could not see through them. Above this layer of sheer beauty, the sun shimmered brilliantly. I marveled at the sight, the result of God's creative mind and intelligent design. To think that He could plan the workings of the universe to create a kaleidoscope of such magnitude caused me to ponder His many unexpected gifts.

While I still enjoyed the view, the captain's voice caught my attention. We were to prepare for landing. The plane gradually began its descent, cutting through the clouds. I wondered what to expect as we made our way through the layer of white. But to my surprise the clouds didn't seem as dense as I expected, nor as thick. For a few short moments the captain guided us through skies less friendly as everything turned white around us, giving no indication of what might be nearby. We had no choice but to trust his instruments and piloting skills. But we'd lost the sun! Now the sky was overcast with indications of stormy weather. The clouds that were magnificent in the sunshine above were now gray and foreboding as they blocked out the sun. I couldn't help musing, "I'd much rather be above the clouds, where everything is bright and glorious."

Soon you and I will be gathered up into the clouds, where on the other side our Father will be sitting on His great white throne in the Holy City, the land of pure delight, ready to receive His faithful children. But in the meantime, we must navigate the unknown, those dark clouds of life. It is a time to completely trust Jesus to see us through. As we lean on Him, the rough patches along the way will seem less fearful. On those days when life isn't treating me so well, I remind myself, "Hold on! It won't be long now."

Bernadine Delafield

Where Was God?

As they talked and discussed these things with each other,
Jesus himself came up and walked along with them; but they were kept
from recognizing him. Luke 24:15, 16, NIV.

"WHERE WAS GOD?" he asked the counselor. His father was hardly what a man—much less a father—should be. Rather than protect his children, he was the one who caused them pain and fear. The home doors meant to keep the family safe at night hid from the neighbors the violence inside. Where was God?

The counselor advised him to ask that it be revealed where God was when he was a boy. This became his fervent prayer: "Where were You, God, when my father was drunk and hit my mother, and I was too little to protect her? Where were You when he punched me? My father's rage so filled the house that there was room for nothing else—not even You. Where were You?"

God answered his prayer. He cried in relief when he saw where God was—and to realize that God had been there all along. Encouraged by his experience, I too prayed, "Where were You when I needed you?"

Then I had a dream that I was being hurt. I felt the pain afresh. I called out for help, but no one came. I ran to the phone and dialed, but the line was dead. It was a sunny day. The apple tree was white with blooms, its branches scraping the window when the wind blew. Then I saw the telephone line swing in the slight breeze—the line to the house had been cut.

"Where were You?" I furiously demanded. "Why couldn't You answer when I called? Then I was shown exactly where God was—in fact, the precise place in the room that terrible day.

"Where was God?" Cleopas asked of his friend on the road to Emmaus. In the shrouded time before the shine of evening stars and moon, they stumbled over holes and stones in their path. As they sought their way through questions and pain Jesus drew near to them, we are told. But their eyes were held back.

As the stranger talked with them, other stars and then the moon glowed too. They no longer stumbled; the road was silvered light. Then suddenly dead coals kindled; flames leapt up in hearts they thought would never hope again. And in the breaking of the bread, they saw that God was there with them in the broken body of the cross. God with us: Emmanuel.

Lisa M. Beardsley-Hardy

A Loving Neighbor

One generation shall commend your works to another,
and shall declare your mighty acts. Ps. 145:4, ESV.

WHEN I WAS a little girl we moved from the country into a small, rural Colorado town on the eastern plains. My mother had never lived in town before and was exceedingly nervous about raising children in this new place rather than in the country that she loved and trusted.

Mother had always been a full-time homemaker and was patient with all of her children. But during this move she had become particularly short tempered, or so it seemed to me. She was always busy—painting, cleaning, and unpacking. One day my brother and I desperately wanted to visit the neighborhood park, but Mom said she didn't have time to take us. So in my 6-year-old logic I decided to put my 4-year-old brother in our trusty red wagon and go to the park without her. Keep in mind that this "city park" was only a swing set and slide, and a mere two blocks away from our new home, but it sat right next to a state highway. With mom's fears about us living in "the city," she was terrified when she turned around and found us missing. She ran next door to ask our neighbor, Mrs. Farnsworth, if she knew of our whereabouts. When she didn't, Mother ran toward the park with a paint stirring stick still in her hand.

Needless to say, when she saw our happy faces she didn't share our joy. I clearly remember just how effectively she used that paint stirrer to paddle our behinds as she put us in the red wagon and promptly took us home. After our rebellious trip to the park, Mrs. Farnsworth became a dear friend to our family. I remember walking into town with this special neighbor several times. She always made a point of letting us play in the park, usually while we ate the Tootsie Roll candies she bought for us. I remember feeling very sad years later when I heard that our precious Mrs. Farnsworth had passed away. She was a jewel to our family. She saw where she could be of help to a busy young mother and extended herself time and again. I hope and pray that I am like her and that I'll always take the opportunity to help young mothers by being the helping hands of Jesus.

Jill Anderson

October 10

"Thou Shalt Not Steal"

Let us hear the conclusion of the whole matter: Fear God, and keep his commandments: for this is the whole duty of man. Eccl. 12:13.

ONE DAY DURING my morning devotions I reflected on the Sermon on the Mount (Matt. 5). In it Jesus gave specific details of what it means to keep the commandments, for keeping the Ten Commandments goes further than a narrow, literal interpretation. Any one of the 10 is easier to break than what one first thinks. I recently had an experience that alerted me to how easy it would be to break the eighth: Thou shalt not steal.

I have never thought of myself as a thief. I give an honest tithe and contribute offerings to many charities and departments of my church's operation. In fact, as a church secretary I handle money weekly on a rotation basis, and I'm not tempted to pocket any of it. I don't have a kleptomaniac streak. However, I had an awakening one day when I went to a hardware store to buy lightbulbs for a friend.

Since all I needed was six packages of 100-watt bulbs, I didn't pick up a basket to carry them in. I collected the six packages off the shelf, but alas, one package slipped out of my hands and fell with a clatter to the floor.

"Oh no," I muttered. "I wonder if the filament snapped in one or both bulbs." It wouldn't be fair to my friend to pay for a package of broken filaments. Shamefully, the idea crossed my mind to put the package back on the shelf and take another one. No one was nearby to hear or see what had happened. But in an instant, my mind flashed with the words *Thou shalt not steal!*

I went to the till and told the clerk that I had dropped one package and wondered if she had a way to test the bulbs to see if they still worked. If they didn't I would pay for the package, but I would have to buy another one to replace it.

She gave me a strange look, but that was OK. I left the store without a tinge of the guilt I would have had if I had yielded to temptation. I delivered the lightbulbs to my friend with a clear conscience.

"Blessed is the [woman] that feareth the Lord, that delighteth greatly in his commandments" (Ps. 112:1).

Edith Fitch

Power in Corporate Prayer

The people of Judah came together to seek help from the Lord; indeed, they came from every town in Judah to seek him. 2 Chron. 20:4, NIV.

WHEN JUDAH WAS attacked by enemies from all directions, he gathered his people and prayed. Later their prayers were answered because all their enemies were destroyed (2 Chron. 20:23). There is power in prayer.

This has been my experience too. My husband and I were on a moving walkway in the Singapore airport when his cart got stuck. I bumped against his back and felt an excruciating pain in my right knee. Upon arriving home in Washington, D.C., we went to a hospital emergency room. An arthroscopic surgery was done in my right knee for the torn meniscus.

The orthopedist said I would be better within six months. Those months passed, corticoid injections were given, and eventually I had a $1,000 Synvisc One injection. Still, I was not well. I was restricted from duty travel, and daily swimming was recommended. I swam 60 lengths of the pool every day except Sabbath, until my swim cap turned yellow because of the chlorine. Nothing helped. Finally I was referred to another orthopedist for a complete knee replacement. Before the surgery, a friend told me of a similar operation that had ended in paralysis. The day before surgery another friend told me that her friend had died of a blood clot. Being a physician, I knew the risks, but their untimely stories definitely frightened me!

Both my Chinese church family and my work colleagues prayed for me. A friend put my name on various prayer request lists. E-mails came from many friends around the world to say they were praying for me. Do these corporate prayers work? The morning after surgery, God helped me walk 40 feet with a walker. The second day, I was able to walk 50 feet *and* up and down some stairs with crutches. The third day I was discharged, walking with a cane. The thirteenth day I was able to drive my car and walk without a cane. Six weeks and two days later, at my second orthopedic visit, I was declared healed.

The orthopedic surgeon performed the operation, but only God brought healing by causing the dissected tissues and skin to speedily return to normal! All this was in response to many prayers. There surely is power in corporate prayer.

Kathleen H. Liwidjaja-Kuntaraf

More Than a Sunrise

Now to him who is able to do immeasurably more than all we ask or imagine, according to his power that is at work within us. Eph. 3:20, NIV.

MY EYES FELT swollen from the ceaseless crying. *How much have I cried in the past 48 hours? It would be easier to count the hours of dry eyes.* I laced my sneakers and headed to the park for a 5:30 a.m. run, my thoughts still swirling with memories of the recently ended relationship. We had dated for quite a while, and the breakup, coming out of nowhere, hit me like a semi running a red light. *Bless me with a sunrise this morning, God. Just so I know You're there. You can do something as simple as that, can't You?*

But as I began my jog, the gray clouds overhead seemed to taunt me. I glimpsed no color, even though I knew sunrise was predicted at 5:42.

Preoccupied with the sky, I didn't even notice it at first. But as I came closer, I instinctively came to a halt. There, directly in front of my path was a small fawn, its chestnut coat specked with ivory polka dots. It stared at me, nervous. The deer and I made eye contact, and it was as if I felt God's arms wrap around me. *There is still beauty in your life,* He told me. *Pause. Embrace this beauty. This is how we pick up the pieces. This is how we remember that love still exists.* Humbled, I bowed my head slightly. *OK, God.*

I continued to run, noticing every bird, every squirrel, every rabbit. I breathed in the floral scents wafting around me, hummed along with the birds serenading me. *Embrace beauty. This is how we pick up the pieces.*

On my last mile flecks of tangerine, rose, and amethyst peeked at me from the expanse of sky that now rose directly ahead of me. I was running into the sunrise. *You already blessed me with the animals, Father. I didn't expect this display, too!*

The answer came clear as a bell. *I want to do more for you than you ask Me for.*

God promised to grant me the desires of my heart (see Ps. 37:4). But He continues to teach me that He knows my desires even better than I do. He knows what will fulfill, teach, and inspire me. *Give me a sunrise,* I asked Him. I imagine Him leaning back, arms crossed, with a teasing smile. *Keep your eyes open,* He says. *I can do so much more for you than a sunrise.*

Addison Hudgins

The School

See, I am sending an angel ahead of you to guard you along the way and to bring you to the place I have prepared. Ex. 23:20, NIV.

"IF YOU WANT TO keep the Sabbath, look for a school run by your church, because you can't continue studying here," said the principal of the municipal school where I had almost concluded my fourth year of elementary school. It was 1960, a difficult period, and all the municipal and state schools held classes on Saturday.

I was 12 years old, and my parents lacked financial resources to afford a private school. Worse, our church did not even have such a school. But my mother looked for an Adventist school, and found one. Thank God, she got a scholarship so that I could finish the year in that school.

We lived in Vicente de Carvalho, and to get to school I had to cross by boat to the seaport of Santos, a coastal city, and then walk some kilometers farther.

One day, when I was coming back from school, I got lost at the pier. As I was never good with directions, I walked from one side to another and did not find the boat station.

It grew dark, and I was afraid of being punished by my parents. This made me cry. The area had many bars and nightclubs. People were smoking and drinking. I was afraid to tell them I was lost. There in the darkness I asked God to send a trustworthy person to whom I could ask for help. When I lifted my eyes, a man stood in front of me. He looked like a good grandfather, although I had never met my grandparents. I felt he was the right person to help me and told him my problem. Immediately, he offered to show me the way. He took me to the boat, crossed the passage with me, and walked with me to the door of my house. Then he went away.

That night was very different from the others. There was peace. Nobody noticed my delay; neither did they ask me anything. My parents did not fight with each other, as was their custom. We went to bed, and I did not have nightmares. There was serenity as never before.

I did not tell this story to anybody, but it is still clear in my mind. Once in a while I ask myself, *Could that man have been my angel? He was different from all the other people. What would he be doing in that place?* I know that one day I will have the answer for this and other stories of protection.

Lourdes S. Oliveira

Longing for Heaven

Let not your heart be troubled. . . . I go to prepare a place for you. . . . I will come again . . . that where I am, there ye may be also. John 14:1-3.

MY HUSBAND AND I were invited to a friend's home. It took a long time to drive there. She lived in a newer, rich part of town close to several shopping malls and the beach. Before we could enter her place, huge security gates had to be unlocked and an alarm had to be deactivated. All her neighbors had similar places: huge security gates, high walls, electric fencing, and systems to keep intruders out. It seemed to me that those people were living in self-made jails while the criminals, who should be behind bars, walked free.

At last we entered the premises, and within those high walls we saw a peaceful, tranquil, serene setting. Three ponds were joined by little bridges, all landscaped with pretty ferns and other foliage all around. A seat for resting and meditating completed this picturesque scene. Looking into this beautiful water feature and garden just made me long for heaven.

Returning home that evening, we unlocked our garage and immediately saw that someone had broken into it. Books, tools, and other things had been thrown on the floor. We saw that the vandals had entered through the side door. The scene upset us so much. To think that the enemy had made entry into our premises again! Before leaving home that morning I had prayed that God would protect our place and keep it safe, and also keep us safe on the busy roads.

I asked the Lord, *Why did You let me down? Why did You allow this to happen?* At 10:00 that same night I flipped the switch for the front porch light, but no light came on. I opened the door to check why the light wasn't burning and saw that the lantern that holds the light was missing. The cords had been cut, and only a hole was left in the wall. I called my husband to come and see, and prayed aloud, *O Lord, come quickly. I'm tired of all this criminal activity on this sin-cursed earth. O Jesus, I long to go home to my mansion in heaven that You have gone to prepare for me.*

I'm so glad no thieves will enter there (see 1 Cor. 6:9, 10). We will live eternally at peace with Jesus, the saints, and with all the angels. I'm longing for heaven and planning to be there. Are you planning to be there too?

Priscilla E. Adonis

Put a Little Love in Your Day

By day the Lord directs his love, at night his song is with me—
a prayer to the God of my life. Ps. 42:8, NIV.

AS THE MIDAFTERNOON SUN wore thin, I decided to take a break from my computer, where I'd been most of the beautiful, sunny winter day. I picked up a favorite book to read a couple of chapters. The sunshine beckoned me outside as I walked onto the patio engulfed now by graying afternoon shadows. Yet, I craved the warmth of the sun.

Farther out in the yard the sun glistened on the oranges hanging from dark-green trees. Sunshine, soft and warm, lingered on the branches and on the grass around the trees. I walked out by the trees to sit in a lawn chair to read and soak in the warmth. But I couldn't stay long. I needed to return to my work. Not far away lay Anneke, my Belgiam shepherd dog, the guardian of the large backyard, who had followed me. She just lay there, occasionally watching me, giving me the space and quietness I craved. Her large black ears were alert for any noise or danger, her soft amber eyes showered me with love.

Pressured by deadlines and multiple items as yet unfinished, I could have walked back into the house to continue my work. I could have left her unnoticed. I could have ignored the rich oranges hanging on the trees. But I didn't. I stopped and soaked in the view of the magnificent trees and noted how uniquely each orange held its space, sometimes swaying in the breeze. I lingered a moment more in the sunlight, and then I called Anneke to me. She acknowledged me with a big doggy smile and lay down at my feet. "Good dog," I told her and patted her tummy, something she cherishes. For a few moments I petted her and talked to her. Then we walked toward the house together. It always makes her day a little happier. It made mine happier, too.

Business! Deadlines! Bills! Phone calls! E-mails! They have a way of seeping through our very soul, crowding out beauty, kindness, and awareness—or at least putting them on hold. I won't remember my busy day, but I will remember the few moments in the sunshine savoring the beauty of the orange trees and stroking and talking to Anneke.

And I have resolved to put a few more moments of beauty, kindness, and love into each day for me, for my family, for the people around me, and for my God. And for Anneke, too.

Edna Maye Gallington

Bowron Portage

You will reveal the path of life to me,
give me unbounded joy in your presence. Ps. 16:11, Jerusalem.

FOR SIX YEARS WE HAD looked forward to camping in North America—the whole time we lived in the tropics. As we swatted mosquitoes 12 months of the year, as we sweated in a city of 8 million, we dreamed of hiking above the tree line, of sliding down snowfields, of seeing purple saxifrage in the crack of a rock, of hearing the whistle of a marmot.

Our son, Garrick, was born while we lived in the tropics, and when we returned to North America we knew we had to change our plans. Instead of hiking in the mountains, we decided to canoe the Bowron Lakes in British Columbia. We looked forward to campfires and stories, loons and moose, quiet paddling and rapids. But first we had to reach the lakes, a mile and a half (2.4 kilometers) from the graveled parking area. Reluctantly we decided to carry the canoe and make a separate trip for our backpacks. We hoisted the canoe over our heads, Larry taking the front because it is heavier. As we hiked along in the afternoon sun, the mosquitoes funneled back, avoiding Larry's head and clustering around my neck. I needed both hands to support the canoe, and a couple more to slap the mosquitoes. And then Garrick began to whine. "Mommy, I want to hold your hand."

"But Garrick, [swat] I don't have a free hand [swat]."

And then he fell. It wasn't far, and he only got muddy, but suddenly Larry and I realized that camping and canoeing aren't fun for everyone. If his first adventure wasn't positive, our son might dread ventures in the wilderness. So we put down the canoe and I rigged up a "fake hand"—a red bandanna tied to my belt loop. Garrick grabbed the bandanna and knew that he was connected to us. He babbled happily.

When we reached Kibbee Lake, we put the canoe down and headed back for our packs. Larry hurried while Garrick and I dawdled. We enjoyed the wildflowers, heard the clatter of dragonfly wings, saw the sun on the leaves, and sang songs. When Larry, laden with a pack, joined us, I hurried off to retrieve my pack. Garrick took his dad's hand, turned around, and started back toward the lake, pointing out fungi and bugs.

The portage didn't seem long when it was filled with laughter.

Denise Dick Herr

A Meeting in Carmel

And how can they believe in him if they have never heard about him?
Rom. 10:14, NLT.

HE WAS ONE OF MY FAVORITE musicians—a singer of ballads with a spiritual bent. Sometimes his songs exhorted us to take care of our world. Other times they awakened our awareness of majestic mountains, streams, and the beauty of living in the west.

A few years ago when my husband noticed John Denver in an auto shop in Carmel, California, I wanted to meet him, so my husband walked over to introduce himself. I held back, hesitant to disturb a celebrity. But John seemed friendly and open to the idea of having my husband take his picture with me. I apologized for taking his time, and he assured me that he was only waiting for his red Porsche to be repaired.

We talked briefly about Carmel and the enjoyment of visiting this lovely place. One does not usually meet a well-known celebrity, but at the same time John seemed so average. His patterned T-shirt revealed a small paunch in his middle. His blond hair and suntan gave him the look of a middle-age surfer. As we posed for the photo, he put an arm around my waist, and I became aware of the fragility of this man. He was of medium height and slight build, and I wondered at the news stories that had him driving fast cars, riding fast horses, and occasionally drinking too much. They seemed out of character for this gentle, melancholy, soft-spoken person; a half smile seemed all he could muster.

We parted company after the photo-taking, but he soon followed us to talk some more. When we left, I told him how much I appreciated his interest in ecological concerns, the topic probably closest to his heart. He smiled with his whole face then. "Thank you," he said.

In October, some months later back in Maryland, the national news reported that John Denver had died while piloting a small experimental plane that dropped into the Pacific not far from where we'd talked that day. This news came not long after hearing of the accidental death of a friend who served God to the end. For days I wondered more about John's destiny than that of my friend. His seemed precarious. In spite of his good works for the environment, had he known anything about the real Christ? Should I have told him about a loving God at our meeting? What good would it have done? Did Christ die for all humans, or just those who had the good fortune to hear about His love from a truthful source?

Ella Rydzewski

Traveling Angels

For the angel of the Lord is a guard; he surrounds and defends all who fear him. Ps. 34:7, NLT.

THERE HAVE BEEN TIMES when today's text has brought much peace and reassurance to me, for traveling long distances with my husband often requires we drive outback roads and camp in remote areas.

A few years ago we journeyed to northern Australia in our four-wheel drive and caravan. Many kilometers would pass, and uncertainties crossed our route, but when the Lord is invited to travel with us, there is comfort. Each day brought new challenges as we met and helped people along the way. There were times we had vehicle problems, but always near places where we, too, could be helped.

After having two front tires replaced, our car developed the shakes. Thinking there was an imbalance, we had that cared for. However, this continued spasmodically to give us trouble.

Then we found ourselves in a very dangerous situation. The gas valve blew while we were filling the car with fuel at a petrol station. Later that problem was somewhat rectified, but because of it our travel was restricted to a slow pace. With this new problem and the increasing shakes, we were anxious to have everything fixed.

After traveling some distance, we stopped in a small town, where my husband was prompted to look under our vehicle. He found that the stabilizing bar, which controls the steering, had come loose to the point of falling off. Once that was tightened, the shakes disappeared. Not long after that, we found that a tap controlling the gas flow was turned off. Low speed had avoided disaster. Praise God, who works in mysterious ways, His wonders to perform.

Further on, an electrical storm struck. Unable to pull off the highway because of flooding, we crawled through sheets of blinding rain until we safely reached the town of Penong, and a parking bay. When we were finally able to get out, we discovered a flat tire! At that moment a man on a motorbike pulled in and, seeing our situation, replaced the heavy tire for us.

God cares, protects, prompts, and guides. We can always trust His wonderful promises. How many angels of the Lord had been with us this day we don't know, but with praise and honor we gave thanks once again to the Lord who delivers.

Lyn Welk-Sandy

He Never Fails

The Lord is close to all who call on him, yes, to all who call on him in truth.
Ps. 145:18, NLT.

FOR TWO WEEKS the words of a chorus I learned many years ago had been reverberating in my mind: "He never failed me yet, He never failed me yet. Jesus Christ never failed me yet. Anywhere I go I want the world to know, Jesus Christ never failed me yet."

There have been times in my life that I knew that God was very near to me. I remember the day I frantically rushed into town to buy a cake for one of my colleagues who was celebrating a birthday. Normally I would have ordered the cake at least the day before it was needed, but this time I had forgotten to do so.

At the first pastry shop where I stopped, they didn't have a whole cake. A trip to two more pastry shops also proved futile. But I had been praying all the while that I would get a cake and make it back to the office before my colleague left for home. With only one more shop to check, my prayer was "Lord, please let them have a cake." I entered the shop, looked in the showcase—and saw it. It was the only whole cake there, and it was beautifully decorated. God answered my prayer and provided a cake to make a friend's birthday a happy one.

Then there was my friend Kenesha, who wanted to go to France as a teaching assistant but needed money for her airfare. Without any funds in sight, she booked a flight for the day she needed to leave in order to be in France on time. The date drew near. Although she and I had often prayed and had contacted many people whom we thought might be able to help with the airfare, we met with no success. Finally, one week before she was scheduled to leave, a donor sent the exact amount she needed! Kenesha flew out according to her plans.

Over the years I have learned that I should talk to my heavenly Father about everything. It is true that sometimes I take things into my own hands and try to work my problems out myself. But invariably when I do this I fail miserably at finding the best solution. At other times, however, when I am tempted to whine and complain, I think of how gracious God has been to me, and I thank Him for being constantly in control of my life. He has never failed me. He will never fail you, either.

Carol Joy Fider

The Cement in Your Life

Let us lay aside every weight, and the sin which doth so easily beset us, and let us run with patience the race that is set before us. Heb. 12:1.

OUR GARAGE APPROACH and sidewalk at the front of the house needed replacing. To remove the old cement, we used a tractor, loader, and log chains. However, in order to wrap the log chain around the pieces, the men had to use a skid steer loader and crowbars to pry them up, giving the men room to slide a chain around the various portions of cement. Removing and disposing of the old cement was time consuming and required a lot of muscle power.

Once the weighty pieces of cement were removed, the carpenters could begin to build forms into which to pour the new concrete. They leveled the gravel and then used a machine to pack the gravel. Only then could the metal rebar rods be arranged to receive the new concrete. The new cement structure will retain its shape and be stronger because it has the rebar rods.

Now they were ready to pour the cement. Trucks brought in the mix and poured it into the forms. Carefully the men leveled the mixture. When at the proper dryness, they troweled it to make it smooth. The end product was a perfectly finished sidewalk and garage approach.

In our lives we carry much weight that can be likened to the old cement. Often our old habits and ways of doing things are hard to remove, but they should be so that they will no longer trouble us. We humans carry old grudges, cherish beliefs that are frequently erroneous, and develop irritating and disgusting habits. Prying them out of our characters and lives is sometimes difficult. It would be wonderful if we could use crowbars and skid steer loaders to work them loose. To have a tractor haul them away would make the process much easier.

Then comes the word we would rather not hear: *but*. But—we don't have the luxury of using power equipment and metal tools to loosen up the "junk" that we wish to have out of our lives. Instead we can turn to a much better helper to clean up our hearts and minds.

We have the privilege of depending upon our Lord and Savior to direct our thoughts, stand by us when we are sincerely trying to change, and give us success. He is more effective than any tools, tractors, or muscle power. His methods are the best. May we learn to lean more fully upon Him and lay aside the negative weights we carry.

Evelyn Glass

The Stressed Seagulls

This is the day which the Lord has made; let us rejoice and be glad in it.
Ps. 118:24, NASB.

ENORMOUS SEAGULLS screeched constantly as they flew around the island. The young ones seemed to be a little calmer, and stood in groups watching our every movement. We were visiting Appledore Island in the Isles of Shoals group in Maine/New Hampshire.

We had a pleasant guide who took us around to see the sights of importance. A famous summer hotel had once thrived there, and the owner's daughter was a great lover of flowers. She had planted a beautiful Victorian garden outside her home. Now replanted with the same types of flowers, the garden was the special enticement on the tour. Later we wandered around the cemetery trails. As we walked, our guide told us that one time a scientist had visited the island, and he did not want her to remove any dead gulls from the paths. She asked him why. He replied, "I am studying the stress life of the gulls." Our guide laughed as she told us, "Can you imagine that? But now he is gone, and I can clear the paths again."

I thought about those screaming gulls. Why were they screaming? Was it stress for them to be continually looking for food? Was the weather a problem for them? Or did our presence stress them? Many of us are not apt to worry about the seagulls' stress as we struggle through our own days. The current message seems to be "You can have it all; you can do it all; and you can be it all." What a challenge to us. Maybe you can do many things, but you will have to pick and choose as to what you will do or be.

Yesterday I had a message on my answering machine to remind me that next week was Vacation Bible School and that I had the first story each day for all the children. It was months before then that I'd been asked to do it. I said, "Yes, certainly," as if a miracle would happen by then to give me the time to prepare. It had been a hectic summer, with weddings, company, classes, and other obligations and/ or choices. Now I needed to face reality. Maybe I could empathize with the screeching seagulls.

Shouldn't we each pray that God would give us the knowledge to make the right choices for the use of our time and give us the strength and desire to fulfill our schedule each day?

Dessa Weisz Hardin

Wait

Therefore, since we are receiving a kingdom that cannot be shaken,
let us be thankful, and so worship God acceptably with reverence and awe,
for our "God is a consuming fire." Heb. 12:28, 29, NIV.

RECENTLY I STOPPED at a local fast-food restaurant to pick up breakfast. I was headed to work early that day and had decided I didn't want to eat my breakfast at home at 6:00. As I pulled up to the drive thru, I noticed they didn't open until 6:30. I glanced at the clock in my car. It was 6:31. Whew, I was glad I hadn't come any earlier, and I hoped they were in fact open.

A cheery voice greeted me and took my order. I drove to the window, paid, and picked up my breakfast. I was on my way in less than two minutes.

It saddens me that on most Sabbath mornings I am the first to arrive at my church. I unlock the door, turn on the lights and wait—and wait—and wait. Where is everyone? Nine-thirty comes and goes, and no one else has arrived.

That morning at the fast-food restaurant, the employees did not arrive at 6:30. They were there and had food prepared and ready for their 6:30 opening.

I know that each workday most people arrive at their place of employment on time. In fact, they arrive before their shift begins so that they can actually start working on time. So why do we treat God with such irreverence and disrespect? Why do we feel that we can arrive late for our weekly meeting with Him?

I am sure that if, when I had arrived at the fast-food spot at 6:31, I had had to wait for them to get settled, turn on their equipment, and cook my breakfast, I would have driven off or never returned again. But since I had such a pleasant experience, I would gladly return.

So how does God feel each week? It's a blessing to know that He is not like us. Most assuredly, if He were, He would not continue to return week after week at the appointed time to find an empty church. But He is there, week after week, and He's wondering, "Where are My children? Why haven't they come to be with Me?"

He, and I—and you, if you attend my church—are waiting. "Let us go to his dwelling place, let us worship at his footstool" (Ps. 132:7, NIV).

Angèle Peterson

Yarn for Africa

And it shall come to pass, that before they call, I will answer;
and while they are yet speaking, I will hear. Isa. 65:24.

I READ IN A MISSION magazine, "Although we work in Africa, it gets very cold, so we are teaching the men and women to knit their own hats and scarves. We need yarn." I therefore put an announcement in the church bulletin asking people to bring their extra yarn to me.

I received yarn, but by the time I was ready to send it, those missionaries had moved to a warmer place and didn't need the yarn anymore. *God, now what am I supposed to do with all this yarn?* I prayed. I decided I would just have to wait until He answered.

Later I read that another missionary family was going to be speaking at a nearby church. I decided to pack all that yarn in the trunk of my car and attend. My husband and I arrived just in time for the church service, but before I could talk to any of them, the woman told the children's story. It was about Margarina, a grandmother who was paralyzed and lying on the ground. First they bathed her sores and got her a mattress, and then a chair so she could sit up during the day. The missionary continued, "I knew it must be boring sitting there day after day with nothing to do. She couldn't read. As I prayed for an idea, the thought of knitting came to me. I asked the African grandma if she knew how to knit, and was surprised when she said yes. Ten years before, someone had come to her village and taught her to knit, but when they moved away and she didn't have any more yarn, she had to stop knitting. Then she became paralyzed. She still remembered how. I had some yarn and knitting needles and was excited that Jesus had given me the idea." Then the speaker showed the children a bright-pink baby hat and booties that the African grandma had made while sitting in her dark, dirt-floored hut.

I was thinking about what I had in the trunk of my car. After church I told the missionary how I had gathered the yarn only to find out the other family didn't need it anymore, but I had been impressed to bring it there that very day. Could she use it?

"Yes, we'd love to take the yarn for Margarina!" she said.

Then she handed me the hat and booties to keep for showing the people at my church. I could now show the children for my own children's story and to those who'd donated the yarn.

Lana Fletcher

There's a Whale in My Bed

How great is your goodness, which you have stored up for those who fear you, which you bestow in the sight of all on those who take refuge in you.
Ps. 31:19, TNIV.

SOME 30 YEARS AGO I purchased my first house—all three levels of it, tucked in the middle of a sunny hillside. It was an exciting time, but it was also a horrific time. Several friends helped me move boxes, hauled the cumbersome washer and dryer, lifted my precious piano, and installed the waterbed. By evening everyone was famished. I had no food in the house, so I took my helpers to a popular pizzeria. We had a wonderful time, but I knew we had to leave early. The waterbed would be filled within the hour, judging by the time it took at my previous house.

When we got to my new home, I rushed upstairs. There was the huge blue mattress—looking much like a whale—propped on the sideboards and on the verge of explosion. We were too late. We heard the dreaded sound, and water gushed out in all directions. It dripped from the upstairs patio deck, flooded the carpeted floors, and ran down the stairs. Devastated, I surveyed my dream house. It was a mess! Then I realized that I had another problem. I had not yet paid for home insurance. Falling to my knees on the soggy carpet, I prayed, "Dear God, please help me." I didn't sleep much that night. Instead I had my own marathon prayer meeting.

I called the insurance office as soon as they opened. After he confirmed my policy number, the agent simply said. "No problem, ma'am. We'll send someone out immediately." With every piece of carpet the workers ripped from floorboards, I exhaled. *Thank You for Your inestimable goodness, gracious Lord. I am not worthy.*

A couple days later as I took a box of moldy clothes to the cleaners, I got another blessing. Updating my new address, I heard an exclamation of surprise from the man in line behind me. "So you're the woman down my street with the flooded house! Your God must have been with you." I turned and fell into discussion with my new neighbor. He reminded me that water pressure changes with altitude. The pressure in my new house on the hill would therefore be much different from my old house on the plain.

The litmus test of a good story is that it ends with a doxology. This one does! "Praise God for His unimaginable greatness."

Glenda-mae Greene

The Misadventures of Apple Picking

A merry heart doeth good like a medicine:
but a broken spirit drieth the bones. Prov. 17:22.

IT WAS A BEAUTIFUL fall day, and my husband, Will, and I were going apple picking. This would be my first time, and I was really excited. I'd picked pumpkins with the kids when they were young, but never apples or any other fruit. Just the night before, Will and I looked on the Internet to find nearby orchards. We were impressed with the Web sites and the activities promoted and decided that we'd bring our granddaughters another time to enjoy the fun. We chose two orchards barely a half hour from where we lived, although in opposite directions.

"I'll call them," Will had said, "just to be sure they're open."

As we drove to the Cider Mill Orchard the next day, the lovely weather, the colorful autumn leaves, and the rural area made the trip extra-special. Sooner than we expected, we saw a large, newly printed sign: Cider Mill Single Family Homes. And while there were many houses under construction, there was no orchard anywhere. "Um, I think that this whole housing development used to be the orchard," I announced.

"Probably so," Will answered. "I forgot to call them before we left."

As we proceeded toward home, I dialed the other number only to find it wasn't a working number. Will still wanted apples and so did I, so we headed to the other orchard. We talked and laughed about losing out on picking apples at the former site. As we approached the area for the second orchard, we started looking for their address. Within seconds I saw a sign, "Closing Soon," but no name for what was closing soon. And though we could see the apple trees nearby, there was no road to get to them.

"For this driving," my husband observed, "we could have bought out the apple section at the grocery store." I nodded in agreement, and we both began laughing again. Soon we were making jokes and laughing about finding no orchards, wasting gas, wasting time, still having no apples, and having to pinch pennies and stay home till payday.

Often our day is ruined when things don't work out as planned. We can become disgruntled or upset. Or we can laugh and enjoy the silliness.

Laughter *is* good medicine! Try it sometime when you feel overwhelmed by the stresses of your life, and see how much better you feel.

Iris L. Kitching

What Do You Need?

Your Father knows what you need
before you ask. Matt. 6:8, NIV.

"BIRTHDAY DINNER at Olive Garden!" chirped Melissa, looking over the menu as she had seen adults do. "This is my favorite restaurant. Let's see, what do I want?" I chuckled at her enthusiasm.

Within a minute or two a tall, slim woman stopped at our table, order pad in hand. Her eyes were red and puffy; her smile wan. Nevertheless, her voice was pleasant and well-modulated. "Hi, my name is Carianne," she said. "May I take your order?"

I turned to ask Melissa what she wanted, but her eyes were not on the menu. Instead, she was studying the woman's face. After a long moment Melissa asked the server, "What do you need?" I blinked. *Where did that come from?* I thought. *What does she need?*

The woman looked down at Melissa. "I need . . ." she began, but her voice faltered as tears chased each other down her cheeks. Carianne cleared her throat. "I need someone to visit my little girl." She explained that her 5-year-old daughter was hospitalized in a city some distance away. Once a week, on her day off, Carianne made a 12-hour round-trip to the intensive-care unit. The rest of the week there was no one to visit her child.

Melissa turned to me, menu forgotten. "We know the youth pastor in that city! Can you call her right now and ask her to make a visit?" (When Melissa gets an idea, that girl wants action.) I took out my iPhone. Within minutes, cell to cell, the youth pastor had the necessary information and was actually on her way to the hospital.

Questions tumbled out one after another from Carianne. "What made you ask that question? How can I ever thank you? What if you hadn't been seated in my section?"

Melissa's face was very serious as she replied, "I was just impressed to ask. Good thing I paid attention to my tuition." (She meant *intuition.*) As we worked our way through a *scrumptitious* meal (one of Melissa's favorite big words), I thought about her question: What do you need?

Later, as we walked out to the car, I knew what the answer was for me. Winging a prayer upward, I breathed, "I need You in my life—always." What do *you* need? If you aren't sure, God can help you figure it out.

Arlene R. Taylor

Fire!

When thou passest through the waters, I will be with thee; and through the rivers, they shall not overflow thee: when thou walkest through the fire, thou shalt not be burned; neither shall the flame kindle upon thee. Isa. 43:2.

MY COUSIN AND I WERE very young the time we took a road trip to a youth congress. I was driving my car on the trip, and before we left I had my car serviced and inspected. We were so excited, because this was the first time we'd gone on a long trip without our parents. Everything seemed to be going smoothly as we rode along deep in conversation.

I noticed that we needed to stop for gas, so pulled into a gas station. But I'd parked a bit too far from the pump for the gas nozzle to reach my tank. My cousin had gotten out of the car and gone into the gas station, so I decided to back my car just a little closer to the gas pump. I started backing up, but when I put on the brakes they didn't work. Panicked, I stomped on the brakes as hard as I could! Instead of stopping, all of a sudden my car knocked over the gas pump! Now fire was shooting up by the car's gas tank.

My cousin came running toward me, shouting for me to get out of the car. Feeling a bit dazed, I got out. Everyone was running around, but mostly speeding away from the station. My cousin yelled that we were in danger of the gas station blowing up!

The firefighters soon arrived. It was like a nightmare. I could not believe that this was happening—I just wanted to disappear. The hardest thing for me was calling my mother to let her know what had happened. She, of course, was concerned about our safety.

My mother and another cousin traveled a good distance to pick us up. Because my car had no brakes, she drove it very slowly to the site of the congress. My cousins and I followed in her car. After we reached the city, my mother drove the car to her mechanic's garage.

The mechanic said he could not believe that the place I'd had my car serviced had inspected my car and had overlooked my brakes. A couple of days later he fixed my brakes so that we could drive safely back from the congress.

I am so glad that I serve a God who has promised to be with me in any situation that might come my way. For truly God is one who keeps His promises.

Bertha Hall

Welcome Home!

*Father, I want those you have given me to be with me where I am,
and to see my glory, the glory you have given me because you loved me
before the creation of the world. John 17:24, NIV.*

IN THE GREATEST HOMECOMING of all time, the resurrected Jesus returns to His heavenly home escorted by an eager, shining cloud of angels. All heaven is waiting to welcome the Savior back to the celestial courts.

As the entourage nears the city, the escorting angels shout out a challenge to the sentinel angels waiting at heaven's gate. "Lift up your heads, you gates; be lifted up, you ancient doors, that the King of glory may come in."

The sentinel angels respond: "Who is this King of glory?" then wait in breathless anticipation for the answer they already know.

"The Lord strong and mighty, the Lord mighty in battle," the escorting angels shout joyously. "Lift up your heads, you gates; lift them up, you ancient doors, that the King of glory may come in," they demand in delight.

Again comes the challenge from the sentinel angels: "Who is he, this King of glory?" (for they never tire of hearing His name exalted).

"The Lord Almighty—he is the King of glory," shout the escorting angels (Ps. 24:7-10, NIV).

The angelic throng sweeps through heaven's wide-open gates, voices soaring in rapturous music. The Son, the beloved Son, has come home! Past the assembled sons of God and the heavenly council He strides, straight to His Father's encircling arms.

"Justice is satisfied!" His Father declares.

Love has conquered. The lost is found. Once more the family of heaven and the family of earth are one.

There will be another homecoming soon, a most glorious homecoming, a victory celebration of the love relationship that already exists between the One who is coming and those who wait for Him.

"I'm coming, My little ones," Jesus promises, "coming to bring you home to My Father!"

Jeannette Busby Johnson

In God's Plan

And ye shall seek me, and find me, when
ye shall search for me with all your heart. Jer. 29:13.

MARGARET AND AN OLDER brother were reared by her mother in a broken home. They rarely went to church, and she was unaware of God or His leading in her life. But she began searching, and for the next several years hopscotched from church to church and from one denomination to another. She didn't know that God already had a church for her—she just hadn't found it yet.

God used an array of events to bring her to a church where she found peace and truth. One was finding some books in a box marked "Free Books" at the local TG&Y store: *Project Sunlight, Bible Readings for the Home, The Great Controversy,* and *The Desire of Ages.* Later a family from church befriended her and answered her questions. One subject was what happened to people after death. After her mother died, Margaret had nearly reached her breaking point.

For so long she had searched for something that would last, something she could invest her life in and never have any regrets. At last she could see that God had been with her through her whole life. She joined the church and claimed the verse "In all thy ways acknowledge him, and he shall direct thy paths" (Prov. 3:6).

Approximately 15 years later I asked Margaret to write her personal testimony and conversion story to be included in the church newsletter that I edited. I knew nothing of the details of her life, so as I read her story my heart leaped for joy. My memory rushed back to the day when I too saw a box marked "Free Books" and felt it needed some religious books to offset the array of novels that it held. I remembered going home, arming myself with religious books, returning to the store, and placing them in the box. Who knew that years later those books would play a part in God's plan to bring Margaret to know and love Him? It seemed like a small thing at the time.

Helen Keller said, "I long to accomplish a great and noble task, but it is my chief duty to accomplish small tasks as if they were great and noble." When we get to heaven, won't it be exciting to hear the testimonies of those brought to the Lord because we took the time to give a Bible study or deliver some literature that would touch a heart searching for God?

Retha McCarty

Which One Will You Be?

For I know whom I have believed and am persuaded that He is able to keep what I have committed to Him until that Day. 2 Tim. 1:12, NKJV.

IT WAS THE DAY AFTER the storm. A terrible tornado had ripped through the town, and not a house was left standing. Everywhere was widespread destruction and loss of life! Two women, neighbors in the small town, stood looking at the remnants of their homes. The shattered fragments of their lives lay in heaps on the ground.

"What will I do?" was the question they both had. "How will I pick up the pieces of my life?" One woman, deeply distraught over the losses she had suffered, continued to stand there looking at the rubbish. Hour after hour, her focus was completely on the losses sustained.

The other woman, deeply grieving over the loss of everything she had ever desired and worked so hard to obtain, cried for the loss, but slowly began to pick up the pieces and move forward. Through her tears and pain, she made her way through the mounds of debris. Her cries went up to the Lord, who helps in time of need (see Ps. 121:1, 2). She trusted that although all may be lost—or appeared to be so—He still had a perfect plan.

She was comforted by one thought that continually ran through her mind, "'For I know the plans I have for you,' declares the Lord, 'plans to prosper you and not to harm you, plans to give you hope and a future'" (Jer. 29:11, NIV). She did not know how she would live or pay her bills, but she knew in whom she believed.

The first woman, sadly, never turned her eyes from her loss and, therefore, never grew beyond it, never overcame, never allowed peace, hope, or joy to fill her again. Like Lot's wife, she could not keep from looking back. And, like Lot's wife, looking back destroyed her.

Both of these women suffered devastation. Both cried and grieved. Help, hope, and new life were available to each of them, yet only one was able to lift up her eyes and see Jesus. Only one was able to say, "Forgetting those things which are behind, and reaching forth unto those things which are before, I press toward the mark for the prize of the high calling of God in Christ Jesus" (Phil. 3:13, 14).

Which one will you be?

Samantha Nelson

The Horrifying Conversation

Judge not. . . . Why beholdest thou the mote that is in thy brother's eye, but considerest not the beam that is in thine own eye? Matt. 7:1-3.

I WAITED FOR MARY, the bank teller that I wanted, for Mary was the mother of one of my son's schoolmates. Her face beamed when she recognized me, and she happily announced, "We have a diagnosis for John! He has cerebral palsy!"

I responded happily to her joy, "Oh, how wonderful!"

Immediately I heard the gasp of those in line behind me. They pulled back, horrified at the exchange they had just overheard. Not knowing the circumstances behind my joy at hearing that a friend's son had cerebral palsy, they judged my response as inappropriate.

It is so easy to judge others by our knowledge and experience without knowing the circumstances behind the situation. These were the circumstances in this case. Less than a week after his birth, John became very jaundiced. When the jaundice was eliminated, the illness left him totally unable to move his arms and legs or to make a sound. For the six years before I met them, Mary and her husband had taken John to an array of specialists, desperately trying to find out what was wrong. Without a diagnosis, nothing could be done to help their child.

I had met Mary and John four years earlier when, at age 6, John joined my son's class in a school for those with disabilities. He came in a wheelchair, unable to move his arms or legs. But John's eyes were bright, aware, and alert, full of fun and intelligence. He followed what happened around him and paid close attention in his classes.

Now, four years later, the search for a diagnosis had finally been successful. Mary was bubbling with joy and hope as she continued talking to me, totally unaware of the horrified responses of those around us. "They tell me he will talk by age 12, walk by 16, and probably be able to graduate with his class at 18. Oh, Darlene, now that they have a diagnosis, they know how to treat him, and my John can have a life!"

We dare not judge others by what we think we know as their life walk is different from ours, and only God knows their situation. May He give us wisdom and discernment!

Darlenejoan McKibbin Rhine

Beauty From God

The heavens declare the glory of God;
the skies proclaim the work of his hands. Ps. 19:1, NIV.

I WAS VERY CONCERNED as I began a class based in evolution, but I was studying for my doctorate and the class was required. Not being familiar with the topic of evolution, I was worried how I would discern God's truth in the midst of many new ideas that could seem to make much sense.

Every week the teachers led discussions of the main ideas presented in the weekly reading assignments. What to do? How do you talk about something you do not believe in? Even more potentially dangerous, I thought, would be bringing into my mind the ongoing confirmation of evolution in the weekly reading. Then I adopted this technique. Before reading, I prayed, asking to see only God's truth, the beauty regarding things He had made.

As I read, I began to see the written material from a different point of view. There were beautiful descriptions of many aspects of nature, animals, and very specific habitats. As I read about the complexity of various species, I marveled at the immense wisdom and divine creativity. Reading of the richness and diversity existing in our world, I soon connected with the fact that God had created everything. I stopped right there, and praised God for His greatness.

When I realized that I was no longer afraid of those textbooks, and that I was able to see the beauty of God within nature as described there, I was joyful! The professors could say that God did not exist, that we are the products of evolution—but I did not care. I knew the truth. And when one professor questioned this point or that, I felt like screaming, "I know. I know why! Because God made things that way!" This answer was enough for me, and my heart was filled with peace, the peace that earthly science could not give.

I continue to be connected to science in spite of believing that in many points it is twisted. When I pray, I can see the God who is responsible for the objects of science. For this reason I continue to make use of it, to understand better the world in which I live and to discover ways of making this world better. I look forward to being able to spend eternity studying and learning more about science and the Creator.

Iani Dias Lauer-Leite

Mother

In everything I did, I showed you that by this kind of hard work
we must help the weak, remembering the words the Lord Jesus himself said:
"It is more blessed to give than to receive." Acts 20:35, NIV.

FROM CHILDHOOD I had the privilege of having a mother who was willing to serve. My infant memories are filled with playing games at the rear of the church and entire evenings sorting clothing to be given to the poor. This taught me the importance of service and sharing.

When I was a child, we moved from Ecuador to Colombia because of my father's business. The first years we lived on the third floor of a building in the center of Cali; it had a large window and I liked to sit and watch what took place near the movie theater in front of the house. After 9:00 p.m. I observed a group of children and young indigents (called "gamines" in Colombia). They walked down the street with cardboard boxes and newspaper to make beds under one of the hedges that would keep them out of the rain.

It was a sad scene. The older ones got the best places and took boxes and newspapers from the younger ones to accommodate themselves, while the younger children had to be satisfied with what was left. Seeing the situation, we decided to help a bit by gathering blankets, newspaper, clothing, and some food. We called the children to give what we'd collected. It was good to see them laugh and share the little they had.

The following day the same thing occurred: the older ones took from the younger, who once again were defenseless. From that time on we gathered up what we could and shared with them. After a time we gained their confidence, and they would shout out to my mother and ask for what they needed. Their faces grew familiar, especially one, a dark-skinned, gracious boy whom we grew to love very much. He even started to call my mom "Mother." Time passed, and the boys grew bigger and did not return to this place.

Their faces and the moments we shared are still registered in my mind. The joy of giving that my mother taught me from childhood brought much joy to our hearts. They are wonderful memories that I still treasure. It is the Lord who gives us the capacity to serve. "It is more blessed to give than to receive" (Acts 20:35, NIV).

Cecilia Moreno de Iglesias

The Orchid Blossoms

So then, just as you received Christ Jesus as Lord, continue to live your lives in him, rooted and built up in him, strengthened in the faith as you were taught, and overflowing with thankfulness. Col. 2:6, 7, TNIV.

I WAS DUSTING THE ledge in our breakfast nook one November morning when I saw it for the first time. It was the largest of 10 tiny buds at the base of the frail reedlike stalk that had sprung from the dendrobium orchid my friend had given me the year before. I remembered that she transplanted it to a new pot that February. And the little plant enjoyed its place in the perfect spot—a fairly dry area with indirect lighting and adequate air movement. It was the picture of promise. I wondered why we had not seen the buds before. After all, our window, which looks out on the golf course, was something we gazed through every day.

A week later we were even more enchanted as pure-white petals formed into a perfect flower. The next day, the petals took on the deep-lavender frosting typical of this kind of orchid. Breakfast became an exciting time as we watched for new developments. Sometimes another bud would open; sometimes a blossom's color changed. Eventually we made a blessings game out of our anticipation and shared novel blessings as each bud blossomed. One morning I commented, "I'm so happy the orchid bloomed again, but I'm even happier that Jesus is coming again."

Another morning, my daughter praised God for the beauty in the symbolic interplay of light and dark—the orchid's white-and-purple markings—as we journey through life, knowing that God is in control of His people.

As I thought about the beautiful orchid, I realized that there were several spiritual lessons in that experience for me. First, there are blessings all around us that we neither take the time to notice nor thank God for. We must live our lives searching for the blessings He puts in our way. When God is in control, everything spells promise.

The transplanted orchid also reminded me that every place where God sends us is the perfect spot. What we do with every moment is significant. Our lives can be the sermons the world hears even if we rarely say a word. Just as the orchid's delightful color permeated the room with loveliness, so will our thankfulness to our gracious Creator pervade our lives.

Carol J. Greene

The Inside View

The spirit of man is the candle of the Lord,
searching all the inward parts of the belly. Prov. 20:27.

IT WAS HAPPENING AGAIN. My colon was bleeding—profusely. This was the third episode. But at least this time I was not in a foreign country, but home with my husband, so we rushed off to the emergency room. As soon as possible, the gastroenterologist did a colonoscopy. She saw an area she thought might be the source of the bleed, but as the bleeding had stopped, she could not be certain. After receiving four units of blood, I returned home, feeling quite well. But 20 hours later my colon was bleeding again. Back to the hospital! This time the doctor ordered nuclear imaging to see where the bleed was originating. Almost as soon as I arrived in the patient room, they drew blood from me, and not long after, it was put back in my veins. This time, however, radionuclide had been added, and off I was whisked to the nuclear medicine department. As I lay on the table with the scanner moving above and around me, I turned my head and watched the computer screen to see what the technician was observing.

It was incredible. There was my colon, and there was the blood flowing into it. It clearly showed the place where the blood should not have been. Within a few hours I was on another table—the operating table, having that section of my colon removed.

But as I lay there on the nuclear medicine table, the thought struck me, *This is how God can see inside of us! Not only can He see the blood circulating, the heart pumping, and all the rest, but He can even look into our minds and see what we are thinking. It really is not so hard—He has allowed people to invent systems that can look inside of us.* Of course, modern medicine has used X-ray technology, MRIs, and CT scans for some time, but to watch something happening inside my own body gave me an insight I'd never thought of before.

God created us. He sustains us through each and every day. And He can even discern what is going on in our brains! Truly, as David sang so long ago, "I will praise thee; for I am fearfully and wonderfully made: marvellous are thy works; and that my soul knoweth right well" (Ps. 139:14). Or as a more modern translation states it: "Thank you for making me so wonderfully complex! Your workmanship is marvelous—how well I know it" (NLT).

Ardis Dick Stenbakken

Doggy Trouble

As a dog returns to its vomit, so a fool repeats his foolishness.
Prov. 26:11, NLT.

EVEN THOUGH MY DOG Rocky is the sweetest and cutest golden retriever ever, he is sometimes mischievous. In our backyard there is a concrete path, grass, and rocks. One day about three years ago my mom was working in her garden with Rocky nearby on the grass chewing on a pinecone. While Mom was working, unbeknown to her Rocky ate several rocks. When she finished the yard work she took Rocky inside, and life went on.

In the next few days little Rocky also ate a spring from a vacuum, a bread twist-tie, drywall, and some Hot Wheels track. A couple days later Rocky stopped eating, and then started barfing up bile, so my mom took him to the veterinarian. At the vet's office they examined him and took an X-ray. The film showed us that Rocky had eaten all of those things! The vet gave us two options: do surgery to take all the stuff out, or let the vet put Rocky to sleep.

You see, the twist-tie had made a hole in Rocky's gut, and the hole had become infected. Of course we let the vet do surgery—even though it was very, very expensive. So we still have our Rocky, and although now he's not so little, he is still as happy as he was before his surgery. Sadly, Rocky still tries to eat grass, pinecones, drywall, and yes, especially more rocks. We named him very well.

Sometimes we are like Rocky, going back to all of those things that will hurt us. Just as Rocky keeps wanting to eat things that put his life in danger, we can fool around with things that are harmful to us—alcohol, smoking, TV, video games, or anything else that can become an addiction. We want to stop our addictions, but like a dog going back to lick its vomit, we keep on going back, even though these things are hurting us. Peter wrote about this as well: "They prove the truth of this proverb: 'A dog returns to its vomit.' And another says, 'A washed pig returns to the mud'" (2 Peter 2:22, NLT). God is the only one who can help us stop our addictions. God is the only one who can help us overcome the sin in our life, and He is willing to help us. As the Bible tells us: "Keep watch and pray, so that you will not give in to temptation. For the spirit is willing, but the body is weak" (Mark 14:38, NLT). All we have to do is ask for help.

Michelle Hebard

The Roses

I am the rose of Sharon, and the lily of the valleys. Song of Sol. 2:1, NKJV.

RECENTLY MY HUSBAND AND I celebrated our twentieth wedding anniversary. Let me tell you, these years have been no bed of roses. On the other hand, perhaps it has been because roses come with beauty and thorns. It has been both a beautiful experience and a painful one. We have faced many trials together, but I can truly say that the good times outnumbered the bad.

We have overcome obstacles and adversity. We have been challenged and stretched beyond our comfort zones. We have gotten ourselves into trouble because of bad choices, but we are still standing by the grace of God. We have dealt with sickness, infidelity, indebtedness, addictions, and generational curses; these are the thorns of life.

Over the years we have grown closer, older, stronger, and wiser. We can love and forgive more readily because we have been loved and forgiven by God. Before, I knew of God but didn't know Him intimately. I heard that He was a merciful God, but now I know for myself that He delights in mercy. He granted me mercy and grace in spite of my character flaws. One of my favorite scriptures is 1 John 1:9, because it is a promise that offers hope: "If we confess our sins, He is faithful and just to forgive us our sins and to cleanse us from all unrighteousness" (NKJV). When we are being cleansed or pruned, it doesn't feel good, but God knows the things that are lying dormant inside that need to be pruned or removed. He knows when we, like a rose, need to be pruned, and He knows just how to do it.

If you and your husband are going through the pruning process, be patient and prayerful. How about the growth process? Are you and your husband growing closer together or further apart? What about the healing process? Can you love even if the thrill is gone? Can you cancel the debt and forgive even when you've been hurt? If you are struggling in your marriage, don't give up, don't get divorced, and don't forget to stop and smell the roses.

These principles apply to any relationship as well, with other family members too. "Therefore, as God's chosen people, holy and dearly loved, clothe yourselves with compassion, kindness, humility, gentleness and patience. Bear with each other and forgive one another if any of you has a grievance against someone. Forgive as the Lord forgave you" (Col. 3:12, 13, NIV). Live, grow, and blossom in Jesus.

Tamara Brown

Learning to Hear God

My sheep hear My voice, and I know them, and they follow Me.
John 10:27, NKJV.

I READ A BOOK ABOUT someone who said God spoke to him. I became frustrated. Even though I grew up in a religious home, as an adult I had never heard God speak to me the way He spoke to this man. So I began to talk to God about it. *Lord, if this man can have an experience like that, I want one as well!*

I was a member of a church in a neighboring city. We used to arrive very early on Sabbath, returning home late in the evening. One Sabbath after lunch I realized I'd forgotten a folder in my parents' car. It had the music I needed for a youth group rehearsal that day. But the car keys were with my father, and he had gone to the town square near the church.

As I went downstairs, a "thought" crossed my mind, *Put sunscreen on your face.* I had been told by the dermatologist that because of a medical treatment I was undergoing, I should faithfully use sunscreen whenever I was going to be exposed to the sun. And it was summer—in Brazil! However, I didn't pay attention to the thought and went down one more stair. *Put sunscreen on your face!*

Why would I need to use sunscreen if I'm going only a block away and coming back right away? I decided not to listen and left.

As I passed the house next to the church, I saw our friendly neighbors in their front yard. I love talking, and we talked for more than an hour. There I was, without sunscreen on my face, under a hot afternoon sun, contrary to both medical and divine advice!

In spite of that, I felt an enormous joy because I noticed that it wasn't just a random thought I had heard, but the still small voice of God! I had expected that God would speak to me about something really significant, but on that day I discovered that the smallest details of my life are more important to Him than I had imagined.

God taught me that I would have to act by faith, obey what He tells me even when I don't understand the why of it. I don't know the future, but my careful heavenly Father already knows what is to happen. And it may not be about something big that He speaks to us, but it will be important. I can guarantee it is worth learning to listen!

Kênia Kopitar

Cut-up Bibles

Your word is a lamp to my feet and a light to my path. Ps. 119:105, NKJV.

COMMUNISM HAD recently fallen in Ukraine, where my husband and I were holding evangelistic meetings to establish new churches. Bibles, which were treasured by people who had been without God's Word for their lifetime, were given to those who attended a prescribed number of meetings.

Each evening two women came to our apartment to "guard" it while we were at the meeting hall, because we, as Americans, were targets for crime.

My husband's translator, Nadya, spoke perfect English, but, being a new Christian herself, was not familiar with the Bible's layout, so could not find the texts quickly. Each day she and my husband spent hours at our kitchen table going over that night's sermon. He used numerous texts when preaching, so placing bookmarks in the many pages was not a viable solution. Finally my practical husband developed a plan. Why not cut the pages from an extra Bible and place them in order in the front of Nadya's Bible? That method worked, but it took a lot of explaining to our guard women.

They gasped, and tears came to their eyes when my husband took his penknife and carefully began cutting pages from the extra Bible. This was not just a book to be used for one's convenience—it was the Holy Word of God that was being defiled! In their era houses had been searched for Bibles, religious books, and even for choir music. Some had gone to prison because of possessing these. Copies were made with muffled typewriters in secluded closets. People who owned copies could be harassed by the authorities or even put in prison.

And here, Pastor Huff was cutting up a Bible! He and Nadya tried to explain that they were sacrificing one Book for the good of many people. It was a hard experience for all of us in the room that day. There may have been other ways to solve this problem, but this was a quick, helpful, and effective tool for the translator to present the gospel to spiritually starved people. The Bible, even a cut-up Bible, lighted the pathway for 511 people in that city who were baptized, and who established a new church in Ukraine, in the former Soviet Union. God's light shines on!

Barbara Huff

Finding Iris

Ointment and perfume rejoice the heart: so doth the sweetness
of a man's friend. Prov. 27:9.

ONE DAY I WAS OUT collecting money for medical missions. At one house a very nice woman answered the door. As we talked, she mentioned that this was a lonely neighborhood. Her neighbors worked all day, so the area was deserted. And no one seemed to talk with one another. She needed a friend. I said that I would like to become her friend. And this is how it began. Iris and I started spending every Thursday evening together as her husband went out that evening to play Scrabble with his friends. I went to her house every Thursday evening at 7:00, and we kept this up for more than 20 years. Oh, how we enjoyed our times together! The joys and sorrows we experienced! The laughter and tears were many. We prayed together and shared our burdens. Thursday evening became the highlight of the week.

Iris had a brother living in Australia, and one of my sons also lived there. They actually lived fairly near each other. Imagine my joy when we both happened to be visiting Australia at the same time. We decided to meet and spend an afternoon together. We met on the beach at Mooloolaba, and some of us decided to go swimming. Iris and her husband, Henry, and my husband Cyril's sister, Jean, sat together on the beach and watched.

As we went down to the water's edge we were stopped by a very tall man wearing a huge hat. He was a coastguard, and proceeded to give us a lecture. Cyril and Henry were strong swimmers, and we assured him that they could cope. He told us how many swimmers had been drowned by the huge waves there. As we reached the water Cyril and Henry struck out into the deep. I sat on the edge where the waves could gently lap over me. In the distance I could see two heads bobbing in the water. The tall coastguard kept an eagle eye on me. Eventually the swimmers returned and "rescued" me. We all had a wonderful time together.

We enjoyed our friendship for many, many years. What precious hours we spent together. But then Iris and Henry moved to another village about 40 minutes away. We phoned each other once a week, but missed the Thursday get-together. I am so thankful for the years of deep friendship that started as a very casual meeting on Iris's doorstep. It is wonderful that God knew that He was giving me a priceless treasure in dear, dear Iris.

Monica Vesey

The Gift of Gap-filling

I looked for someone among them who would build up the wall
and stand before me in the gap. Eze. 22:30, NIV.

I HAD JUST STARTED working as a volunteer family therapist at Charis, a Christian counseling center in a tiny, economically deprived town in Fife, Scotland. The prayer team had invited me to an evening on which they would pray for me and ask God to bless my ministry. The day of the prayer meeting I'd been busy, and we were running late. I was tired, stressed, and frustrated. As we drove along I was complaining because I felt that all I ever did was fill gaps. Whenever I volunteered to help I would say, "I'll just fill in the gaps until you know what everyone else wants to do." And I was usually happy to do that. But somehow my identity felt lost in the "gap-filler" label, as if I was some kind of home-maintenance product.

The prayer team had been praying specifically for me before the meeting. They came with passages of Scripture, messages, encouragement, blessings, and insights. But one woman was a little hesitant. "I know this sounds kind of funny," she said, "but I feel God is calling you to be a gap-filler." *M'mm, that's interesting—I've just been complaining about being one of those.* She continued. "Maybe it's because without someone filling the gaps, things fall apart." I looked at the old walls of the building where irregular Scottish rocks had been carefully piled together. There was no way they could be fitted snugly to keep out the winds and wild weather, so mortar had been carefully inserted between the stones to keep the building safe, strong, and warm. I looked at a small, wooden cross that stood on a table. Yes, Jesus had also been an amazing gap filler: He filled the gap between earth and heaven, death and life.

Most of my gap-filling activities are not courageous, dramatic, or life-saving. A cake for a funeral. A freshly laundered tablecloth. A bag of toothbrushes for a local homeless project. The scripture reading. A dish for the potluck. Maybe a few words of friendship and encouragement. A simple prayer. But although gap-filling is invisible, it's also essential and it needs people who are flexible enough to fill the different-shaped gaps—like the mortar in the stone wall.

I wonder if there's a spiritual gift of gap-filling designed for those of us who do this work. And maybe Jesus would say, "Blessed are the gap-fillers, for they prevent things from falling apart." What gap is God calling you to fill today?

Karen Holford

Fallen Soldiers, Risen Savior

He is not here; he has risen, just as he said.
Come and see the place where he lay. Matt. 28:6, NIV.

THE MEDIA REPORTS tell of soldiers who gave their lives for others. Countless soldiers from the United States, Canada, and other countries have died since the war in Afghanistan began. Men and women, fighting for something they believed in: a better life. Many of the fallen were children themselves who fought, knowing they were sacrificing their lives for their fellow citizens. Yet they served.

Journalists traveled to faraway countries to report on the peacekeeping efforts and the day-to-day experiences of the soldiers. No comfortable beds, no air-conditioning, no Jacuzzis, no hockey. Away from loved ones, missing holidays, the births of children, and other significant life events. Some of the reporters lost their lives in the process. Yet they reported.

Tragedy struck Haiti in January 2010, as it was devastated by a massive earthquake. Thousands of people lost their lives. Children wandered around—some wounded—without parents. Parents didn't know if their children were dead or alive. Families were torn apart; many had no means to bury their dead. Homes destroyed, jobs gone, only the clothes on their backs. Christian brothers and sisters were among those who had fought the good fight. Yet they died.

There is another battle going on closer to home, and your life is at stake. We are living in the midst of the battle between good and evil. You see, war broke out in heaven because Lucifer (Satan) wanted to be like God. In fact, he wanted to *be* God, so he and his angels were cast down to earth. Since then Lucifer has waged war against God. Lucifer tempted our foreparents and they sinned, which separated us from God. But God, in His wisdom, had already devised a plan to save us. God the Son laid divinity aside, put on humanity, and came to earth as a baby. He knew saving us meant giving up His life. Yet He came.

In the fullness of time Jesus was nailed to a cross and took what we deserve so that we could have eternal life with Him. Satan thought that he had won when he saw Jesus hanging between heaven and earth. Jesus was put into a tomb guarded by Roman soldiers. Yet He rose. God loves us with such unconditional love that He laid down His life for us. Yet He lives.

Sharon (Brown) Long

The Parable of Old Gray

I am the way, and the truth, and the life.
The only way to the Father is through me. John 14:6, NCV.

OLD GRAY, a brindled cat, arrived at my neighbor's house one morning. Since they already had 10 cats, putting out a little additional food was no big deal. Old Gray had found a home. But in the beginning Gray would always eat and run. One could never approach her. She suspiciously watched every move of her enemy, the humans who had befriended her.

"Well," rationalized Cheryl, my neighbor, "she must have been abused by her former owners. Perhaps she even ran away."

As time went on, we made no progress in taming Gray. We would call to her softly, kindly, but she gave no response. Instead, she would look at us blankly with what I now interpret as a sad, very sad, look in her eyes.

Several years have passed. Cheryl and Glenn have moved to Florida. Gray is still hanging around waiting for her Kibbles and Bits, but contributing nothing to the relationship.

One day as I watched her distance herself from me, I couldn't help thinking, *This is how so many of us distance ourselves from our loving God.*

As I called in my sweetest voice to Old Gray, the words of a beloved hymn flooded my mind: "Softly and tenderly Jesus is calling, calling for you and for me; at the heart's portal He's waiting and watching, watching for you and for me." All who answer Jesus' call embrace the love and care of a protective Father. If Old Gray were to respond, she would enter into a friendship manifested by the love and protection of a caring human.

To this very day, Old Gray has resisted. For years, how many of us have also resisted that tender call of Jesus? As rings true with Old Gray, our basic needs are also met. The essentials. Oh, if only we would enter into life with Christ, who came that we may live *abundantly.*

The gift of life is there for each of us, so plain and simple, but we try to make it complex and complicated. Therefore we keep putting off Christ's gentle call: "Come home, come home, ye who are weary, come home." Like Old Gray, many will continue to wait and resist. What a blessing it is to be able to walk unafraid, knowing that our Savior is guiding our footsteps.

Patricia Buxton Flores

Deal or No Deal

If you fully obey the Lord your God and carefully follow all his commands . . . the Lord your God will set you high above all the nations on earth. Deut. 28:1, NIV.

"THE BANKER offers Rs.1,750,000. Deal or no deal?" asked the moderator. The contestant, encouraged by the family, said, "Deal." Quickly changing her mind, she blurted, "No deal," giving heed to her husband's suggestions.

Deal or No Deal is a television game show I watch occasionally. There are 26 boxes with amounts ranging from 1 rupee to 5 million rupees. The contestants choose one of the boxes, not knowing what it contains. Then they call for other boxes to be opened. At the end of each round the banker offers a deal based on the amount left. Those who play till the end without accepting the offer get the amount in their chosen box, even if it is just one rupee.

The contestant of that day, not accepting the previous offers from the banker, came to the most crucial point of decision. There were only two boxes left: the one she had chosen and one other. The amounts on the screen showed Rs.500 and Rs.5,000,000. None had a clue which box contained the more coveted amount.

The audience was spellbound when she said "No deal," to the offer of Rs.1,750,000. Now she would get only what was in her box. *What if her box contains only 500 rupees?* I wondered. *Wouldn't she be wise to accept the deal?* In fact, her box did contain only Rs.500.

The moderator asked, "Why were you so greedy? Wouldn't you be better off with Rs.1,750,000? If you have to yield to your husband's suggestion, why didn't you let him play?"

His questions made me think. God, in His infinite wisdom, has made a deal with us. He says, "If you love Me and keep My commandments, I will be your God and you will be My people. You will inherit the Promised Land and live with Me forever." But we are greedy. We are often misguided. We love the world and the temporary pleasures it offers.

We have heard it said, "Life is a game; play it." How we play it is very important. We will win the game only if we give heed to right counsel. God gave us the power of choice as well as the pros and cons of our choice. Won't it be wonderful to accept His deal and enjoy the prize He offers us?

Hepzibah Kore

God's Gifts to Us

There were few people left in the villages of Israel—
until Deborah arose as a mother for Israel. Judges 5:7, NLT.

THROUGH THE PAGES of Scripture, God inspired its writers to note not only the victorious attributes of men, but their falterings as well. And being the respecter of all persons, God revealed women of faith and their attributes as well. Among these noteworthy women one discovers a spectrum of qualities:

Deborah: a judge of Israel. A discerning woman, she refused to be ruled by fear. Her leadership was invaluable.

Priscilla: Working in tandem with her husband in business, she provided a welcoming home, training, teaching, and support of fellow Christians.

Dorcas: a woman known for her good deeds, generosity, and compassion for the poor.

Eunice and Lois: a mother and grandmother duo who provided spiritual nurture for the boy in their lives, Timothy.

Elisabeth: Despite years of disappointing barrenness and heartache, she remained faithful to God.

God used women in multiple capacities. He gifted and empowered them. And today is no different. Among the women in the world, who attend any one of your churches, can be found a woman (or women) who raise money for missions or devastated areas, those who feed the homeless, conduct Bible studies, or tenderly tend to the needs of their neighbor or friend suffering from ill health or a broken heart. There are women who mentor other people's children, young wives and mothers, or new Christians. Many women have ministries that go unnoticed.

We have inherited a legacy from women who were involved in sharing God's love, living as women of faith. In this sense "legacy" is active, not just a noun. For as in times gone by, God remains faithful. He continues to provide giftedness, inspiration, and empowerment to each of us.

So I can't help wondering, on a scale of one to 10 (with 10 being most active), what my rating for using for Him the gifts God has given me is. And what might yours be?

Lynn Nicolay

The Ever-present God

The name of the Lord is a fortified tower;
the righteous run to it and are safe. Prov. 18:10, NIV.

ON MY WAY TO the Philippines for our daughter's graduation, I went through China. When I had been in New York, the gentleman at the boarding gate told me that he did not think I could go the Philippines without a visa. "I checked on the Internet and called the embassy, and they said I did not need one," I told him. He was not convinced, and I almost missed my flight. I was the last to board, but happy, and thanked God I was on my way.

We had to clear immigration when we got to China, and the line was very long. I went to find someone to help me, as I did not want to miss my connecting flight. Because of the language barrier I was sent back to the first line. I finally went up front and I told them that I was connecting to Manila and would miss my flight if I did not get cleared immediately.

The immigration officer looked at my ticket and said, "Oh, ma'am, you are supposed to be in the other line, as you are connecting to Manila at a different airport, and the ride will take 40 minutes." The airline had not informed me I was to change airports in Beijing. Now I was in full panic mode: *What am I going to do in this strange country if I miss my flight?*

When I got to the other line, the attendant did not seem to be in a hurry. Finally she realized my dilemma and rushed through the process. As I ran to catch the bus, a lovely English-speaking woman came from nowhere and took me to the bus and told me what to do.

I missed my flight, and there were no other flights to Manila that day. I was told the flights were fully booked for the coming week, but they would try to put me on standby.

So back to the United Airlines office at the first airport, but they could not help me. I was disappointed, but then I said, "God knows why I missed my flight. I leave it to Him."

A friend I met helped me buy a new ticket to Manila on a different airline. That night in the hotel room I thanked God for being with me all the way from Washington. He is trying to teach us when we go through certain experiences, but we have to remember that He is always with us, working in ways we cannot even imagine. He placed people in my path to help me. If today is not turning out the way you planned, God still has a master plan for you. He will take care of all your needs. I found proof of it, and I did arrive in time for graduation.

Judith Mwansa

A Childlike Faith

Except ye be converted, and become as little children,
ye shall not enter into the kingdom of heaven. Matt. 18:3.

IT WAS A DARK, early-winter evening, and there was an air of expectation in the tiny church of biblical Berea as we prepared for our first Revelation seminar. We couldn't advertise on radio or television, or even in the local newspaper, but we had all invited friends and neighbors, and even mere acquaintances. However, this was Greece. Would anyone come?

Long before starting time, the door opened, and a thin, elderly, poorly dressed little man came in. We hurried to welcome him, handing him a new Bible and a copy of the first lesson. Then we chatted quietly. After a while he asked if he might recite a poem he had written about Jesus. Of course, we willingly agreed. So he walked to the front of the church and sang his poem, his own composition, without the help of written words or music. It was simple, childlike, and deeply moving.

He left after the meeting, clutching to his heart his precious Bible and the second lesson. He radiated joy. He was almost illiterate, but he was sure that his little granddaughter would be more than willing to help him study his lesson.

The following evening he returned, carrying his Bible carefully and with lesson number two completed. This continued for several meetings, but then, one night he didn't come. In fact, we never saw him again. What could have happened? A few days later we phoned his home and spoke to his daughter. This is what she told us: On his return from the seminar he had studied his lesson as usual, with the help of his willing granddaughter. Later, when the family went to bed, he chose to spend a little longer with his Bible. He was feeling a bit cold, so they wrapped him snugly in a warm blanket and left him sitting at the table, reading haltingly. It was a cold night, and his family was surprised to see him the following morning, still bowed over his Bible. But he was not reading. He had slipped peacefully into his last sleep. He now awaits the glorious resurrection morning when he will see his precious Jesus face to face.

Would that we all had more of his simple, childlike faith and love for Jesus, for of such is the kingdom of heaven.

Revel Papaioannou

The Lamb

Aaron went to the altar and killed the young bull
which was for his own sin offering. Lev. 9:8, 10, TEV.

Then he shall kill the lamb. Lev. 14:13, NKJV.

He must kill the lamb for the guilt offering. Lev. 14:25, NIrV.

None of you may eat blood, nor may any foreigner residing among you eat
blood. . . . The life of every creature is its blood. Lev. 17:12-14, NIV.

WHEN HAVE YOU taken time to really read Leviticus? After reading it, did you think to pray a prayer of thanksgiving that you are living in the post-Old Testament era?

Blood is valuable. Hospitals have blood banks to supply patients in emergencies. Some students regularly give blood for a little extra spending money.

As I think of my life, I'm afraid a lot of perfect, innocent little lambs would have had to suffer for my sins if I lived in the Old Testament times. Years ago, when I was secretary for M. L. Andreasen, he made it a point to cover the sanctuary service and all of its rituals thoroughly. One of the illustrations he used to tell his students was to picture him walking down the road to the Temple leading a little lamb. He imagined that his brethren would say, "I wonder what Andreasen has done now!"

I'm thankful I do not have to shed blood for my sins. Just the sight of blood makes me faint. When I go to the doctor or hospital, I must be sure to alert them to my problem. Can you imagine someone with my malady having to see the blood of a lamb every time I sinned?

Every day I thank Jesus for His blessings—His loving care and protection, my food and water, my loved ones, His church, the blessings of fellowship with other believers, His gifts of nature, His work that instructs, inspires, comforts, and gives hope for the future and, above all, that Jesus, the Lamb, shed His precious blood for me so I don't have to kill an innocent lamb to obtain forgiveness for my sins. "When Christ came," "he did not enter by means of the blood of goats and calves; but he entered the Most Holy Place once for all by his own blood, thus obtaining eternal redemption" (Heb. 9:11, 12, NIV). For that we can all give thanks!

Rubye Sue

When You Call, He Answers

Call unto me, and I will answer thee, and shew thee great and mighty things, which thou knowest not. Jer. 33:3.

DURING MY LAST year in college God helped me to trust and cling to His promises. In spite of being a working student, I survived until I graduated as a Bible instructor and elementary school teacher.

A year before I graduated from Mountain View College in the Philippines, Mrs. Vevencia Gayao, then the head of the Education Department, told me, "You cannot graduate unless you enroll for a summer class." A new curriculum had been imposed by the Department of Higher Education for the coming school year.

I spent many sleepless nights, considering what to do. I was a working student taking subjects toward my degree. It would mean many hours working and studying at the same time. I continued praying, trusting, and believing God's promises.

My work supervisor encouraged me by saying, "God will work miracles for you." I had no way of knowing that she had submitted my name to the college administrative committee for financial assistance. Then one day before summer classes started, I received a memorandum from the registrar's office saying, "Your summer class is paid and you can enroll now."

I was so happy to learn that I could take the required summer classes! I also found out that a Dr. Block, a philanthropist from the United States, had sent sponsorships for deserving students who needed help. I still do not know this man, but my comfort is that God answers when we call.

Today, I am happily serving God at the Adventist University in Zurcher, Madagascar. My husband and I are glad that we can share blessings with students who need help financially. May we also be a blessing to answer the needs of others.

I personally experienced the truth of "For there is not a word on my tongue, but behold, O Lord, You know it altogether" (Ps. 139:4, NKJV). God knew my need and moved someone to meet it. I also know the truth of "Call unto me, and I will answer thee, and shew thee great and mighty things, which thou knowest not" (Jer. 33:3). You can trust Him!

Evelyn G. Pelayo

God Was Guiding Us

I will instruct you and teach you in the way you should go;
I will guide you with My eye. Ps. 32:8, NKJV.

MY HUSBAND AND I have felt so blessed over the years to have had five children, eight grandchildren, and three great-granddaughters. When we learned that two little great-grandsons were about to join our family, we were delighted. They arrived eight days apart, in the same town, many miles from our winter home, and we were determined to go to meet them. We would need to fly, and since airline regulations had changed since we had last flown, we were a bit nervous about that. We also knew that the town we would be flying in and out of was prone to fog in the winter, but we prayed for guidance and set about making our plans.

Our first shock came when we priced the tickets, but my sister-in-law heard of an outstanding special and that information saved us $400. A big blessing! Then we had to decide when to leave and return. We finally settled on a Thursday departure, but just could not decide whether to return on a Tuesday or Wednesday. There was a prayer meeting series going on in our community that we did not want to miss. We knew if we returned on Wednesday we'd be too tired to attend, so decided to return on Tuesday.

Thursday was a very pleasant day for flying and layovers, and the long weekend was a dream. It was wonderful to meet our two little great-grandsons, who were so sweet and cuddly. We took many pictures, and of course, enjoyed visiting with the parents of the little boys, as well as many of the rest of our family. Time flew by, and before we knew it, it was Tuesday morning and time to return to our southland home.

Always lurking in the back of my mind was the fear that the airport might be fogged in early in the morning. However, as we arrived we saw clear skies and a lovely sunrise. All was well. When our daughter called the next morning, she said, "Mom, the airport is closed. You would never have gotten out this morning, because of the fog."

When we were planning our trip, God knew that we needed to return on Tuesday, and I feel He directed us the entire time. I invite you also to turn all your concerns over to God, knowing that He knows what is in the future for each of us. He will direct our paths.

Anna May Radke Waters

Reviving Hope
in the Institution of Marriage

Enjoy life with your wife, whom you love, all the days of this meaningless
life that God has given you under the sun—all your meaningless days.
For this is your lot in life and in your toilsome labor under the sun.
Eccl. 9:9, NIV.

EVEN AT THE RIPE AGE OF 90 years young and still counting, my father is a strong man, both physically and spiritually. He is a World War II veteran who served his country well enough to protect and provide for his family. He married his school sweetheart and affectionately named her Baby Sweet. I suppose he named her that because she birthed him 11 sweet babies. As a child I remember every Sabbath eve he would polish his shoes and then paint and polish our dress shoes in preparation for church the next day. As a U.S. Army veteran, he learned the importance of a good shoeshine as a part of good grooming. He was a true soldier to the bone. He faithfully marched us to church to learn the teachings of the Bible. Where I grew up in Georgia his name is engraved on the cornerstone of New Hope Community Church. My parents' marriage gave me a model to live by. I witnessed some of their trials and triumphs. Through it all, they were faithful. They started a Bible study ministry in the community and invested many of their resources in order for it to grow. Most important, they instilled in us a thirst for truth.

After 67 years of marriage, God called His Baby Sweet to her final rest a week before Mother's Day. At her memorial service, a local evangelist credited her spiritual journey to their ministry.

My father is now a widower, and no longer able to lead Bible studies. However, he remains faithful as he struggles on a different battlefield. This battlefield is not on the foreign soil of a European country. It is on domestic ground, a battlefield called Alzheimer's. It's an uphill battle, but he is faithful, and he has not given up on life. He regularly partakes in praise, prayer, and worship services. There is still a glimmer of light in his eyes and pep in his step. Like a soldier, he marches mechanically in his safe zone at home with the help of Christian caregivers. Each day that God gives him is a gift, a testimony to the community and an opportunity to be a witness that "great is your faithfulness" (Lam. 3:23, NIV). May we each be so faithful!

Fartema M. Fagin

When God Answered My Prayer at Midnight

Be careful for nothing; but in every thing by prayer and supplication with thanksgiving let your requests be made known unto God. Phil. 4:6.

MY MOTHER WAS VERY ILL—not the kind of illness common to seniors, but a severe and debilitating mental attack. The doctors did determine that the medication she had been taking since surgery years before should not have been taken for such a long period of time.

I traveled to my parents' home in the hopes that I could help bring her back to reality, and also to relieve my father of the constant strain of managing her. Until I arrived, I did not realize the severity of the situation. It was heartbreaking to see my mother in such a state of mind. Neither Dad nor I could break through the barrier that separated us from her.

I went to bed in agony of mind. My mother, always so kind and loving to her family, was a completely different person with no sense of family around her. I knew divine help was the only answer. As midnight drew near, and desperate for some help, I cried to God to help my mother, to give her a good night's rest, and also to reveal to me some way that she would come around and be herself once again.

The answer came almost immediately. Her room was adjoining mine, and I could hear any sound from her room. She began snoring and this told me that she was sleeping. As I lay hearing sounds from her room, it sounded like music from heaven. The next day my father said she had slept better than she had in ages.

Following my return home to my own family, every time I called to check on her the report was better than the time before. Once again she began enjoying life with the family. She also enjoyed the many summers that she spent time at my home.

She lived more than 20 years after this experience, outliving my father by six years. As I look back on this event, I think of Hezekiah and how he was given an additional 15 years. "Thus saith the Lord, the God of David thy father, I have heard thy prayer, I have seen thy tears: behold, I will heal thee" (2 Kings 20:5). I thank God for the additional years given to my mother. Just as God heard Hezekiah's prayer, I believe he heard my heart's cry and answered in a most remarkable way.

Miriam L. Thompson

Driving Dangerously

God is our refuge and strength, a very present help in trouble. Ps. 46:1, NKJV.

I CAME AROUND A corner and was stopped—by the traffic police. The officer asked for my documents: driver's license, car registration, and insurance. I promptly gave them to him. He read, paused, and looked at me. I wondered why the stare. I soon discovered that my car registration had expired in June. It was now November. I went into complete shock—I had never missed a deadline before. I humbly yet firmly insisted that this had never happened before. Ignoring me, the officer called his partners, and soon a squad of police descended. A tow truck was called. I was ordered out of my car and told to remove my things. I would be fined for driving without a road license, charged the cost of the tow truck, the storage of the vehicle, its release, and of course, obtaining my up-to-date document. The sum was more than $25,000, local currency. I had no money! I had just completed university. My last paycheck had been 15 months before. I earnestly explained my dilemma to the officer, but to no avail.

I was now sobbing uncontrollably. The officer suddenly led me across the road. "Again, what is your situation?" I explained. I prayed. I cried to the most high God. I needed a miracle.

The next moment, the same prosecuting officer suddenly stopped a passing car, took out his ATM card, handed it to me along with his pin number, and told the driver to take me to the nearest tax office where I could update the expired document. I could not believe it—this was a true miracle! The car took me to the tax office and back. As I thanked the "taxi," the driver kindly pointed out he was *not* a taxi but just stopped to help out a citizen in distress. Another miracle! Upon returning to the car, I learned that the officer had recovered his money, for a church elder had sent some money via a taxi. Another miracle! Still sniffling and shaken, I prepared to drive off, the prosecutor/rescuer officer wishing me well.

Despite this, another officer issued me a traffic ticket with a fine of about $10,000. I started crying again. The miracle officer said not to worry. On the date to pay the traffic fine, the clerk checked the system repeatedly. No ticket was listed. Still another miracle!

God does not always answer exactly as we pray. But this I know: God is indeed a very present help in times of trouble.

Keisha D. Sterling

Disaster Averted

*For He shall give His angels charge over you, to keep you in all your ways.
Ps. 91:11, NKJV.*

HORRIFIED, I WATCHED as my car slid backwards down the icy driveway, headed directly toward the car parked across the street below. I could imagine the two vehicles smashed by the impact, and I was powerless to stop it.

Accumulating snow had been predicted, with the possibility of power outages. Twice I'd been without power for several days. My sister lived about an hour's drive away and while sometimes her electricity went off, too, the company that served her was more prompt in restoring things. So I had decided to join her to wait out the storm.

That morning I had met with a group to celebrate a friend's birthday. The festivities were nearly over when the first snowflakes drifted down. I lost no time in rushing home, gathering my things, and heading up the mountain, driving through falling snow the entire way. I made it to the top of my sister's steep, snow-covered driveway, breathed a prayer of thanks, put the car in park, and took the key out of the ignition.

We had unloaded the trunk, and I had just opened the back car door when the car started to roll. It was gaining momentum, heading toward disaster. Suddenly it was as if someone unseen took control. The front wheels turned, redirecting the back of the car toward the yard next door. It stopped against a rise, barely missing a small tree. I stood in wonder, relief flooding over me. A neighbor came to our rescue, and we were soon settled and snug inside my sister's home.

As expected, snow piled up, roads were icy, and traffic was stopped or delayed. Fortunately, neither of our homes lost power. Though stranded, we enjoyed the time together.

Reflecting on the fact that we had been behind the car just moments before it began moving, we cringed, thinking of what might have happened. We were safe, the cars were spared, and once again we had the assurance of God's protection and care.

There are times we feel utterly unworthy of God's interest in us. We are so small in the great scheme of things, and often fail to fulfill even our own expectations. Yet time after time He intervenes to let us know that indeed each person matters to Him. And if that does not give us the assurance needed, we have only to behold the cross of Christ, and that is enough.

Lila Farrell Morgan

Hurry!

The angels urged . . . , saying, "Hurry!" Gen. 19:15, NIV.

"HURRY." It's not a simple word. It's a lifestyle.

I am certain that most people reading these words will identify with me when I affirm that hurriedness is a lifestyle.

If you are like me, you try to do two or three things at the same time, and you try to achieve as much as possible. You make sure that in 10 minutes you accomplish several tasks and that not one minute is wasted. To save time, we always multitask. Our right hand fixes our hair, our left arm is trying to dress us, and our right foot is looking for the shoe. But in reality, our mind is not thinking about what our right or left arm does, or how to balance either foot, because while all of these actions are going on, we are thinking about how much money we'll withdraw from the bank, and figuring out when we can visit a sick friend. This is the "Hurry" lifestyle.

There are days and weeks in which we feel that if we don't speed up, we'll be run over—who knows where or how—and in order to avoid this we take time out of the other things we call irrelevant so there's time to do what we think we must.

We have lost so many "times": our time to rest, our time to socialize, our time to recreate, our time to reflect, and worse yet, our time to be alone with God.

Each time we come out of a "time crisis," we think that tomorrow will be better, that next week we'll have more free time, that next month will be calmer. These are all illusions because tomorrow, next week, or next month come and go with another long agenda!

There is a Bible verse that gives me great relief. It's found in 2 Peter 3:8: "But do not forget this one thing, dear friends: With the Lord a day is like a thousand years, and a thousand years are like a day" (NIV). This tells me how to measure time and that how I live my time is something worldly; that in heaven we will enjoy time—not as something that is harmful but as something that is a delight.

I invite you to slow down, to allow your soul to be soothed, and to prepare yourself to spend the rest of your time in heaven.

Susana Schulz

335

Trudy

They will neither harm nor destroy on all my holy mountain, for the earth will be filled with the knowledge of the Lord as the waters cover the sea.
Isa. 11:9, NIV.

IT WAS NOVEMBER and my husband, John, and I were making the long drive from Ontario, Canada, to our second home in West Palm Beach, Florida. It had become an annual trip. We are snowbirds—retirees from the north who winter in warmer climes. We like driving because we can stop and visit with relatives and friends along the way. Now we were going to see my sister in Maryland.

While driving down the long, bumpy road to her house in the woods, we were amazed to see a feathered sentinel blocking our way. It was a large wild turkey, almost four feet tall, with iridescent brown and purple plumage, standing directly in front of the car bumper.

We were stuck and could not move. My husband suggested that I open my door to distract the bird. But the turkey was too smart for that. It moved to the driver's side and peered into the car, its gray-blue snood and red beak visible through the window.

Then we came up with a plan. We fed the bird an apple, then some bread, and finally a piece of cauliflower. While she was still eating, we managed to get to the house.

Listening to us explain the reason for our delay, my sister smiled. She told us that the bird was why she had canceled her security system. No stranger could enter her property with it around. We found out that my sister had named the bird Trudy. Perhaps that was because in Germany, our homeland, a male turkey is a *trudhau* and a female turkey is called *trudhene*.

As we stayed at the house, Trudy got to know us. She followed us everywhere. We seemed like family. Even the three-legged stray cat let Trudy eat her food. I began to think about how it will be in the new earth where nothing will hurt or destroy.

Isaiah 11:6 says that "the wolf will live with the lamb, the leopard will lie down with the goat, the calf and the lion and the yearling together; and a little child will lead them" (NIV). My paraphrase is: There will come a time when not only will the lion eat with the lamb but the turkey will also eat with the cat and a little child will lead them all. I can't wait to see the new earth restored. Can you?

Emilie Howard

God in a Box

You have granted [her] heart's desire and have not withheld the request of [her] lips. Ps. 21:2, NIV.

MANY TIMES throughout my life God's presence has been very real to me. I have been blessed in the physical realm to know that God was near. One time in particular stands out to me more than the rest.

It was right before Thanksgiving 2006, and my husband and I were attending Andrews University. As most students who are working their way through school, we didn't have a lot of money, and that fall we had many needs. We had invited my mom and step-dad to Thanksgiving dinner along with numerous students who didn't have funds to get home for the holiday.

During a quiet moment in my tiny kitchen I had some alone-time with God. I was thinking how nice it would be to have matching dishes for our dinner. Also, at this time, our youngest daughter had outgrown her shoes, and we couldn't afford to buy new ones. I was thinking, *God, it surely would be nice to have matching dishes and some shoes for our girl.* No more than a thought. These desires were not voiced to anyone. Merely a mother's heart echoed in her mind.

The next morning when I went outside on the porch I saw a box. Not knowing who had put it there or what was inside, I was excited to open it. Being a poor college student brings excitement over things like that. So I brought the box inside our 750-square-foot house and began to open it. It held a plastic bag that I couldn't see through and something beneath that. Underneath the bag was a set of matching dishes! They weren't brand-new, but it was a full eight-piece set with all the trimmings! My throat began to tighten. I opened the bag. To my great joy I found six pairs of shoes that just fit our little girl!

As tears rolled down my face, I whispered, *God! How? How can You love me this much?* I didn't even say it out loud. It was just a thought!

There He was. Larger than life. My God. My King. In a box of dishes and a bag of little girl's shoes. My heart soared, knowing that the King of the universe had just sat with me as I opened a cardboard box full of His love.

Tanya Kennedy

When God Whispers

Share with the Lord's people who are in need. Practice hospitality.
Rom. 12:13, NIV.

DO YOU EVER wake up and have someone on your mind and feel they may need a phone call or a visit? That happened to me the Monday before Thanksgiving. As I woke up, my friend Louise came to mind. Louise was a wonderful family friend whom I'd known most of my life. Even though we didn't see each other frequently, we had kept in touch over the years. She was elderly now and I knew she was beginning to experience health problems.

My loving mama had passed away in February of that year, so this was the first Thanksgiving we had experienced since her death. She and Louise had stayed in close contact with each other through the years. So when I woke up thinking about Louise, I felt it was God impressing me to call her.

As the week of Thanksgiving pressed on, I continued to think of Louise. Then on the day before Thanksgiving, I felt God urging me, "Call Louise!" I remember saying, "Yes, Lord, I will sit down and call her now."

So I did. Louise's grandson answered the ring. He told me that Louise hadn't been doing well, but he would tell her I was on the phone. A moment later Louise said, "Hello." She was so happy to hear from me, and my heart soared with joy to hear her voice. She was always a sweet person, generous with her time, and very loving and patient. I said things to her that I hadn't said in a while, telling her how much she meant to me and my family. We shared so much and expressed our love for each other. It was just a wonderful conversation, and I felt so good afterward.

Thanksgiving came and went. I was doing chores the next week when the phone rang. It was Louise's daughter calling to tell me that Louise had taken a turn for the worse, and had passed away.

As sad as I felt, I was also overjoyed that our sweet Lord had impressed me to call her. This has happened to me many times in the past. I know it is our Lord talking to me, and without fail there has always been a need for which just a phone call, a card, or a visit has made all the difference for someone.

Jean Dozier Davey

God's Tender Care for His Creatures

Are not two sparrows sold for a copper coin? And not one of them falls to the ground apart from your Father's will. Matt. 10:29, NKJV.

I ARRIVED AT school at 7:15 a.m. that Friday and began my daily routine of unlocking the library and teachers' lounge. In order to get to one door I had to go through another door in a storage area. As I entered the storage area I heard something fall, and thought it might be a rat. I looked around, and to my surprise, I saw a tiny kitten in a large box. I have no idea how it got there.

I put the box outside near the wall in the shade. What should I do with this helpless little creature of God's? Without care it would surely die. The school was having a long weekend since the next Monday was a holiday weekend in the United States. My heart was saddened as I thought of this little kitten dying of starvation and heat. I hoped a student would take it home.

Since it was Friday, school finished at 12:10. The students left. The schoolyard became quiet. It was about 2:00 when I saw a most heartwarming sight. A mother cat gently clasped her mouth around the kitten's neck and took it away from the box to a safe place under the steps. I said, "Thank You, Jesus, You are so wonderful. Thank You for answering my prayer, even though it wasn't the way that I expected." God knows best, and we should always trust His leading.

As I thought of this experience, it reminded me how special we are in the sight of God. He is concerned about the tiniest details of our lives. Matthew 10:30 states, "But the very hairs of your head are all numbered" (NKJV).

What lesson can be learned from this experience? Whatever my needs, I can trust God to provide for me. I am encouraged to make my requests known to God who knows what I need. If we apply this knowledge to our daily lives, it will free us from much unnecessary worry.

In the United States this is the season when we take time to express our thanks to God for His many blessings. Among these blessings is His care for all His creatures. "Give thanks to the Lord, for he is good; his love endures forever. Who can proclaim the mighty acts of the Lord or fully declare his praise?" (Ps. 106:1, 2, NIV). Let us give thanks!

Janice Fleming-Williams

Two Extra Weeks

And it shall come to pass, that before they call, I will answer; and while they are yet speaking, I will hear. Isa. 65:24.

OK, LORD, what am I going to need these two extra weeks for? This was the question that popped into my head as I walked toward the hospital operating room to deliver our son by Cesarean section.

My C-section delivery had been carefully scheduled for the Monday after Thanksgiving. I had worked out the plan and discussed it with my doctor, who'd given his approval. It would give my husband, who was in Jamaica, ample time to arrive before the delivery of his firstborn.

Now here I was, at 37 weeks gestation, and two weeks before our scheduled date, going into the OR to have the baby, as he needed to be delivered soon. My doctor had been kind enough to give us a day so my husband could travel to be with me and witness the birth of his son. The trade-off was that I had to remain on the labor and delivery floor so the baby could be continuously monitored.

I was given two doses of spinal anesthesia that did not work, so had to have general anesthesia, and my son was immediately whisked off to the neonatal intensive-care unit (NICU). He was a scrawny little thing who had a hard time regulating his temperature and blood glucose. Apparently he had stopped growing inside of me, hence his need to be delivered early. He spent a week and a half in the NICU, and even when he came home, we were warned not to take him to public places. If he became ill, he would have to be hospitalized again. When he was 5 weeks old, we got clearance from his pediatrician to take him to church and have him dedicated, and when he was 6 weeks old, we were able to fly home to Jamaica with him.

God in His wisdom altered my well-made plans and delivered our son two weeks early. I do not know if otherwise the problems at delivery would have been the same (they may have been worse). What I do know is that when we left with him for Jamaica it was very clear that we had needed the two extra weeks for him to grow strong and big enough to travel.

This is just one experience in my life where God has intervened before I even knew I needed to call on Him. Trust Him today—He has your back.

Raylene McKenzie Ross

My Miracle Mouthguard

But my God shall supply all your need. Phil. 4:19.

I HAVE A DISORDER known as TMJ, short for temporomandibular joint, a joint that is located in the jaw. If you suffer from this disorder, you know how painful it can be. After nearly a year of active treatment, I continue to wear upper and lower mouthguards (or appliances/splints) daily, and will need them for the rest of my life.

I had usually kept a good care routine, but broke it one day while Christmas shopping with my daughter and granddaughter. I took out my lower appliance so that I could eat, and placed it in the pouch on the back of the stroller, as I didn't have its case with me. When we got back to my daughter's home, I checked the pouch. The appliance was gone. I was clueless. I prayed earnestly to find it as such appliances can be costly in time and money.

I waited days, hoping for it to turn up, and kept praying—with no success. Finally I called my doctor's office to let them know I had lost it. I thought the replacement would cost around $330, and was sweating that. I was shocked to learn the cost would be nearly $1,000! My only option was to rely on one mouthguard for the time being, so I ended the call.

I sat on my couch and cried out to God in desperation, *Help, dear Lord! What am I going to do?* Almost the moment I ended my prayer, the phone rang. It was the doctor's office. The voice on the other end said, "Dr. Spencer wants to give you an early Christmas gift! He is going to pay for your day splint!" All I could do was cry and repeatedly say, "Thank you!"

I wrote a note to the doctor expressing my sincerest appreciation, and praising God for His and the doctor's generosity. It seemed so inadequate for such an amazing act of kindness. How wonderful our God is! He has a thousand ways of answering our prayers of which we know nothing!

Every time I wear my day splint I remember the One who gave it to me. It's a daily reminder of God's attentive care. Have I become the perfect Christian as a result of that amazing instant answer to prayer? Well, reader, you already know the answer to that question. But I am keenly aware of my enormous need and His tremendous love. My summation is this: never doubt His love for you.

Joan Green

A Meditation for Gathering: Call for the Wailing Women

Look over the trouble we're in and call for help. Send for some singers who can help us mourn our loss. Tell them to hurry—to help us express our loss and lament, help us get our tears flowing, make tearful music of our crying. Listen to it! Listen to that torrent of tears out of Zion: "We're a ruined people, we're a shamed people! We've been driven from our homes and must leave our land!" Jer. 9:17-19, Message.

JESUS' CALL IS for women who are not afraid to cry out! Where are the wailing women who will prostrate themselves before God and petition for deliverance? Lord, we "look over the trouble we're in and call for help. Send for some singers who can help us mourn our loss."

Where are the women who shed tears not only on behalf of themselves, but for all those who need a word and a touch from the Lord? "Tell them to hurry—to help us express our loss and lament, help us get our tears flowing, make tearful music of our crying."

For we have backslidden; we have made excuses. We have turned up our noses and passed by our sisters in need. We have been so busy getting our hair done and our nails polished that we have forgotten about exhibiting the fruits of the Spirit. I feel a wail, even now, in my spirit! "Listen to it! Listen to that torrent of tears out of Zion."

Women, clasp your sisters' hands and open up your mouths and cry aloud together as God speaks to us today. Women, hear the word of the Lord; open your ears to the words of His mouth. Teach your daughters how to wail; teach one another a lament (see Jer. 9:20, Message). Women are longing for safety and security, yearning for healing and wholeness, hoping for restoration of love and family in their homes.

Oh, where are the wailing women? We are here—knees bent, heads bowed, hands lifted, hearts open. Let all the women cry aloud in word, in prayer, and in song.

For the Lord will record our tears and list them in the book of life. God sees and cares. He will raise us up and deliver us.

We acknowledge our Jehovah-God; and as Jehovah, He is also love. We greet Him today with the assurance that He has loved us with an everlasting love. We ask God to embolden our faith community to be a resounding chorus of love, hope, and consolation for all women.

Michelle Riley Jones

Love With No Limits

Can a mother forget the baby at her breast and have no compassion on the child she has borne? Though she may forget, I will not forget you! Isa. 49:15, NIV.

WHILE MY HUSBAND studied theology we lived in a house with a lovely spacious backyard, a nice lawn, and a gorgeous mango tree in front of our land. And in our backyard a burrowing owl made its nest. She has been given this name because she digs a hole in the earth and deposits her eggs there.

From my kitchen window I could watch the owl daily. She stayed immobile, never moving from the entrance of the hole, keeping safe her precious legacy. It was like this every day. When my son cautiously tried to approach to see the eggs, mama owl was ready and prepared to attack, opening her wings, and charging menacingly. Sometimes she flew to demonstrate what would happen if he got closer.

Once I saw something that impressed me with the care that this little owl has for its brood. It was late afternoon. There had been a lot of rain and strong winds. And this zealous mother, just a little apart, sheltering below the branch of a bush, remained constant and observant, always looking at her nest.

Immediately I remembered God's care for us, His children. With love He keeps constant watch over us, and He is always ready to defend us when the enemy tries to attack. In the storms and adversities of life He continues there by our side—firm, considerate, even though we can't see Him. In these hours we might think that He has abandoned us, but in fact, like that careful mother, He is under the very next branch. It is from there that He pays attention to each step we take. He has a much better view of our situation than we do, and He is always ready to help.

Looking at that little owl and thinking about her devotion to her young, I thought of my son who was sleeping at that moment and of how much I love him. I don't forget him for even a minute. The words of today's text about God's care and love comforted my heart: "Though she [the mother, I, the little owl, or whomever] may forget, I will not forget you!" It is very good to feel as loved children of the Lord!

Patrícia C. de Almeida Santos

God Is Speaking to You

Be still, and know
that I am God. Ps. 46:10.

ABOUT 5:00 ONE MORNING we were awakened by a drumming sound. The loud noise seemed to be coming through the vents. Assuming that something had gone wrong with our heating system, my husband rushed to the basement to turn off the thermostat. We listened and speculated about the noise for a half hour, because the idle thermostat did nothing to quiet it. Later my daughter, Leah, said, "It sounds like a woodpecker is in our vents." We thought she had a point, since the noise was loudest in her room.

Over the course of the week, the noise sporadically came and went. At our request a technician came in, but he was unable to solve our problem. Judging from the location of the noise, he suggested that a bat, a squirrel, or some type of bird was getting into the chimney. His advice was to change the cap on the chimney, and he mentioned that once he had rescued a goose from inside a customer's chimney.

While pulling into our driveway the following week, I saw a goose on our roof! So I suggested to my family that maybe a member of the goose family was stuck in the chimney. We waited for the noise to return, and one morning it started again. My husband rushed outside to look up on the roof, and to his surprise saw a woodpecker tapping at the chimney. The sound could be heard both inside and outside our home. A woodpecker was the culprit. She had caused the ruckus while making a nest under our porch.

That incident made me think. Leah had suggested a woodpecker was on the roof, and we should have considered her suggestion instead of busily speculating and brushing off the idea.

Oftentimes we do not hear when God is talking to us. Is God trying to get your attention? Ellen White has the solution: "In the midst of this maddening rush, God is speaking. He bids us come apart and commune with Him" (*Education*, p. 260). She wrote this many years ago. Think about how much more noise there is today with MP3s, iPods, radios, and TVs everywhere—and just more people. It is difficult to find a quiet place. We must be intentional in seeking to listen to God and His still small voice. Let us quietly wait on God. He needs our attention, and we need to hear Him. I urge you right now to practice your God-listening skills.

Margo Peterson

The Inga and the Açaí

The righteous shall flourish like a palm tree,
he shall grow like a cedar in Lebanon. Ps. 92:12, NKJV.

FROM THE CONDOMINIUM where I live I can see numerous trees. Some are big with thick trunks; others are thinner. In the backyard of our house we have an Inga, a tree with a thick, strong trunk. Its branches spread over the garden and give us shade on hot days. It is as majestic as a cedar. In the front yard is a set of Açaí saplings. They are a typical fruit palm of the region. Their trunk diameter doesn't exceed 5.5 inches (14 centimeters), and their height measures almost 40 feet (12 meters). Actually, their stems look very fragile, and compared to the other large trees in the Amazon, they just look like sticks.

In the northern region of Brazil the season from December to March is winter, the rainy season, when it rains throughout the whole day. At any moment storms begin. Gigantic clouds suddenly empty their rain, causing floods and disasters for the city.

In one of these sudden storms our Inga, strong and resistant, could not handle the strong winds and intense rain, and broke completely. Its branches stretched along the road. To keep the tree from damaging the electrical wires, we had to call the fire department to remove it. Later when I looked at the garden in the front yard, I saw that the Açaí saplings, which appeared very fragile and thin, remained intact. I could not understand how a beautiful, strong tree, which stretched out its leafy branches, would break while the thin Açaí saplings would stand firm. But then I remembered a botany class in which the professor explained that the palm stalk is very flexible. The smaller stalks can handle more wind. However, the trunks of large trees become hollow and at any moment crumble.

I pondered why the psalmist used the palm as a reference. I don't find them beautiful, and they do not have a captivating fragrance. Moreover, they are droopy. But the dictionary says that to flourish is not only the act of giving flowers, but also of prospering!

Many times the difficulties and storms reach us. Let's remember that while the cedar is distinguished for its grandeur and height, the palm endures the storms. By Christ's side, the just will never be helpless.

Mariana Sampaio

Introduced

Teach me your way, Lord;
lead me in a straight path. Ps. 27:11, NIV.

HOW DID THEY KNOW each other? She was in Jordan at that time, and he was in Virginia.

In 2008 I went home to the island of Polillo in the Philippines. As I walked around the town I noticed many preschool children who were underweight and malnourished. Led by Ailen, five other elementary teachers and a midwife had formed a volunteer group that taught children from birth to age 5 and carried on a feeding program for both children and nursing mothers.

Emer, one of the teachers, had a burden for her daughter who was ready to have a family but was not married. I heard her tell this to the group, so I responded, "I have a son." That very day she gave me a picture of her daughter, her address, and phone number. I sent this information to my son who, at first, was very skeptical.

However, the two soon began chatting on the Internet, happy to know more about each other. They discovered that their parents are Christians and belong to the same church; that both are from Polillo, although Jon was born in Tucson, Arizona, and currently lived in Virginia Beach. At the time of their meeting via the Internet, Princess, a nurse, was working in Jordan. After the couple found out they were compatible, they decided to meet in Polillo. She flew to Manila from Jordan, and Jon flew from Virginia to the same airport, where Princess and I met him. A few months later their relationship culminated in a wedding witnessed by 500 friends, relatives, and families. I was glad Emer led the way for each of us to know each other.

I have a friend who entered the United States as a yoga minister. She told me that many of her friends had taken her to Christian churches to worship, but they had never introduced her to Christ-centered Bible studies. We were led by the Holy Spirit to study and finish a set of Bible lessons.

The best Person to introduce anyone to is Jesus. He will also lead you to the right place at the right moment in His own time. One of the Gospel stories tells of some Greeks who came to the disciples. "They came to Philip, who was from Bethsaida in Galilee, with a request. 'Sir,' they said, 'we would like to see Jesus'" (John 12:21, NIV). May we, at all times, tune our hearts to His own leading, introducing others to Jesus.

Esperanza Aquino Mopera

The Angry Bull and Three Men

Our help is in the name of the Lord, who made heaven and earth. Ps. 124:8.

THE BARGE *SAMARITANA II* descended the Rivera River of Iguape along the south coast of São Paulo, Brazil. My husband, a missionary pastor who worked on that Christian social assistance boat, was at the helm and we, close by, were talking and contemplating the scenery. Traveling with us were my husband's brother and his family.

It was a typically hot summer day. My husband needed to anchor the barge in the port of Iguape to buy fuel and food.

As Iguape was close to the sea, we decided to go to the beach. He anchored the barge along the side of an uninhabited island that we had to cross on foot. The island was covered by undergrowth, and when we were halfway down the path, we saw a herd of bulls. My husband carried our baby in his arms. My brother-in-law had our oldest daughter by the hand, and I held the hand of our 3-year-old son.

Then I observed that one bull stood out from the others. He was quiet, with his head erect in attack position. His sharp horns were turned forward. As I swept the island with my eyes I shouted to my husband, "The bull is going to attack!" There was no protection against that bull. Only God could help us.

The bull came like a fury, its horns still in attack position. Everyone ran. But when I tried to run, my right leg sank into a narrow, deep hole. I was caught, and fell. Pulling my son in front of me, I covered him with my body to protect him. My back was to the bull, and I froze, waiting for the attack. When the bull was just a few meters from me, I heard men shouting. I looked back and saw three men brandishing their work tools against the bull. It resisted the men, but finally they scared him away from the area.

Then the men, their tools in their arms, picked up the trail that led to the sea and disappeared in the solitary island.

Who were they and how did they arrive in the exact moment to help us? For more than four decades my husband and I have asked this same question—even though we knew that only God could answer.

Adair Ottoni Raymundo

"You Are Most Welcome"

I can do all things through Christ
which strengtheneth me. Phil. 4:13.

THREE YEARS AGO my 5-year-old grandson, Donwayne, did me a favor. I can't remember what it was or what he did, but what I'll always remember is what he said when I thanked him: "You are most welcome." I'm sure I smiled, thanking God for the good training and common courtesies my daughter had taught him. Now when anyone thanks me for something, I am often tempted to repeat his words, "You are most welcome."

My grandchildren are the light of my life. They bring me so much joy, especially when I see how well brought up they are. Courtesies, no matter how small, bring out the best in all of us. Words are links to our memory. When they are wrapped in courtesy, they are particularly special.

I can understand why more than 2,000 years ago Jesus allowed Himself to be surrounded by young children, telling those who listened that these little ones were citizens of heaven. I can also understand why three of the Gospel writers (Matthew, Mark, and Luke) recorded His words: "But Jesus said, Suffer the little children, and forbid them not, to come unto me: for to such belongeth the kingdom of heaven" (Matt. 19:14, ASV).

Ellen White tells us even more. "Jesus was ever a lover of children. He accepted their childish sympathy and their open, unaffected love. The grateful praise from their pure lips was music in His ears, and refreshed His spirit" (*The Desire of Ages*, p. 511).

Ellen White also wrote directly to mothers who are often wearied by taking care of their precious children. She gave them comfort, inviting them to lay their burdens at the Savior's feet, and urged them to lead their little ones to their Master for a blessing. Jesus came down to the level of small children, she said. "He, the Majesty of heaven, did not disdain to answer their questions, and simplify His important lessons to meet their childish understanding" (*The Desire of Ages*, p. 515).

Jesus still knows how important child care is. He also knows how challenging it is. Today's text is a promise to each of us as we help the children of our homes, churches, and communities. We, with Christ's help, can handle anything that comes our way.

Verona Bent

Dead Batteries

See what God has done!
Num. 23:23, NIV.

I'VE ALWAYS BEEN fascinated with how God can transform a disastrous situation into an occasion to praise Him, especially if we remember to pray first. The timeless words of a well-known hymn come to mind: "O what peace we often forfeit, O what needless pain we bear, all because we do not carry everything to God in prayer."

December 8 is Mother's Day in the republic of Panama. As one of our yearly community outreach projects, the executive directors of 4Real Women International decided to take some love to a shelter for pregnant teens. The girls get to spend their pregnancy there, and are allowed to remain until their baby is 6 months old. Most of these girls are severely underprivileged. Some have been rejected by their families, and a number of them are rape victims. Because of their circumstances, many are forced to drop out of school, making their future seem even bleaker. We knew that several private businesses periodically contributed to these shelters, but we also knew that the vast majority of the donations were baby items. So this was the perfect occasion to remember these special mommies and to remind them of God's unconditional love.

After spending a few minutes handing out the gift bags and getting to know the girls, we found it was time to leave. Of course I wanted to take some pictures to keep in our records, but imagine my dismay when I turned on my camera to find that the batteries were dead. I tried a few more times and kept getting the message "Please replace batteries," just before the screen went black.

I calmly announced what was happening, but maybe the girls could sense that this problem would be quickly resolved, because they remained seated in the living room, looking over their gifts and chatting happily. I prayed silently while I simultaneously engaged the center's director in a conversation and removed the batteries. I put the dead batteries back in and turned on the camera. No change. I praised God for the miracle He was about to perform, removed the batteries, and put them back in. The screen lit up. "Run!" I yelled at the girls. Giggling, they obediently bunched up and I was able to take two pictures of these beautiful teens. Every time I look at those pictures, their happy smiles remind me of God's faithfulness.

Isn't God amazing? Trust Him today. He's still in the miracle business!

Dinorah Blackman

God's Glorious Power

But this precious treasure—this light and power that now shine within us—is held in a perishable container, that is, in our weak bodies. Everyone can see that the glorious power within must be from God and is not our own. 2 Cor. 4:7, TLB.

DIFFERENT WORDS can describe the "perishable containers" mentioned in this verse. The King James Version calls them "earthen vessels," and several other versions call them "clay pots." These all imply something plain and fragile, which draws attention to the contents within rather than the container holding it. Thus weak human beings can display God's glorious power.

As I was growing up, deep emotional wounds, health problems, and self-doubt hounded me at every step, and I was painfully aware of my weaknesses. Then a few years ago, in the midst of a personal crisis, the Lord brought me to a deeper surrender that opened a floodgate of blessings, beginning the most amazing journey of my life.

For years I had longed to write music, but had no training in music composition and had never written a song. I thought I would have to wait until heaven to realize this dream. In His great love, God started giving me ideas for melodies and lyrics, and I met a talented arranger in Malaysia who brought these simple songs to life. Then the Lord unfolded every step in developing a CD called *My Peace* that soon followed. As I waited on Him, He provided a graphic arts designer, Greg Baron, a professional soloist, and led me to the right duplication company. I met many wonderful people. As I look back I marvel at what God did throughout this amazing project.

Different people have told me that this music encouraged and blessed them. I have been humbled and amazed that Jesus was able to use this "earthen vessel" to be a channel of blessing to others. Through His power the impossible became possible, and my inadequacies made it more obvious that the inspiration came from God.

What things in your life make you doubt yourself and sense your weakness? Would you like to see God transform these inadequacies for His own glory so that others may see Jesus in you and praise Him for His goodness and grace? Pray today that He will use you too, so that others will see His glorious power.

Teresa (Proctor) Hebard

You *Are* God's Glory

But we all, with unveiled face, beholding as in a mirror the glory of the Lord,
are being transformed into the same image from glory to glory.
2 Cor. 3:18, NKJV.

DID YOU KNOW that as you live your life consecrated to your Lord, you actually *are* His glory? And, just how could this happen?

Let's visualize the scene of Jesus praying in Gethsemane just before His crucifixion. As He knelt there on the ground pleading with His Father, He made an amazing declaration—that the glory He had received, He had given to all those who believed in Him (see John 17:20-22). That's us. Today. Right now. We certainly have to ask *What does God's glory entail? How can this be explained? Is it a glorious light shining from heaven? a wave of indescribable, unviewable brightness before our eyes? Or something totally different?*

Just before Moses constructed two additional tables of stone (the first had shattered when he threw them to the ground), with the Ten Commandments written on them, he made a bold request of His Lord: "Please, show me Your glory" (Ex. 33:18, NKJV).

Right then the Lord descended in a cloud and proclaimed, "The Lord, the Lord God, merciful and gracious, longsuffering, and abounding in goodness and truth" (Ex. 34:6, NKJV).

Oh, now we have the answer to the question: how can *we* be God's glory? We become transformed into "the same image" of God when we show concern and relieve suffering, as we minister to individuals who desperately need the Lord, as we demonstrate graciousness even when our family and friends do not measure up to our standard.

In the narthex of one church, after the Communion service, a member knelt before an older woman and washed her feet. The elderly person had expressed her disappointment that she'd missed that portion of the service. Do you think this woman who washed the feet of this other, totally out of schedule, could be classed as a person who lived God's glory? How about the couple who offered their front yard as a burial place for a dog owned by two grieving women who wanted a place to lay their beloved pet where they could come and weep over him?

You have received and you live God's glory. How could your privileged life be any more rewarding, exciting, and satisfying?

Myrna Tetz

"See You Soon!"

For the Lord Himself will descend from heaven with a shout,
with the voice of an archangel, and with the trumpet of God.
And the dead in Christ will rise first. 1 Thess. 4:16, NKJV.

ABRAHAM WAS seated on a front-row pew in the church when my daughter introduced us. As soon as I spoke to him, he said, "I recognize your voice—you are Sally Phoon, the woman from the radio program *Spirit-filled Moments.*"

Years before, a debilitating nerve disorder had left Abraham blind, so he always sat in front where he could hear best. A year before he had listened to my radio program over the Hope Channel in Singapore. On it I shared short devotional thoughts, and through this program he had become acquainted with our church and began attending.

Despite his blindness, Abraham lived a full life. He offered to take me out for lunch at a very special hotel that served Penang food (Penang food is super-delicious!), but we were leaving Singapore so we promised to do that the next time we visited. A few months later my daughter sent me the sad news that Abraham had died and was finally resting in Jesus.

The 2010 Christmas season will remain etched in my memory for as long as I shall live. Nine days before Christmas my mother was snatched away from us, losing her battle to cancer. It was not an easy thing to discuss the subject of death as we watched her dying. Tears would come as we anticipated a separation, but we thanked God for the resurrection morning; thanked God for the hope we have in Christ; thanked God for the peace that passes all understanding as we go through these unavoidable times when we have to say goodbye.

I hate saying goodbye. To those who believe in Christ, I would rather say, "See you soon!" It won't be long until the last trumpet call will sound and those who are asleep in Jesus will rise. What a morning that will be!

As the graves open and those who are dead in Christ rise to meet Him, I will be looking for my parents, for Abraham, and for many dear friends who have gone before, resting in Jesus. I will look for Abraham and say, "Come, I'm collecting my rain check. Let's feast at the banqueting table, Abraham. It's going to be even better than Penang food!"

My heart is longing for that day. Yes, come quickly, Lord Jesus!

Sally Lam-Phoon

Belonging!

If we live, we live for the Lord; and if we die, we die for the Lord. So, whether we live or die, we belong to the Lord. Rom. 14:8, NIV.

BELONGING TO A FAMILY is a precious privilege. As I reflect on an experience that happened to my grandparents on my father's side, it reminds me how God directs and leads in our lives, and we belong to Him. In 1901 they, along with their parents and siblings, made a life-changing decision to emigrate from Freudenthal, Russia, to the United States. They traveled by train to Bremen, Germany, where they planned to board a ship to America.

A baby had just recently been born to my grandparents, and unfortunately it became sick as they traveled by train. So my grandparents decided to stay in Bremen, hoping the baby would recover, but urged their parents and siblings to proceed with their plans, which they did. How hard it had to be to bid goodbye and watch that ship leave the harbor without them, not knowing what the future held.

Sadly, after just 18 days of life, the baby passed away and was buried in Germany. My brokenhearted grandparents decided to proceed with plans to sail to America and join their family. Boarding the *Kaiser Wilhelm der Grosse,* they arrived at Ellis Island 15 days after their parents and siblings did. From there they traveled by rail to Colorado. When their train finally arrived at the station where they thought their parents would meet them, no one was there. They waited and waited, and . . . waited, finally alarmed that they had gotten off at the wrong place with no money to travel on. How frightened they became. Both cried bitterly. Still mourning the death of their dear baby, they had endured a long trip across the ocean, a hard ride halfway across the United States, only to be left at the train station—alone! Of course they spoke no English, so they could not ask for help. After waiting for most of the day, their parents finally arrived. How relieved and happy they were! Tears of joy flowed. What a reunion! Their parents had been given wrong information on the train's arrival time.

Being a child of the King, belonging to Him, we will have no disappointment! He will come for us. We belong to Him, and He will be at the "right place, at the right time!" What a grand reunion that will be. Praise God!

Ginger Bell

Even Sunglasses

For your Father knoweth what things ye have need of, before ye ask him.
Matt. 6:8.

I DO NOT WEAR prescription glasses or sunglasses. But for years, every time I visit the ophthalmologist I am told that even with 20/20 vision I need to wear sunglasses to protect my eyes, as I have a small growth because of the glare from the sun.

Running late one day, I hurriedly ran through the store racks looking for an affordable but unusual outfit to wear to Fashion Week. When I found one and went to try it on, I took off my sunglasses and put them over a clip in the dressing room, only for the handle to break and the entire thing to fall. I was really mad because the glasses were not even a month old.

That Tuesday afternoon when a girlfriend visited I relayed the story, and in exasperation exclaimed, "I don't ever want a cheap pair of shades again! I want one that costs *hundreds* of dollars and will last for *years!*" Then Thursday, just two days later, I spent the night with some other girlfriends. (One of them was going through a transition and needed support.) We had a late night and much fun, and then this friend told me that she had bought new sunglasses. She said she could have gotten a second pair, or a discount coupon, but instead chose new shades that cost more than $700. She was happy about them—I could see that—but not that excited.

As we left the house the next morning, I encouraged her to wear her new sunglasses. She put them in her handbag. As we walked, she stopped and said to me, "Somehow, I feel impressed to give these to you." She went on to say that she was not even sure why she had bought them when she already had a good pair. In addition, the style was not to her liking—but it was more to mine. At that point she took the glasses out of her bag and handed them to me.

What happened next was even more amazing! She breathed a sigh of relief and exclaimed, "Now I feel relieved."

I said, "Are you serious?"

She was.

I was amazed because she had no clue what had happened earlier in the week, and amazed that God had used Angie to honor a simple desire for a pair of sunglasses! They even came with a one-year manufacturer warranty, and free eyewear servicing. Oh, what a God!

Nadine A. Joseph

Helga or Heather

I praise you because I am fearfully and wonderfully
made; your works are wonderful, I know that full well. Ps. 139:14, NIV.

I'M NOT FOND of mornings like this. When I don't get out the door on time and my hair does this greasy, floppy, uncooperative thing. When I spend far too long trying on three pairs of jeans one after the other. When the longer I look in the mirror, the louder that bullying voice shouts. Words like "fat" and "gross" and "ugly" and "unmotivated" and "pathetic" sneak into my otherwise kinder vocabulary and leave me feeling, well, most of those things. Mornings when it's only Monday and the war has already begun. In actuality, the war never ends. It just ebbs and flows, depending on who's in charge. It's usually Heather or Helga, depending on the day. I'm usually either accepting or acidic, kind or critical, compassionate or controlling.

Heather is the young girl who has never seen a fashion magazine or longed to be anyone else but herself. Helga is the calloused critic. She picks me apart and reminds me of everything I've done wrong. Ever! Helga was loud enough for long enough to introduce me to anorexia and bulimia. She could not admit flaws. Tough on the outside, falling apart on the inside. She was convinced that organized, efficient, and productive were her important virtues. She was sad, but unwilling to say it out loud. She was apparently "perfect," but unable to see any worth in herself.

Heather is learning that perfection is a myth, a lie, one I've believed too easily, chasing my own tail in circles. Now I'm learning to let go and accept myself. When people try to compete with me, to prove they are prettier, or thinner, or more perfect, I bow out. That's right. I let them "win," because that's not winning anyway. The game is silly, and I'm not playing anymore. Bowing out doesn't mean giving up or letting myself go. It means that I've recognized that today's standard for perfection is completely unreachable, and I'm choosing to take the grace offered to me instead of killing myself just to look like I have it all together. I can be content. I can be whole. I can accept the gift of grace and end the perpetual swim upstream.

What if I am *everything* I need to be? What if I have *always* been everything I need to be? First Corinthians 1:3 says, "May God our Father and the Lord Jesus Christ give you grace and peace" (NLT). God has already given us grace and peace. Actually taking it is a choice. Every day.

Heather Bohlender

Because I Asked

And all things, whatever you ask in prayer, believing, you will receive.
Matt. 21:22, NKJV.

I DISCOVERED QUITE by accident that Christian Edition (CE), a dedicated men's chorus based in southern California, would be in my area Friday evening. I went early to the church where they would be singing. They are one of my favorite singing groups, and I wanted to be certain of finding a good seat where I could both watch them and listen. I chose an aisle seat in the second row and sat back to await the beginning of the program. A quiet tranquillity settled over me as they sang. Their calm, relaxing music filled me with awe and reverence, and I rejoiced as they sang praises to our Lord in heaven. Eventually the members of the chorus retired to a side room for a brief break while an offering was being taken. Mr. Calvin Knipschild, founder and director of the organization, sat down in the pew in front of me.

I leaned forward, tapped him on the shoulder, and asked hopefully, "Are you going to sing 'Daystar' this evening?"

"Hadn't planned to" was his quick reply.

"Any chance you could change your plans?" He chuckled. CE was filing back into the auditorium, singing as they came. Mr. Knipschild stood facing them as they completed their song. Then he gently knocked on the nearby piano, said something to the accompanist, and then turned to the group and spoke softly to them. I watched and listened as the pianist began playing and the soloist stepped forward and began to sing, "Lily of the Valley, let Your sweet aroma fill my life . . ." "Daystar"! The group had sung the song for so many years that they had abandoned it in favor of newer music. But they were singing it now! To me it seemed akin to what the angel choir in heaven must sound like. A quiet peace settled over me as I basked in the melodious sounds, and I mentally recommitted to the Lily of the Valley to continue to be His witness, as the song suggested.

The CE chorus had just sung one of my favorite songs, and they'd sung it for me—simply because I asked. That started a whole chain of thought. If we here on this earth, being so imperfect, are willing to give good things to one another, how much more eager is our heavenly Father to give us good gifts; but we need to ask Him (see Matt. 7:11).

Barbara Horst Reinholtz

Awards Banquet Faith Gift

Ask and it will be given to you; seek and you will find; knock and the door will be opened to you. For everyone who asks receives; the one who seeks finds; and to the one who knocks, the door will be opened. Matt. 7:7, 8, NIV.

AROUND CHRISTMASTIME every year at my work, we have an awards banquet to honor those with significant accomplishments. To entice attendance, they raffle off big prizes during the event. I told my husband, "This year we will attend, since I have no excuse not to."

We agreed to stay through dinner and the awards portion, then leave before the band started playing. As in every previous year, 10 tickets were given to each employee to put in the raffle boxes. This year they were giving away a tool set, a flat-screen TV, gift cards to restaurants and department stores, a weekend getaway, and an iPad. When we saw the prizes, we knew which one we wanted. You see, just the week before, my in-laws had been in town and had shown us the iPad they'd purchased. We really wanted one. So we put all 10 tickets in the iPad raffle box and instantly, mentally, and in faith claimed our prize.

Throughout the night we chatted with other couples in the room and asked them which boxes they'd put their tickets in, and they asked us the same. Of course, my response was "We are going to win the iPad." They were thinking to themselves, *Yeah, right.* They laughed at our faith, but we knew the power of God. What I didn't know is that during dinner my husband was calling on God with a specific prayer. It was for God to show me that He was working in our lives, because for a year straight we had received some huge blessings. My husband prayed, "Lord, just in case Traci thinks that all the blessings we've received are by chance, show her this night, in the midst of hundreds of people, that we have Your favor. Amen."

When it came time for the raffle, they announced all the prizes, saving the iPad for last—trying to stall my victory. At last I heard, "And the winner for the iPad is . . ." I stood up ready to claim my prize before they could even announce the winner, and everyone laughed. Then the name on the envelope was read, and it was mine! God wants us to have the desires of our heart, and all we have to do is ask. "Delight yourself also in the Lord, and He shall give you the desires of your heart" (Ps. 37:4, NKJV).

Traci S. Anderson

God Is Faithful

And a little child shall lead them.
Isa. 11:6.

I HAVE HAD THE JOY and the challenges of taking care of aging parents. My loving parents took such good care of me I always felt it was only natural to do the same for them in their sunset years. The last three years have been more challenging as my mother, in particular, suffers from renal failure and chronic diarrhea.

This past Christmas, after yet another of many hospitalizations, her physician informed us there was nothing else he could do for her diarrhea. She came home, and through the holiday festivities, family visits, and joys of the season it was evident to me as a nurse that because of the effect of her illnesses, my mother was fading. I felt utterly helpless. Everything she ate went right through her, and she was already quite frail. No medication helped.

One afternoon I once again got down on my knees to pray. I thanked God for the privilege and the joys of still having my parents alive. My children get to see them every day. I get to hug and thank them for all they have done for us. I didn't even ask God to extend her life, only to give my mother relief from the symptoms ailing her and to give me the wisdom to assist. That very evening my 11-year-old daughter, Cynthia, came to me and said, "Mommy, I think I know what's wrong with Grandma." My daughter loves TV medical programs and often goes online to research diseases, since she desires to be a doctor one day. She went on to show me her research on a disease called Habba syndrome. I was dumbfounded as I read and saw all of my mother's symptoms.

The next day I sent the information to my mother's gastroenterologist. He gladly prescribed the treatment for this illness, for he admitted that he knew of nothing else to prescribe for her. To our amazement, with only one dose of the medication, she had immediate relief from diarrhea that had lasted consistently for three years! She has regained her strength and is back to enjoying life. We praise God for His intervention through a child.

I have always found comfort in prayer. God has a way of answering, often in ways we cannot fathom or understand. One thing is for sure: God is faithful. He hears us when we pray, and sometimes He answers through a little child.

Lisa Lothian

Friday Evening Honesty

Trust in the Lord with all thine heart;
and lean not unto thine own understanding. Prov. 3:5.

DIRECT DEPOSIT was my usual pay method—in fact, I have not been to the bank to carry out a transaction for seven years. Now it was Friday evening at the height of the busy holiday season. I went to the bank drive-through and cashed a check for $400 from my deposit.

On awaiting the completion, my coworker drove up in the lane next to mine. I saw her, but she did not see me. The handling of the bank's caddy was proving to be quite a challenge to her, so I offered to help. Through my instructions she was able to push the "send" button with her transaction. While we waited, we made small talk.

Finally my completed transaction was returned via the bank's caddy. I quickly retrieved my receipt, said a thank-you to the teller and a goodbye to my coworker.

I had driven about 500 feet when I noticed that the slot for my driver's license in my open wallet was empty. The bank's cash envelope was not in my possession either. *Oh, no!* The bank teller had not executed my transaction correctly.

Dodging through the Friday evening rush-hour traffic, I made a U-turn, and quickly parked beside the drive-through lanes. My heart raced, but I still felt calm. As I walked up to the window, all the tellers were beckoning with their hands, "Come, come, come." Their faces showed relief, urgency, perplexity—a need to tell me something.

My teller exclaimed, "You left your envelope with your cash and driver's license in the caddy. The customer behind you saw it, and sent it back to me." I was awestricken, dumbfounded, and grateful. How could this possibly be? Could this be real, in this day and age? A person returning $400 in cash?

On Monday when I saw my coworker, I was about to tell her what had happened. But she told me, "I witnessed everything, and was in a position to help safeguard your possession."

In the same way the all-omnipotent God protected my money and driver's license through the Spirit collaborating with a human, He will continue to manifest Himself. All we need to do is allow God. What a show of honesty!

Pauline A. Dwyer-Kerr

Trust in the Lord

Do not let your hearts be troubled. You believe in God; believe also in me. My Father's house has many rooms; if that were not so, would I have told you that I am going there to prepare a place for you? And if I go and prepare a place for you, I will come back and take you to be with me that you also may be where I am. John 14:1-3, NIV.

WHEN I WAS IN COLLEGE, my boyfriend, whom I wholly trusted, greatly disappointed me. It was the most disenchantment I have ever had. That year, as others celebrated Christmas, I wept as if someone had died. In fact, it felt like a death. I felt as if my life were going to be meaningless without him, and my sadness drove me to leave the church for some time. After I graduated, I went to live with my aunt in the heart of the city.

The first Sabbath I joined my aunt and her family at their church, intending to hide the fact that I had not been to church in years. But the following Sabbath I went back to my routine of not going to church.

I had seen a small school nearby, so I went to their office to ask whether I might teach there. The head teacher accepted my request, and asked me to bring my documents the following day. I began teaching there the next week. The schoolchildren gave me a lot of respect, which made my life comfortable. I knew the Lord was using them to bring new life in my heart so I would be able to proclaim His love once again. I had turned away from Him for a long time.

God started to work some miracles in my life, and after a few months I received an unexpected call from one of the church elders from the village where I used to live. He told me of a scholarship for young women. They had decided I should go for it, as I had been an active member in that church. I would still need a lot of money to continue my education, but I was thrilled to say yes! I came from a disadvantaged family and truly needed help. Some relatives promised financial contributions, but when the time came, only one gave it.

My brother tried hard to get money for my ticket to go back home, but he couldn't get enough. *Another obstacle in my life,* I thought. Four days before my traveling day, I got a call to get ready for the journey, as everything had been arranged by my church in that region.

Trust in the Lord! Only he gives the peace, joy, and satisfaction you need. We can trust His promises for the home He has prepared for us as well!

Atango Margaret Omon

Rainbow Sightings

My help will come from the Lord. . . . He will not let you fall; your protector is always awake. . . . The Lord will protect you from all danger. . . . He will protect you . . . now and forever. Ps. 121:2-8, TEV.

I have placed my rainbow in the clouds. It is the sign of my covenant with you and with all the earth. Gen. 9:13, NLT.

WHAT WOULD MY NEXT MOVE BE? There were unanswered questions, even from those in authority, so I had to search for myself. It was self-preservation. Should I continue with my plans to go home for my four weeks' holiday? I thought I needed a break, a time to think and rejuvenate before returning to deal with this ordeal I was in. We had little support from higher authorities, especially since we had to be supportive to our clients and to each other. I made my decision. I would go home and have a better time to think about my future.

The plane ride was long, but I managed to sleep through it. I had a wonderful welcome from my sister and our family friend, who wasn't aware I was coming. Nor did my mom know. They kept her in the kitchen, allowing me to sneak in, then encouraged her to come into the other room. When our eyes met, she screamed! That is the last time that I'll do something like that as Mom was unable to eat, and kept talking about it, all the while shaking her head.

As my holiday proceeded, I took a trip to our twin island, Tobago. On our way to Charlottesville I saw a lovely rainbow and then another arched over it. *A double rainbow.* I'd never seen anything like it before, and smiled. *This is God reminding you that all will be well, Susan, as I have promised, when you return to England.*

My holiday was coming to a close. It went by so fast, but it was full of fun and reflection, one of the best holidays I'd had in a long time. On the way to the airport I felt anxious, but there it was again: that rainbow with another rainbow arched over it. As I looked away, it was gone again. Then I heard Mom say, "Susan, look!" There was yet another bright rainbow, and we both smiled. Mom was reminding me of God's promise as well and how He had already worked out a plan. "For I know the plans I have for you . . . plans for good and not for disaster" (Jer. 29:11, NLT). God was so creative in His rainbow sightings to assure me that He will never leave me nor forsake me. Be reassured today that He has sightings and plans for you, too.

Susan Riley

"Joy Cometh in the Morning"

Weeping may endure for a night,
but joy cometh in the morning. Ps. 30:5.

I AM AT A HAPPY time in my life. In fact, I have never known such joy. There are days when I just can't contain the joy—even in the troublesome times such as the suicide attempt of my young son, the death of my mother, or my youngest sister's cancer scare. God has given me such peace and joy during these times. But this joy has not always been there, nor has the peace. I had to learn to trust God's Word. For example, today's scripture that tells us that "weeping may endure for a night, but joy cometh in the morning."

At the darkest time of my life I found this scripture to be true. Twenty-two years ago my first husband left me and our three children. I had no place to go, and my children had no father. I felt like my world had crumbled. How could he leave me? He was the father of my children! The first man I ever knew! Some days I just cried and cried. I thought I would never be happy again, and I had no desire to live. Furthermore, I had no plan for my life.

It was only when I learned to trust the Bible and its promises for me that things started turning around. Only when I learned to depend wholeheartedly on God did things work out. There were days I had no food for my children, and at night we had no heat. The kids had to sleep with their clothes and coats on to keep warm. But when I learned to go to God and to pray, He provided those things we needed. I watched God perform miracle after miracle. This would bring joy—the joy that was so overwhelming.

God eventually blessed me with a new husband and two more children, a new home, and all the food I could eat. And I had the warmth of a good man. So when I am sad, or dark times come, I just think of the goodness of God.

Many texts tell us about this joy. One of them is Psalm 16:11: "You will show me the path of life; in Your presence is fullness of joy; at Your right hand are pleasures forevermore" (NKJV). I think also of a song we sing in church that says, "The joy of the Lord is my strength." It is this joy that brings me through. Knowing that God has my best interests at heart, and He wants what's best for me—more than I want it for myself—brings me peace and joy in the morning, and noon, and night. "For the joy of the Lord is [truly] your strength" (see Neh. 8:10, NKJV).

Avis Floyd Jackson

Green Shoelaces

Then the Lord said to him, "What is that in your hand?" Ex. 4:2, NIV.

THE PAIR OF OLIVE-GREEN brogues hugged my feet like a second skin. I'd been watching for them for some time, waiting for the sales. Now they were marked down to less than half price, and finally I could afford them. I congratulated myself on my bargain as I slipped them off and watched the sales assistant place them in a bed of tissue paper and put the lid on the box.

Each time I wore the shoes I was careful not to step on their matching satin laces. I was conscious of how easily the delicate material could become damaged, for despite searching in a number of outlets, I had been unable to locate another pair of green laces.

The years passed and, as anticipated, the laces began to fray.

Then one week in church, we were asked to fill a shoe box with gifts for an unknown boy or girl whose circumstances were less comfortable than our own. Soap, crayons, hairbrush, comb, toothbrush, notebooks, sturdy toys, a ball, things that did not require batteries or electricity, were to be placed in the box. A date was given when the boxes would be collected and shipped. Straightaway I started to consider what I might include in my shoebox.

The next day I went into the cupboard where I kept my shoes to look for a suitable box. I had recently transferred most of my shoes into clear, plastic containers, retaining only one or two cardboard shoeboxes. One of them held my favorite pair of green shoes. I'd held onto this box because of its unusual design, but now it was time to put it to better use. I began to empty the box, and as I lifted out the tissue paper I saw a small, brown envelope tucked into one corner. I opened the envelope and shook into my hand—you've guessed it—an extra pair of waxed, olive green shoelaces. All this time they had been right under my nose!

This experience has taught me two things. We frequently ask God to meet our needs while failing to recognize that letting go of some cherished "prop" is the key to receiving His blessings. Second, we mistakenly assign value to His gifts based on the opulence of their packaging. Often God wraps His most precious offerings in plain, brown, everyday paper.

"Then the Lord said to him, 'What is that in your hand?' 'A staff,' he replied. The Lord said, 'Throw it on the ground'" (Ex. 4:2, 3, NIV).

Avery Davis

Encounter in the Target Checkout Line!

I have loved you with an everlasting love. Jer. 31:3, NIV.

IN FRONT OF ME LAST December 23, in a long checkout line at Target, was a father pushing his little girl in the shopping cart while holding a purchase in his hand. Suddenly, with a big smile, the little girl reached out her hand to me and said with a big grin, "Hey, do you know that Santa Claus is coming tomorrow night?"

I shook her little hand and said, "I've *heard* that! Have you been a good little girl all year?" Immediately her smile faded, she dropped her eyes, let go of my hand, and frowned.

"Actually," she said very slowly, shaking her head, "I haven't been all that good."

Trying very hard not to laugh, I said, "Well, let's hope Santa rewards your honesty."

At this her dad smiled and said, "Yes, she's very, *very* lucky that Santa loves bad little girls, too." I don't know what the child had done that caused her father to describe her as "bad," but I was glad that he made it clear that love was available in spite of her behavior.

For my part, I was fascinated by her. That precious child was so filled with excitement about the fabled coming of Santa Claus that she couldn't help sharing it with me, a perfect stranger. Obviously it was the foremost thought in her mind, and therefore the information bubbled uncontrollably from her mouth. The transparent, honest evaluation of her past behavior was so refreshing that I wished I could hug her! I also admired her dad for letting her know that she was loved even when she misbehaved.

Throughout the Christmas season I found myself thinking about that encounter in the Target checkout line. Wouldn't it be wonderful if this Christmas we *all* were like that little girl! What if we were so excited about the soon coming of Jesus that we couldn't help reaching out our hand to perfect strangers and tell them the good news? What if the anticipation of seeing our Lord and Savior were our foremost thought, making the joy of it bubble uncontrollably from our mouths? And even though we may not have been all that good this past year, would not our transparency and honesty demonstrate the power of God in our lives?

And then . . . oh, yes . . . then . . . *everybody* would see how very, very "lucky" we are to serve a God so wonderfully full of unfathomable grace that He loves even us bad little girls, too!

Ellie Postlewait Green

A Rose Melody
in the Winter Forest

For a child will be born to us, a son will be given to us; . . . and His name will
be called Wonderful Counselor, Mighty God, Eternal Father, Prince of Peace.
There will be no end to the increase of His government or of peace.
Isa. 9:6, 7, NASB.

IT IS CHRISTMAS EVE, and I wish I could be somewhere far away into the wood-
land where peace might exist. Maybe there I could escape all the rush of Christmas,
which often centers on buying costly presents. If Christmas means peace, I can't
sense it this rainy, cold night. The church service is over, but where is peace? And
while I walk home I wonder, *Father, why shouldn't I do it? Why shouldn't I go with
You for a night walk into the woods?*

In the past days rain has melted nearly all the snow, and the temperature is that
of an average winter day. It will likely not snow. At home I quickly dress in warmer
clothes, and several minutes later I leave the streetlights of the village behind me;
the night wraps me in its dark-blue world. Through fields and meadows I walk into
the silence. Trees are lined up on both sides of my path; their leafless branches draw
a delicate pattern against the night sky. From the distance the forest seems to be a
black wall, but when I reach it I am able to distinguish the silhouettes of the single
trees like black cutouts. As I enter, the forest seems to embrace me with a protecting coat, and peace fills my heart as gently as the breeze whispering in the branches.

*Father, it's a night of a special memory—a night that reminds me anew of Your
greatest miracle.* With humbleness the Creator of the universe embraced humanity
as He became visible, lying in a manger. A Baby was born, unrecognized by the
world, yet He was God leaving eternity to come to us. Most likely we will never understand it completely. His abundant love gave everything, gave Himself, in order
to unite heaven with earth and Himself with us.

I draw a deep breath, since again peace dwells in my heart. And it's already
midnight, time to go home. I think of the warmth that will receive me there and of
the scented candle that fills my room with the fragrance of roses: "Lo, how a Rose
e're blooming from tender stem hath sprung! . . . Isaiah 'twas foretold it, the Rose
I have in mind . . . To show God's love aright, . . . when half spent was the night."

Jaimée Seis

Valued Customer

Praise the Lord, my soul, . . . who redeems your life from the pit
and crowns you with love and compassion. Ps. 103:2-4, NIV.

I AWOKE THIS CHRISTMAS morning wondering what gifts I should give my children. They are age 27 and 22, both single and living with us. They are both in transition. The elder is between jobs and thinking of going back to school. The younger one has just finished college and is preparing for his licensure examination. At the moment there is nothing for them to do, and watching them with more leisure time than work irks my husband and me to the max.

So here am I, contemplating what I should give them. It's too late for Christmas shopping, and I did not want to give them things they don't need or even want. Shall I give them a few dollar bills as I promised myself several times in the past? Or just a Christmas card, or a Christmas letter? After all, it is the thought that counts, isn't it? But the more I think and pray, I realize I can't do that despite their past performance, or my vows. My heart cannot afford it. Christmas is about giving and loving, not punishing. And surely it will not make me any happier.

The thought that God loves me and heaps favor upon favor on me, continually filling my life with so many blessings affirms this idea. I have no doubt that I have disappointed Him countless times, yet He does not hesitate to lavish extravagant gifts on me. He allowed His only Son to suffer pain and hardship so I may have a chance to be with Him for eternity. Even when I don't think of Him, but I spend time in silly activities, He is always there, ready—and longing—to give me what I need most: comfort, guidance, wisdom, a perceptive heart, hope, whatever my need happens to be.

Being a parent has helped me understand God's heart a little bit. Several times He fumed over the rebellion, defiance, and stupidity of His favored people, the Israelites, yet in His next breath He promised to take care of them, to restore what they lost. He pleads with them to return to Him because He knows this is their best chance to overcome the enemy. Oh, what love!

So here am I, preparing my simple gift for my young adult children, the ones the Lord gave me to love. The amount is several times more than what I had originally intended, but I know this will make me happy. After all, I am a recipient of so much more favor and love.

Ana Teorima Faigao

Even Before Praying

Before they call, I will answer; and while they are yet speaking, I will hear. Isa. 65:24.

MY FAMILY AND I traveled to Florida at Christmas. The idea was to spend six months studying English. My daughters and I would stay there, and my husband would go back to Brazil to work and help us from a distance.

At that time the difference between the United States dollar and Brazilian money was very large. We decided we would not furnish the apartment, but would live very economically during these six months so we could fulfill our dream of learning English. As soon as we arrived in Florida we received a sofa, a table, and a mattress from fellow church believers. But we still didn't have chairs. Without chairs we couldn't sit around the table to eat our meals.

It seems like such a foolish thing, but I hated not being able to eat at a table, and not having chairs. Sitting at a table and staying after a meal to talk with my family is very precious to me. For this reason, after a while with no chairs I began to feel depressed. Then one night I talked to God. I said, "Lord, You know my heart. You know what I am feeling, the distance from my house all furnished in Brazil, and how much I miss my husband. I would like to ask You to help me find four chairs. I know this is a rich country. There must be many chairs abandoned someplace. Please, Lord, this is a simple request, but You know that these chairs will make a difference in my life. I ask and thank You in Jesus' name, amen."

It seemed like such a little thing with which to bother God that I decided to open my heart to Him. Soon after praying I went to bed. The next morning, as I was taking my younger daughter to school, my neighbor called to me, saying, "I don't know if you will want this, but yesterday my husband found four chairs in good condition." My eyes filled with tears, and I told her about my prayer.

Later her husband told me that even as I was praying for the chairs, they were already in their house. They hadn't bothered us then because it was already night.

Dear friends, don't be afraid to ask our wonderful God for what you need today. He cares for and about little things. Ask with all your heart, and He will answer. Thus you can testify about God's love to other people.

Ivani Viana Sampaio Maximino

Rocking Chair Memories

*I remember thee upon my bed, and meditate on thee in the night watches . . .
in the shadow of thy wings will I rejoice. Ps. 63:6, 7.*

HEAT FROM THE fading embers drifted into every corner of the room. Old-fashioned lights bubbled on the Christmas tree. Our feet propped comfortably on the footstool, my husband pulled me into a tight snuggle. Once-steaming bowls of corn chowder sat empty on the end table. Our New Year's weekend at our favorite mountain chalet would end tomorrow as we headed back to the city.

"Tell me about your favorite Christmas," my husband coaxed.

"Well, my family tradition embraced my married sister and her family as we celebrated each Christmas at the old Mission Inn in Riverside, California. I remember the shiny hardwood floors and old English decor, and especially the creamed onions and the candied yams."

"How about you?" I asked.

"Well, as we had a house with a high ceiling, each Christmas Dad brought home a tree that reached to the ceiling. I loved those trees—except one year. That year Dad brought home a tree half the size. As my 8-year-old eyes surveyed that tree, Christmas was ruined! I ran to my room and cried my eyes out. Eventually Mom persuaded Dad to take the tree back and bring home the traditional giant tree. For me, Christmas became Christmas once again."

"Do you remember another Christmas?" he inquired.

"Yes, when Mom opened a sack of Pillsbury flour and found a small booklet with Christmas cookie recipes. She and I spent an entire afternoon baking every recipe. My favorite was the piecrust stars, sprinkled with sugar. I still have that booklet—somewhere."

Memories. How we rush on down the road, forgetting the memories that once joyfully filled our hearts. Rocking chair memories, I call them.

A friend of many years told me, "Be sure to fill your mind with beautiful memories. You never know when grief or illness will steal your present joy." Those words proved true for her in the last months of her illness, as I placed a fragrant rose on her pillow each day.

I invite you, dear reader, to fill your mind with beautiful thoughts and beautiful memories. Savor those experiences.

Edna Maye Gallington

The Coffee Mug

A generous person will prosper; whoever refreshes others will be refreshed.
Prov. 11:25, NIV.

I AM PICKY ABOUT my "coffee" mugs. They have to be the right shape, the right weight, the design has to be appealing, and the inside has to be a light color. I had a drawer full of mugs at work—some I loved, some I didn't, plus one for every mood and season!

It was just after Christmas, and I was sitting in the staff room one afternoon sipping tea out of a relatively new mug that was quickly becoming my favorite. One of my colleagues admired the cup and asked where I had bought it. She then went on to say that she had received pajamas and a robe for Christmas with the identical color and design. We laughed, and I assured her that my mug had not been bought as part of a pajama set.

When I went back to my office a thought started to repeat itself in my mind, *Jill, go and give Esther your mug.*

What? Give away my beautiful mug? Yes, Jill, give your mug to Esther. *But, but, but . . .* I came up with all sorts of excuses to keep my beloved mug.

I quickly realized how selfish I was being over a silly mug. Without any more thought I marched down to Esther's office and gave her my mug. I told her how much fun it would be for her to sip coffee out of a mug that matched her pajamas and robe. She didn't really want to take it, but I insisted.

The next morning, Esther appeared in my office with a little card and a book of poetry as a way of thanking me.

After saying, "Have a great day," Esther left my office, but right away she turned around and came back. Standing in my doorway, she said, "I haven't told anyone this except my husband, but I am scheduled for a lung biopsy in two weeks. The gift of your mug yesterday meant so much to me. It represented more than a mug. It told me that people care about me. It means so much to me, and I don't know how I can ever thank you."

As we hugged and talked for a few more minutes, I was overjoyed that I had listened to God and His prompting to give away my mug. I'm not sure who received the bigger blessing!

Jill Rhynard

A Penny for My Thoughts

Blessed are they that mourn:
for they shall be comforted. Matt. 5:4.

AFTER A CHRISTMASTIME visit my father drove on to spend time with other relatives before heading home to Michigan. An icy highway well past midnight, just four days after Christmas, turned out to be the last stretch of road that wonderful man would travel on this earth. Twenty years later the memory is still difficult. But God had rapidly come to my rescue, and in ways so tailored to my particular needs, that I feel some joy recalling that portion of my grief-filled days.

Each day I walked a mile to and from work. While walking, I would try to think of anything to avoid thinking of my father, but he would enter my mind, causing deep sadness. I found myself questioning God about Dad's state at death—had things been right between him and God? Then my delightful heavenly Father began to speak to me in the language of pennies. It didn't make sense at first, but cent by cent I began to recognize God's loving presence. Whenever questions about my father's readiness to die came to mind, I saw a penny on the ground. Every single time there would be a penny within a small radius of where I was. Each one was, for me, God's immediate confirmation that I needn't worry.

I shall never forget a more recent time God gave me a penny for my thoughts that was absolutely jaw-dropping. Kneeling by my bed in the dark, I was thinking about a young man I had known who had mysteriously disappeared. Later his body was discovered along a roadside, an obvious homicide victim. I found myself wondering about his state with God at the point of death, and was extremely distressed. Remembering my father, I found myself praying that the young man, who had been turning his life toward God, was resting safe in Jesus, and I longed for a penny from God to confirm it. But there couldn't be pennies on the floor where I knelt—could there? I "walked" my knees around the carpet hoping to feel one, when right in the middle of my deep concentration I was rudely interrupted by a thought totally disconnected from my immediate concerns. My neighbor popped into my mind. *Why am I thinking of her?* I tried returning to my sad thoughts, but Eliane was in my head again, this time with her fat little dog. I sighed, annoyed, but then immediately praised the Lord for His miracle. He had indeed provided a penny for me. The fat little dog? Her name was Penny!

Christine B. Nelson

My Special Notebook

Give thanks to the Lord, for He is good, for His lovingkindness is everlasting.
Ps. 136:1, NASB.

WHEN WE PASS through sad moments in life, it is comforting to remember how we have been able to handle them in the past. That's the reason I have a special notebook in which I write every request I ask of God. If He answers me, I write it the exact day it happens. I also write words of gratitude and praise to my Lord when He gives me things I didn't even ask for, but in His mercy He provided. Many times I silently read them over and instantly I feel re-comforted. It's my special treasure.

One special life episode that I recorded was when I wanted to teach in the faculty of dentistry in my city. I sent my resume to the person in charge of the department. After he read it, he said he would call me, because he thought it was excellent. Three times, on different occasions, I was called for interviews. I always received the same answer: "We will call you."

After the last meeting we had, I felt very disappointed. Knowing those feeling weren't healthy, I decided to empty my heart to my best friend, my Lord, asking His will to be done. I wrote it as a letter, explaining what I felt and what I was expecting. Specifically, I wrote that this would be the last time I went there for an interview. If they called me for the job, I would go. Otherwise I wouldn't.

Surprisingly, it happened. I left the country for Christmas holidays and when I returned, after the plane landed, I turned on my cell phone. I had three messages from the university telling me they needed me urgently. In amazement, I said: "Oh Lord, how amazing You are! And my soul knows that well!"

Of course that day I immediately wrote in my notebook a testimony to an answer of my God, the same God that heard His people in the wilderness. *Lord, praised be Your name always!*

Many times I hear my friends say that after praying they think God doesn't hear them. I encourage them to get a notebook and write all the needs they have and present them to the Lord. Like the people of Israel, we forget how amazing is the God we serve! This is a special way to keep in mind all the gifts we receive.

María Gabriela Acosta de Camargo

No Dumping Zone

A soft answer turneth away wrath.
Prov. 15:1.

ONE OF MY FACEBOOK friends had posted an unbecoming status update, and one of her friends responded with a story entitled "The Law of the Garbage Truck" that was particularly interesting. Since we all have run-ins with these garbage trucks, I was reminded of a very poignant experience.

My husband and I were vacationing with his mother in New York City. As usual, there was much to do. When in a strange country my husband continually challenges himself (and me, of course) by using the local bus system to become familiar with the environment. On New Year's Eve our travel arrangements were no different: we were using the bus. However, returning home late, my husband saw another bus that he'd observed passing through our neighborhood and decided we should hop on it. We did. On approaching our stop we used the bell signal to stop, but the driver continued driving. We tried for the next stop, but again the driver did not stop. Someone else who was obviously foreign to the area wanted the following stop and used the signal. You guessed it: again no stop. Then the driver, visibly agitated, became abusive. Unknowingly, we appeared to be flaunting the system, and this brought on the driver's ire. He assumed we knew that the bus was not supposed to make short stops in that neighborhood. After going some distance the driver had to pick up passengers, so we exited, to the cheers of other passengers. As we disembarked, the driver continued to be abusive.

At that point I felt like giving him some choice remarks. However, my husband prevented this by calmly wishing him a happy new year. *That* was so unexpected that the driver, mouth agape, was left in midsentence. As we walked away my husband explained that the driver may have had a rough day, and we did not have to respond in kind to his cruel remarks.

Today, and each day of the coming year, you will meet people who are ready to dump their garbage on you. Do not dump back. God wants you to help them clean up the mess they have in their lives. It is your Christian duty to speak kindly to someone today. Just ask yourself, "What would Jesus want me to do?" The answer: create for that person a No Dumping Zone.

Happy New Year!

Brenda D. (Hardy) Ottley

Author Biographies

Jodie Bell Aakko writes from Colorado. She has served as teacher and principal in Seventh-day Adventist schools for 17 years. She is a wife and mother of two daughters, and spoils her cats, Simba and Penelope. The cat Sunshine, mentioned in the story, now lives happily with a former student from the school. **Jan. 30.**

Betty J. Adams, a retired teacher, lives in California. Betty is the mother of five, grandmother of seven, and great-grandmother of three. She has written for *Guide* magazine and her church newsletter, and is active in community services. She enjoys writing, her grandchildren, scrapbooking, and traveling—especially on mission trips. **Mar. 25.**

Taiwo Adenekan writes from Gambia, West Africa, where she is a teacher and the local women's ministries leader. She was born into a Muslim family; her mother was the second wife. She became a Christian at a Christian teachers' college. She lost her first husband early in life, after two children. Now remarried, she is blessed with two more children. **Mar. 18.**

Priscilla E. Adonis, who writes from South Africa, was the women's ministries coordinator for her local church for many years and chaplain for the federation. She enjoys text-messaging Bible verses early each morning to people far and wide. Recently widowed, she was married almost 41 years. Her children live in the United States, so she often feels lonely. **Apr. 22, Oct. 14.**

Shirley Cadiz Aguinaldo directs four ministries at the South Philippine Union Conference in Cagayan de Oro City, Philippines. She is a registered nurse, holds a master's degree in public health, and has worked as a nursing clinical instructor. She loves singing, teaching, mentoring, writing, making friends, and hosting TV family programs. **Apr. 20.**

Sally j. Aken-Linke started writing stories for her family and friends when she was 6 years old. Today she writes devotionals, articles, and blogs. Sally and her husband, John, love to sing at church and share Jesus with all they can. They often thank God for the blessings of their children, grandchildren, friends, and family who live throughout the U.S. They reside in Norfolk, Nebraska. **Jan. 26.**

Shanter H. Alexander hails from the beautiful island of St. Lucia and has served as teacher and school counselor with the mission's Department of Education since 1997. She is passionate about ministry and is currently pursuing graduate studies at Andrews University in Michigan. She enjoys reading, writing, public speaking, travel, cooking, and quiet time. **Feb. 9.**

Minerva M. Alinaya has been in the field of education for 30 years, handling primary, secondary, and tertiary students. Presently she works as the high school principal of Patnubay Academy, a private nonsectarian school in Cavite, Philippines. She wants to establish an adult literacy class to teach basic skills in reading and writing and, at the same time, share with the students the Word of God. **Apr. 30.**

Jussara Alves is a mother of four, an educator, and an evangelist to children. She lives in Bahia, Brazil, and enjoys reading, walking, doing crafts, and working with children. **June 6.**

Jill Anderson grew up in the rural, ranching, eastern plains of her native Colorado; she now lives in beautiful Estes Park, Colorado. Married for 23 years, she is the mother of 16-year-old Ivy and grandmother of five through her two stepsons. She loves reading, writing, camping, hiking, and entertaining friends and family. **Oct. 9.**

Traci S. Anderson lives in Huntsville, Alabama, with her husband, Jeremy. She enjoys cooking, spending time with family and friends, and relaxing on the weekends. She works for a government contractor as a project coordinator, but looks forward to becoming a full-time entrepreneur doing God's work, and to starting a family. **Dec. 16.**

Beulah E. Andrews, originally from Trinidad in the West Indies, now lives in California. She retired from the California public school system after 23 years of rewarding service as a special education teacher, and now teaches part-time. She enjoys reading, gardening, music, traveling, and volunteering in her church. **Aug. 28.**

Lydia Andrews, a certified nurse midwife, lives in Huntsville, Alabama, with her husband of 45 years. During their 10-year assignment in Africa she established the first B.S. in nursing program at Valley View University, Ghana, and now teaches nursing at Oakwood University. Lydia has three adult children, and enjoys reading, cooking, music, travel, and her four grandsons. **Apr. 13.**

Suzi David Arandas, a history professor, is married and lives in São Paulo, Brazil, with her husband, Robson, and daughter, Rebecca. She enjoys being in church, organizing and decorating her house, having family reunions, and trips to the coast of Brazil. **Aug. 7.**

Ester Figueiredo Araujo is a university professor, a member of the Academia Itacoatiarense de Letras, and of the scientific committee in the city of Itacoatiara, Amazonas, Brazil. She has three children, two biological grandchildren and two adopted ones. She works in the children's department at church and likes to read, go on walks, visit people, and write. **June 10.**

Raquel Queiroz da Costa Arrais is a minister's wife who has developed her ministry as an educator for 20 years. She is the associate director of the General Conference Women's Ministries Department. She has two sons and two daughters-in-law and one grandson, Benjamin. Her greatest pleasure is to be with people, sing, play the piano, and travel. **Jan. 22, Oct. 2.**

Edna Ashmeade, of Stamford, Connecticut, is a retired learning and language development specialist and a member of the Kingsboro Seventh-day Adventist Temple Church. She has a published program, Rights/ Rites of Passage Initiative for Children and Young Adults. She is in a doctoral program and is completing her dissertation. **Aug. 25.**

Lady Dana Austin lives in the apple capital of north Georgia: Ellijay. She enjoys the outdoors and loves to go white-water rafting, cycle, swim, and run. She feels most inspired on the lake, and has just completed her first novel. She continues to minister to women with specialized tea ceremonies, and is an emergency responder in her community. **Mar. 9.**

Darlen Cibeli Martelo Bach lives in Brazil, where she is a bank employee. She is the church secretary and conductor of the choir. She enjoys painting and reading, and has been married for five years. **Mar. 6.**

Carla Baker is women's ministries director for the North American Division of Seventh-day Adventists in Silver Spring, Maryland. She also served as women's ministries director of the Southwestern Union Conference, in Texas, and at a local church for many years. Carla conducts leadership training and has developed resources for local churches, including the new DVD Bible studies, *Journey of Joy: Healthy Emotions, and Holy Hearts.* **Jan. 13.**

Jennifer M. Baldwin writes from Australia, where she works in risk management at Sydney Adventist Hospital. She enjoys Scrabble, crossword puzzles, and being involved in church. She has contributed to this devotional book series for more than 15 years. **Apr. 8.**

Renee Baumgartner wrote this story while working as communication director for Gimbie Hospital in Ethiopia. She enjoyed blogging while there. She loves people, nature, and most important, her Savior. Although Renee is from southeast Pennsylvania, she is currently enjoying graduate school at Andrews University in Michigan. **May 22.**

Dana M. Bassett Bean is an educator who lives in Bermuda with her husband and her two children. Her favorite time is summer when she can swim, read, write, and travel. **Apr. 5.**

Lisa M. Beardsley-Hardy is world director of education for the General Conference of Seventh-day Adventists, with headquarters in Maryland. She works with the Adventist Accrediting Association and is editor in chief for *Dialogue*, a journal that is published in English, French, Spanish, and Portuguese for Adventist university students around the world. **June 1, Oct. 8.**

Dawna Beausoleil, a retired teacher, lives in northeastern Ontario with her husband, John. She enjoys reading and singing, and has published an array of short writings. Recently she joined the local art club to take up painting again. Her biggest goal and earnest prayer is that others may see the love of Christ reflected in her life. **Apr. 3.**

Ginger Bell lives in Brighton, Colorado, with her pastor-husband, assisting in his ministry and in the church office. She leads women's ministries for her church and is the director for the Rocky Mountain Conference. She enjoys gardening, decorating, reading, and being with her family, which includes four grandchildren. **Dec. 12.**

Sylvia Giles Bennett lives in Suffolk, Virginia, with her husband, Richard. They have two adult children and two grandchildren, Kennedy and Derrius. Sylvia is a member of the Windsor Seventh-day Adventist Church. Her hobbies include reading, writing, and the simple things of life. **Mar. 22.**

Verona Bent and her husband are farmers in Top Hill, Jamaica, planting acres of tomatoes, cucumbers, carrots, and peppers. She has six adult children and seven grandchildren. Going to the Bellevue Adventist Church is one of her favorite activities. **Dec. 7.**

Annie B. Best, a retired teacher in Washington, D.C., is a widow, mother of two adult children, and grandmother of three. She enjoys reading and listening to music. Working as a leader in the children's departments of her church inspired her to compose a song that was published in *Let's Sing Sabbath Songs*. **Mar. 1.**

Cynthia Best-Goring lives in Glendale, Maryland, where she is the principal of a pre-K-6 elementary school. Her passion lies in helping children learn, teachers teach, and all to become acquainted with our heavenly Father. She is a wife and mother of two adult children. Cynthia's hobbies include writing, playing the piano, and reading. **Mar. 16.**

Selena Blackburn, who lives in Washington State, is a wife, mother, grandmother, nurse, and so much more. She believes that the only balance to this life is God's grace. She was thrilled to write for this book as she longs to share the sweetness of the grace heaven blesses her with again and again. **Mar. 14.**

Dinorah Blackman writes from Panama, where she lives with her husband and young daughter, Imani. **Dec. 8.**

Cintia García Block is originally from Argentina, but grew up in different parts of Africa where her parents worked as missionaries. Years later she went back to Argentina to study psychology and marry a good Argentine husband. She was successful on both counts. Presently she lives in Ontario, Canada, where she is a homemaker and the proud mother of two children. **Sept. 6.**

Juli Blood is happily married with two sons and a desire to stay in God's plan for her life. Hebrews 6 speaks to her heart when it emphasizes the need to dig deeper into the Scriptures for a greater understanding of God. It is her prayer that every woman find her worth, strength, and joy in her personal relationship with Jesus. Juli lives in Pennsylvania. **Jan. 7.**

Julie Bocock-Bliss is pursuing her master's degree in library and information sciences at the University of Hawaii at Manoa. She is an active member of the Honolulu Japanese Seventh-day Adventist Church in Manoa. She is "mommy" to three cats, and loves reading, traveling, and crafts. **Sept. 16.**

Patricia Hook Rhyndress Bodi lives in Michigan and has been active in women's ministries for 20 years. She loves travel and has visited all seven continents. Walking with Jesus is her passion. **Apr. 25.**

Heather Bohlender attends Union College in Nebraska, but will always call Colorado home. She enjoys Ultimate Frisbee, snowboarding in the Rocky Mountains, and a healthy game of dodge ball. She authored the 2011 young adult devotional *Honestly, I'm Struggling*. **Dec. 14.**

Fulori Sususewa Bola writes from Papua New Guinea, where she is a lecturer in the School of Education at

Pacific Adventist University. She loves to work with women and to help out in the student-organized outreach programs. **Mar. 26.**

Evelyn Greenwade Boltwood is a mother of two young adults and grandmother to two grandsons. She is the Pathfinder and Adventurer coordinator for western New York. Her passions are youth ministries, camping, reading, inspirational writing, and traveling. She is a member of the Akoma Women's Community Gospel Choir, which raises scholarships for young women. **May 3.**

Tamar Boswell, a registered nurse, resides in Bermuda. She loves to pray for others, and gets excited when she sees answered prayers—especially in the lives of unbelievers. Her interests include travel, reading, experimenting with vegetarian recipes, and participating in community outreach programs. **Jan. 24.**

Althea Y. Boxx, a Jamaican, is a registered nurse. She has published her first book, a devotional entitled *Fuel for the Journey*, an inspirational nugget for life's uphill climb. Althea believes that nothing is as contagious as enthusiasm. Her hobbies include reading, writing, traveling, and photography. **Feb. 5.**

Elizabeth Boyd, a physical therapist, served as a traveling therapist in the early days of the traveling health care industry, and is founder and owner of Traveling Medical Professionals, Inc. Now retired at her farm in Harpswell, Maine, she enjoys horses, writing, hospitality, and music. Weekends are filled with coaching young people in Bible study and prayer activities. **Aug. 27.**

Wendy Bradley lives in a small town near the New Forest in Hampshire, England. Her husband, David, died in 2007, and now she has taken up her writing again. God has put around her the most wonderful set of friends, who have encouraged her back to driving after a gap of 12 years. They have allowed her to become *herself*, and are always on her side. **Sept. 9.**

DeeAnn Bragaw counts it all joy to have the privilege of sharing with both adults and children a passion to experience God's Word in a fresh way. A speaker, author, and educator, she loves to bike, hike, laugh, and learn. DeeAnn lives in Colorado. She can be contacted at her Web site: www.deeannbragaw.com. **Feb. 14, July 4.**

Ani Köhler Bravo is a retired secretary who worked at the Brazil Publishing House and wrote the 2007 daily devotional book for juniors. She lives with her husband and son in Engenheiro Coelho, Brazil, and serves her church by leading women's ministries. She enjoys reading and says that a day doesn't have hours enough to read all the books she wants. **Jan. 25.**

Marcela Bittencourt Brey, a lawyer, pastor's wife, and native of São Paulo, Brazil, currently lives in Inhambupe, Bahia. She likes to work with children, youth, small groups, and women's ministries. She also enjoys giving Bible studies. Cooking, painting wooden boxes for crafts, walking with her husband, and caring for their puppy are her hobbies. **June 11.**

Tamara Brown is a native of Ohio, who now resides in Murfreesboro, Tennessee. She strives to be faithful to God and others, and to be focused and skilled. She and Robert have been married for 21 years and have a son, Robert II. She believes that the home is a woman's first ministry. In addition, she promotes health ministry and couples ministry. **Nov. 6.**

Vivian Brown and husband, Jimmy, have three adult children and six grandchildren. Vivian has served in Sabbath school, with children's choirs, Revelation seminars, women's ministries, and technology. Now retired from teaching, she volunteers as a computer teacher at a senior center and sings in the Women's Praise Chorale. She lives in Madison, Alabama. **Sept. 1.**

Marielena (Mary) Burdick was a 15-year-old sophomore at Campion Academy when she wrote this devotional. When she finishes school, Mary would like to work as an agent in the behavioral analysis unit of the Federal Bureau of Investigation. Her home is in Montrose, Colorado. **Aug. 14.**

Maureen O. Burke is a busy retiree in New York, serving her church as an elder, interest coordinator, and Sabbath school teacher. She enjoys giving Bible studies, reading, music, writing, entertaining, and helping others through what she calls the "ministry of encouragement." She also volunteers at the central public library. **Jan. 5.**

Jennifer Burkes loves the Lord first and foremost! She was baptized in 2006 and is the women's ministries leader of the Grants Pass Seventh-day Adventist Church. She lives in Grants Pass, Oregon, with her husband, James, and daughter, Krista. She works at the community college as a department secretary. **Feb. 18.**

Helen Dick Burton lives in Littleton, Colorado. After home, church, music, and Sabbath school activities are completed, she dreams up artistic and writing projects. Colorado's economy has had her job hunting, and God gave her a small business of teaching a few beginning piano students—children and adults. **Sept. 30.**

Joy Butler, originally from New Zealand, is a wife, mother of three married children, with one grandchild. She has worn many hats, including teacher, chaplain, departmental director, speaker, and writer. Now retired, she looks forward to doing more writing. **May 6.**

Nancy Buxton is the women's ministries director for the Mid-America Union of Seventh-day Adventists in Lincoln, Nebraska. She has been married to Bob for 42 years. They have two married children and six grandchildren. **May 17.**

Elizabeth Ida Cain writes from Jamaica, where she works as an administrative assistant at a new motor vehicle dealership. She attends the St. John's Seventh-day Adventist Church, where she is a member of the women's ministries association. She enjoys writing and is a floral-arranging art designer and instructor. **Feb. 4.**

María Gabriela Acosta de Camargo writes from Venezuela, where she is a pediatric dentist with a private practice, and also teaches dentistry at the University of Carabobo. At church she is in charge of the music department. She has written for journals in dentistry and is writing a book to help students. She is married and has two boys. She plays tennis and enjoys playing the piano. **Dec. 30.**

Ruby T. Campos is a secondary school teacher in a Seventh-day Adventist academy in Leyte, Philippines. She has taught for 18 years, and was recently appointed principal of a new academy. She loves nature, and her hobbies include gardening, photography, reading, and writing. Ruby is single. **Sept. 22.**

Gloria Carby is director of the Kingsway Early Childhood Centre in Oshawa, Ontario, Canada. She enjoys observing and documenting the interaction of preschool children with their peers. **Oct. 5.**

Antonia Castellino is married and lives in the English Midlands. She has two grown children and two grand-children—her pride and joy. She is a retired teacher who, with her husband, founded the Harper Bell School, an elementary church school in the Midlands. She enjoys walking, nature, music, visual arts, and Bible study. She is active in her local church. **Feb. 13.**

Aucely Corrêa Fernandes Chagas lives in Campo Grande, Mato Grosso do Sul, Brazil. She teaches nursing and enjoys reading, plants, and handicrafts. **June 15.**

Judy Gray Seeger Cherry, a graduate of Union College, lives on a farmstead in Nebraska with her husband, Earl. Between them they have six children and seven grandchildren. She is church and school treasurer, and church organist. Her hobbies are visiting their grandchildren, doing puzzles, and watching car races. **July 14.**

Suhana Benny Prasad Chikatla, a doctor, was born in India. She has two master's degrees and a Ph.D. A member of the Cody Road Adventist Church in Mobile, Alabama, for the past nine years, Suhana has been a youth leader. She serves as an executive council member for the Gulf States Conference Women's Ministries Department. She is married to Royce Sutton. **July 26.**

Caroline Chola lives in Pretoria, South Africa, and is the women's/children's ministries director of the Southern Africa-Indian Ocean Division of Seventh-day Adventists. She and her husband, Habson, have five adult children and one granddaughter. She enjoys gardening. Her passion is to see women discover their potential and use it to the glory of God. **July 20.**

Birol Charlotte Christo is a retired teacher and office assistant. She was the first coordinator of Shepherdess International of the Southern Asia Division of Seventh-day Adventists. She lives with her husband in Hosur, Tamil Nadu, India. She enjoys gardening, sewing, making crafts, and keeping in touch with her five children, 12 grandchildren, and one great-grandchild. **July 3.**

Rosenita Christo writes from India and works at the Southern Asia Division of Seventh-day Adventists as editor of *New Southern Asia Tidings* and the coordinator of Adventist Volunteer Service. She leads the church choir, has written articles and editorials, and coauthored a Bible study guide with her husband, Gordon. She likes singing, listening to music, and reading. She has two married children. **Apr. 11.**

Rosemarie Clardy and her husband enjoy the blessings of country living while raising their three boys—and caring for many pets—in Candler, North Carolina. They volunteer at church and school. **Aug. 6.**

Sherma Webbe Clarke writes from Bermuda, where she serves as women's ministries director. Her many interests include sewing, photography, sign language, and traveling. She and her husband, Ricardo, have four adult children and one canine companion. **Aug. 26.**

Sandy Colburn and her husband live in a rural setting in central Tennessee, where he is a family practice physician and Sandy manages a small equestrian boarding facility. They are involved in church planting and enjoy seeing how God is leading in that. Their son is a surgery tech in an emergency veterinarian practice, and their daughter is a veterinary tech. **May 9.**

Gilsana Souza Condé writes from Juiz de Fora, Brazil. She is 29 years old and an early childhood teacher at an Adventist school. She is also an assistant Sabbath school teacher for her church. **June 12.**

Minéia da Silva Constantino has worked for six years in the children's and adolescents' ministry of the Adventist kindergarten Sao Pedro de Mogi Guaçu, São Paulo, Brazil, where she is a teacher and coordinator of the Galilee Project (Social Action of the Adventist Adolescent). She is also an environmental engineer, and she praises God with her voice and talents. **June 18.**

Rose E. Constantino is associate professor at the University of Pittsburgh School of Nursing. She and her husband, Abraham Constantino, Jr., M.D., live in Pittsburgh, Pennsylvania. They have three sons. **May 26.**

Reba Cook lives in a little community called Rulison, between Rifle and Parachute, Colorado, and has been married to husband, Dan, for 35 years. They have two adult sons and a daughter-in-law. Reba enjoys doing the Lord's work in her community service center, helping people with food and clothing. She has a passion for reaching kids for the Lord. **Sept. 23.**

Patricia Cove writes from Ontario, Canada, and is a semiretired teacher, a sailor, gardener, writer, and lover of nature. Her husband, children, and their offspring are her greatest treasures. She is an active church elder whose favorite activity is sharing the good news of the gospel with others. **Jan. 20.**

Hilary E. Daly, originally from London, England, is a high school science teacher at Takoma Academy in Maryland. As the daughter of an English professor and writer, she grew up making the pen her friend. When she is not freelance writing, Hilary enjoys writing poetry, reading biographies, doing puzzles, and drama. **Sept. 29.**

Jean Dozier Davey and her husband, Steven, live in the beautiful mountains of North Carolina. She retired in 2003 from a career as a computer programmer. She enjoys spending time with family, cooking, reading, taking walks in Pisgah Forest, sewing, organizing, and encouraging others. **Nov. 27.**

Avery Davis, originally from Jamaica, lives in England, where she is actively involved with children's and women's ministries in her local church. She is the mother of Theresa, Sarah, and Grace, and is currently working on a book of conversations with women. **Dec. 22.**

Marlyn L. DeAugust resides in Niles, Michigan, and was the director of women's ministries at the Niles Philadelphia Adventist Church. She is a physical therapist assistant and enjoys working with the elderly. She has one child, Jonathan, of whom she is very proud. She enjoys singing, reading, and exercising outdoors. **June 19.**

Bernadine Delafield coordinates NET evangelism for the North American Division of Seventh-day Adventists and produces Adventist Preaching, a DVD sermon series by gifted preachers for churches without speakers. She is a mother and the grandmother of three. Flowers, gardening, and music round out her life. She lives in Maryland. **Oct. 7.**

Sinikka Dixon is an Adventist sociologist with a Ph.D. from the University of California, Riverside. She is multicultural and multilingual, with publications in her professional field of social inequalities, aging, and community studies. She loves to read, travel, and participate in water and snow sports. Now retired, she lives on Prince Edward Island, Canada, with her husband. **Feb. 1.**

Joan Dougherty-Mornan writes from Ontario, Canada, where she enjoys discovering God between the pages of the Bible and in life's experiences. She has two daughters and a son. Her hobbies are reading, writing, crocheting, and keeping busy for Christ. **Sept. 27.**

Louise Driver, now retired, lives in Idaho, where her three sons and four grandchildren also live. She is the librarian at the Caldwell elementary school, where two of her grandchildren attend. Her hobbies are singing, music, reading, gardening, and traveling to historical places. **June 29.**

Clody Flores Dumaliang writes from Los Angeles where she is a mental health counselor, social worker, and educator. A hospital volunteer, she enjoys providing emotional and spiritual support to hospital patients. She is also active with children's ministry in her church. She is married to Bonn, her grade school classmate, and they have a teenage daughter, Victoria. **Sept. 21.**

Pauline A. Dwyer-Kerr, a native of the beautiful island of Jamaica, resides in Florida. She has a doctorate and is a professor. Pauline has served in the church as an elder, in Sabbath school, in communication and family life, on social committees, as receptionist, and as a church clerk. She has sung in the church choir and led their singing group. She loves travel and the outdoors. **Dec. 18.**

Valsa Edison, a retired higher secondary school teacher, is a pastor's wife in India. She is the director for children's and women's ministries and has published articles in *Shepherdess International*. Her hobbies are reading, writing, gardening, cooking, and listening to music. In 1991 she was awarded the Best Teacher Award. She and her husband have two daughters. **June 8.**

Ruby H. Ennis-Alleyne writes from Guyana, South America, where she is the assistant treasurer for the Guyana Conference of Seventh-day Adventists. She is the family ministries leader, an elder in her local church, and loves young people and hospital ministry. She and her husband, Ashton, have three adult children. **June 3.**

Doreen Evans-Yorke is a Jamaican-Canadian mother of three young adults. She spent 16 years living and working in three countries in Africa and derived many blessings from her experiences there. She now lives in Montreal, Canada, where she works as a child life specialist. **Feb. 3.**

Fartema M. Fagin is a retired social worker and is now an adjunct instructor at a community college in Tennessee. She and her husband have three sons, two daughters, and four grandchildren. She enjoys singing, reading, and writing. **Nov. 20.**

Ana Teorima Faigao was born and raised in the Philippines, but now resides in Maryland with her family. She is married to Howard Faigao, publishing director for the world church. She has been fighting multiple myeloma or cancer of the bone marrow since 2006. She enjoys writing and has kept a blog of her cancer journey. **Dec. 25.**

Gloria Stella Felder is an accountant who lives in Atlanta, Georgia, with her pastor-husband. They share a family of four adult children and five grandchildren. Gloria enjoys music, writing, speaking, playing Scrabble, and spending time with family, especially her grandchildren. She has written articles and a book of poetry, *My Inspiration,* and is working on a second book. **Feb. 8.**

Mona Fellers has been a paramedic for 26 years and works in Gilpin County, Colorado, as a paramedic/quality assurance leader and a deputy coroner. She loves living at 10,300 feet. She is also children's and women's ministry leader at her church. She is married with two daughters, three dogs, one cat, and a rat. God has certainly given her a gift with small wild animals. **Aug. 31.**

Carole Ferch-Johnson was the first women's ministries director for the South Pacific Division of Seventh-day Adventists. She is editor of *Going Places,* the author of numerous articles, the book *Women Like Us,* and coauthor with Ardis Stenbakken of *Bible Studies for Busy Women.* She is a church officer in Australia with special responsibilities for the support of women pastors. **May 11.**

Ellen Rezende Festa is a professor in Brazil, married to Sérgio Festa, a pastor. She likes reading, studying the Bible with people, walking, listening to good music, and spending time with her family. She is the mother of two children, Lucas and Letícia. **June 20.**

Carol Joy Fider is chair of the Department of English and Modern Languages at Northern Caribbean University in Jamaica. She serves as women's and prayer ministries director for her church, as well as church elder and Sabbath school teacher. She enjoys cooking, gardening, and mentoring young people. She and her husband, Ezra, have two adult daughters, Carla and Carlene. **Feb. 19, Oct. 19.**

Margaret Fisher and her husband, Floyd, live in Daytona, Tennessee. She loves to write, especially poetry. She has had a few articles and several poems published, one for *Guideposts* and several for *Southern Tidings.* She and Floyd have five children and 16 grandchildren. She enjoys playing the piano in church. Her hobbies are knitting and crafts. **Sept. 26.**

Edith Fitch is a retired teacher living in Lacombe, Alberta, Canada, and volunteers in the archives at Canadian University College. She enjoys life and thanks God for every new day. **Apr. 27, Oct. 10.**

Janice Fleming-Williams, an elementary school teacher and certified family life educator, has been teaching for more than 35 years. She serves as associate family life leader at her church and has been working for the church school since 1981. Janice and her husband, Gordon, live on St. Thomas, United States Virgin Islands, and are the parents of two adult sons. **Nov. 28.**

Lana Fletcher lives in Chehalis, Washington, with her husband. They have one married daughter. Their younger daughter was killed in a car accident in 1993. Lana is the church clerk. She loves gardening, does the bookkeeping for her husband's business, makes Creative Memories albums, helps with a Loss-of-a-Child support group, and journals her prayers. **Feb. 7, Oct. 23.**

Patricia Buxton Flores lives in Trenton, New Jersey, and is a member of the Morrisville Presbyterian Church. As a mother of four adult children, grandmother of eight, a widow, and retired teacher, she keeps busy volunteering. She presents workshops on storytelling and entertains in libraries, schools, and at summer camp with her collection of international folktales. **Nov. 12.**

Linda Franklin writes from British Columbia, Canada, where she gains object lessons from her greenhouses in the spring and summer months. During fall and winter she often travels with her husband, Jere, as he speaks to churches and at camp meetings. She recently published the story of their son's healing from a serious burn accident, *Rainbow in the Flames.* **July 16.**

Edna Maye Gallington has put aside the deadlines of a career in public relations to write creatively from her patio in southern California. She is the author of *Watching From the Shadows*—24 biblical women tell their stories. She is working on a devotional book and a children's book, and loves spending time with her Bible. www.ednagallington.com **Oct. 15, Dec. 27.**

Claudette Garbutt-Harding lives in Orlando, Florida. She and her husband, Dr. Keith R. Harding, have been together in ministry for 34 years. They have two young adult children. Claudette loves to teach and work in women's ministries. Her greatest joy is to help prepare others for the soon coming of Jesus. **Mar. 12.**

Yan Siew Ghiang writes from Singapore, where she was employed as assistant administrator with a construction project. She attends Balestier Adventist Church in Singapore, but recently has been to west Malaysia to be involved with the Pathfinder Club. She has been an assistant pastor, a chaplain, Bible teacher, and Voice of Prophecy coordinator. **May 16.**

Carol Wiggins Gigante, a former day-care provider, is a teacher at heart. She is an avid reader, photographer, flower lover, and bird lover, and works as a freelance proofreader. Carol resides in Beltsville, Maryland, with her husband, Joe, their dog, Buddy, and cat, Suzannah. They have two adult sons, Jeff and James. "Even so, come, Lord Jesus!" **Jan. 3, Sept. 28.**

Evelyn Glass and her husband, Darrell, live in northern Minnesota on the farm where Darrell was born. They have three grown children and two grandchildren. Evelyn writes a weekly column for the local paper and is active as a speaker and a community volunteer. She also belongs to a local writers' group and a quilting group. Evelyn is the author of a series of Bible studies, *Women in the Bible and Me.* **July 9, Oct. 20.**

Jothi Gnanaprakasam writes from India, where she is the women's ministries director for the Erode Nilgiris Section. This is her first contribution to the devotional book project. **May 14.**

Beverly P. Gordon lives with her husband and two sons in Downingtown, Pennsylvania. Dr. Gordon is a professor of psychology, a registered nurse, and family ministry coordinator for her church. She has presented seminars, sermons, and keynote addresses for academic and religious settings. Her hobbies include gardening, music, reading, word games, and chess. **Feb. 27.**

Paula Graham is a teacher at Miracle Meadows in Salem, West Virginia. She has been a missionary in Korea and Costa Rica. Her passions are God and helping hurting people. **Jan. 16.**

Roxie L. Graham-Marski and her husband, Eser, recently relocated from Texas to northwest Nebraska to be closer to her parents and grandparents. A few of her hobbies include writing, horseback riding, reading, traveling, and visiting with family and friends. She loves animals and shares her life with several. Roxie is grateful to the Lord for His goodness. **June 30.**

Cecelia Grant is a Seventh-day Adventist medical doctor retired from government service, living in Kingston, Jamaica. Her hobbies are traveling, gardening, and listening to good music. She has a passion for young people, to whom she is always giving advice. **Mar. 8.**

Mary Jane Graves lost her husband, Ted, to cancer in 2009, after 58 years of happy marriage. She is looking forward to the day when they can be together again. She lives in western North Carolina and is involved in her church. She enjoys gardening, reading, writing, family, and friends. **Feb. 2.**

Elaine Gray lives in Toney, Alabama, and works at the Eva B. Dykes Library on the campus of her alma mater, Oakwood University, as the circulation/technology manager and systems administrator. A Red Cross volunteer, she also enjoys gardening, photography, giving Bible studies to children, singing with her group, and the First Church Inspirational Choir. **Feb. 28.**

Ellie Postlewait Green, a retired registered nurse, has coauthored three books and published more than 300 articles. She has conducted 18 evangelistic series at home and abroad and serves as head elder and lay pastor of the Sharon Seventh-day Adventist Church in Charlotte, North Carolina. She and her husband enjoy their two children and three grandchildren. **Dec. 23.**

Joan Green is a semiretired mother of two adult daughters and has four grandchildren. She writes from Boise, Idaho, and enjoys writing, reading, speaking, traveling, friendship evangelism, a growing relationship with the Lord, and spending time with family. **Nov. 30.**

Carol J. Greene writes from Palm Bay, Florida, where she has a telephone ministry and is a link in a prayer chain at her church. She delights in being the grandmother of four and spends much of her personal prayer time on their behalf. **Nov. 3.**

Glenda-mae Greene, a retired university educator, writes from her wheelchair in central Florida. Her passion is helping other women write their stories of God's grace. **Feb. 10, Oct. 24.**

Gloria Gregory is a minister's wife and mother to two daughters. She works as director of admissions at Northern Caribbean University in Jamaica, and is convinced that her mission is to help others unearth their full potentials and use them to honor God. **Sept. 4.**

Venessa Stinvil Gutierrez is a licensed optometrist. She lives in New York with her husband, four adult children, and one granddaughter, and is health ministries director in her local church. One of her greatest passions is working with an organization called AIMM to help a hurting world find solace in her Savior. **Aug. 24.**

Gloria Durichek Gyure is a retired English teacher, technical writer and editor, and systems engineer. She lives in Denver, Colorado, with her husband, Joe, in a house with a yard she describes as a romantic xeriscape garden. She loves gardening, reading, traveling, and pondering the God-given things that make life worthwhile. **Aug. 23.**

Bertha Hall, an educator, recently moved with her husband from Mississippi to Florida, where he is the pastor of two churches. She believes that each person is precious in God's sight and was born to fulfill a special mission, and she loves activities that promote preparing souls for the second coming of Jesus. She likes to play putt-putt and Bible games, and to travel. **Mar. 4, Oct. 27.**

Jean Hall enjoys sewing, cooking, gardening, helping make quilts to give away, and traveling with her husband of 61 years. They were missionaries in eastern Asia for 25 years. Now retired, they volunteer for Adventist Development and Relief Agency overseas and in the United States. She writes from Lebanon, Oregon. **Apr. 4.**

Dessa Weisz Hardin lives in Maine with her husband, where she enjoys the ocean. She is interested in traveling, writing, art, and music, and is teaching herself to play the piano. An added dimension is grandparenting. She also enjoys the devotional book and hearing from friends who have been blessed through it. **May 30, Oct. 21.**

Dawn Hargrave writes from Australia. She and her husband had been married 42 years when he died in April 2008. They have two daughters and two grandchildren. Before her retirement she worked as a financial officer and in clerical positions. She accepted Christ as her Savior after the birth of their first daughter. She discovered her talent for writing only in recent time. **Aug. 4.**

Peggy Harris is a member of the Beltsville, Maryland, Seventh-day Adventist Church. She developed and is chair of WASH (Women and Men Against Sexual Harassment and Other Abuses); the Web site: www.w-a-s-h.org. She is active as an insurance agent and has published several books. She has two children and two grandchildren; her husband, Mel, died in 2011. **May 8.**

Marian M. Hart, a retired elementary school teacher and nursing home administrator, works with her husband in property management. A member of the Battle Creek Tabernacle in Michigan for 35 years, she has served in many church capacities. Six grandchildren make her a proud grandmother. Marian enjoys knitting, reading, growing flowers, and spending winters in Florida. **Jan. 18.**

Beverly D. Hazzard, the daughter of medical missionaries, was born in England and grew up with her two brothers in Jamaica, Ohio, and British Columbia. A retired nurse administrator and published author, she lives in Kelowna, British Columbia, Canada. She has two adult children and three grandchildren. **July 19.**

Michelle Hebard, age 12, lives in Colorado with her parents and brother, and a golden retriever named Rocky. She enjoys volleyball, basketball, swimming, running, reading, playing with Rocky, singing, playing her flute, and a lot of other activities. She loves God and wants to serve Him in any way she can. **Nov. 5.**

Teresa (Proctor) Hebard is a wife and the mother of Daniel and Michelle. She enjoys long walks in nature, singing, playing the piano, and creating delicious, healthful recipes. She loves living in Colorado and hiking in the beautiful Rocky Mountains. **Dec. 9.**

Cheryl Henry-Aguilar writes from Wilmington, North Carolina, where she owns and operates a five-star day care and an after-school program. A product of Christian education, she attended both Andrews University and Loma Linda University. Cheryl enjoys photography and traveling with her daughter, Antannia. **April 6.**

Muriel Heppel, from British Columbia, Canada, is a retired teacher who moved north to an area where she'd taught many years before. Now a widow, she enjoys traveling, reading, bird-watching, and helping others through her prayer warrior ministry. She has one son. **May 13.**

Denise Dick Herr teaches English at Canadian University College in Alberta, Canada. She loves to read and travel—especially with her family. **Jan. 2, Oct. 16.**

Vashti Hinds-Vanier is retired from a nursing career that spanned more than 40 years. Her published work, *School Daze and Beyond*, includes lessons contained in this story. Her hobbies include travel, cake decorating, gardening, and crocheting. She was born in Guyana, South America. **July 15.**

Denise Hochstrasser is married and the mother of three adult daughters. She lives in the mountains of Switzerland, and loves to sit in her garden high above Lake Thun. She has been ministering to women for more than 20 years, and is now women's ministries director of the Euro-Africa Division of Seventh-day Adventists in Bern. She enjoys reading books, swimming, and traveling. **June 21.**

Roxy Hoehn is a happy grandma who helps the economy in Topeka, Kansas, for she loves to shop for her 11 very special grandchildren. **July 1.**

Marian C. Holder is the coordinator for the homebound ministry at Pioneer Memorial church in Berrien Springs, Michigan. She has one adult daughter and two grandchildren. **July 25.**

Karen Holford, a freelance writer and family therapist, lives in Auchtermuchty, one of the oldest recorded places in Scotland. Her husband is president of the Scottish Mission. She loves creative and interactive worship, making quilts, and walking in the Scottish countryside. **Apr. 12, Nov. 10.**

Jacqueline Hope HoShing-Clarke has been an educator since 1979 as principal, assistant principal, and teacher. She now serves Northern Caribbean University in Jamaica as the head of the Teacher Education Department. She and her husband have two adult children. Jackie enjoys writing, flower gardening, and housekeeping. **Feb. 16.**

Emilie Howard and her husband, John, served as missionaries in the Congo for six years and traveled the world when John was director of ADRA Canada. Milly loves painting, and her work has been displayed in the German embassy in Ottawa. Now in retirement, she enjoys the relaxation and inspiration of painting while overlooking her lagoon in either Florida or Stoney Lake, Canada. **Nov. 25.**

Addison Hudgins, a native of Maryland, enjoys writing, singing, running, baking, and spending time with loved ones. She was a student at Union College, studying English, journalism, and music, when she wrote this devotional. She dreams of eventually being a stay-at-home wife and mother who writes professionally. **Oct. 12.**

Barbara Huff was an administrative assistant in the Euro-Asia Division of Seventh-day Adventists working primarily in public relations before retiring in 2000. Barbara enjoys planning various programs for the Port Charlotte, Florida, Adventist Church, where she and her husband are members. **Nov. 8.**

Gloria P. Hutchinson, a registered nurse, lives in Palm Bay, Florida, and is a member of the Palm Bay Seventh-day Adventist Church. She has a passion for their children, and is active in the Sabbath school and children's ministries departments. She loves reading, spending time with the children, and surfing the Internet for information to enhance these church ministries. **Sept. 11.**

Cecilia Moreno de Iglesias is the women's ministries director for the Inter-American Division of Seventh-day Adventists and worked for 15 years as the director of women's ministries in Colombia. She has 20 years' experience teaching in primary and secondary schools and universities. Cecilia has been married 27 years to Pastor Pedro Iglesias Ortega and is the mother of two children. **Nov. 2.**

Shirley C. Iheanacho is retired and enjoys traveling with her soul mate of 42 years, speaking, writing, visiting, singing to the sick and shut-ins, helping and encouraging fellow travelers, sending e-mails to friends, playing handbells, and singing in the choir. She is grateful to God for the gift of her daughters, Ngo, Chi, and Aku, and her two grandsons. **Mar. 29.**

Amanda Amy Isles is a young Seventh-day Adventist woman from the nature isle of the Caribbean, Dominica. Currently she lives in St. Lucia, where she attends Monroe College pursuing a bachelor's degree in business management. **Mar. 3.**

Avis Floyd Jackson is the mother of five and lives in Pleasantville, New Jersey. She runs a party planning business out of her home. Avis has been the women's ministries director in her local church for the past six years. She says she is an Adventist by calling. **Dec. 21.**

Junet S. Jackson lives on the beautiful island of St. Vincent and the Grenadines. She is a secondary school English and social studies teacher. She enjoys writing plays, singing, reading, teaching children, and leading the youth in Sabbath school. Her lifetime dream is to become a speech and language pathologist and to go on mission trips to Africa. **Mar. 10.**

Joan D. L. Jaensch and her husband, Murray, live in South Australia. They have two married sons, two granddaughters, two grandsons, and one great-grandson. She is a retired factory purchasing officer, and served 31 years with Saint John Ambulance. She has filled many roles at church and enjoys cooking, gardening, and reading. **Sept. 3.**

Donette James is a staff nurse who lives and works in the United Kingdom. She studied in the West Indies College (now Northern Caribbean University). At church she is involved in the health department and sings in the choir. She especially enjoys working with the youth and the elderly. Instrumental music and reading give her much comfort. **Feb. 20.**

Sanjo Angella Jeffrey is originally from Jamaica but now teaches at a secondary pupil referral unit in London. She has served in many church offices and was dean of women at Northern Caribbean University. A lay Bible worker, she has also contributed to the *Collegiate Quarterly*. Her hobbies are reading, writing, talking with the elderly, and running. **June 22.**

Velda M. Jesse is director of women's and children's ministries of the Belize Union. She works tirelessly in this capacity because of her love and commitment to the work of the Lord. She is the wife of Pastor Luis Jesse and the mother of three (two boys and one girl). A business administrator by profession, she has worn the hat of a teacher for more than 13 years. **Feb. 15.**

Greta Michelle Joachim-Fox-Dyett, from Trinidad and Tobago, is a wife, mother, artist, writer, teacher, blogger, radio announcer (with Resurface Radio on the Adventist Internet radio station), and member of the women's ministries council. Most important, she's a child of the most high God. **Feb. 23.**

Elaine J. Johnson has been married to her best friend for 44 years, and they live in Verbena, Alabama. She is a retired preschool teacher, active in her small country church, and enjoys writing, reading, and electronics. **June 23.**

Jeannette Busby Johnson, from Hagerstown, Maryland, thinks retirement is so great that she's done it twice (and is working on a third) after several decades of playing with words at the Review and Herald Publishing Association as editor of *Guide*, acquisitions editor, and assistant vice president of the Book Division. She has three married children, four grandchildren, and two dogs: Ludwig and Lola, one of whom is elderly and dignified—the other one, not so much. **Apr. 1, Oct. 28.**

Karen J. Johnson worked in Seventh-day Adventist education for 34 years; 18 of those years were in boarding academies as teacher, dean, and school principal. She was also the vice president for advancement at Walla Walla University for 16 years. She is now the president of the Rocky Mountain Adventist Healthcare Foundation in Denver, Colorado. **Sept. 25.**

Madeline Steele Johnston is a retired missionary to Korea and the Philippines, and served with her husband, a seminary professor, at the theological seminary of Andrews University. She is the mother of four and grandmother of six. She and her husband serve jointly as associate head elders of Pioneer Memorial church. She has written numerous articles and some books. **Aug. 29.**

Michelle Riley Jones serves as the minister of music and worship for the Capitol Hill Adventist Church in Washington, D.C. She is also a liturgist for the first ecumenical African-American Lectionary (www.theafricanamericanlectionary.org), a collaborative partnership with Vanderbilt School of Divinity. Michelle is married and has a beautiful stepdaughter named LaChelle. **Dec. 1.**

Nadine A. Joseph was the acting dean for commuter students at the University of the Southern Caribbean, and a part-time lecturer in the School of Social Sciences. Presently she is at Adventist International Institute of Advanced Studies in the Philippines pursuing a Ph.D. in educational administration. She is also working on publishing some of her own work. **Feb. 26, Dec. 13.**

Liliane Calcidoni Kafler has degrees in law and international relations and a master's in business administration. She is an international director of products and services in São Paulo, Brazil. Liliane likes preaching in churches, writing, and traveling. **June 14.**

Barbara Ann Kay lives on Sand Mountain in the northeast corner of Alabama with her husband. She has adult children and precious grandchildren. Her ministry combines nature photography and writing and can be found at gardenofgraceandhope.com. **Feb. 25.**

Tanya Kennedy is a recent graduate of Andrews University, where her husband graduated from the seminary. At the time she wrote this devotional, she was awaiting a job in Colorado. She is the author of a children's book and plans to write more, for her passion is writing. She has four children and a stepson. **Nov. 26.**

Lynette Kenny is a wife, mother of four school-age children, business partner, Sabbath school teacher, and registered nurse, but most of all a daughter of the King of the universe. She enjoys painting, writing, photography, and being out in nature. She has been published in *Signs of the Times*, and writes from rural Australia. **May 4.**

Edith Kiggundu, Ph.D., is a visiting assistant professor in the faculty of education at Memorial University of Newfoundland. She is a Ugandan, but now lives in Canada with her husband, Fred, and three children. She is a Sabbath school superintendent, adult Bible lesson teacher, and prayer ministry leader. She is a prayer warrior and enjoys singing and studying the Word of God. **Sept. 2.**

Gayle A. Kildal writes from a small rural town in Alaska, where she has lived most of her life. She is married to her best friend, and they have four adult children. They attend the Glennallen church (membership six to 10), which holds services once a month in a rented church. Gayle is an administrative assistant at a community college, and is working on her associate's degree. **Mar. 7.**

Cathy Kissner has been married to her husband, Michael, for 36 years. They have two adult children and two grandchildren. (Their son, Marcus, was deployed to Afghanistan at the time she wrote this.) She has served the Colorado/Wyoming area as Adventist community service director for 15 years. Her hobbies include riding her mules into wilderness areas for camping. **June 5.**

Iris L. Kitching enjoys life with her husband, Will; they live in Maryland. Their favorite pastime is laughing together. She continues to work in the presidential section of the General Conference of Seventh-day Adventists as administrative assistant to two vice presidents. **Apr. 7, Oct. 25.**

Kênia Kopitar is a Brazilian who lives in New York City. She loves being with children, talking with people, and meeting with God in dawn's silence and through His creation. **Nov. 7.**

Hepzibah Kore served as the union and division director of women's ministries and Shepherdess ministries of the Seventh-day Adventist Church for 17 years and continues as the Shepherdess coordinator and the adult literacy project manager. She and her husband live in Hosur, India. She finds fulfillment in ministering to women, especially through literacy. **Nov. 13.**

Betty Kossick and her husband live in Jasper, Georgia. Their free-spirited life has allowed them to share the joy of Jesus. She is the author of an autobiographical book, *Beyond the Locked Door*, and *Heart Ballads* (available via amazon.com), and cowrote 14 books and 15 chapbooks with other authors. Regardless of growing older, she avidly continues as a freelance writer. **May 19.**

Patricia Mulraney Kovalski lives in Collegedale, Tennessee, but spends many months each year with her family in Michigan. She enjoys walking, swimming, crafts, reading, and traveling. **May 18.**

Kay Kuzma, Ed.D., a wife, mother, friend, and author of more than 30 books and hundreds of articles, is founder of Family Matters Ministry. She taught university students for 27 years, developed a daily and a weekly radio feature, and has presented various television programs on 3ABN. She and her husband spend most of the year in Kauai, Hawaii, and enjoy nine grandchildren. **Jan. 4.**

Mabel Kwei lives in New Jersey and is a retired university/college lecturer. For many years she served in Africa as a missionary with her pastor-husband and three children. She reads a lot, loves to paint, write, and give talks, and spends much time with the very little children in her church and her community. **Feb. 24.**

Sally Lam-Phoon serves the Northern Asia-Pacific Division of Seventh-day Adventists as children's, family, and women's ministries director as well as coordinator for a unique leadership program. Her passion is to help people unleash their potential as they seek to live out God's purpose. Married for 40 years to Chek-Yat, a gospel minister, she has two married daughters and one granddaughter. **Aug. 10, Dec. 11.**

Iani Dias Lauer-Leite lives in Bahia, Brazil. She is a college professor and enjoys helping in music and prayer ministries at her church. **Nov. 1.**

Temitope Joyce Lawal is a pastor's daughter and Sabbath school secretary for her local church. She has worked for nine years as a payroll officer-administrative secretary at the Adventist hospital in Ile-Ife, Nigeria. She loves singing. **Aug. 13.**

Loida Gulaja Lehmann sold religious books in the Philippines for 10 years, then went to Germany, where she and her husband are active members in the International church in Darmstadt. Both support lay ministries, and are helping plant churches in the Philippines. Her hobbies include traveling, collecting souvenirs, nature walks, and photography. **July 11.**

Débora Maurlia Nascimento Leite, a retired public official in Brazil, is married with two daughters, Carollina and Camilla. She has been treasurer of her church, and likes to read and do domestic chores. Her greatest dream is to again see her third daughter, Daniella, who is already resting in the Lord. **Oct. 4.**

Kathleen H. Liwidjaja-Kuntaraf, M.D., M.P.H., has been the associate health director at the world headquarters of the Seventh-day Adventist Church since 1995. Prior to this, she worked in eastern Asia in Adventist hospitals and as assistant ADRA director and health director. She and her husband, Jonathan, have authored five books. They have two adult children, Andrew and Andrea. **Oct. 11.**

Sharon (Brown) Long, originally from Trinidad, lives in Edmonton, Canada. She is a social worker and worked with the Alberta government for 30 years. She and her husband, Miguel Brown, attend the West Edmonton Adventist Church and have four adult children and two granddaughters. Sharon enjoys entertaining, shopping, and serving others. **Nov. 11.**

Rhodi Alers de López writes from Massachusetts. Her ministry, ExpresSion Publishing Ministries, aims to inspire others to a closer relationship with Jesus. She's an author, singer, songwriter, and speaker, and leads a prayer ministry. She also has a bilingual Web site: xpressionpublishingministries.com. **Mar. 2.**

Lisa Lothian is a registered nurse in New York. She is married and has twins, whom she and her husband homeschool with great delight. She enjoys gardening, praying, reading, and finding creative ways to witness to others. **Dec. 17.**

Shari Loveday, a wife and mother, is a homemaker living in Maryland. Her hobbies and interests include writing poetry, songs, and plays. Through sewing and other crafts Shari does dressmaking and creates home decor. She loves the Lord with all her heart and seeks to offer herself to Him as a living sacrifice and a willing vessel. **July 18.**

Violeta Mack-Donovan lives in St. Thomas, Virgin Islands, and teaches Spanish at the University of the Virgin Islands. She is the Sabbath school superintendent at her church and likes to share her personal spiritual experiences with others. **July 24.**

Alice Mafanuke is audit manager at Grant Thornton Camelsa Chartered Accountants. She is married with four children. She enjoys preaching, reading, and sharing God's Word. She was the Voice of Prophecy and personal ministries director at her local church and is now the women's ministries leader and Sabbath school teacher at Harare City Centre church in Zimbabwe. **May 15.**

Rhona Grace Magpayo, a part-time optician, has a passion for helping people and has participated in optical mission trips abroad. Rhona and her husband, Jun, a retired master chief of the United States Navy, have two adult children. They attend Sligo Seventh-day Adventist Church in Silver Spring, Maryland. Rhona loves singing with the Sligo Friends Singers. **Mar. 30.**

Hanan Jacob Maniwa is a student at the Middle East University, Lebanon. She was born in Nzara, in South Sudan. Her mother died when she was 7, and three years later she lost her father, too. Her uncle, who had lost all his siblings, raised her. God granted her a scholarship through the South Sudan Field, the Middle East Union. She enjoys singing and reading her Bible. **Apr. 26.**

Rozenia Cerqueira Marinho holds a master's degree in curriculum and instruction and a bachelor's in accounting. She works at Andrews University in Michigan as manager of the multimedia center. She is from Brazil, is married to Robson Marinho, and they have two daughters. She has moved 30 times in 11 different states. **Sept. 24.**

Tamara Marquez de Smith writes from Ocala, Florida, where she lives with her husband, Steven, and daughters, Lillian and Cassandra. At the time of writing this devotional, it was her last year to serve as the lead teacher of the kindergarten-primary Sabbath school class. Tamara looks forward to where God will lead her family next. **May 2.**

Marion V. Clarke Martin, a recently retired physician, is grateful for myriad blessings. She lives in Panama, where she enjoys reading, classical and sacred music, interior decorating, and her three grandchildren. **May 27.**

Margaret Masamba is a Malawian with more than 15 years' experience in teaching and administration. She holds a diploma and a Bachelor of Science degree in agriculture, Master of Science in family and consumer sciences, and a postgraduate diploma in education. She serves as the director of Malawi Union communication, education, children's and women's ministries. She is married to Chauncy. **Aug. 8.**

Ivani Viana Sampaio Maximino is mother to three daughters: Camila, Caroline, and Catherine. She and her husband, Roberto, have gained a new son, Sandro. She loves family gatherings on Saturdays, and likes to read and go jogging. She is a deaconess and helps decorate the church at Brazil Adventist University Academy, São Paulo, Brazil. **Dec. 26.**

Mary L. Maxson is an associate pastor in Paradise, California. Her responsibilities include seven ministries and discipling young adult women. For creativity she prevents her landscaping from being demolished by the deer and squirrels that often pass through their property. She loves flower gardening and creating cards on the computer to send to church members. **Jan. 9.**

Madge S. May is a registered nurse who has worked in Canada—from Quebec to Alberta's northland—Saudi

Arabia, and Florida, where she now lives. This article was the preamble of a testimony she gave at her church in Plant City. **Aug. 16.**

Lorena Mayer is from Argentina but lives in Switzerland with her husband, Reto, an associate treasurer at the Euro-Africa Division of Seventh-day Adventists. She has worked with the United Nations since 1998, while also doing communication projects for the Seventh-day Adventist Church. She speaks several languages, loves photography, writing, reading biographies, and time with her husband. **Aug. 30.**

Retha McCarty is retired and lives in Gladstone, Missouri. She enjoys reading, writing poetry, crocheting, and bird-watching. She sews quilt tops for her daughter's "Bags of Love" project in Tennessee. She has been the church treasurer since 1977, and publishes a church newsletter each month. **Mar. 21, Oct. 29.**

Catherine McIver, a social worker, lives in Maryland with her college sweetheart husband of 32 years. They have one grown son. She is the women's ministries leader for Restoration Praise Center in Lanham, Maryland. She enjoys singing, music, gourmet cooking, reading, photography, swimming, traveling, and entertaining. **Sept. 8.**

Judelia Medard writes from the island of St. Lucia in the Caribbean. A high school teacher, she is involved in women's and youth ministries. She loves reading, empowering at-risk girls, and volunteering. She is persuaded that nothing shall separate her from the love of God, and like the lotus flower, she digs her roots deeply into Him when the mire of life threatens to overwhelm. **Sept. 20.**

Gay Mentes lives in Kelowna, British Columbia, and enjoys writing, art, photography, and working with flowers. Being "Grama" to Callah is a delight in her life. **Aug. 21.**

Annette Walwyn Michael writes from St. Croix in the United States Virgin Islands. She is a retired English teacher who has replaced the classroom with many family, church, and community activities. Her husband, Reginald, their daughters and grandchildren, continue to enrich her life. She has written and published Caribbean literature. **July 2.**

Quilvie G. Mills is a retired community professor. She and her husband, a former pastor, are members of the Port St. Lucie church in Florida, where she serves as a musician, Bible class teacher, and member of the floral committee. She enjoys traveling, music, word games, reading, and teaching piano. **June 24.**

Falada Dorcas Modupe is a vice principal and school guidance counselor who served as the women's ministries secretary for the South West Nigeria Conference. Her husband is the conference stewardship, communication, and trust services director. They are blessed with children, and her highest interest is engaging in Bible studies. **Mar. 5.**

Susen Mattison Molé grew up as a missionary child in India and enjoyed moving from place to place. She has two daughters, who are in college, and enjoys hiking, writing, reading, painting, playing her cello, and food from different cultures. She continues to travel with her doctor/Navy husband, as she has for many years. **Mar. 11.**

Marcia Mollenkopf, a retired teacher, lives in Klamath Falls, Oregon. She enjoys being involved in her church and has served in adult and children's divisions. Her hobbies include reading, writing, music, and bird-watching. **Apr. 2.**

Esperanza Aquino Mopera retired from nursing after an accident disabled her upper right arm. She now works with 20 volunteers in the mission field in Polillo, Quezon, Philippines. As soon as her therapy is completed she will return to the island. The church's women's ministries still continues the feeding project mentioned in the devotional. **Dec. 5.**

Frances Osborne Morford passed away in Colorado in June 2011. She was married to her high school sweetheart for more than 60 years and spent 30 of those years in South Africa, Uganda, Ethiopia, Lebanon, Egypt, and South Sudan. She taught English and Bible alongside her math instructor husband. They had two children, three grandchildren, and one great-grandson. **Jan. 28.**

Lila Farrell Morgan is a widow with five adult children and five grandchildren. She attends the church in North Carolina of which she and her physician husband were charter members more than 50 years ago. She enjoys walking, nature, baking, table games, family, and friends. Reading is also an important part of her life, with the Bible and *The Desire of Ages* heading her list of favorites. **Nov. 23.**

Chynsia Morse writes from Rock Tavern, New York. This is her first devotional submission. **July 8.**

Nanzelelo Motsi, 27 years old, is happily married to Ronald Motsi, a pastor. They have one daughter, Adiel Joelah, and currently serve in Zimbabwe. She enjoys reading, writing, traveling, and socializing with people. She holds a degree in journalism and media studies. Previous publications include a book, *Media for Peace.* **July 10.**

Joelcira F. Müller-Cavedon became an Adventist Christian while living in Hong Kong, but was baptized when she went back home to Brazil. Her daughter and son-in-law are theology graduates in the ministry in Brazil. Joelcira has remarried and now lives in Germany. She and her husband are working to form an international church in the Stuttgart region. **Apr. 23.**

Lillian Musgrave and her family continue to enjoy the beauty and uniqueness of northern California, close to family and friends. She belongs to Sierra Christian Writers, and in addition to her church responsibilities and family activities, she enjoys writing stories, poems, songs, and music. **June 28.**

Judith Mwansa comes from Zambia. She is married and works for women's ministries at the General Conference of Seventh-day Adventists in Maryland. She and her husband are blessed with children, and her oldest son recently married, gaining them another daughter. Judith enjoys music, the beach, and the things of nature God has wonderfully created. **Nov. 15.**

Anne Elaine Nelson is a retired teacher who corrects testing for schools. She is author of the book *Puzzled Parents.* Her four children have blessed her with 13 grandchildren and three great-grandchildren. She lives in Michigan, where she stays active in her church. Her favorite activities are sewing, music, photography, and creating memories. **May 31.**

Christine B. Nelson has edited her church's monthly newspaper, *Church Chatter,* for four and a half years, and has been secretary for the Stetson University Art Department for 14 years. Reading, watching ice skating, poetry, and *Pride and Prejudice* are among her favorite things. She and her husband, Len, have lived in Florida since 1991. Their grown son, Brian, also lives in Florida. **Dec. 29.**

Samantha Nelson is a pastor's wife who loves serving alongside her husband, Steve. She is also the vice president and CEO of The Hope of Survivors, a nonprofit organization dedicated to assisting victims of clergy sexual abuse and providing educational seminars to clergy of all faiths: www.thehopeofsurvivors.com/. They live in Nebraska. **Jan. 6, Oct. 30.**

Judith P. Nembhard, a former English teacher in high school, college, and university, served in administration at all three levels. She writes from Chattanooga, Tennessee, where she is a freelance writer and a member of the Chattanooga Writers Guild. She enjoys reading, and shares the pleasure regularly with residents in an assisted living facility near her home. **May 20.**

Lynn Nicolay, who lives on the western slope of Colorado, is a registered nurse married to a surgeon. During the past six years they have had the privilege of doing medical mission trips. They have three adult children and four grandchildren. **Nov. 14.**

Suely Luppi Novais lives in Maringá-Paraná, Brazil. She is married and the mother of two precious treasures, Felipe and Lara. A teacher for many years, she is now an educator of her children, the Adventurers group, and a primary class at the church. She enjoys reading and loves to cook. She is working toward a master's degree from the state university of Maringá. **July 21.**

Diane Shellyn Nudd graduated from Michigan's Andrews University with a degree in communications, and has lived in the South ever since. She is a telecommunications advertising producer at Life Care Centers of

America, corporate headquarters in Cleveland, Tennessee. She served as a board member for the Chattanooga Chamber of Commerce and produced a call-in talk show. **Jan. 10.**

Beryl Aseno Nyamwange and her husband, Joe, have been to various countries as missionaries; they currently live in South Africa. Beryl loves to write, and is an avid reader who likes to play Scrabble. Cooking and baking, especially vegetarian recipes, are her other hobbies. Beryl is a very good swimmer. She has been keeping a daily spiritual prayer journal for the past 18 years. **Apr. 17.**

Elizabeth Versteegh Odiyar of Kelowna, British Columbia, Canada, has managed the family chimney sweep business since 1985. She has three adult children. Beth enjoys mission and road trips. She loves being creative: sewing, cooking vegan, decorating, and organizing, and would love to be an artist. She has filled many positions in her local church, and is still a Pathfinder at heart. **July 12.**

Joyce O'Garro, a retired laboratory technologist of 20 years, took care of cancer patients. She is a qualified teacher who has taught from kindergarten to college, and a pianist who at age 79 still teaches piano. She has two adult daughters, one son-in-law, and three grandchildren. Her hobbies are reading and organizing and planning programs. **Jan. 12.**

Sal Okwubunka lives in Nigeria and is a counseling psychologist. She is a former director for the Adventist women's ministries in the East Nigerian Union. Sal has four children and 10 grandchildren. **Sept. 15.**

Lourdes S. Oliveira has been married for 37 years, and is the mother of three children and grandmother of one. A retired civil servant, she lives in Hortolândia and Serra Negra, São Paulo, Brazil. She likes to read and listen to music. She is trying to learn how to deal with the computer. **Oct. 13.**

Neide Balthazar de Oliveira was born in Brazil and for several years coordinated the primary class in the Central church of Cotia, São Paulo, Brazil. She enjoys walking, listening to music, reading, and cooking. She loves her family a lot! **Feb. 6.**

Atango Margaret Omon was born in Obbo, Magwi County, Sudan. She has two brothers and one sister. During the civil war of Sudan, her family left for Uganda. After her father died, she grew up in a refugee camp, where she experienced many difficulties. Right now her church is sponsoring her at Middle East University in Lebanon. She likes to listen to music and to sing. **Dec. 19.**

Jemima Dollosa Orillosa lives in Maryland with her husband, Danny, and what she loves most is doing mission work. Each year she organizes trips for 20 to 35 people. They build, provide free medical and dental care, and hold evangelistic meetings. She loves children, traveling, and visiting with family and friends. Jemima is originally from the Philippines. **Jan. 17.**

Sharon Oster lives in Colorado with her recently retired pastor husband, Jerry. Diagnosed with multiple sclerosis several years ago, Sharon has taken medical retirement from the special school district. She enjoys spending time with her three children and seven grandchildren. **Aug. 2.**

Brenda D. (Hardy) Ottley lives with her husband, Ernest, on the island of St. Lucia in the Caribbean. A teacher at heart, she teaches both secondary school and university students. She is engaged in radio ministry with her husband at Rizzen 102fm/Rizzen102.com, as well as family, couples, and communication workshops. **Dec. 31.**

Hannele Ottschofski lives in southern Germany with her husband, a retired pastor. She has four adult daughters and loves to spend time with her grandchildren. Her interests include music, sewing, and editing German devotional books for women. **Jan. 23.**

Ofelia A. Pangan and her husband, Abel, celebrated their fiftieth wedding anniversary in 2009, and they thank God for His goodness. They are blessed with three professional children and 10 grandchildren. Ofelia loves reading, gardening, teaching a Sabbath school class, playing Scrabble, and being with her loved ones. She writes from Clovis, California. **Mar. 24.**

Revel Papaioannou works with her retired-but-working pastor-husband of 55 years in the biblical town of Berea, Greece. They have four sons and 14 grandchildren. She has held almost every church position and is now Sabbath school superintendant, teaches the adult Bible lesson, cleans the church, and cares for a tiny garden. When possible, she hikes and reads. **Nov. 16.**

Carmen Virgínia dos Santos Paulo holds a degree in Portuguese and is doing postgraduate studies in linguistics and education. An Adventist since her youth, she enjoys praising the name of the Lord and talking about His love to others. She likes to read and write poetry. **June 13, Aug. 9.**

Eliana Nunes Peixoto lives in Rio de Janeiro, Brazil. She likes traveling and exploring the cultural side of each place she visits, and praying for her husband, daughters, grandchildren, and sons-in-law. It is a habit she does not want to break. **July 30.**

Evelyn G. Pelayo is the assistant librarian at Adventist University Zurcher in Madagascar. She is married and they have two sons. Her hobbies are reading, gardening, baking, and sharing with others in need. **Nov. 18.**

Yara Bersot Pellim is a 19-year-old student of accounting sciences. She lives in Guarulhos, São Paulo, Brazil, with her parents and older sister. She plays piano in church and also works with children in Sabbath school. This is the first time that she has written a devotional. She loves playing and listening to musical instruments, and reading. **June 25.**

Maria Vicência Salviano Pereira lives in Macapá, Amapá, Brazil. She was married 50 years to the first-baptized Adventist in Amapá. She was a church elder, and loves music, visiting, and doing work for ADRA. She enjoys plants and her dogs, Lury and Lully. **July 29.**

Ester Loreno Perin lives in Mato Grosso, Brazil, and is married with two children whom she loves as God-given jewels. She likes to read, walk, and take care of her dogs and birds. She is a deaconess and a small-group leader. In 1972 she had a prayer published in a book. She has always liked to read very much. **Feb. 17.**

Betty G. Perry lives in Fayetteville, North Carolina, with her semiretired pastor-husband. They have two adult children and five grandchildren. An anesthetist for 34 years, she also is semiretired. Her hobbies include sewing, new recipes, piano, interior decorating, and arts and crafts. **Jan. 31.**

Angèle Peterson lives in Ohio and enjoys relating everyday occurrences to her spiritual life. She's been told that her inspirational e-mails always appear in her friends' and families' in-box at the right time—to God be the glory. **Oct. 22.**

Margo Peterson writes from Eagan, Minnesota. A former mortgage loan specsalist and underwriter, she now is a substitute teacher. She volunteers as an English as a second language (ESL) teacher. She enjoys reading, walking, traveling, working with the young people at her church, and spending time with her family. **Dec. 3.**

Karen Phillips, the single mother of four children, is a human resource/safety manager in Omaha, Nebraska. She is active in her church choir, teaches in the beginner's class, and was nominated as a church elder. She devotes time to prayer journaling, walking her two dogs, traveling, and ministering to others. Spending time with her children is her favorite pastime. **Jan. 11.**

Maureen Pierre lives in Meridianville, Alabama. She is a teacher and enjoys gardening, decorating, and writing poetry. She loves reading God's Word and finding interesting nuggets from its pages. **May 23.**

Carla Pietruska has a degree in business administration and has been a primary teacher in church. She enjoys spiritual retreats and the campouts the church has for the youth. Her hobbies are photography and traveling. She writes from Germany. **July 27.**

Birdie Podder, a retiree, is from northeast India and settled in south India. She has two adult children and four grandsons. Her hobbies are gardening, cooking, baking, telling stories, writing articles, and composing poems. She has a handcrafted card ministry for those who need comfort and encouragement, and to glorify God's name. **Jan. 15.**

Beverly Campbell Pottle retired after 18 years as an administrative assistant at Andrews University and 14 years as a missionary with her family. She enjoys writing, local history, genealogy, travel, friends around the world, birding, and walking. She lives in Michigan. **Sept. 12.**

Donnell Powell writes from Goldsboro, North Carolina. She recently retired from Hillsborough County schools in Tampa, Florida, where she was a teacher, librarian, and human relations specialist. Donnell has three adult children and six grandchildren. She enjoys reading, writing, travel, and conducting miniworkshops. **July 23.**

Euclídea Assis Rabelo is a member of the Lourenço Seventh-day Adventist Church, in Rio de Janeiro, Brazil, and a Bible instructor and Sabbath school promoter. She enjoys time spent with her four grandchildren, and cooking, selling natural products, and participating in church activities. **July 22.**

Adair Ottoni Raymundo writes from Brazil, where she is a physiologist, teacher, and educational trainer. She was a professor and missionary pastor's wife in Brazil, Portugal, and Canada. Now widowed, she has two daughters, four grandchildren, and two great-grandchildren. She enjoys reading, crocheting, and growing flowers. **Dec. 6.**

Barbara Horst Reinholtz is a happily retired senior citizen in Michigan who enjoys the luxury of spending quality time with her husband. They have three married children, two grandchildren, seven "granddogs," and two "grandhorses." She enjoys her friends and family, choosing her own daily activities, and cooking and baking for ailing, bereaved, or lonely church members. **Dec. 15.**

Darlenejoan McKibbin Rhine was born in Nebraska, grew up in California, schooled in Tennessee, and now lives in Washington State. She holds a bachelor's degree in journalism and is retired from the Los Angeles *Times.* She attends the new Anacortes Adventist Fellowship on Fidalgo Island, where she lives. **Jan. 8, Oct. 31.**

Jill Rhynard is a recently retired health professional who wrote a health column for 32 newspapers. She lives in Vernon, British Columbia, Canada. She is an elder in her local church, head of the healthy relationship team, and on the worship committee. Jill loves her friends and enjoys traveling and scrapbooking. She has two married sons. **Dec. 28.**

Karen Richards writes from England, where she is a teacher of children age 4 and 5. She is married and has two grown daughters. She helps take care of her elderly parents and believes that God teaches us many lessons through His wonderful creation. Sadly, the little dog described in her devotional, which they rehomed about 10 years ago, recently passed away. **Sept. 18.**

Ione Richardson writes from Oregon City, Oregon. She is a pastor's wife, mother of Paul and Kari, a local church elder, Oregon women's ministries assistant, teacher, Bible instructor, and soloist for D.C. Naval Security Station chapel services. She also produces *Bouquets With Love, Jesus: Paraphrased Bible Promises.* **Sept. 10.**

Susan Riley, who was born in Trinidad and Tobago, now lives in England. She is a mental health nurse and works on a child and family unit. She loves corresponding, writing poems, and walking—especially along the river where she lives. Although she is a nurse working with children, one of her dreams, her aim, is to be a freelance writer. **Dec. 20.**

Sweetie Ritchil writes from Bangladesh, where she is the treasurer for the Union Mission. She has served the church in financial areas, worked with children's Sabbath school—writing songs in Bangla—and is women's ministries and Dorcas director. She loves reading the Bible, writing articles, and finding ways to help the helpless children, students, and mothers. **Aug. 12.**

Dinorah M. Rivera was born in the Dominican Republic and has lived in several countries of Central America, in Puerto Rico, and the United States. She is a commissioned minister and ordained elder of the Seventh-day Adventist Church. She has been married to Edwin C. Rivera for 35 years, and is a mother of four and grandmother of three. **June 27.**

Taniesha Robertson-Brown writes from the island of Jamaica, where she and her husband are studying. Both are teachers, and in the future hope to make further contributions to Adventist education in the Turks and Caicos Islands. Her joys include spending time with family and friends, working with the youth in church, and gardening. **May 12.**

Charlotte Robinson was born and grew up in Arkansas, and raised her family there also. She and her husband, George, have three children. Charlotte, George, and all three children work at McKee Foods (the manufacturer of Little Debbie snacks) in Gentry, Arkansas. Charlotte also cleans three post offices. Downtime is spent going to church with her family. **Jan. 19.**

Avia Rochester-Solomon writes from Jamaica, where she is a lecturer at Northern Caribbean University. Her husband, Darren Solomon, inspires and motivates her to write. She is passionate about cooking, literary works, and the outdoors. She loves the Lord and loves telling others about His goodness. **Mar. 17.**

Avis Mae Rodney is a justice of the peace for the province of Ontario, Canada, where she resides with her husband, Leon. Avis is the mother of two adult children and continues to be awed by the blessings of her beautiful grandchildren. She enjoys early-morning walks, gardening, reading, and spending time with family and friends. **Jan. 27.**

Eva Matos Rodrigues lives in Paulo Lopes, Santa Catarina, Brazil, with her three children. She is a seamstress and loves to pedal her bike. She decided to tell her testimony because she knows that many people hear voices and do not know how to get free. **Aug. 22.**

Zuila V. N. Rodrigues is a pastor's wife, and both she and her husband are retired. They have three adult children and four grandchildren. She enjoys writing and walking in nature where she lives in Brazil. **Mar. 27.**

Hazel Roole is retired and lives in central Florida, praising God for the extra years He has granted her. She is a deaconess at the South Brevard church and works with the nursing home ministries and the feeding program. **July 5.**

Juliette Rose writes from Cape Town, South Africa. She is a high school teacher and the mother of two daughters. A first-time contributor to the devotional book project, she loves the Lord and is a fourth-generation Adventist. **Mar. 23.**

Raylene McKenzie Ross is a labor and delivery nurse who works in Newark, New Jersey, but lives in Spanish Town, Jamaica. She and her husband, Leroy, have a son, Zachary, who makes her life more interesting than she ever could have imagined. She serves her church in Spanish Town in the health ministries department. She likes to sew, scrapbook, and read. **Nov. 29.**

Peggy Rusike is a published writer who grew up in Zimbabwe but now lives in England. She is a single mother who was blessed with three children, and recently she gained a beautiful granddaughter. **Feb. 11.**

Ella Rydzewski is a freelance writer living in Clarksville, Maryland, with her husband, Walter. She has published more than 200 articles, most of them during the 10 years she worked at the *Adventist Review*. **May 28, Oct. 17.**

Leah A. Salloman is a pastor's wife who works at East Visayan Conference in Tacloban City, Philippines, as a church school teacher. She just graduated, earning a master's degree from the Adventist International Institute of Advanced Studies. She enjoys women's ministries, reading, baking, and developing programs in the church. She has two grown children, Shawn and Glay. **Apr. 9.**

Kollis Salmon-Fairweather, originally from Jamaica, West Indies, lives with her husband in Florida. She served as an elder, Sabbath school superintendent, health and temperance leader, personal ministries leader, and chorister in her home church. She is retired from the practice of nursing, but remains active. Her hobbies include cooking, reading, singing, and people-watching. **Aug. 20.**

Mariana Sampaio, a pastor's daughter, is not yet 20 years old, and has lived in various cities of Brazil. She plays the flute for church and participates in the youth Sabbath school. She plans to be a doctor to testify about Jesus to others. **Dec. 4.**

Deborah Sanders lives in Alberta, Canada, and is married to Ron, her high school sweetheart. For Deborah every day is an epiphany day, and she loves writing and sharing devotionals with others in the family of God. Ron is her helpmate in sharing God's love. They have two blessed children, Andrea and Sonny. She is looking forward to meeting you in Paradise! **May 24.**

Hilda José dos Santos lives in Lins in the interior of the state of São Paulo, Brazil. She is a caring mother and grandmother who enjoys "spoiling" her grandchildren. She likes caring for her small orchard. She also visits and prays for the sick. **Aug. 19.**

Patrícia C. de Almeida Santos is a pastor's wife from São Paulo, Brazil. She likes to work with children, read, write, cook, and wander in nature with her family. She has one son. **Dec. 2.**

Dorothy D. Saunders is a 79-year-old widow living in Pennsylvania. She is a substitute teacher in Philadelphia, and under the mayor's commission on literacy she volunteers tutoring adults. As an elder and coordinator for persons with disabilities, each month the church bulletin carries her article reminding members of their responsibility to persons with disabilities. **Sept. 13.**

Susana Schulz is from Argentina. She has three adult daughters and three grandchildren. A missionary spouse, she has studied people and languages and cultures. She was the first women's ministries director for the South American Division of Seventh-day Adventists, and director of the Adventist Colleges Abroad at River Plate University. She works in the General Conference Education Department in Maryland. **Nov. 24.**

Jennifer Jill Schwirzer wears many hats. Some are: running a private practice in mental health counseling in Philadelphia, Pennsylvania, conducting a music and speaking ministry, and cooking a mean gourmet vegan meal. **May 21.**

Shirley P. Scott has been registrar at Oakwood University in Huntsville, Alabama, for 15 years, and director of women's ministries at South Central Conference for seven years. She and husband, Lionel, Sr., have been married for 45 years. She has three adult children and is a grandmother. Her deepest desire is to establish a women's center to train and develop women to become Christian leaders. **Oct. 3.**

Marie H. Seard is enjoying retirement in Tennessee with her husband of 52 years. She is happy to have her son, daughter-in-law, and two grandchildren only 40 minutes away. She likes to have guests for Sabbath dinner. As a contributor to this project for several editions, she enjoys writing, sending cards, and shopping. **Mar. 28.**

Victoria Selvaraj is a retired nursing superintendent living in Chennai, Tamil Nadu, India. Her husband is a pastor, and she accompanies him in God's ministry as the director of women's ministries. They have a daughter and a son. She loves to sing, write articles, conduct Bible exams, give Bible studies, and spend time with her granddaughter. **Mar. 13.**

Donna Lee Sharp writes from Yuba City, California, where she is involved playing the piano in three different churches, children's ministries, two care homes, and a nature club. Her hobbies are bird-watching, gardening, flower arranging, and traveling to visit her far-flung family. **Aug. 17.**

Donna Sherrill lives in Jefferson, Texas. She is retired from working out of the home, but does some home health care and enjoys working in her garden and yard. **Mar. 19.**

Jaimée Seis was born in 1964 in Germany; she was already happy in her childhood days to know that Jesus was with her and therefore would like others to experience God as a loving Father too. As a freelance writer she has written articles, sermons, and books in order to make His abundant love known. **Dec. 24.**

Ardis Sichangwa works as a teacher in a public high school in Walsall, England. She is married with two teen-age sons. She enjoys traveling, reading, singing, and writing songs and short stories. **July 13.**

Bessie Siemens was a retired missionary librarian who remarried her sons' father and enjoyed old age with him. They both enjoyed their grandchildren and great-grandchildren. Her hobbies were sewing, and her husband loves giving his services to church building projects. Bessie died March 19, 2011. **Feb. 12.**

Rose Neff Sikora and her husband, Norman, call the beautiful mountains of North Carolina their home. She retired recently from a 45-year career as a registered nurse. She enjoys walking, writing, and helping others. Rose has one adult daughter, Julie, and three grandchildren: Tyler, Olivia, and Grant. **July 7.**

Daisy Simpson, for more than 40 years, was a member of an Adventist church in Queens, New York, but now attends Purdue Adventist Church in Los Angeles. She has been a choir member, deaconess, Sabbath school secretary, treasurer, and teacher. She also worked as a counselor and instructor in prison ministries. She enjoys gardening and giving Bible studies. **Sept. 5.**

Kay Sinclair writes from Palm Bay, Florida, where she and her husband have retired. She is the mother of four adult sons and the grandmother of five. She enjoys singing, cooking, baking, and doing crafts. **June 7.**

Heather-Dawn Small is Women's Ministries Department director at the General Conference of Seventh-day Adventists. She has been children's and women's ministries director for the Caribbean Union Conference, located in Trinidad and Tobago. She is the wife of Pastor Joseph Small and the mother of Dalonne and Jerard. She loves air travel, reading, and scrapbooking. **Jan. 29, Sept. 14.**

Yvonne Curry Smallwood resides in southern Maryland and enjoys crocheting, journaling, and spending time with her granddaughter, Jordan. Her stories have appeared in several publications. **Apr. 14.**

Thamer Cassandra Smikle writes from Jamaica. Presently she serves with her pastor husband in the Crofts Hill district of churches. They have three children: Akeelah, Crystal, and Wayne, Jr. She is an auditor at Jamaica Customs Department. Her hobbies are singing, writing, and listening to gospel music. **Apr. 29.**

Lynn C. Smith was born on the beautiful island of New Providence, Bahamas. She and her husband have had the wonderful privilege of serving together in ministry in Bermuda, the Cayman Islands, the Bahamas, and now the Turks and Caicos Islands. One of her passions is reading, and recently she began writing about her experiences after a medical emergency. **Jan. 14.**

Peggy Miles Snow retired from the Adventist Health System as the administrator of skilled nursing facilities in three states. She volunteers at Huguley Memorial Hospital in Fort Worth, Texas, and has served her church as children's teacher, deaconess, and elder. She enjoys swimming and reading American history. She has four children and four grandchildren. **Apr. 24.**

Tammy Sommer lives in Cookeville, Tennessee, and is the mother of a 2-year-old son. Before his birth she taught in a Seventh-day Adventist school for eight years, primarily in the K-2 classroom. Currently she is a stay-at-home mom. This is her first devotional contribution. **May 5.**

Débora de Souza lives in Amazonas, Brazil. She is a psychopedagogist and pastor's wife who likes to be involved in the programs and activities of the churches. The couple has two children. Her hobby is reading educational books. Her great desire is to see Jesus return soon. **June 16.**

Érica Cristina Pinheiro de Souza is a teacher and a pastor's wife. They have two children, Gabriel and Lílian Raquel. She loves working for God and children, and loves to read. Érica is a carioca (native of Rio de Janeiro, Brazil) and lives there now. **Aug. 18.**

Sylvia Stark lives in east Tennessee and works as a stained-glass artist, among other creative endeavors, and any other kind of honest work that comes her way. She is a fourth part of a bluegrass band, Back Porch Harmony, which travels to churches raising awareness and support for Adventist World Radio. She has also been published in *Guide.* **June 26.**

Verlyne Starr and her husband, Wayne, have been married for 36 years. They have two children and four grandchildren. She is an associate professor in the School of Business and Management at Southern Adventist

University, Collegedale, Tennessee, and gives weekly Bible studies to women at a shelter for homeless women and children in Chattanooga. **June 2.**

Ardis Dick Stenbakken edits this series of devotional books as her principal ministry since retiring from women's ministries. She and her husband, Richard, live in Colorado, where they can view the Rocky Mountains. She is especially proud of their two children and their spouses. Two grandchildren live nearby, while the other two live in Maryland, so Ardis likes to visit there! **Mar. 31, Nov. 4.**

Keisha D. Sterling is a health-care provider who works in Mandeville, Jamaica, and is a doctorate of pharmacy student at the University of Technology. She serves local churches in the areas of women's health and education. She enjoys young people, writing, presenting, and community outreach. Sleeping, avocados, pineapple, and ackee delight her. **May 1, Nov. 22.**

Rubye Sue and her husband, Bill, enjoy living on the campus of Laurelbrook Academy in Dayton, Tennessee, in the summer. In the winter they appreciate the sunshine in their home in Avon Park, Florida. They enjoy traveling, seeing old friends, and meeting new ones. **Nov. 17.**

Loraine F. Sweetland is retired in Tennessee. She does court-appointed special advocate work for the Cumberland County Juvenile Court. As an officer of the court, she works with children who have been removed from their parents. She lives alone with her little dog, Sugar. She began and coordinates a food club as an outreach to her church, www.adventistbuyingclub.org. **June 9.**

Arlene R. Taylor is regional risk manager and corporate compliance officer for three Adventist Health hospitals in northern California. A brain-function specialist, she engages in research through her nonprofit corporation, Realizations, Inc., and with the St. Helena Center for Health. She is an internationally known author and speaker. Her electronic Brain Bulletin is: www.arlenetaylor.org. **Jan. 1, Oct. 26.**

Edna Thomas Taylor is a conference women's ministries coordinator, former church women's ministries leader, and proud mother of two daughters and a son. A musician, she also enjoys reading, writing, and working with *Legacies* (young women) to share God's love with them. She lives in Florida and has three granddaughters. **Sept. 17.**

Patrice Hill Taylor is a speech/language pathologist who attends Church of the Redeemer, Presbyterian (U.S.A.) in Washington, D.C. She served as chair for the forty-ninth anniversary committee of their church and is a member of the education committee and pastoral nominating committee. She loves to sing and to read devotionals. She is a member of the church choir. **Aug. 5.**

Myrna Tetz is retired and lives in West Kelowna, British Columbia, Canada. She works part-time as a consultant editor for *Ministry* magazine. She was managing editor of the *Adventist Review*. Her husband, Bob, is also retired, but continues to pastor churches as requested. They have a daughter, a son, and three grandchildren. **Dec. 10.**

Rose Joseph Thomas is the mother of Samuel Joseph and Crystal Rose. She and her husband live in Altamonte Springs, Florida. She works at Forest Lake Education Center (FLEC). **Feb. 21.**

Sharon M. Thomas, a retired public school teacher, is an adjunct instructor at a community college in Louisiana. She and her husband, Don, a retired social worker, enjoy traveling, playing Scrabble, walking, and bicycling. Sharon also enjoys reading and quilting. **Apr. 21.**

Stella Thomas works at the General Conference of Seventh-day Adventists in Maryland. She has a passion to share God's love with the world and wishes to see many in God's kingdom. **May 29.**

Andrea Thompson is a member of the Takoma Park Seventh-day Adventist Church's women's ministries. She is a Filipino who, with her husband, spearheaded a prison ministry. They go to the Philippines each December and return to the United States in May. This story is about one of their members, Glenda H. Sobremisana. **June 4.**

Bula Rose Haughton Thompson, a fraternal twin, writes from Mandeville, Jamaica. She has been a dental assistant for 34 years and works for the Southern Regional Health Authority. She is married to Norman, a lecturer at Northern Caribbean University. Her hobbies are sewing, singing, reading, and meeting people. **Apr. 16.**

Ethlyn Thompson, from Kingston, Jamaica, recently retired from a career in real estate and food service. (She started the first, and largest, restaurant in Jamaica.) Married, with four children and four grandchildren, she is the music director at her church in Constant Spring, an elder, organist and pianist. Her hobbies are gardening, cooking, and floral arranging. **July 31.**

Miriam L. Thompson lives on a farm with her husband in Pugwash, Nova Scotia, Canada. They have two adult children, and her hobbies are quilting, reading, gardening, and taking long walks out in nature. She appreciates the devotional book that she receives every year from her daughter. **Nov. 21.**

Ena Thorpe is married with three adult children and four grandchildren. She is a retired registered nurse who is very active in her local church. She also loves spending time with her grandchildren and friends. Her hobbies are Scrabble and Sudoku. She lives in Ontario, Canada. **Aug. 15.**

Joey Norwood Tolbert lives in Ooltewah, Tennessee, with her husband, Matthew, and their 3-year-old daughter, Lela Joy. Joey works at Network 7 Media Center and is an adjunct teacher in humanities. She is a member of the musical group Message of Mercy, and enjoys spending time with her family, writing music, singing, and having tea time with her daughter. **May 25.**

Denise Tonn lives outside Flagstaff, Arizona, in a little cabin surrounded by national forest. She has worked as a lifeguard, a biology research tech, a biology teacher, and a 911 dispatcher, and is now a stay-at-home mama. She enjoys swimming, basketball, and reading anything she can get her hands on. **Mar. 15.**

Nancy Van Pelt is a certified family life educator, speaker, and best-selling author of more than 40 books. For 25 years Nancy has traversed the globe teaching families how to really love each other. Her hobbies include getting organized, entertaining, having fun, and quilting. She and her husband live in California and enjoy a highly effective marriage. **Aug. 3.**

Agnes Vaughan is a business instructor at a college in Charlotte, North Carolina. She enjoys reading and working on various arts and crafts projects. She is mother of two daughters and the proud grandmother of one granddaughter. **Jan. 21.**

Monica Vesey is a committed Christian and daughter of missionary parents. She lives in Berkshire, England, with her husband and daughter. She taught for many years, helping countless children overcome dyslexia. She and her family are regular worshippers at the Seventh-day Adventist church and key members of the local community. **Nov. 9.**

Heidi Vogt, a recent transplant to the alpine high country of Colorado from her beloved Pacific Northwest, praises the Lord for her lifelong blessings of God's natural world. Learning, research, reading, writing, and hiking are hobbies. Whether as a wildlife biologist, author, paralegal, community volunteer, or accountant, she lives for the Lord each day. **Oct. 6.**

Nancy Vyhmeister is a wife, mother, and grandmother in California. Retired from the university classroom, she still works with words—student papers, editing projects, and a biography of her mother. Keeping up with friends and family around the world takes time also. She loves cooking and enjoys yard work. **July 6.**

Mary Wagoner-Angelin lives in Ooltewah, Tennessee, with her husband, Randy, and their two daughters. Mary is a social worker at a psychiatric hospital. She volunteers with the Make-A-Wish Foundation, the local library, and MOPS (mothers of preschoolers), and at church as a young adult leader. Her hobbies are humor therapy, exercise, and collecting vegan recipes. **Apr. 15.**

Dolores Klinsky Walker (and her husband), having launched their three children into adulthood, has found great satisfaction in mentoring released prisoners and tutoring English as a second language students. A prolonged convalescence temporarily switched her from "doing" to "being," and revealed the treasure of time alone with God. **Apr. 10.**

Cleopatra Wallace was born in Jamaica, but now lives in Georgia, where she works as a nurse. She enjoys cooking, gardening, and helping, but most of all telling testimonies of the mighty power of God. **July 17.**

Kathy Walter writes from central Florida, where she is a visiting infusion nurse. Hers is a personal prayer ministry, for at the end of the day she talks to the Great Healer about each of her patients. She and her husband have two adult children. **May 7.**

Anna May Radke Waters is a retired administrative secretary from Columbia Adventist Academy. She enjoys playing table games and making friends. She has too many hobbies to list, but at the top of what she enjoys are her children, eight grandchildren, five great-grandchildren, and her husband, with whom she likes to travel. She also enjoys answering prayer requests for Bibleinfo.com. **July 28, Nov. 19.**

Sheila Webster lived in Chesapeake, Virginia, until she was a young adult, and now lives in Chesterfield, Virginia. She holds a degree in social work from Norfolk State University, and for most of her career has worked with children. She is the author of a poetry book, *A Poem for Every Season*, and her autobiography, *Discovering God for Yourself*. **Aug. 11.**

Daniela Weichhold is originally from Germany, but works as an administrative assistant at the European Commission Headquarters in Brussels, Belgium. She enjoys the cultural diversity of her workplace and her adopted hometown. She likes cooking, the outdoors, playing the piano, and singing. She likes to do medical missionary work as an entering wedge to share God's love. **Oct. 1.**

Lyn Welk-Sandy lives in Adelaide, South Australia. She works as a grief counselor and assists Sudanese refugee families. Lyn has spent many years as a pipe organist and loves church music and choir work. She enjoys nature, photography, and caravanning around outback Australia with her husband, Keith. Lyn is a mother of four and has 12 dearly loved grandchildren. **June 17, Oct. 18.**

Shirnet Wellington, an administrative assistant in Miami, Florida, is Jamaican by birth and a teacher by profession. She served as an education officer before migrating to the United States with her pastor husband. They have two sons: one a pastor, the other a pilot. Her hobbies include writing, reading, gardening, and encouraging other ministers' wives in their role. **Sept. 19.**

Penny Estes Wheeler has been blessed by a family she treasures and work she enjoys. She loves scrapbooking, growing flowers, and travel. There will never be enough time to do all she wants to do, read all she wants to read, and see all the places she wants to see. She and her husband live in Maryland. They have four adult children and three grandchildren. **Mar. 20.**

Beth-Anne Nicole White is a K-2 teacher in Cookeville, Tennessee. Her hobbies are reading, writing, backpacking, canoeing, and spending time with friends. Her desire is to be God's handmaiden wherever He places her, and to live a life that reflects abundant joy in Christ Jesus. **Sept. 7.**

Sandra Widulle is married and has two children. She loves to express her thoughts in writing. In her local church in Germany she is engaged in the children's division and uses her creativity to decorate the church showcase. **Aug. 1.**

Melanie Carter Winkler has written short stories, articles for magazines, and devotionals. She has a passion for music, writing, and spreading the gospel using her talents. She is involved in children's, youth, and women's ministries at her church. She lives in western Australia. **May 10.**

Wendy Wongk, a registered nurse, is a lover of God, family, travel, friends, and things of the Lord. She has three sons and four grandchildren, and writes from Danville, Georgia. **Apr. 18.**

Maxine Young is a writer from Queens, New York, who has been published nationally. She is writing a devotional, which is exactly what God has led her to do. **Apr. 28.**

Leni Uría de Zamorano is the mother of two adult children who have given her and her husband, Luis, two granddaughters. She is a member of the Florida Adventist Church in Buenos Aires, Argentina, where she plays the piano and organ and teaches a Sabbath school class. She likes to travel, do handwork, play the piano, and translate from English to Spanish. **Feb. 22.**

Candace Zook is a mother of three and grandmother of six. She recently returned to Indiana from the mission field in India, and is writing her first book—about India. **Apr. 19.**